SAMUELSON FRIEDMAN

ALSO BY NICHOLAS WAPSHOTT

*The Sphinx: Franklin Roosevelt, the Isolationists,
and the Road to World War II*

Keynes Hayek: The Clash That Defined Modern Economics

*Ronald Reagan and Margaret Thatcher:
A Political Marriage*

Older: The Unauthorized Biography of George Michael
(with Tim Wapshott)

Carol Reed: A Biography

Rex Harrison

The Man Between: A Biography of Carol Reed

Thatcher (with George Brock)

Peter O'Toole: A Biography

SAMUELSON FRIEDMAN

The Battle Over the Free Market

Nicholas Wapshott

W. W. NORTON & COMPANY
Independent Publishers Since 1923

For information about permission to reproduce selections from this book,
write to Permissions, W. W. Norton & Company, Inc., 500 Fifth Avenue,
New York, NY 10110

For information about special discounts for bulk purchases, please contact
W. W. Norton Special Sales at specialsales@wwnorton.com or 800-233-4830

Manufacturing by LSC Communications, Harrisonburg
Book design by Ellen Cipriano
Production manager: Beth Steidle

Library of Congress Cataloging-in-Publication Data

Names: Wapshott, Nicholas, author.
Title: Samuelson Friedman : the battle over the free market /
Nicholas Wapshott.
Description: First edition. | New York, NY : W.W. Norton & Company,
[2021] | Includes bibliographical references and index.
Identifiers: LCCN 2021005100 | ISBN 9780393285185 (hardcover) |
ISBN 9780393285192 (epub)
Subjects: LCSH: Samuelson, Paul A. (Paul Anthony), 1915–2009. |
Friedman, Milton, 1912–2006. | Economics—United States—History—
20th century. | Free enterprise. | Keynesian economics. |
Chicago school of economics. | Economists—United States.
Classification: LCC HB119.A2 W25 2021 | DDC 330.15/53—dc23
LC record available at https://lccn.loc.gov/2021005100

W. W. Norton & Company, Inc., 500 Fifth Avenue, New York, N.Y. 10110
www.wwnorton.com

W. W. Norton & Company Ltd., 15 Carlisle Street, London W1D 3BS

1 2 3 4 5 6 7 8 9 0

For Louise

Contents

SAMUELSON
FRIEDMAN

1

The Land of Oz

Newsweek changes hands and the new editor, eager for controversy, pits Paul Samuelson against Milton Friedman. As stagflation bites, Keynesianism is put to the test

Vincent Astor,[1] the reclusive head of the American branch of the New York real estate family, had been unwell since he caught a cold when staying at Cliveden,[2] the country home of his British cousin William Astor.[3] The vast, gloomy house teemed with history. It was at lavish weekend parties there in the 1930s that William's parents, Waldorf[4] and Nancy,[5] had hosted the "Cliveden Set," the elite clique of senior government ministers, newspaper editors, and aristocrats who in the Thirties favored appeasing Adolf Hitler.[6]

Vincent Astor, aged sixty-six, was visiting his English cousins with his third wife, Brooke, ten years his junior and affectionately known by him as "Pookie." She had caught up with her husband in London after attending, on the arm of the Catholic Archbishop of New York, the coronation of Pope John XXIII in the Vatican. Their brief English sojourn over, Brooke and Vincent, still sniffling from his cold, boarded the SS *United States* bound for Manhattan.

The sea journey appears to have fired Vincent's imagination. He had inherited the Astor fortune at the age of twenty after his father, John Jacob

Astor IV,[7] drowned on the maiden voyage of the RMS *Titanic*. Popular tales of John Astor's sangfroid when the "unsinkable" liner began taking on water offered a flicker of grace under pressure in an otherwise bleak scene of disaster. Reports told of the tall, good-looking, phlegmatic multimillionaire escorting his pregnant wife Madeleine to a lifeboat before heading to the ship's kennels, where he liberated all the canine inmates, including his own Airedale terrier, Kitty. The suggestion that, while awaiting his fate at the cocktail bar, Astor had quipped, "I ordered ice, but this is ridiculous," may not have been true, but the story fixed in the public imagination an image of Vincent's father as a collected character who embraced premature death without complaint.

On Vincent's return from his English visit, he and Brooke made for the Astor family seat of Ferncliff, set on the Hudson River nearly a hundred miles north of New York City. He sought out a screening in nearby Poughkeepsie of a new British movie, *A Night to Remember*,[8] that retold the story of the Titanic sinking, to see how the filmmakers portrayed his father's understated heroism. He also wished to see how the freeing of Kitty was depicted. Echoes of his father's mortality were to stalk him through his life. While climbing the stairs to the theater's balcony, Vincent suffered chest pains that were later diagnosed as the symptoms of a minor heart attack.

Returning to Manhattan, Vincent's health worsened. On the night of February 3, 1959, he and Brooke were due to attend a dinner party. Feeling unwell, Vincent urged his wife to go on her own. Returning home, she found him in bed, struggling to breathe. Brooke Astor called Vincent's personal physician, Connie Guion, who decided that his condition was stable and that there was no need to move him to the hospital. Around midnight, Vincent died, with the two women fretting at his bedside. This tragic turn had far-reaching consequences, not just for Brooke Astor, who lived another five eventful decades. Vincent's death was the first act in a string of incidents that would inadvertently construct a stage for one of the most significant and bitter duels in the history of economic thought.

Vincent Astor left the vast bulk of his $134 million fortune ($1.2 billion in 2020 dollars) to Brooke, the first $2 million without strings. Half of what remained was invested to provide her with a vast income, the other half tied up in the Vincent Astor Foundation, established in 1948 "to alleviate human misery." The foundation was to be wholly administered by Brooke and the income distributed according to her wishes. She took her work for the Foundation seriously and relished her task playing Lady Bountiful. "Money is like manure," she liked to say. "It should be spread around." Among the many notable properties the Astor Foundation owned were the landmark St. Regis Hotel on Fifth Avenue, Manhattan, and *Newsweek* magazine.

After taking advice, the widow Astor decided she had little interest in becoming either a grand hotelier or a press magnate, and both the St. Regis and *Newsweek* were put up for sale. The magazine had been set up in 1933 by former employees of Henry Luce's conservative *Time* magazine as a more liberal alternative. By the late Fifties, however, it had lost its zing. As Ben Bradlee,[9] *Newsweek*'s Washington bureau chief at the time, recalled, it had become a staid business weekly, run by Malcolm Muir Sr. and Jr.— father and son, and editor in chief and executive editor respectively—"as an adjunct of the Chamber of Commerce for [their] business friends" and was produced "without energy or idealism." "It had none of the brilliance or zest of *Time*, and none of the excesses of [Henry] Luce," the journalist David Halberstam[10] wrote.

When Brooke Astor decided to sell the magazine, the Muirs believed that as trusted friends of Vincent they would be given first option to buy, and they began raising money. Norton Simon,[11] chairman and CEO of the canned tomato and fruit company Hunt Foods, was also rumored to be interested in the acquisition. Bradlee, however, had other plans. He and Osborn Elliott,[12] *Newsweek*'s managing editor, began exploring more palatable alternatives and found a likely buyer in Phil Graham,[13] publisher of the *Washington Post*.

The energetic and charismatic Graham, who was married to Katharine

Meyer, the daughter of the *Washington Post's* proprietor, was always looking for distraction from the clinical depression that dogged him, and he
responded to an initial approach from Bradlee and Elliott with enthusiasm.
"Why don't you come on over? Now!" he said. Since being handed the *Post*
to run by his wife's father, Graham had been on the lookout for a property
that he could transform and call his own. *Newsweek* appeared to fit the bill.
It was a prominent news brand that would sit neatly alongside the *Post* to
become a potent rival to the burgeoning *Time*. It would need flair, imagination, and hard work, which Graham felt he could provide. So a bid was
prepared and, on March 9, 1961, amid a snowstorm that engulfed New York
City, Phil and Kate Graham waited in their Manhattan apartment in The
Carlyle Hotel for news from the Astor Foundation board. The larky Brooke
Astor favored the sale to Graham from the start and argued his case to the
rest of the board. And so it was that for the sum of $15 million ($129 million
in 2020 dollars) *Newsweek* changed hands.

The editorial direction of the magazine changed at once. As Bradlee
explained, "All of a sudden the magazine shed its Chamber of Commerce,
pro-business, pro-Republican establishment cast, and staked out new ground
for itself. Younger, more creative, less cynically biased than *Time*. Fairer, less
preachy, and more fun."[14] Under its new editor in chief, "Oz" Elliott, *Newsweek* gradually changed to a more liberal and entertaining news weekly for
a general readership. To distance itself from the right-leaning *Time*, Elliott
set about replacing, in his words, "the predictably conservative views" of
contributors to reflect the progressive attitudes of the Sixties. Elliott hoped
a broader approach to *Newsweek's* opinion columns would invite much-
needed controversy—and therefore public attention—to the changed magazine. And he continued refreshing *Newsweek's* content after Graham died
by suicide in August 1963.

Having brought in the old warhorse Walter Lippmann,[15] a giant of
American journalism and a seasoned columnist, in October 1962, and
Emmet Hughes,[16] a former speechwriter to President Dwight Eisenhower

who had turned on his old master, in early 1965, Elliott decided to replace the magazine's business columnist, Henry Hazlitt,[17] who alternated with Yale's professor of economics Henry Wallich,[18] a former member of Eisenhower's Council of Economic Advisers. Hazlitt was an old-school conservative, opposed to the federal government manipulating the economy, which, since the end of World War II and the adoption of the revolutionary ideas of the British economist John Maynard Keynes,[19] both political parties had embraced to minimize unemployment. Elliott thought Hazlitt's views "antediluvian" and set about finding a distinguished economist who would reflect the Keynesian thinking of the administration of President Lyndon B. Johnson.[20]

The obvious candidate was John Kenneth Galbraith,[21] the Canadian-born Harvard economics professor, who through a series of best-selling books, such as *The Affluent Society*,[22] had become America's best-known left-leaning public intellectual and most celebrated economist. Galbraith's ambition to see his progressive ideas put into practice had led him to work for Democratic presidents Franklin D. Roosevelt, Harry S. Truman, and John F. Kennedy.[23] He was tall and slim, with a pronounced drawl and lofty manner that echoed his patrician views. Elliott was convinced that such a stellar figure would be a newsworthy catch and would give a clear sign that *Newsweek* was heading in a new direction. Not only was Galbraith well connected in the worlds of politics and economics, he had been a close friend of the assassinated Kennedy and of the dead president's immediate social circle, which included Phil and Katharine Graham, whose boisterous parties at their Georgetown home had made it Camelot's[24] most glamorous salon.

Galbraith was not interested. Never one to underestimate his own worth, he saw himself as far more than a columnist for a news magazine and was reluctant to become tied to a weekly deadline. Used to writing at book length, Galbraith told Elliott he simply could not confine himself to the thousand words or so that a *Newsweek* column would allow. But Galbraith's protestations disguised a more complex truth.

When in 1961 President Kennedy invited Galbraith to find a head for his new Council of Economic Advisers, the mission proved to be a veiled rebuff to Galbraith, who expected the role to fall to him. Kennedy made clear he favored the Professor of Economics at the Massachusetts Institute of Technology, Paul A. Samuelson,[25] who had helped Kennedy understand the economic choices before him during the 1960 campaign. But Samuelson had little appetite to move with his young family from Boston to Washington, D.C., and he declined the invitation. Samuelson found the young president hesitant. "People had JFK all wrong," Samuelson recalled. "They thought of him as a dashing, deciding type. He was an extremely hesitant person who checked the ice in front of him all the time."[26]

Kennedy asked his top aide and speechwriter, Arthur Schlesinger Jr.,[27] to sound out whether Galbraith would still take the post, but by this time Galbraith was having second thoughts of his own. As Schlesinger recalled, the president-elect was "far from distressed" when Galbraith finally said no. Galbraith was anxious his impact on the Kennedy administration would be overwhelmed by other voices. As he put it, "I didn't wish to come every day to the same discussion of the same questions around the same oak table, mostly with the same people, not all of whom I wished to see."[28]

Having failed to persuade Galbraith to join his team, Kennedy nonetheless invited him to sketch out the main tenets of the new administration's economic policy, to be announced in his inaugural address in January 1961. Galbraith drew up a list of wider aims the new administration should embrace, including an extension of civil rights, an increase in spending on education and health, an attempt to tackle widespread poverty, a more ethical foreign policy that would eschew support for foreign dictators, and an increase in financial and technical aid to poorer nations. But when Kennedy delivered his first address to the nation as president, Galbraith discovered that the new president's innate caution had prevailed. Many of the economist's more radical suggestions were absent from the speech.

The assassination of Kennedy less than two years later distanced Galbraith from the Democratic leadership as power shifted to Kennedy's vice-president, Lyndon Johnson. Galbraith was not a Johnson man and, in the absence of an invitation to join the new administration, Galbraith decided to continue to write books and give lectures. Before long, Galbraith found himself at odds with Johnson over the war in South Vietnam. As Galbraith's biographer Richard Parker described it, Galbraith moved "from being a senior administration insider to being a passionate government outsider and critic."[29]

The *Newsweek* column would have given Galbraith a perfect platform from which to oppose Johnson's adventurist policies, but it was not to be. Galbraith declined Elliott's offer, so Elliott turned to Samuelson. Like Galbraith, Samuelson was an economist who had become well known far beyond academia, having written in 1948 the definitive (and vastly popular) Keynesian economics textbook titled simply *Economics*. But Samuelson told Elliott he was not interested. "You have to realize that as a result of my textbook I'm well-to-do and don't need the money," he told Elliott. Elliott countered that while he was sure that the few extra thousands a year that *Newsweek* could pay would not change Samuelson's life, a *Newsweek* column would provide even more luster to Samuelson's reputation as the foremost theoretical economist in America. When Elliott pointed out that *Newsweek*'s weekly readership was fourteen million, Elliott recalled, "Samuelson's ears pricked up and he said yes." It was agreed he would be paid $400 a column, or $3,450 in 2020 dollars. By the time the columns began, however, in September, the fee had risen to $750, or $5,800 in 2020 dollars—$98,600 per year for seventeen columns. Samuelson was told he was in complete control of the content and could even write the column's headlines, if he wished.

Elliott's plan was to have a triumvirate of economists taking it in turns commenting on the news. As he recalled, "I had a liberal economist [Samuelson], a centrist [Wallich] and still a dull right-winger [Hazlitt]." What Elliott felt *Newsweek* needed was a young conservative economist to replace the superannuated Hazlitt. He also toyed with the idea of just having two economics columnists, right and left—Samuelson and another—and sounded out Samuelson[30] about writing every other week. Samuelson replied that he was too busy revising his *Economics* textbook. Once every three weeks was agreed.

Since publication of Keynes's revolutionary *General Theory* in 1936, conservative economics had been in retreat. And so were conservative economists. By the mid-Sixties, the Keynesian revolution in economic management of the American economy that was credited with ending the Great Depression was still in the ascendant and, faculty by faculty, Keynesians had replaced conservative economists in almost all major American universities. Finding an articulate, young economist who would counter Samuelson's viewpoint would not be easy. But there was one lively professor, based in the conservative economic redoubt of the University of Chicago, who caught Elliott's eye: Milton Friedman.[31] To Elliott's despair, when he approached Friedman in the summer of 1966, he too said he was "too busy to write for *Newsweek*." Elliott was disappointed. But he was unaware that Friedman's formidable wife, Rose, was arguing *Newsweek*'s case.

"Though agreeing that this was a worthwhile project, my husband was very reluctant to undertake the assignment," recalled Rose. "He thought he would have difficulty finding enough issues which he could discuss clearly in the space allotted to a column. . . . He felt that it would take too much time and thus interfere with his research, which was, along with his teaching, his main task."[32] Rose Friedman understood how a column in a prominent news magazine would lift Friedman's profile and she suggested to her husband that truly great economists found time to spread the word.

Usually, she told Friedman, research and dissemination of ideas were left to two different sorts of people. But not always. "John Maynard Keynes, for example, did both," she told him. And, like Keynes, Friedman harbored an ambition beyond mere theoretical economics. "The task of explaining the relationship between political freedom, for example, and a free market economy, or the consequences of the spread of government into more and more areas of our lives, has not been performed very well," Rose recalled. "I felt that my husband's special abilities and knowledge put him in a particularly good position to do so."[33]

Friedman drew up a list of topics he might tackle and wrote a couple of sample columns, to see if the length and tone that *Newsweek* demanded was within his reach. He sent the trial columns to his friend, the Chicago economist George Stigler,[34] who agreed with Rose that Friedman would not run out of ideas and so urged him to accept the *Newsweek* position. Still undecided, Friedman called his friend Samuelson, whom he had known from his Chicago undergraduate days. Friedman recalled that, after a long conversation, Samuelson "strongly urged me to agree."[35] By encouraging Friedman to write for *Newsweek*, Samuelson was suggesting that of all conservative economists, Friedman was the most appropriate opponent.

Snagging Samuelson and Friedman was a journalistic coup for Elliott, the deal even making news in the *New York Times*.[36] And Elliott's "innovative" decision to field a strong team of disparate economists received an accolade the following year when he was awarded a G. M. Loeb Award for Distinguished Business and Financial Journalism.

The scene was set for the most articulate and persistent verbal contest between major economists since Friedrich Hayek[37] first challenged John Maynard Keynes to a duel by learned journal in 1931. Neither Elliott, nor Samuelson, nor Friedman could have imagined that the series of alternating columns would continue for the next eighteen years, a time in which the Keynesian intellectual hegemony would be fundamentally challenged.[38]

The long series of Samuelson and Friedman columns, that over time amounted to a running debate about the current state and the future of economics, remain unprecedented in their contribution to the way economics is popularly understood.

The duel would not have lasted long had it not been for the generosity and civility of Samuelson and Friedman, who, though ideological enemies, were personal friends. Both offered very different approaches to thought and writing, which reflected on their very different viewpoints. Samuelson's literary style betrayed his personality. His were the contributions of an established, successful, confident leader in his field whose responses to challenges were largely generous, if sometimes gently patronizing. By contrast, Friedman was something of a street fighter whose right jabs were designed to score points as much as to persuade his endlessly skeptical rival. Friedman's intention was political, to alter events as they were happening by reason and advocacy. Samuelson tended to the long and broad view, reluctant to engage too readily in every passing controversy.

Friedman put the success of the *Newsweek* venture down to the personal affection and respect the two men had for each other. "Though Paul and I have often differed sharply on issues of public policy, we have been good personal friends and have respected each other's competence and contribution to economics,"[39] Friedman wrote. Samuelson returned the compliment in a letter to Friedman: "I hope it will be said of us that, though we disagreed on much, we understood wherein our logical and empirical differences were based and that we were pretty good at preserving amiability, friendship, and respect throughout."[40]

2

Born Again in a Chicago Classroom

From humble beginnings in Gary, Indiana, Samuelson's
precocious ability at math leads him to be taught by the
free-market economists of the Chicago School

Paul Samuelson and Milton Friedman were similar in many ways. Both were born Jewish, both married fellow members of their university class, both achieved their first degrees from and shared graduate classes at the University of Chicago. And there were personal links, too. At Chicago, Samuelson was taught economics by Aaron Director, Friedman's wife Rose's brother. Samuelson used to joke that Director was "the only man alive who could (later) speak of 'my radical brother-in-law Milton Friedman.'"[1] But despite similarities in their home backgrounds and their personal life experiences, from which their views and vantage points were largely derived, the two men were very different.

Paul Anthony Samuelson was born on May 15, 1915, in Gary, Indiana, at the southernmost tip of Lake Michigan, where, in his words, "Appalachian coal brought by rail met Minnesota iron ore, brought by ship,"[2] to be processed in Gary Works, the largest steel plant in the world. Samuelson's father, Frank, and his mother, Frank's first cousin Ella Lipton,[3] had migrated to the United States from "that little part of Poland that's between Lithuania and East Prussia."[4] Frank Samuelson was a pestle-and-mortar pharmacist, whose customers were largely first-generation immigrant steel workers from Poland, Czechoslovakia, Croatia, Russia, and other parts of eastern Europe. Frank Samuelson spoke to his customers in Slavish, a pidgin language which combined the common words in his patients' many home tongues.

Gary was a boomtown, even before demand for steel for armaments and war materiel soared after the U.S. entry into World War I, and Frank Samuelson would ride the economic prosperity of the 1920s. "That led to considerable affluence," recalled Paul, the second of Frank and Ella Samuelson's three sons. "I wasn't underprivileged. Never knew a hungry day in my life."[5] What is more, Gary's boom was linked to government activity. Growing up in Gary, he recalled, was "a pretty good preparation to become, in later life, an economist. Not a businessman, but an economist, because I experienced the boom of wartime heavy spending."[6]

When he was seventeen months old, Samuelson was sent to live with foster parents on a hundred-acre farm in Porter County, near Gary. The move would puzzle him for the rest of his life, though he suspected his parents may have wanted him to escape Gary's poor air quality. The farmers he was billeted with, "Uncle Sam" and "Aunt Freda," neither of them blood relatives, raised Samuelson as their own until he was five or six years old. "This whole adventure cost one dollar a day for food, lodging and love from someone who was not my DNA,"[7] he said. Asked in old age why he thought his parents had abandoned him at such a tender age, Samuelson could only speculate. "I think maybe my mother was a premature feminist who didn't relish primarily cooking and so forth. Maybe I was a difficult eater. But at seventeen months, how can you tell?"[8] He appears to have borne his parents no grudge, nor does being raised by Sam and Freda appear to have left any lasting psychological scars. Instead, Samuelson seems to have learned from his brief experience as an orphan. Life on the farm was primitive. "I know what it was like to have no indoor electricity, no indoor central heat, and of course no indoor plumbing. It meant the privy and the chamber pot," he recalled. "Going shopping in Valparaiso, which was only five miles away, involved harnessing the horse to the buggy and killed most of the morning."[9]

Samuelson was a highly intelligent boy who, despite the lack of obvious intellectual stimulation in the farmyard, soon began to devour books from the library.[10] He went to the local taxpayer-funded school, which had high standards, and he proved to be smart enough to skip grades. Samuelson went on to attend about eight schools in all, including in Florida, where his parents also briefly lived. In 1923, the Samuelsons took Paul back into the family and returned to Chicago, where he studied at Hyde Park High School. He began to display an early interest in the way the economy worked. With the market in stocks booming through the Twenties and sucking in ordinary Americans looking to make a buck, he started following the stock market and helped his high school algebra teacher pick winners from the stock report in the newspaper. Alas, there is no record of whether Samuelson's stock picks turned a profit.

At age sixteen, displaying a precocious ability in mathematics, Samuelson was allowed early admission to the University of Chicago and discovered there, in his first lecture on his first day, the subject that would fascinate him for the rest of his life. He liked to say, "I was born on January 2, 1932, when I walked into the first University of Chicago classroom." Economics was a perfect match for his intellect; he never considered another subject, or another career. "What incredible luck, while still adolescent, to stumble onto the subject that was of perfect interest to me and for which I had special aptitudes," he recalled.

Among the first ideas he learned about in his early days at Chicago were British economist Robert Malthus's[11] theory "about how people will always produce so many children that by the law of diminishing returns the population will always grow so that wages are held down to a minimum. I found that very interesting, but found it very simple. And I thought there must be some complications that I didn't understand,"[12] he recalled.

Samuelson's first teacher in economics was Aaron Director,[13] whom

Samuelson found "very conservative, very iconoclastic, but very interesting to me." Samuelson concentrated his studies on economics and was taught by giants of the Chicago School,[14] such as Frank Knight,[15] Jacob Viner,[16] Henry Simons,[17] and Paul Douglas.[18] Samuelson was, by all accounts, a pleasure to teach. Viner described him in a report at the time as "a sober, careful and extremely able student, equipped with extensive mathematical technique, zealous, original and independent, without the belligerencies and the arrogance that so often marks young men with keen minds and the knowledge that they are superior in mental capacity to their classmates."[19] In 1935 Samuelson graduated, after just three years, with a bachelor's degree. The following year, he completed his master's.

One of Samuelson's earliest contributions to economic theory was a diagnostic tool used to analyze business cycles, called the multiplier-accelerator, later known as the Hansen-Samuelson model,[20] which attempted to explain the reasons market economies proceed in an established cycle, from boom to bust, and so on. He observed the effect of outside influences on an economy, such as foreign investment, and how such exogenous factors contribute to the ebb and flow of the business cycle. He concluded that neither Keynes's multiplier nor J. M. Clark's acceleration principle was adequate to explain business cycles and he offered his own explanatory formula.

When in 1935 Samuelson won a Social Science Research Council Training fellowship—a newly established, well-remunerated scholarship awarded to the eight top graduating undergraduates in economics in the United States—his life took an unexpected turn. The only condition to the prize was that Samuelson should leave the University of Chicago. As he put it, the proviso meant he was "bribed to leave" Chicago.[21] "Thank God I got that bribe, because I think it would have been a terrible mistake to have stayed there,"[22] said Samuelson.

Leaving Chicago suited Samuelson, who for some time had felt that Chicago School economics had only a glancing connection to reality. In the Thirties, while the Depression raged and millions of jobless begged for

work, the Chicago faculty kept to their intellectual last, insisting that nothing governments could do would alleviate the human suffering. "The niceties of existence were not a matter of concern, yet everything around was
closed down most of the time," he recalled. "If you lived in a middle-class
community in Chicago, children and adults came daily to the door saying,
'We are starving, how about a potato?' I speak from poignant memory."[23]
He could not square what he was being taught with the human devastation around him. "What I was learning in class could not rationalize for
me that almost every bank in my neighborhood in northern Indiana and
Illinois went broke and that almost all the money that my older brother
had earned to go to college was lost."[24] Moreover, "I did not have a wealthy
family and they could have used the income that I would have produced if
I had worked, but it was pointless to look for work."[25] Another of his earliest memories of real life economics, the recession of 1919–1921, was how
employers had imported workers from Mexico to break a strike. Like John
Maynard Keynes before him, Samuelson was appalled by the scourge of
mass unemployment he witnessed and found the Chicago School's claims of
impotence in the face of such misery to be crocodile tears.[26]

Compelled to leave Chicago, Samuelson thought the best place to continue his studies was either at Columbia University, in New York, or at Harvard, in Cambridge, Massachusetts. "Without exception, my mentors in
Chicago said to go to Columbia," he recalled. "I was never one particularly
to accept advice of my elders and betters. And kind of by miscalculation I
picked Harvard."[27]

At Harvard, Samuelson was taught by a group of exceptional German
and Austrian intellectuals escaping the tyranny of Nazism, among them
Wassily Leontief,[28] Joseph Schumpeter,[29] Gottfried Haberler,[30] and Alvin
Hansen,[31] known as "the American Keynes" for his adept, early, and highly
influential exposition of Keynes's 1936 masterwork, *The General Theory*, to
American economists. The terms of Samuelson's fellowship meant he could
not study for a PhD, so he holed up in the Harvard library writing a succes-

sion of groundbreaking papers on mathematical economics. "By the time I was twenty-five, I had more publications than my age,"[32] he recalled.

In 1936, Samuelson set out on his doctoral thesis, which Harvard finally awarded him in 1941. The ideas Samuelson offered in his PhD dissertation, "Foundations of Analytical Economics," were so demanding that, after mounting his defense in the viva voce examination against the stern probing of his supervisors, Schumpeter and Leontief, Schumpeter turned to his colleague and asked, "Well, Wassily, have we passed?"[33] Samuelson later adapted the dissertation into his first book, *Foundations of Economic Analysis* (1947), which soon became a standard work describing how mathematical methods can best be applied to economics. In July 1938, Samuelson married fellow midwesterner Marion Crawford, a graduate student in economics at Harvard, who was Schumpeter's assistant and a protégée of Leontief.

Having shown himself in possession of a brilliant mind, Samuelson might have expected the Harvard economics department to secure him a place in the faculty once his fellowship was over. Instead, in the fall of 1940 Samuelson was, it seems rather grudgingly, offered by the Harvard economics department a lowly instructorship, which he reluctantly accepted. But almost immediately something came up that turned Samuelson's head. In the summer of 1937, while a Harvard Society Junior Fellow, he had started what was to become three years of teaching undergraduates at the Massachusetts Institute of Technology (MIT). At MIT he had attracted the attention of an assistant professor of economics, Harold Freeman, who helped recommend whom MIT should appoint to its faculty. In those days, MIT could not match the prestige of Harvard and was best known for its engineering courses. Its economics department had a mediocre reputation and did not offer graduate courses.

Just hours after Samuelson accepted the Harvard post, Freeman counteroffered with an assistant professorship at MIT, with the promise that he could build a doctoral program from scratch, so long as he started teaching immediately. Samuelson told Harvard he was also considering a post at

MIT and waited for Harvard to respond, but when after twelve hours there appeared to be no hint of a counter-counteroffer, Samuelson accepted the MIT post. His choice would turn out to be life changing. "I really thank Darwin or whoever runs the universe that I wasn't stuck at Chicago," he said.[34] Some believe Samuelson's decision to abandon Harvard for MIT resulted from the unsympathetic view of him held by Harvard's professor of economics, Harold Hitchings Burbank,[35] who, unluckily for Samuelson, was both hostile to the use of mathematics in economics and anti-Semitic. Others thought Samuelson's arrogant, independent attitude and his rejection of Harvard's lukewarm embrace were to blame.

Samuelson himself thought it was a little of both. He recalled:

> Anti-Semitism was omnipresent in pre–World War II academic life, here and abroad. So, of course, my WASP wife and I knew that would be a relevant factor in my career at Harvard. But by 1940, times were changing. Perhaps I had too much of William Tell's hauteur in my personality to ingratiate myself with the circles who gave limited weight to merit in according tenure.[36]

When deciding whether to choose MIT over Harvard, Samuelson also took advice from his old statistics and mathematical-economics mentor at Harvard, Edwin Bidwell Wilson.[37] "He wrote me that when in 1907 he got an offer to be the head of the physics department at MIT and left Yale, people thought he was crazy. But it was one of the best moves he ever made," Samuelson recalled. "That carried weight with me."[38]

Samuelson joined MIT as an assistant professor in economics in 1940. World War II had broken out in September 1939 and it seemed only a matter of time before Franklin Roosevelt would take America into the war on the Allied side. Just twenty-five years of age, Samuelson considered joining the armed forces, but he suffered from hypertension and knew the condition would automatically make him ineligible to serve in uniform. He therefore volunteered for special scientific war work, an occupation that would allow him to continue teaching at MIT.

From 1944 onward, Samuelson lent his keen mathematical skills to the war effort in a small wooden shack, Room 20 of MIT's Radiation Laboratory, known as the Rad Lab, which had opened in November 1940. In 1941, the Lab was tasked by the newly created Office of Scientific Research and Development (OSRD) to develop a radar system that would allow fighter aircraft to detect enemy planes; a radar-based automatic gun-aiming system for antiaircraft batteries; and a long-range radio navigation system for military aircraft.

The end of hostilities in 1945 brought Samuelson new challenges. Ralph Freedman, the head of MIT's economics department, approached him with a project. "Paul, we've got this requirement that every student must take as an elective requirement two full semesters of introductory economics. And they hate it," Freedman said. "Would you take a light teaching load for a few months and write an interesting text that they'll enjoy? . . . It doesn't have to be long, it just has to be interesting." Samuelson barely gave the idea a thought. "I said, sure, why not?"[39] Four years later, Samuelson published the result of his labors: a textbook, *Economics: An Introductory Analysis*, which would revolutionize the teaching of economics and establish Keynesianism as the mainstream approach to macroeconomics for generations of economists the world over. As Samuelson recalled, "I knew it would sell well. But what I didn't know is that it would sell well for fifty years and set a new pattern."[40]

The first edition of Samuelson's *Economics* was unashamedly—and in the circumstances, provocatively—Keynesian. Of all the great economists cited, only Keynes, "a many-sided genius," was given a potted biography to make him come alive to readers. The key elements of Keynes's *General Theory* were all present: Kahn's multiplier (the notion that every new pound added to the economy by government would be respent by the recipient, then spent again and again by successive holders so that the effect was not of one pound spent but several), the propensity to consume, the paradox of thrift, and countercyclical fiscal policy. The formula to assess aggregate demand (GDP = C + I + G, where C = Consumer spending, I = Investment, and G = Government spending) was described and explained, as was, for the first time, the Keynesian cross income-expenditure diagram, plotting the intersection of aggregate demand and incomes. (The diagram adorned the cover of the first three editions.) Samuelson turned the traditional means of understanding economics on its head by putting macroeconomics ahead of microeconomics.

The unalloyed Keynesian message of Samuelson's textbook brought him into the political crosshairs for the first time. The immediate postwar period saw the start of the Cold War, which sparked a flurry of anticommunist activity in the United States, culminating in the hectoring congressional hearings of Senator Joe McCarthy's Permanent Subcommittee on Investigations, intent on purging communists from public life. Although Keynes was neither a communist nor a socialist, his innovative ideas came under suspicion because they promoted government-funded spending to create jobs. To some, this was akin to communism. The Canadian economist Lorie Tarshis[41]—a student of Keynes who joined the Stanford faculty and whose *The Elements of Economics* (1947) became the first American textbook to promote Keynes's theories—was an early victim of the anticommunist hysteria. A campaign was launched to have Tarshis's book banished from American campuses, and although Stanford resisted calls for Tarshis's dismissal, other schools were less brave and buckled to the pressure to boycott the book.

When William F. Buckley Jr.,[42] fresh from publishing *God and Man at Yale*, his sensational diatribe against the "Godlessness" of liberal educational institutions, suggested there was something unsound, un-American, and almost Marxist about promoting a Keynesian line to students, Samuelson found himself suspected of communist tendencies. He eventually came under critical scrutiny from anxious members of MIT's governing Corporation. He was only saved from sharing Tarshis's grisly fate by the personal intervention of the MIT president, Karl Taylor Compton,[43] a physicist, who wrote to Corporation members who had raised an eyebrow, threatening that he would resign if any of them started interfering with the freedom of expression of any member of the MIT faculty. The witch-hunting ceased.

With the threat of ideological censorship removed, Samuelson prospered at MIT. In 1947, the American Economic Association named him the economist under the age of forty "who has made the most distinguished contribution to the main body of economic thought and knowledge," largely for *Foundations of Economic Analysis.*

The following year, Samuelson published *Economics: An Introductory Analysis.* The book became an immediate best seller, revised about every three years, and a source of envious amusement to Samuelson's colleagues. His friend George Stigler once introduced him with the words, "Samuelson, having achieved fame, now seeks fortune."[44] As the royalties poured in, Samuelson found himself rich enough to pay off the mortgage on his home. For the middle-aged professor, the textbook was more than a money-spinner. "Let those who will write the nation's laws if I can write its textbooks,"[45] he would later remark.

In 1951, Samuelson first unveiled his ingenious synthesis of economics old and new. In *Principles and Rules in Modern Fiscal Policy: A Neo-Classical Formulation,* he spelled out how government policy could minimize unemployment by countering the natural ebb and flow of the business cycle. He said the success of public works programs during the New Deal had been overestimated and that cutting taxes as a means of stimulus had been underestimated. The key to taming the business cycle was fiscal policy: a mixture of public spending and tax changes. He did not mention the role money and the Fed might play in maintaining the appropriate money supply. For Samuelson in 1951, in a period of economics he later referred to as "Model T Keynesianism,"[46] money did not matter. His decision to ignore monetary theory—the assumption that the supply of money in an economy is directly related to inflation—was to become the core of his disagreement with monetarists like Friedman.

In the 1955 edition of *Economics,* Samuelson introduced to a wider world his "neoclassical synthesis," by which he melded Keynesian thinking with liberal economics, the pre-Keynesian approach to economics that relied upon the forces of the free market to over time deliver an equitable equilibrium. He wrote:

> In recent years, 90 percent of American economists have stopped being "Keynesian" economists or "anti-Keynesian" economists. Instead they have worked towards a synthesis of whatever is valuable in older economics and in modern theories of income determination. The result might be called neoclassical economics and accepted in its broad outlines by all but about 5 percent of extreme left wing and right wing writers.[47]

Samuelson was being optimistic. By declaring the division between Keynesians and conservative economists over, he hoped it would become so. But the gulf between Keynesians and market economists was too deep and too heartfelt.

It was Samuelson's reputation for making economics understandable and his proximity to Boston that led Kennedy to recruit him as an economic adviser in the glamorous Massachusetts senator's 1960 presidential campaign. At their first meeting, Samuelson made little effort to ingratiate himself. He had already offered his advice on economics to two giants in the Democratic Party, Adlai Stevenson,[48] governor of Illinois, who in 1959 was considering a third run for the presidency, and Averell Harriman.[49]

Samuelson was blunt with Kennedy. "I'm not for you," he said, "I'm for [Adlai] Stevenson." Kennedy said, "I don't want your vote. That's one vote. But I'm thinking of making a run for [the White House] and if you think you have good ideas for the country, here's your chance."[50] Samuelson had reservations. "I believed his father, old Joe Kennedy, to be an S.O.B. and an appeaser and a bigot," he said. And he doubted the seriousness of the poor little rich kid whose White House run was in part to fulfil his father's dream of having at least one of his four sons become president. He also doubted Kennedy's seriousness. Although Samuelson had given evidence on economic matters to senatorial committees on which Kennedy sat, he had never seen the young senator attend.

But Samuelson agreed to help Kennedy, not least because he thought so little of the alternative advice Kennedy would be given. Samuelson recalled thinking, "This country is too important to be run by the advice of economists like John Kenneth Galbraith and Walt Rostow."[51] Despite Samuelson's initial misgivings, there was also a rapport between the two men. As Samuelson recalled, "Our styles and chemistries clicked."[52] Samuelson was surprised by Kennedy's studied informality, "although I never called him Jack."[53] After being served a Bloody Mary, Samuelson recalled, "I had prepared my stomach for tenderloin steak."[54] Instead, "We had franks and beans."[55]

Samuelson soon got the measure of Kennedy, who, while being "a very smart listener," liked a little drama injected into his briefings. "I learned that every adviser to the king has a need to bamboozle him a little bit, because you won't get his enthusiasm up unless you exaggerate," recalled Samuelson.[56]

Notwithstanding Kennedy's instruction in economics for a year at Harvard, Samuelson set out to teach Kennedy the subject afresh, and, in true Camelot style, he conducted the first brief class with the new president, shortly after the 1960 election, on an outcrop of rock at the Kennedy family's compound at Hyannis Port, Massachusetts. Samuelson then wrote an assessment of where the American economy had reached and what needed to be done next in *The Samuelson Report on the State of the American Economy to President-elect Kennedy*, which was delivered to Kennedy on January 5, 1961.

Kennedy inherited from Eisenhower an economy with high unemployment, running at about 5 percent, and spare capacity in idle factories and plants. The high price of the dollar, which was fixed by the Federal Reserve, meant American exported goods were expensive. How could this be remedied? Samuelson told Kennedy that in similar circumstances in the Thirties Keynes had recommended tax cuts to pump cash into a failing economy to raise aggregate demand. In his pioneering work during the Great Depression, Keynes had offered several remedies to governments who wished to avoid a downturn, chief among them public works funded by public spending, with borrowed money if necessary. But Keynes also recommended, in *The Means to Prosperity* (1933), reducing taxes to increase aggregate demand. It was a proposal Samuelson would adopt in his 1951 paper, *Principles and Rules in Modern Fiscal Policy: A Neo-Classical Formulation.*

Kennedy, who had campaigned on cautious economic policies, was surprised that Samuelson should recommend that if unemployment rose to the "critical 7.5 per cent level," taxes should be cut "3 or 4 percentage points . . . to every income class." The new president was taken aback. "I've just campaigned on a platform of fiscal responsibility and balanced budgets and here you are telling me that the first thing I should do in office is to cut taxes?" he said. Samuelson replied that while a tax cut of about $10 billion in total would do the trick, he wanted Kennedy to be even more radical. "I thought we should have devalued the dollar on taking office and blame it on Eisenhower,"[57] he said. "But it wasn't in the cards to do that and as a result we spent a whole decade defending the indefensible until the dam broke after considerable time after Kennedy was dead."[58]

It was inevitable that Samuelson would be sounded out about joining the Kennedy administration full time. But he was reluctant to throw himself into government and inhabit the incestuous world of Washington, D.C. And when Samuelson was formally approached to head up Kennedy's Council of Economic Advisers, he declined. He did not relish the potential disruption to his personal life, nor the idea of abandoning the highly productive working rhythm he had established at MIT. Regularly revising his economics textbook, along with his faculty duties, and writing learned papers at the rate of about one a year was quite enough. Samuelson's nephew, Lawrence Summers,[59] recalled that "Paul took pride in saying he never spent more than three consecutive nights in Washington."[60]

Samuelson's responsibilities as a young father also kept him in Cambridge. Asked how many children he and Marion had, Samuelson replied, "First we got one, then we got two, then we got three, then we got scared."[61] They were to have six children in all, including triplet boys. At one frenzied period, the Samuelsons were sending 350 diapers a week to the laundry.

In light of Kennedy's brief presidency, Samuelson's decision proved to be sound.[62] Presidential economics advisers are transitory figures and many survive only a brief time. Samuelson would likely have been rebuffed by Kennedy's accidental successor, Lyndon Johnson, meaning he would have had to make a hurried retreat to Cambridge. MIT appreciated the devotion, rewarding him in 1966 by promoting him to Institute Professor.

The approach from Oz Elliott to contribute regularly to *Newsweek* came as a surprise to Samuelson. He was already overloaded with work and other commitments, but it was clear to him that writing a column on economics for a general readership would give him enormous influence worldwide. He was sorely tempted to accept the offer. And to write alternately with Friedman added the sort of edge that Samuelson relished. But neither he nor Friedman could have imagined that the columns would constitute an informal debate on the future of economics that would continue for nearly two decades.

3

Paradise Lost

Brought up poor in New Jersey, Friedman finds his
feet studying economics in Chicago, where he meets,
befriends, and first challenges his lifelong rival

Milton Friedman's parents, like Samuelson's, were Jewish immigrants from Central Europe. While Samuelson's family departed from a sliver of Poland between East Prussia and Lithuania, Friedman's came from Beregszász in Carpathian Ruthenia, which at the time was part of Hungary. In the redrawing of borders stemming from the two world wars, it became briefly Czechoslovakia. It is now Berehove, Ukraine.

Jenő Saul Friedman and his wife Sára Ethel (née Landau) arrived in New York City at the very start of the twentieth century, when both were in their teens. Living first among Jewish immigrants in Brooklyn, New York, Jenő, with few obvious skills, hired himself out as a day laborer and continued in manual jobs for the rest of his life.

Milton Friedman was born on July 31, 1912, in Brooklyn, the last child and second son of Jenő and Sára's four children. When he was a year old, the family moved to Rahway, New Jersey, a tree-lined small city about twenty miles from Manhattan and five miles west of Staten Island. There, Sára Friedman set up a business selling "dry goods"—dietary staples such as dried beans, flour, whole grains, and rolled oats. As Friedman recalled, "The family income was small and highly uncertain. Financial crisis was a constant companion. Yet there was always enough to eat, and the family atmosphere was warm and supportive."[1]

Tragedy struck the family when Jenő died shortly before the precocious Friedman, not yet sixteen, graduated from Rahway High School in 1928. Sára was left to support the family, but it was made clear to Milton that his father's death would not interfere with his education. "It was taken for granted that I would attend college," Friedman recalled, "though, also, that I would have to finance myself." Growing up in a family where money was always tight left a lasting impression on him. Even when he had become a highly successful, Nobel Prize–winning multimillionaire, Friedman always reversed the charges to journalists telephoning him for a quote.

He won a scholarship to study mathematics at Rutgers University, New Jersey, at the time a private college, where he supplemented a modest allowance from his mother by waiting on tables, serving in a retail store, and taking part in the odd entrepreneurial venture, including selling green Rutgers ties to freshmen, dormitory to dormitory. Math came naturally to Friedman and his earliest ambition was to become an actuary for an insurance company. "I took actuarial exams because that was the only way that I knew of that a person could make a living using mathematics,"[2] recalled Friedman. "Only after I got into college and started taking economics courses, as well as mathematics courses, did I discover that there were alternatives."

Friedman graduated from Rutgers in 1932, when the American economy was already deep into the economic recession at the start of the Great Depression. The national economic tragedy made the subject of economics a hot topic among students and those interested in politics. Always ready for a scrap, Friedman reveled in the heated arguments and counterarguments about who was responsible for the 1929 stock market crash, how and why the slump took hold, and what, if anything, Franklin D. Roosevelt's new Democratic administration could do about it. Friedman discovered a passion about economics and abandoned his actuarial ambition. As he explained,

"If you're a 19-year-old college senior, which is going to be more important to you: figuring out what the right prices ought to be for life insurance, or trying to understand how the world got into that kind of a mess?"[3]

On graduation, Friedman faced a fork in the road. Brown University offered him a scholarship to study mathematics; the University of Chicago offered a scholarship to study economics. He picked Chicago over Providence and on his first day of studies, thanks to the banality of the administrators who sat students in the classroom in strict alphabetical order, he found himself next to Rose Director, the sister of the lawyer and Chicago economist Aaron Director.[4] As Friedman recalled, "The most important event of that year was meeting a shy, withdrawn, lovely, and extremely bright fellow economics student, Rose Director. We were married six years later."[5] Rose was to become not just a devoted wife and mother to Friedman's children, Janet and David,[6] but his constant collaborator, coauthor, loyal critic, and fiercest defender.

Another meeting around this time was also to prove significant: in the fall of 1932, in the recently completed Social Science Research Building at the University of Chicago, he met for the first time Paul Samuelson, who, although three years younger, was, thanks to his precocity, a year above Friedman at Chicago. Friedman had been made aware of Samuelson's evident genius by Director, who taught him. The rivalry appears to have been intense from the start. And not just in their competing intellects. Rose Friedman harbored a smoldering resentment about the differences in life chances that Friedman and Samuelson enjoyed and, even when the two men were in their nineties, would grumble about Samuelson's "privilege."

While Samuelson was studying at Chicago on a full-fee-paying scholarship, Friedman received a stipend for tuition fees but was dependent upon a $300 loan from his sister for rent and subsistence. While Samuelson never had to work on campus to make ends meet and spent every summer at the beach at Lake Michigan, Friedman had two part-time jobs, waiting lunchtime tables at a restaurant on campus and all day Saturday in a shoe store.[7]

Samuelson, irritated by the Friedmans' complaint, protested that he had wanted to work while at the university but did not because, having won a scholarship that covered most of his expenses, he felt it wrong to compete with friends who needed jobs. "I wanted to work summers to pay for my education," he recalled many years later, but "I had friends who would apply to 800 companies and not get one nibble unless you knew somebody."[8]

Friedman achieved his MA in economics from Chicago in a single year, in 1933, then spent the following year at Columbia University, studying statistics and mathematical economics on a fellowship under the supervision of Harold Hotelling,[9] and being taught by Wesley C. Mitchell[10] and John M. Clark.[11] But he felt most at home at Chicago, having found a group of economists who shared his skeptical view of the discipline as currently taught. The Chicago School—George J. Stigler, Henry Simons, Lloyd Mints,[12] Frank Knight, W. Allen Wallis,[13] and Jacob Viner—shared with Friedman an instinctive suspicion of government intervention in the economy and a preference for rules-based rather than discretionary government actions. (Suspicious of politicians' motives when making economic decisions, the School preferred to limit government actions by defining specific measures to be taken only when certain economic conditions existed.) After Columbia, Friedman returned to Chicago to work for $1,600 a year ($30,100 in 2020 dollars) as a research assistant to the economist Henry Schultz,[14] one of the founders of the new discipline of econometrics—which measures elements of the economy, such as the relationship between an individual's income and consumption—who was completing his book *The Theory and Measurement of Demand.*

It was in 1934 that Friedman had his first and only encounter with John Maynard Keynes, by then the world's most famous economist. While checking for errors in Schultz's book in draft form, Friedman found himself at odds with the legendary Arthur Pigou,[15] the eminent Professor of Economics at Cambridge, England, and his ideas about the elasticity of demand, the extent to which demand for a good changes as the price alters.

The highly confident Friedman, still a graduate student, was confined to bed with a heavy cold and noted what he believed to be an error in Pigou's reasoning. Without a second thought, Friedman wrote a sharp critique of Pigou's conclusions and sent it to Keynes—who, among his many other duties, was editor of the Royal Economic Society's *Economic Journal*—with a view to publication. Keynes showed Friedman's article to Pigou, who said Friedman's argument did not hold up. Keynes decided not to publish.

Undeterred by Keynes's rebuff, Friedman sent the article to Frank Taussig,[16] editor of Harvard University Economics Department's *Quarterly Journal of Economics,* who, after a recommendation from Harvard economist Wassily Leontief, published it in November 1935. Pigou sent Leontief a riposte to Friedman, who was then given a chance to respond to Pigou's retort. For a young economist to elicit a response from such a distinguished, world-renowned economist as Pigou drew attention among Chicago economists to Friedman's exceptional abilities—and his exceptional nerve. And the Pigou exchange introduced the highly disputatious Friedman to the highly charged world of academic controversy. He found he thoroughly enjoyed it.

Unable to find a permanent position at Chicago, in the summer of 1935 Friedman followed the tide of young economists filling the many well-paid jobs provided by the Roosevelt administration for the assessment and application of its New Deal policies. Friedman was taken on by the National Resources Committee in Washington, D.C., to research how Americans spent their incomes, work that would eventually find its way into Friedman's 1957 book, *A Theory of the Consumption Function.* In the fall of 1937, Friedman switched to the National Bureau of Economic Research (NBER) in New York, where he was made assistant to Simon Kuznets,[17] who was researching the incomes of professional Americans to provide the federal government with the first accurate assessment of total national income.[18]

Part of Friedman's workload was to complete a study Kuznets was undertaking into professional qualifications, in particular the difference in salaries between doctors and dentists. Although dentistry required three more years of study, doctors charged a third more than dentists. Friedman was aware that Jewish émigré doctors, many of them fleeing Nazism, found that when they arrived in America it was hard to find a job due to the residency requirements imposed by the American Medical Association (AMA), a condition that ostensibly was to do with maintaining the quality of doctors but in practice operated as a restraint on trade. Having finished his investigation, Friedman handed his startling conclusions to Kuznets: the licensing of doctors to practice through the AMA was harmful to doctors and patients alike.

Friedman's paper was so controversial that, at the insistence of a NBER board member, the study remained unpublished. Samuelson, who became aware of the flap, was scathing about the poor judgment displayed by Friedman in his conclusion. "Only Milton Friedman could argue—argue seriously—that therefore everyone should be able to practice surgery,"[19] he recalled.

Years later, Friedman reflected on his time working for Roosevelt's New Deal. There was in the Thirties a great amount he found laudable in Roosevelt's scattergun approach to intervention in the economy, in which a range of different, disparate approaches were tried to reduce unemployment and restore demand in the broken economy. "We witnessed at close range the collapse of bank after bank in Chicago during our first graduate year there," he wrote. "Like our teachers and fellow students at Chicago, and indeed most of the nation, we regarded many early New Deal measures as appropriate responses to the critical situation—in our case not, I hasten to add, the price- and wage-fixing measures of the National Recovery Administration and the Agricultural Adjustment Administration, but certainly the job-creating Works Progress Administration, Public Works Administration, and Civilian Conservation Corps."[20]

With the economy broken, businesses going bust by the day, and no jobs available, working for the government, or independent bodies set up to monitor government programs, was a good option for the Friedmans. While he later concluded that much of FDR's trial-and-error approach to market intervention had been pointless, he could hardly deny that the New Deal had worked to his and Rose's benefit. He recalled:

> Ironically, the New Deal was a lifesaver for us personally. . . . Absent the New Deal, it is far from clear that [Rose and I] could have gotten jobs as economists. Academic posts were few. Anti-Semitism was widespread in the academy. . . . We were on the verge of beginning our careers, and though young and naturally optimistic, our outlook and habits throughout our lives were greatly affected by the depression.[21]

Friedman wasn't offered an academic post until he went to Wisconsin-Madison University for a year as a visiting professor in 1940, "and anti-Semitism helped make that only a one-year appointment,"[22] Friedman recalled. Roosevelt was slowly preparing the American people to fight against Germany and Japan, and Wisconsin was home to a large population of German-Americans who felt differently. Friedman made little attempt to disguise his belief that America should aid beleaguered Britain, the last remaining democracy in Europe, in its fight against the Axis tyranny. But Friedman found himself caught between rival factions on the Wisconsin economics faculty when, having written a report on the teaching of statistics at the school that disparaged the faculty members responsible for the subject, his appointment as an assistant professor was heavily opposed, then rejected. Chief among Friedman's detractors was Walter A. Morton,[23] who, according to Rose Friedman, was "regarded as anti-Semitic and strongly pro-German." (Morton denied the charge.)

Just as Samuelson had encountered anti-Semitism at Harvard and had crossed the Charles River to MIT to avoid it, so Friedman decided to shrug off Wisconsin-Madison University's insult and find employment elsewhere. He soon found a research project to intrigue him: Columbia economics professors Carl Shoup[24] and Ruth Mack[25] invited him to join them for the summer in Norwich, Vermont, on behalf of the Carnegie Foundation and the Institute of Public Administration. His task was to explore how best to raise taxes in a wartime economy without the additional costs being passed on by businesses to consumers and by workers demanding higher wages, which would result in a rise in general prices. When the report, *Taxing to Prevent Inflation*, was completed, Friedman was offered a post at the Division of Tax Research at the U.S. Treasury Department in Washington.[26] Friedman spent the next two years inventing ways to collect taxes in wartime, a conundrum that was also being hotly debated in Britain by Keynes[27] and Hayek.

A question raised by Friedman was to what extent taxes should be raised as a means of limiting rising prices. When recommending to Congress a tax hike of $87 billion, which he considered "the smallest amount that is at all consistent with successful prevention of inflation," Friedman found himself adopting the same logic being propounded in London by Keynes. "The most striking feature of this statement is how thoroughly Keynesian it is," Friedman recalled. "I had completely forgotten how thoroughly Keynesian I then was."[28]

In later years, Friedman would distance himself from his single most important contribution to the war economy: the invention of the payroll withholding tax. By taxing Americans at the source, out of their pay packet, there was no way to evade income taxes. He recalled:

It never occurred to me at the time that I was helping to develop machinery that would make possible a government that I would come to criticize severely as too large, too intrusive, too destructive of freedom. Yet, that is precisely what I was doing. Rose has repeatedly chided me over the years about the role that I played in making possible the current overgrown government we both criticize so strongly. That is in jest, since withholding would have been introduced had I been involved or not. The most I accept blame for is helping to make it more efficient than it otherwise might have been.[29]

Friedman was also involved in work more obviously applied to the art of war.

> You've got an antiaircraft missile. It's possible to produce it in such a way that you can control how many pieces it breaks into when it explodes. Should you have a lot of little pieces, so there's a high probability of hitting, but it won't be as harmful to the object hit? Or, should you have a few big pieces, each of which will destroy the plane you're shooting at if it hits it, but the probability of hitting it is less?[30]

In 1943, the Friedmans returned to New York City at the invitation of W. Allen Wallis to join the Statistical Research Group at Columbia University, where Friedman would work for the rest of the war.

The year after war ended, in 1946, Friedman's work with Kuznets, coauthored with Kuznets as *Income from Independent Professional Practice*, was submitted to Columbia as his PhD thesis. In 1946, on the departure of Viner from Chicago to Princeton, Friedman was offered a teaching post in the Chicago economics department and he returned to his spiritual home. With like-minded colleagues, he became an integral part of the group that established Chicago as the home of market-based economics and who were deeply skeptical of the Harvard-led Keynesian orthodoxy that had swept through economics.

But Friedman's return to Chicago was overshadowed by Samuelson's apparently effortless, irresistible progress. Jacob Marschak,[31] known as "the father of econometrics," persuaded Chicago's chancellor, Robert Hutchins,[32] that if the university could snag both Friedman and Samuelson, it would leave the economics capitals of Cambridge, England, Harvard, and Stockholm far behind. There then followed a long wooing of Samuelson. He was offered a full professorship and a larger salary than he was getting—a figure that kept increasing as the negotiations continued. Samuelson was in two minds and, having first turned down the position, accepted it before turning it down again.

Part of his reluctance was the antagonism he was likely to face from the conservatives in the Chicago department over his devotion to Keynes. Behind the scenes, opposition was growing to Samuelson's appointment. Marschak wrote to Hutchins in despair, "Since macroeconomics—which is, after all, the foundation of all economic policy other than that of doing nothing[—]is considered a Keynesian heresy, I have a difficult stand in the department in defending his candidature."[33] Friedman, who joined the department on September 1, joined the chorus of disapproval, writing to Stigler that he was "very low" about the prospect of Samuelson returning to Chicago. "The Keynesians have the votes & the means to use them," he wrote. "[Frank] Knight is bitter & says he will withdraw from active participation in the dept."[34] In the end, Samuelson decided to stay put, much to Friedman's relief. But the incident revealed the intensely political nature of the personal rivalry that already existed between the two men.

It was around this time that Friedman, in collaboration with a colleague from the National Bureau of Economic Research, Anna Schwartz,[35] set out on research into the role of money in the history of the U.S. economy. Their work together would become the central plank of Friedman's lifelong interest in the subject. The resulting *Monetary History of the United States, 1867–1960*, published in 1960, turned on its head conventional wisdom about the reasons for the Great Depression, blaming not the stock market bubble and the overheated economy, which were suggested by Keynes, but the failure of the Federal Reserve to provide enough money to keep the economy moving. While the conventional view was that the federal government had rightly tightened the cost of borrowing to put an end to the rampant speculation in stocks that had led to the Crash of 1929, Friedman, by trawling through the monetary data, came to a different conclusion: had the Federal

Reserve eased interest rates earlier, many of the businesses which had gone bust could have borrowed to remain open.

Friedman was becoming well known in America. But his fame had not reached Europe, where an invitation came out of the blue from Friedrich Hayek. And not to Friedman but to his brother-in-law Director. Director was instrumental in having the University of Chicago Press publish Hayek's highly influential *The Road to Serfdom* in the U.S. in September 1944 after no mainstream American publisher would take it.[36] Now Hayek was inviting Director and others to a powwow in an out-of-season skiing hotel on top of a mountain in Switzerland. It was to be, literally, a summit to decide how to reinvigorate the intellectual case for the free market in the face of creeping collectivism.

Hayek was on a mission. He believed that, notwithstanding the victory of the democracies over the tyrannical Axis nations, liberty was at risk. The Keynesian revolution in economics had legitimized and emboldened the government sector to overrule market messages and directly manage economies, through state spending on public projects. Vast government building programs had been the trademark of Nazism, which also put the state in charge of the economy. Hayek had a knack of spotting the big picture. In 1931, he had moved to London to personally try to halt Keynes in his tracks. Now he was going to lead a ragbag army of nonconformist, maverick, conservative, and libertarian intellectuals with the aim of reviving the fortunes of free-market economics in the face of creeping socialism in Western nations encouraged by the need for a command economy during wartime. He sent his call to arms to a disparate gaggle of rank outsiders and members of the awkward squad, inviting them to spend a week discussing what should be done to halt the tide of rampant statism.

Director didn't take Hayek's alarm too seriously. Hayek had already spelled out the dangers of accidental socialism in *The Road to Serfdom*. But the prospect of a week in Switzerland, all expenses paid by a group of Swiss bankers, seemed a good idea. It would be a great chance for him and his pals to play cards for a week. So he invited his brother-in-law Friedman and Stigler to join him, suggesting that, while the meeting was ostensibly "a junket to Switzerland . . . to save liberalism,"[37] it was a good excuse to escape their wives and play bridge for ten days.[38] Stigler told Friedman to "train Aaron on bridge, and let's find a fourth liberal and teach him."[39]

On this Swiss sojourn at the Hotel du Parc in the Swiss village of Mont Pèlerin, near Vevey, in April, 1947, Friedman discovered a world beyond the United States inhabited by sympathetic thinkers, many of whom were to become his natural allies and eventually his disciples. He recalled:

> Here I was, a young, naïve provincial American, meeting people from all over the world, all dedicated to the same liberal principles as we were; all beleaguered in their own countries, yet among them scholars, some already internationally famous, others destined to be; making friendships which have enriched our lives, and participating in founding a society that has played a role in preserving and strengthening liberal ideas.[40]

Friedman had glancingly met Hayek in Chicago on a tour promoting *The Road to Serfdom*. In Switzerland, he got to know Hayek better and the important place he held in the early counter-Keynesian firmament. It was on Mont Pèlerin, too, that Friedman met the irascible Ludwig von Mises,[41] a giant figure in Austrian economics, whose belligerence and independence of mind had so offended the Nazi puppets in Vienna, it had led to his banishment. After a time kicking his heels in Switzerland, by 1940 he had washed up in New York, where, thanks to the William Volker Fund,[42] which promoted free-market ideas, he had landed a professorship at New York University. "Mises was a person of very strong views and rather intolerant about any differences of opinion," Friedman recalled. And because he liked nothing better than a no-holds-barred intellectual tussle, Friedman noted with glee that "our sessions were marked by vigorous controversy."[43]

Rather than a place to play bridge with his pals, Friedman found on Mont Pèlerin members of his own truculent tribe, a group of passionate, argumentative freethinkers intent on countering a socialistic wave engulfing the postwar governments of the West. "The place is unbelievably wonderful," he wrote to Rose. "We've been meeting three times a day. . . . It's pretty wearing, but also very stimulating."[44] They embraced politics and philosophy, too. Friedman, who had never confined his own thoughts to economics, was inspired by wide-ranging discussions on such disparate issues as: the role of religion and morality in maintaining a free society; the role of the monopolistic power of trade unions; and whether governments should try to make society more equitable through income taxes.

Although Friedman did not attend any of the next ten Mont Pèlerin annual meetings, the breadth of thinking he encountered at that first gathering proved an inspiration. Among the many turning points in Friedman's life, Mont Pèlerin was very significant.[45] And although Friedman and Hayek differed over the value of Austrian economics, in time Friedman became Hayek's heir apparent, less for his economics than for the scale of his ambition to overturn the progressive Keynesian consensus and shrink the government sector.

The differences between Friedman and Hayek over economics became evident in 1950, when Hayek applied to join Chicago's economics department. Hayek imagined his Austrian School dimension would be a natural fit with the rest of the conservatives in the Chicago School. But the logic of Austrian economics was as far from the Chicago School's reasoning as the Chicago School was from Keynesianism.

Inspired by the teachings of von Mises, Hayek believed an economy should be totally free of government intervention, except to ensure the efficient working of the market through light regulation. He thought no one knew enough about the workings of the economy for government involvement to be anything but reckless interference. Friedman, and much of the Chicago School, promoted the virtues of free-market forces but concentrated their energies on determining how an economy works most efficiently, for instance through study of the price mechanism and incentives for growth.

To Hayek's embarrassment, the Chicago economics faculty rebuffed his overtures and he was obliged instead to accept a post in a minor department, the Committee on Social Thought. The Chicago School "didn't want him," recalled Friedman. "They didn't agree with his economics. . . . If they had been looking around the world for an economist to add to their staff, their prescription would not have been [Hayek,] the author of *Prices and Production*."[46]

Friedman soon came to experience at firsthand the lingering bitterness between Keynesians and the conservative holdouts who attended Mont Pèlerin meetings. The rift between left and right in economics, born of the bitter duel between Keynes and Hayek in 1931, had permanently soured the atmosphere between the two sides and continued to cause otherwise well-mannered academics to insult each other. At the height of the Keynes Hayek clash in the Thirties, Pigou, the professor of economics at Cambridge, complained that since the Keynes and Hayek debate the quality of intellectual discourse at Cambridge had devolved into "the method of the duello," with the quarrel "conducted in the manner of Kilkenny cats." He asked, "Are we, in our secret hearts, wholly satisfied with the manner, or manners, in which some of our controversies are carried on?"[47] In the two decades after that, however, the political divisions in economics remained poisonous.

In the academic year 1954–55, Friedman entered the lion's den by accepting a Fulbright Visiting Fellowship to study for a semester at Gonville and Caius College, Cambridge, England. For Friedman to visit Cambridge, the world capital of Keynesian thought, was in some part an act of courage as, in the eyes of Keynesians, "classical" economists like him were antediluvian outcasts. As one observer put it, to Keynesians, "free-marketeers seemed to occupy something like the eighth ring of the Inferno, the special place for soothsayers, diviners, and magicians, where they are condemned to walk backwards with their heads twisted around."[48] And the Keynesians' contempt was dutifully returned to them by free-market economists.

In the run-up to publication of his revolutionary *General Theory* in 1936, Keynes had surrounded himself in his redoubt in King's College, Cambridge, with vociferous acolytes, who after his premature death in 1946 fiercely defended what they believed to be the true Keynesian faith. The "Cambridge Circus," as they were known, were a band of trusted students and dons who freely discussed economics with their hero Keynes and, through a series of intimate seminars, had helped revise *The General Theory*. Many of them had, since the death of Keynes, moved far to his left, with many, such as the formidable Joan Robinson,[49] embracing public ownership, high taxation, and collective provision, and even praising command economies of totalitarian regimes such as communist China.

The Circus felt secure on home territory and were amused by the short, sharp American[50] with antiquated views. The amiable Friedman got on well with Keynes's disciples and was invited into the cozy world of college high-table dinners and early evening sherry parties. Among the Circus members Friedman came to know: Richard Kahn,[51] who had mathematically proven Keynes's notion of the wealth-spreading "multiplier" effect of new spending in an economy; Joan Robinson, wife of fellow Circus member Austin Robinson;[52] and Hayek's translator and early collaborator turned Keynesian, Nicholas Kaldor.[53] Friedman also met Harry Johnson,[54] Keynes's Canadian disciple and biographer, and Dennis Robertson,[55] the most prominent holdout against Keynes and his ideas in Cambridge, who shared Friedman's belief in the importance of monetary theory.

But while Friedman took the many cultural differences in his stride, Rose Friedman was appalled by the stark gulf between Keynesians and the few laissez-faire economists left in Cambridge. "What disturbed us most was the bitterness and hostility that the two groups exhibited toward each other and the almost complete absence of any intellectual dialogue between them," she recalled. A similarly hostile divide was evident between American economists, too. "We were accustomed to being in a minority with respect to our political and economic views on most campuses in the United States at this time," she explained. "However, we have never been on a campus in the U.S. where the cleavage was as deep or as emotional as it was in Cambridge."[56]

The Circus was unfazed by Friedman's cocky confidence and relished the chance to take him on in public. Joan Robinson not only went out of her way to give a lecture directly challenging one of Friedman's favorite topics—freeing currencies from the straitjacket they had been confined to by Keynes at Bretton Woods[57]—she invited him to attend as her guest. In her talk, she robustly defended Keynes's decision to tie the price of currencies to each other. Before World War II, governments had fixed the price of their currencies—and therefore the prices of their exports and imports—to their domestic needs. But the result was often painful. By pegging the pound sterling at too high a price directly after World War I, Britain's Conservative government had provoked mass unemployment as British exporters struggled to find customers prepared to pay such a high price. Having delivered her talk, Robinson invited Friedman to the stage to defend his contrary point of view: that currencies should be free to float on the market. It was a high point for Friedman, who enjoyed the ensuing argument—and the attention given to him and his ideas in the heart of Keynesianism.

Friedman found his eight-week Cambridge stint "extremely stimulating and instructive, and led to my forming close professional friendships that paid dividends."[58] But Rose found it uncomfortable to live, however briefly, in a community that so openly held market economists in disdain. She thought the London School of Economics, where Hayek had taught, "much healthier and more congenial than that of Cambridge."[59]

As an avowed Keynesian, Samuelson was intimate with the Circus and was embraced by them as one of their own. He regularly wrote letters to all the main protagonists—Austin Robinson and his wife Joan, Dennis Robertson, Piero Sraffa, John Hicks, Roy Harrod, Richard Kahn, Lionel Robbins—and they replied in the friendliest terms. As time passed and Keynesianism developed, he would describe himself as "a Keynesian, but a somewhat disillusioned one, believing that as the 20th century progressed, governments tended to become overlarge and under-efficient, failing to meet the human needs that we do-gooders extol,"[60] and as "a cafeteria Keynesian. . . . I might go to mass every week, so I'm a good Catholic, but I don't regulate my family size the way the Pope would like to."[61]

Samuelson never regarded Keynesianism as a religion, and criticized colleagues who did.[62] Asked what sort of economist he was, he would respond, "I call myself a post-Keynesian. The 1936 Model A Keynesianism is passé. Of course, it doesn't mean that it wasn't right for its time."[63] And throughout his life he was prepared to criticize Keynes the Master, even when cavorting among members of the Circus. He attended a gathering of Keynesians in Cambridge, England, in 1983 to celebrate the 150th anniversary of Keynes's birth. "Everybody was there," he recalled, "and they all stood up and said, 'I am still a faithful Keynesian. I am still a true believer.' I was a bit rude. I said, 'You remind me of a bunch of Nazis saying, I'm still a good Nazi.' It's not a theology: it's a mode of analysis. I think I am a different Keynesian than I was ten years ago."[64] But when asked to rank Keynes as an economist, Samuelson did not blink. "I still think he was the greatest economist of the twentieth century and one of the three greatest of all time."[65] Asked to name numbers two and three, he replied, "Adam Smith and Leon Walras."[66]

It was perhaps the sublime confidence in his own intellect that allowed Samuelson to change his mind as often as he liked, an admirable trait that separated him from those, like Friedman and Hayek, who, having decided a line to pursue, kept digging down. Samuelson once wrote to Friedman, "Now I must eat my words. As you know I hate to change my mind, but

I hate worse to hold wrong views, and so I have no choice."[67] As he would remind Friedman on a later occasion, "No paper of mine that is a decade old could represent my present views."[68] It was a self-assurance that Samuelson shared with Keynes himself, who, when challenged on his changing views, would respond: "When my information changes, I change my views. Don't you, Sir?"[69]

4

Counter Keynes

Friedman finds his life's mission: to wrest economics from the ideas of Keynes. In his economic utopia, unbridled capitalism would triumph and order would be restored

After visiting Britain, the Friedmans traveled to Madrid, Spain, and spent a family skiing vacation in Switzerland before going to Edinburgh to visit the home, then the grave, of the Scottish founder of free-market economics, Adam Smith. The ever-suspicious Rose Friedman saw the hidden hand of Keynesians in the poor state of Smith's last resting place. "The burial plot, though larger than any other in the cemetery, was the most barren and neglected," she wrote. "Milton felt the neglect was more likely a result of bachelor Smith's having no descendants other than the decline in the acceptance of his philosophy, as I did."[1]

The Fifties were a busy and productive decade for Friedman. In 1953, he published a collection of works, *Essays in Positive Economics*, whose central essay, "The Methodology of Positive Economics," addressed a theory expounded by J. M. Keynes's father, John Neville Keynes, about the objectivity of economics and whether it should, like a physical science, describe the world as it is, or whether, like philosophy, it should adopt a set of subjective criteria by which to assess outcomes of changes in policy. In the paper, Friedman laid down fast principles that would guide him the whole of his career: above all, as an evangelist for his views, he grasped the value of a theory that in its apparent simplicity was easy to understand.

Hayek, for one, found Friedman's essay troubling. "One of the things I most regret is not having returned to a criticism of Keynes's [*General Theory*],"[2] Hayek confessed in the 1990s, "but it is as much true of not having criticized Milton's [*Essays in*] *Positive Economics*, which in a way is quite as dangerous a book."[3]

In the essay *A Theory of the Consumption Function* (1957), Friedman questioned one of the basic tenets of Keynesian thought, the relation between spending and income, which Keynes dubbed "the consumption function." Friedman contended that individuals responded to permanent changes in their income rather than temporary changes, so a short-term tax cut, intended to increase consumption by providing more money for a person to spend, might have little effect in boosting the general economy because cautious individuals, aware of the temporary nature of the cut, might save rather than spend their tax windfall. Friedman considered this book "my best scientific contribution, though not the most influential,"[4] but it added considerably to Friedman's reputation among economic theorists.

In 1960, Friedman and Anna Schwartz concluded their years of research into a century of American monetary data, *A Monetary History of the United States, 1867–1960*, which turned on its head the conventional wisdom about what caused the Great Depression. The traditional view suggested that too much money chasing too few goods—and too few stocks—had led to unsustainably high prices of both stocks and goods, ending in a stock market bubble that burst in the Crash of 1929. But a careful perusal of the contemporary financial data, Friedman and Schwartz argued, suggested a quite different cause: that the tightness of money in circulation—with interest rates kept deliberately high by the Federal Reserve—had led to the string of bank collapses that froze the financial system, spooked the stock market, and triggered the market collapse.

The book was not merely a piece of revisionist economic history that became universally accepted as correct; it argued that mismanagement of the control of the supply of money, above all, changed the direction of the economy. At the heart of their argument was the long-abandoned quantity theory of money, which suggested that the more money in circulation, through low interest rates and cheaper borrowing, the more the value of money would decrease. Similarly, the less money in circulation, because of high interest rates, the more money would maintain its value over time. In their *Monetary History*, Friedman and Schwartz revived the long-ignored quantity theory in an incarnation that would fast become known as "monetarism."

Friedman was delighted by the warm reception his and Schwartz's argument received. "It played a more important role in changing the tide of professional opinion by presenting extensive evidence from history on the consistent relation between monetary changes and subsequent economic change,"[5] he explained. It was an "important contribution to the ongoing controversy between Keynesianism and what had come to be dubbed 'monetarism.'"[6]

IN JUNE 1956, Friedman had been invited by the Volker Foundation to deliver a series of lectures at Wabash College, in Crawfordsville, Indiana. The talks, when published five years later as a book, *Capitalism and Freedom*,[7] became Friedman's first comprehensive defense of unbridled capitalism, and it was soon viewed as a bible for conservative economists and politicians working to trim the size of the state. The book also introduced Friedman to the joys of writing a best seller. In the next fifteen years, the book would sell 400,000 copies, allowing the Friedmans to buy a summer vacation home in Vermont they called "Capitaf" in tribute to the source of the funds.[8]

Capitalism and Freedom was Friedman's personal manifesto. At age fifty, he had assembled his insights into money and the role of government into a coherent world view that was not merely a repudiation of Keynesian economics but a critique of the system of democratic government that America had enjoyed since the founding of the Republic. His judgment was that there could be no political freedom if the market was not allowed to operate freely. All attempts to temper the market, however well intended—such as progressive income taxes designed to make society more equal or subsidies or tax breaks to encourage racial or gender equality—were doomed because they hampered the efficient operation of capitalism, which, when left to its own devices, was sure to maximize the benefits to society.

The book's opening line made clear Friedman's intended target. The golden boy of American liberalism, the new young president, John F. Kennedy, had the previous year, at his inauguration, inspired Americans with his appeal to "ask not what your country can do for you—ask what you can do for your country."[9] Friedman dismissed the fine words from the personification of progressive thinking as patronizing claptrap. It confirmed a world view, he said, in which "the government is the patron, the citizen the ward, a view that is at odds with the free man's belief in his own responsibility for his own destiny."[10] Kennedy's call to arms to defeat common enemies and unite the world behind America was dismissed by Friedman as implying "that government is the master or the deity, the citizen, the servant or the votary."[11]

He continued:

The free man will ask neither what his country can do for him nor what he can do for his country. He will ask rather 'What can I and my compatriots do through government' to help us discharge our individual responsibilities, to achieve our several goals and purposes, and above all, to protect our freedom?[12]

And free men would ask a second question:

How can we keep the government we create from becoming a Frankenstein that will destroy the very freedom we establish it to protect? . . . Government is necessary to preserve our freedom, it is an instrument through which we can exercise our freedom; yet by concentrating power in political hands, it is also a threat to our freedom.[13]

After half a lifetime observing the federal government at work, Friedman concluded that almost nothing good could be achieved by government. Starting with evidence from his revisionist history that it was feckless members of the federal government's Federal Reserve, not failures inherent in capitalism, that had set off the Great Depression, Friedman heaped blame on almost all successive efforts by government to ameliorate the lives of the American people.

Progressive income tax had not made the rich and the poor more equal. Social welfare payments had merely exacerbated poverty. Public housing and slum demolition programs had "worsened the housing conditions of the poor, contributed to juvenile delinquency, and spread urban blight."[14] Government support for farmers by fixing market prices in agricultural produce had "become a national scandal"[15] that had done little to help dirt-poor farmers. The minimum wage had not lifted the incomes of the poor but had thrown Americans out of work. Grand publicly funded schemes such as the interstate highway network and vast hydroelectric dams were merely "tributes to the capacity of government to command great resources."[16] Labor unions, set up to protect the rights of their members and collectively bargain for better wages, could no longer be considered "on the side of the angels."[17]

Chapter by chapter, Friedman laid out his vision of how an economy, freed from tinkering by politicians, could eventually make everyone more prosperous and fulfilled than the existing mixed economy, part private, part government system. Instead of government spending, government regulation, and government as the patron of last resort, Friedman offered an idyllic

world in which the market alone would purge the old evils of unemployment, racism, income inequality, and poor education that repeated government efforts had failed to cure. Keynesianism was dismissed as logically
flawed, in that new money pumped into an economy through government
spending on borrowed money provided a false and temporary sense of prosperity that undermined true progress.

As one liberal commentator observed, "Whatever government did, he
wanted to undo: farm parities, tariffs, rent control, minimum wages, industry regulation, social security, public housing, conscription, national parks,
the post office, public roads, and the licensing of the professions."[18] In assessing the faults in existing government policies, the strong strain of contrar-
ianism in Friedman's character came to the fore. As Groucho Marx[19] sang
in *Horse Feathers*:[20]

> *Your proposition may be good*
> *But let's have one thing understood:*
> *Whatever it is, I'm against it.*

Capitalism and Freedom was a tour de force, a flagrant bid for attention that slaughtered liberal sacred cows and deposed progressive household gods. It marked the moment when Friedman showed the extent of his
revolutionary thinking. He was reaching far beyond economics, injecting
the moribund political philosophy of conservatism with a vibrant strain of
libertarianism.[21] While debates about economics between Samuelson and
Friedman would continue, Friedman served notice on his old rival that he
had moved on to a grander scheme, in which economics played a relatively
small part.

It is a mark of Friedman's slender reputation in 1962 that, though *Capitalism and Freedom* was reviewed in some learned journals and in *The Economist* in London, no major American general publication thought it worth
noting. It was, for Friedman, more evidence of the pronounced liberal slant

in the American press. "It is inconceivable that a book of the same kind on the other side of the subject would have failed to have been reviewed in [the *New York Times*, the *New York Herald Tribune*, *Newsweek*, etc.],"[22] he said. Although it would take Samuelson several more revisions of his *Economics* textbook before Friedman was given full credit for his many endeavors, by the ninth edition in 1973, Samuelson commended *Capitalism and Freedom* to students as a "rigorously logical, careful, often persuasive elucidation of an important point of view."[23]

From this point on, Friedman redefined himself as an evangelist for capitalism with the aim of transforming the Republicans from a moderate party into a dynamic vanguard for radical libertarianism that often ran counter to traditional conservative values. As Friedman pointed out, old conservative prejudices, such as race hatred, had no place in capitalism, which was a disinterested system that treated all people alike.

Friedman's libertarian beliefs often ran counter to traditional conservative principles. Old-school Republicans were above all patriotic and believed in public service as a sacred duty. For Republicans, joining the armed forces represented the height of personal devotion to the nation, and the military draft, in which citizens were obliged to serve in uniform, was the ultimate call to duty. Particularly during the Sixties, with American troops fighting in Vietnam in large numbers, those who opposed the draft in protest marches were mostly dismissed by conservatives as "peaceniks," or conscientious objectors, or individuals who were fearful for their lives. Draft dodgers were universally castigated by Republicans as un-American traitors, even when the children of conservatives—George W. Bush,[24] Mitt Romney,[25] Newt Gingrich,[26] Rudy Giuliani,[27] and Dick Cheney[28]—found ways to avoid compulsory military service.

Friedman took the dodgers' side.[29] For him, compulsory military service was an impertinent demand from an overweening state. He considered the draft "inequitable, wasteful, and inconsistent with a free society" and conscription "a weapon . . . to discourage freedom of speech, assembly, and protest."[30] He was anxious that a large standing army supported by the military-industrial complex threatened essential freedoms. Instead he suggested armed forces recruited from volunteers.

Similarly, Friedman scandalized his conservative friends by advocating the legal sale of mind-bending drugs. "Do we have the right to use the machinery of government to prevent an individual from becoming an alcoholic or a drug addict?" he asked. His answer: "We have no right to use force, directly or indirectly, to prevent a fellow man from committing suicide, let alone from drinking alcohol or taking drugs." The huge profits from the illegal drug trade corrupted the police, who were meant to put an end to the black market in drugs. Thus, legalizing drugs would both reduce crime and make police more honest. "Can you conceive of any other measure that would accomplish so much to promote law and order?"[31] he asked.

Friedman also championed freeing parents from having to send their children to government-run schools,[32] a system that meant parents could only exercise control over schools through the political process.[33] His solution? Education vouchers provided to parents by government equivalent to the cost of sending a child to a public school that could be spent at independent schools. He hoped his proposal would break the monopoly of teaching unions in public schools and give parents a real choice.[34]

FRIEDMAN WAS ENGAGED in a long political struggle across many fronts, but even by the early Sixties, in his early fifties, he remained little known outside of academia, and even then he was little regarded outside of a small coterie of economists who did not subscribe to the Keynesian consensus. His next step, however, would bring him into direct contact with high politics for the first time, burnishing his reputation among conservatives while confirming for liberals and moderate Republicans his lack of judgment.

To remain popular with voters, in the years after World War II the

Republican Party had, like many conservative parties in western Europe, adopted popular social and economic policies of their opponents. But a rump of Republicans, often living far from the cosmopolitanism of the coasts, had quietly resisted the changes. By the early Sixties, these backwoods conservatives had started to flex their muscles, leading to the presidential campaign of Arizona senator Barry Goldwater.[35] In late 1963, Friedman joined Goldwater's campaign as an economic adviser in a race that would see a resurgent traditional conservative movement challenge the patrician Republican leadership, represented by the New Yorker Nelson Rockefeller,[36] whose surname was a byword for wealth and privilege.

Friedman had taken a liking to the contrarian Goldwater when he was introduced to him by Bill Baroody,[37] who would later lead the conservative think tank the American Enterprise Institute. Goldwater was self-evidently an authentic figure, rough around the edges, and had a mind—and ideas— of his own. Friedman was impressed by Goldwater's adherence to basic conservative principles, his willingness to champion unpopular positions, and his readiness to forgo political expediency.[38]

The Goldwater campaign was an attempt to provide Americans with a radical conservative option in the face of the progressive approach to problems adopted by successive administrations of both stripes. To win his party's nomination, Goldwater had to overcome vehement opposition from the cozy, complacent eastern Republican establishment, which had become used to running the Republican Party like a fusty men's club. But Goldwater was popular among the party's grassroots and trounced the smooth Rockefeller at the party convention in San Francisco in July 1964, emerging as the party's unlikely champion in the election that November against President Johnson.

Goldwater offered voters a crisp conservative message that rang true with Friedman. The East Coast political establishment, however, liked to portray Goldwater as a dangerous extremist, to which Goldwater joked,

"Sometimes I think this country would be better off if we could just saw off the eastern seaboard and let it float out to sea."[39] Friedman thought the "bias of the press and the intelligentsia against Goldwater" to be grossly unfair. The candidate offered a catchy riposte when charged with being a worrisome fanatic: "Extremism in the defense of liberty is no vice. Moderation in the pursuit of justice is no virtue."[40]

But one of Goldwater's "extremist" positions "in the defense of liberty" looked likely to make him unelectable: his promise to use America's full military arsenal to subdue the communist regime in North Vietnam, which, backed by its powerful allies Russia and China, had for years been waging a guerrilla war against its faux-democratic neighbor South Vietnam. Johnson—who would himself ramp up the war in Vietnam after the election—was delighted to paint his opponent as a trigger-happy warmonger who might inadvertently lead the United States into nuclear war. The president's knockout blow was a television commercial, dubbed "The Daisy Ad,"[41] in which a young girl counts as she picks petals from a flower while a somber man's voice counts down the launch of a nuclear missile.

Friedman was unafraid of being associated with a candidate the liberal establishment thought beyond the pale and found himself in great demand as a shill for Goldwater, ready to appear on television or in press interviews to put a respectable intellectual gloss on Goldwater's apparently extreme positions. It confirmed to Friedman that the odds were heavily stacked against those who articulated conservative views. He recalled:

> I talked to and argued with groups from academia, from the media, from the financial community, from the foundation world, from you name it. There was an unbelievable degree of intellectual homogeneity, of acceptance of a standard set of views complete with cliché answers to every objection, of smug self-satisfaction at belonging to an in-group. The closest similar experience I have ever had was at Cambridge, England, and even that was a distant second.[42]

In November 1964, Goldwater was defeated in a landslide, with Johnson sweeping the field except for Goldwater's home state of Arizona and five deeply conservative southern states. For Friedman, the defeat offered a lesson in the inequities of practical politics he would never forget. And his involvement with the Goldwater campaign, though highly controversial, was noted by *Newsweek* editor Osborn Elliott, who was looking for a lively, argumentative, provocative conservative economist to counter the views of his new Keynesian hire, Paul Samuelson.

And so it was that Friedman entered the ring with Samuelson to continue an intellectual duel that had begun in England in 1931 between Keynes and Hayek. While the Keynes Hayek prizefight lasted barely four months, the Samuelson Friedman debate started in *Newsweek* in 1965 lasted nearly five decades. And as with the Keynes Hayek clash, there was to be no knockout blow. No one even fell to the canvas. But the intensity and passion of the original dispute soon became evident. The direction of the next fifty years of economic theory was at stake and with it the role of the federal government as the manager of the American economy.

5

Dueling Columnists

Their competing *Newsweek* columns soon revealed
the profound divide in economics that had first been
defined by the clash between Keynes and Hayek

The ability to maintain a steady and novel stream of subjects to engage
readers is a regular columnist's principal concern. At first, Samuelson
and Friedman both thought writing a weekly column in *Newsweek* would
mean that the fountain of ideas would before long run dry. But both men
soon adapted to the rhythm, at first writing every three weeks, then, when
Henry Wallich joined the Federal Reserve board, every other week. As the
pace quickened, both discovered that the task became easier and that their
rapport with readers improved.

"When first deciding to write for *Newsweek*, I wondered whether I
might run out of topics to comment on. I need not have worried,"[1] explained
Samuelson. His lingering concerns about being inspired in time for the fort-
nightly deadlines was cured by the act of writing itself. The columns became
a means of thinking aloud. "How do I know what I really think until I read
what my pen is writing?"[2] Samuelson asked. And both men wrote quickly
and cogently. As Samuelson put it, "Having a facile pen helped."[3]

The fact that the two men who had known each other so long were
pitted against each other proved a point of amusement to them both,

and something of an inspiration, too. As both were intensely competitive and highly articulate, the contest for readers' attention—and approval—produced good copy.

Both men were aware that a great deal more was at stake in the columns than merely measuring events against their current views. Keynes may have triumphed over Hayek and classical economists after publication of *The General Theory*, but by the time Samuelson and Friedman locked horns thirty years later, the Keynesian hegemony was under pressure. "The layman has a vision of economists as a quarrelsome tribe who never agree," wrote Friedman.

> There is an element of validity in this vision. Paul Samuelson and I, for example, disagree frequently, strongly and publicly on matters of public policy. . . . Disagreement among economists on public policy seldom reflects a difference in economic analysis proper but rather in judgment about quantitative magnitude, goals to be pursued, or the time span to be considered, or political considerations outside economics.[4]

Samuelson concurred. Differences of opinion were the spice of intellectual life. It was nothing personal. "Professor Friedman is an able scholar and a forceful spokesman for the libertarian form of conservative economics," wrote Samuelson. "He is also an old friend. Yet my liberal mind is not persuaded by a considerable number of conservative arguments."[5] For readers searching for the truth, Samuelson had an answer: "I define a truth to be that which at least two out of three *Newsweek* experts on economics are agreed upon."[6] And he suggested that readers who violently disagreed with his views or those of Friedman should calm down. "If you don't like the economics you read in *Newsweek* today, wait a week: something different, maybe better, is sure to turn up,"[7] he said.

While pompous journalists like to elevate the importance of their mundane trade by suggesting that they are writing "the first draft of history," all journalism, including column writing, is ephemeral. Who wants yesterday's papers? It suited Samuelson to pretend that he had not been pitted against Friedman to maximize sensation. "I do not deem it my function to press my value judgments on those with different ethical views," he wrote. "My duty as an economist is to present as accurately and objectively as I can what will be the likely costs and benefits from each proposed policy decision."[8] But he was under no illusion that genuine debate about the fundaments of economics was his main concern. "These analyses of the passing economic scene [are] deliberately written so as not to present a debaters' view," he wrote. "Conversion of the reader was farthest from my mind. Instead of trying to press reality into the distorting confines of simple sermons, I [wanted] to bring out the interesting variety of economic problems."[9]

The Samuelson/Friedman ding-dong emerged as a national fixture in politics that galvanized supporters into two distinct camps—left and right, liberal and conservative, established and radical. Week by week, column by column, both men were obliged to address the twists and turns in the federal government's economic policy thrown up by the news. But their weekly contributions, seen as moving pictures, betrayed profound differences not only in their economics but in their world views.

Samuelson, like Keynes, had an elegant pen, and the care and pleasure with which he chose his words is evident. Like Keynes, he could draw upon a deep hinterland of knowledge way beyond the dry stuff of economics. Like Ronald Reagan, who began his weekly radio broadcasts with a joke, Samuelson liked to start his columns with a humorous quote, then, having raised a smile, he moved to the substance of his mini-essay.

So when, for example, in 1966, commenting on whether the federal government was applying the right fiscal remedies, Samuelson found himself hovering between two minds, he wrote that "like Oscar Wilde, who spent the morning putting in a comma and the afternoon taking it out, I am oscillating."[10]

He could mix it with intellectual giants. And he credited readers with having as broad and deep an intellectual hinterland as he did.

Before Jean-Jacques Rousseau,[11] people generally made the mistake of regarding children as little adults. Since Sigmund Freud,[12] there has been no excuse for failing to recognize adults as merely grown-tall children.

Among the many regular sources Samuelson would summon were the *New Yorker* writer E. B. White,[13] the British imperialist author Rudyard Kipling,[14] the malign Italian political philosopher Niccolò Machiavelli,[15] the English utopian Samuel Butler,[16] and Charles Dickens,[17] the chronicler of the free market in full spate in London at the height of the industrial revolution. And there was a stream of references to Old Testament figures and stories.

Friedman approached writing in a different way. Not only did his columns display little cultural erudition, but, in comparison to Samuelson's broad brush and often lofty approach to problems, Friedman liked to engage with the reader directly and make his case in practical terms. He was less interested in elegance and verbal fireworks than in expressing himself with clarity and persuasiveness. "Friedman is not a great literary stylist," observed one political commentator, "but he learned to write serviceable prose accessible to the common reader. And he cultivated a glibness that gave his arguments, once dismissed by liberals as 'flaky,' a convincing ring."[18] While Samuelson may be thought of as a Keynesian high priest with highfalutin phrasing to match, Friedman was a door-to-door free-market evangelist, hoping to convert the unwashed one proselyte at a time.

So long as the debate remained leveled at fellow economists, Samuelson retained a distinct advantage. While he always maintained the dignity and demeanor of America's supreme economics professor, Friedman the insurgent liked to duck and weave. Samuelson the incumbent rarely missed the

chance to diminish Friedman the challenger's standing. Among most economists, Friedman was little more than a gadfly. And a faintly absurd one at
that. Samuelson piled on, describing Friedman's challenge to the Keynesian
orthodoxy as "a man with a foil attacking a battleship."[19] But Samuelson did
not underestimate his rival. "He's about as smart a guy as you'll meet. He's
as persuasive as you hope not to meet,"[20] he would later observe.

Jokes about Friedman's preoccupation with the money supply to the
exclusion of all other elements of the economy and the sleight-of-hand
with which he could employ logic were legion. "Milton knows how to spell
banana, but he doesn't know when to stop," quipped one economist. "I wish
I could be as sure of one thing as you are of everything," joked another.
"Everything reminds Milton of the money supply," wrote Samuelson's MIT
colleague Robert Solow.[21] "Well, everything reminds me of sex, but I keep
it out of the paper."[22] Samuelson explained the slipperiness of Friedman in
argument thus: "To keep the fish that they carried on long journeys lively
and fresh, sea captains used to introduce an eel into the barrel. In the economics profession, Milton Friedman is that eel."[23]

While in private, in conversation, and in correspondence the pair used
jargon and special knowledge, in their journalism they were restricted to
arguments that could be understood by intelligent readers untrained in the
complexities of advanced economics. Samuelson was stripped of his ability to
call in his defense erudite concepts and technical terms, or make logical leaps
through mathematical equations, as he did in his learned papers, because
few readers would be able to understand him. Friedman, however, had developed a straightforward style that avoided unnecessary intricacies in favor of
an apparently common-sense approach to problems an average reader could
grasp. And while they would play up their differences in print, in private
they were often in agreement. "Where Milton Friedman and I disagree, we
are quick to be able to identify the source and texture of our disagreements
in a way that non-economists cannot perceive,"[24] recalled Samuelson.

In the limelight of their weekly columns, collegiate behavior was abandoned, which benefited Friedman. It was not so much that he was prepared to hit below the belt as that he was happy to put aside barely comprehensible economic theory and make the sort of case ordinary Americans made at home when discussing money and the economy. The money supply was a case in point. That too much money chasing too few goods leads to rising prices is a basic tenet of economics. So an argument that suggested that if the government created a lot of new money the result would likely be short-lived prosperity followed by inflation seemed a reasonable contention. But Samuelson would remind readers that kitchen-table analogies were misleading because a national economy does not work like a domestic budget.

Samuelson confessed to being at a loss to know how best to handle Friedman's highly effective, disruptive debating technique and admitted that when preparing for face-to-face debates with his nemesis, "he always had fear in his heart."[25] And whatever the upshot of a debate, Friedman had the knack of ensuring that it appeared that he had won. "If you looked at a transcript afterward, it might seem clear that you had won the debate on points," Samuelson recalled. "But somehow, with members of the audience, you always seemed to come off as elite, and Milton seemed to have won the day."[26] It was little wonder that George Shultz[27] said of Friedman, "Everybody loves to argue with Milton, particularly when he isn't there."[28] The *Financial Times* journalist Sam Brittan[29] admired above all Friedman's intellectual candor and courage in the face of disapproving conventional opinion. "Part of his appeal lay in his willingness to come out with home truths that had occurred to many other people who had not dared to utter them," he wrote. "Friedman would then go on, however, to defend these maxims against the massed forces of economic correctness."[30]

Martin Anderson,[31] who became one of Reagan's top economic advisers, watched Friedman perform with envious fascination. He wrote:

To meet Friedman is to encounter a ball of controlled energy. The alert, quick eyes are friendly. At first he listens quietly, intensely. As long as he totally agrees he listens, but that usually isn't for long. At the first sign of the slightest break in your logic, or your facts, he pounces with a bewildering array of questions, statements, and relentless logic. And it's all done in such a friendly earnest way that even the intellectually shredded thoroughly enjoy the encounter.

Friedman is the intellectual's intellectual. He makes people think, and he almost always does it in such a way that it gives them pleasure.[32]

The economist Robert Solow, who counted Samuelson as his best friend, was less admiring, but could not deny Friedman's exceptional qualities. He wrote:

Milton was an ideologue, a True Believer, not given to skepticism or self-doubt. There are many of those, but he was an ideologue equipped with a very sharp and quick mind. And, what is not the same thing, he was a superb debater and a happy warrior: relentless, plausible, tactical, convincing, good with an audience, always smiling. When we argued, he would often say: "Bob, I don't understand you." What he meant was: "How can you be so stupid?" But he would not say that.[33]

Friedman learned from Keynes that for a theory to capture the public imagination it must be easy to understand. Many thought Keynes's monumental *General Theory* confusing and hard to grasp. But the main takeaway from Keynes's revolutionary thinking was simple and did not require a reader to plough through the book. Keynes posed the key questions: Should governments try to prevent unemployment? How could there be widespread unemployment in an economy with unused productive capacity? How can governments restore aggregate demand in an economy when it collapses? Friedman explained:

What you need to do is to have a very simple theory that gets at the fundamentals. No theory is successful if it's extremely complicated and difficult, because most phenomena are driven by a very few central forces. What a good theory does is to simplify; it pulls out the central forces and gets rid of the rest. So Keynes's *General Theory* was the right kind of theory.[34]

Friedman's notion linking changes in the supply and velocity of money to inflation was simple and persuasive: inflation is caused solely by changes in the money supply and the rate at which money chases goods. Samuelson, by contrast, had no need nor inclination to oversimply his arguments for effect. The proofs of theories he wrote and published so prolifically defied simple explanations. They were heaped with mathematical equations describing the complex interrelationships between factors in an economy. Samuelson explained, "Like eggs, there are only two kinds of theories: good ones and bad ones. And the test of a theory's goodness is its usefulness in illuminating observational reality. Its logical elegance and fine-spun beauty are irrelevant."[35]

WHATEVER SUBJECT the two men were writing about, both traced the fundamental difference in their views to the schism between Keynes and Hayek that had emerged thirty years before. At the core of their disagreement, and that of the two main opposing factions in economics, left and right, was a fundamental difference about whether governments should intervene in the market and whether any intervention could achieve its intended aims.

Hayek's thinking about economics was based upon his own experience in Austria in the aftermath of World War I, when the Hapsburg Empire was dismantled and its territory divided. Austria was left the decapitated head of an empire that no longer existed and the economy soon fell into chaos, with rampant inflation terrorizing the Austrian population, including Hayek and his family. Hayek was given a job by von Mises, who was head of the Austrian government body administering Austria's enormous war debt.

Hayek discovered at firsthand the horrors of hyperinflation. His salary was set at five thousand old kronen a month. But inflation was so severe that, to keep pace with rising prices, the second month Hayek was paid fifteen thousand kronen, and by July 1922 a million kronen a month. In *The Economic Consequences of the Peace*, Keynes had predicted the postwar hyperinflation that Hayek and his fellow countrymen were enduring. "By a continuing process of inflation, governments can confiscate, secretly and unobserved, an important part of the wealth of their citizens," Keynes wrote. "Lenin was certainly right. There is no subtler, no surer means of overturning the existing basis of society than to debauch the currency."[36] For Austrians like von Mises, who had drawn attention to the shortcomings of a command economy in his *Socialism: An Economic and Sociological Analysis*, published in Vienna in 1922, the prospect of Lenin's violent Bolshevik revolution spreading westward to Austria sent a chill down the spine.

Mises and Hayek avidly read a series of articles written by Keynes for the *Manchester Guardian*, in which Keynes turned his mind to inflation and currency values. Mises warned Hayek that Keynes supported "a good cause with some very bad economic argument." But Hayek found Keynes's fresh thinking about old problems to be invigorating. In particular, Hayek was fascinated by Keynes's thoughts about governments intervening in an economy to keep prices and the price of currencies stable. "We must free ourselves from the deep distrust which exists against allowing the regulation of the standard of value to be the subject of deliberate decision,"[37] Keynes wrote. "In the modern world of paper currency and bank credit, there is no escape from a 'managed' currency, whether we wish it or not. Convertibility into gold will not alter the fact that the value of gold itself depends on the policy of the Central Banks."[38]

Keynes also challenged the assumption among economists that over time an economy would come to rest at an equilibrium in which, "in the long run," a constant supply of money would result in stable prices. Keynes argued that it was not the supply of money that was the key to stable prices—the quantity theory of money—but the velocity of money in the system, which could change without notice, leading to constantly changing prices. The impatient Keynes found "in the long run" far too distant a prospect to be helpful when formulating public policy or when commiserating with the victims of inflation or deflation. In what would become one of his most famous quotes, Keynes wrote, "In the long run we are all dead."[39]

In Britain in the years after World War I, the return by the government of the price of the pound sterling to its prewar parity was causing millions to be thrown out of work. As with the elusive equilibrium that was over time meant to match constant currency values with constant prices, so Keynes was skeptical of the claim that, left to its own devices, a market would reach an equilibrium in which all those of working age would be employed.

The British government had in 1918 fixed the pound at such a high value that British exporters found themselves priced out of the market. Between 1918 and 1920, the British government cut its expenditure by 75 percent. In the following decade, unemployment never fell below a million and by 1933 reached more than three million—or 20 percent of Britain's working population. The failure of the government to find work for its people led to civil unrest, mass protests, including a general strike of all workers in 1926, and the coal miners' Jarrow March in 1936. With an intransigent chancellor, Neville Chamberlain,[40] resisting all pleas to devalue sterling, Keynes began to explore how a government might act to put the unemployed back to work.

"The more troublesome the times, the worse does a laissez-faire system work,"[41] Keynes declared in 1924. He suggested that a truly laissez-faire economy was a myth, an intellectual construct, a will-o'-the-wisp. In the real world, there were endless inhibitions, regulations, and constraints on the operation of a truly free market that could never be overcome. The very existence of a government perverted the free market by directing taxpayers' millions into the economy. The choice of where and how to spend taxpayers' money was a means of directing the economy and could be strategically targeted. He hinted that those who put their trust solely in the freedom of the market were more interested in economics as an act of faith than as a means of assessing objective fact. He wrote:

> In considering how to [stimulate investment at home], we are brought to my heresy—if it is a heresy. I bring in the State; I abandon laissez-faire. . . . It entrusted the public weal to private enterprise unchecked and unaided. Private enterprise is no longer unchecked—it is checked and threatened in many different ways. . . . And if private enterprise is not unchecked, we cannot leave it unaided.[42]

Keynes said a government could deliberately reduce interest rates and issue government bonds to flood the economy with money. The government could also directly employ the jobless in public works programs. But Chamberlain ignored his advice. Keynes was quickly coming to the conclusion that the market, left to its own devices, was an inappropriate mechanism to ensure prosperity for all. "It is obvious that an individualist society left to itself does not work well or even tolerably,"[43] he wrote.

Keynes's interventionist thinking gathered speed. "We have stuck in a rut. We need an impulse, a jolt, an acceleration." He proposed, as "the ultimate cure of unemployment," that £100 million ($1.5 billion in 2020 dollars) should be spent immediately on public housing, improving roads, and a refit of the electricity grid. He was aware that the outcome of such a comparatively large public investment was far from certain. But the situation was so dire that anything was worth trying. "Let us experiment with boldness on such lines, even though some of the schemes may turn out to be failures, which is very likely,"[44] he wrote.

Faced with what he saw as the failure of the free market, Keynes did not embrace its antithesis: socialism. He thought free enterprise to be "in many ways extremely objectionable," but, a Liberal by political affiliation, he had no intention of undermining it. "I think that Capitalism, wisely managed, can probably be made more efficient for attaining economic ends than any alternative system yet in sight," he wrote. And in a lecture pointedly titled "The End of Laissez-Faire," delivered at Oxford University in November 1924—and at the University of Berlin two years later—he wrote, "The important thing for Government is not to do things which individuals are doing already, and to do them a little better or a little worse, but to do those things which at present are not done at all."[45]

Forty years later, Samuelson was to make an identical point, invoking the founder of the Republican Party, Abraham Lincoln:

> Lincoln is supposed to have said somewhere, "I believe the government should do only that which private citizens cannot do for themselves." . . . I think Lincoln meant to imply in his formulation that there is needed a certain burden of proof that has to be established by anyone who proposes that the government do something. Why? Lincoln did not say.[46]

In his battle with Keynes, Hayek had drawn attention to the downside of intervening in the market. If the free operation of the market "is distorted by the creation of artificial demand," he wrote, "it must mean that part of the available resources is again led into a wrong direction and a definite and lasting adjustment is again postponed." He went on:

> The only way permanently to "mobilize" all available resources is, therefore, not to use artificial stimulants—whether during a crisis or thereafter—but to leave it to time to affect a permanent cure by the slow process of adapting the structure of production to the means available for capital purposes.[47]

Austrians like Hayek believed a government that reduced interest rates merely to promote economic activity was storing up trouble for later. Such intervention interfered with the "natural equilibrium" between savings and investment. If capital goods, such as machine tools not needed by the market, were bought with artificially cheap money, the relationship between savings and investment would hurtle out of kilter. A central bank that kept interest rates artificially low would promote a downward spiral of reducing interest rates, ending with an economy in disarray and a recession.

MANY YEARS LATER, Hayek went further, and, in 1944, in a wartime tract—*The Road to Serfdom*—warned that government intervention in an economy could jeopardize democracy by transferring key choices from citizens to government officials. But in a passage that would come to haunt him, Hayek drew a line between what he thought was legitimate state activity and what he considered to be dangerous government overreach.

The Road to Serfdom went on to sell millions of copies and, taken up by the Volker Foundation in the U.S., quickly became a bible for those who champion the free market. But like the Bible, even true believers can fail to read it carefully. One passage is worth quoting at length because the complexity of Hayek's thoughts is often oversimplified or ignored, even by his devotees. Writing not from the comfort of prosperous postwar America but from a cold, draughty room in war-torn, bankrupt, austerity-ridden Britain, Hayek's remarks may come as a surprise to those who think themselves to be Hayekians and Hayek to be an absolutist when it came to government intervention.

> There is no reason why in a society which has reached the general level
> of wealth which ours has attained the first kind of security should not
> be guaranteed to all without endangering general freedom. . . . There
> can be no doubt that some minimum of food, shelter, and clothing,

sufficient to preserve health and the capacity to work, can be assured to everybody. . . .

Nor is there any reason why the state should not assist the individual in providing for those common hazards of life against which, because of their uncertainty, few individuals can make adequate provision.

Where, as in the case of sickness and accident, neither the desire to avoid such calamities nor the efforts to overcome their consequences are as a rule weakened by the provision of—where, in short, we deal with genuinely insurable—the case for the state's helping to organize a comprehensive system of social insurance is very strong.

There are many points of detail where those wishing to preserve the competitive system and those wishing to supersede it by something different will disagree on the details of such schemes; and it is possible under the name of social insurance to introduce measures which tend to make competition more or less ineffective. But there is no incompatibility in principle between the state's providing greater security in this way and the preservation of individual freedom. . . .

There is, finally, the supremely important problem of combating general fluctuations of economic activity and the recurrent waves of large-scale unemployment which accompany them. . . . But, though its solution will require much planning in the good sense, it does not—or at least need not—require that special kind of planning which according to its advocates is to replace the market.

Many economists hope, indeed, that the ultimate remedy may be found in the field of monetary policy, which would involve nothing incompatible even with nineteenth-century liberalism. Others, it is true, believe that real success can be expected only from the skillful timing of public works undertaken on a very large scale. This might lead to much more serious restrictions of the competitive sphere, and, in experimenting in this direction, we shall have to carefully watch our

step if we are to avoid making all economic activity progressively more
dependent on the direction and volume of government expenditure.
But this is neither the only nor, in my opinion, the most promising
way of meeting the gravest threat to economic security.

In any case, the very necessary effort to secure protection against
these fluctuations does not lead to the kind of planning which constitutes such a threat to our freedom.[48]

Hayek sent a proof copy of *The Road to Serfdom* to Keynes, who read
it on board an ocean liner crossing the Atlantic en route to, among other
things, the Bretton Woods conference in New Hampshire, over which he
was presiding. In his letter of congratulations, Keynes was, as ever, encouraging to his rival, though he remained unconvinced by the general thrust
of Hayek's argument. He went straight to the weakest point in Hayek's reasoning: that a civilized society is honor bound to provide its citizens with
the basic necessities: food, healthcare, and housing. Writing from the Clar-
idge Hotel in Atlantic City, Keynes told Hayek, "It is a grand book. We all
have the greatest reason to be grateful to you for saying so well what needs
so much to be said. You will not expect me to accept quite all the economic
dicta in it. But morally and philosophically I find myself in agreement with
virtually the whole of it; and not only in agreement with it, but in a deeply
moved agreement." Then came the stiletto.

I come to what is really my only serious criticism. You admit here and
there that it is a question of knowing where to draw the line [between
the private sector and government activity]. You agree that the line has
to be drawn somewhere; and that the logical extreme is not possible.
But you give us no guidance whatever as to where to draw it.

It is true that you and I would probably draw it in different places.
I should guess that according to my ideas you greatly underestimate
the practicability of the middle course. But as soon as you admit that

the extreme is not possible, and that a line has to be drawn, you are, on your own argument, done for, since you are trying to persuade us that so soon as one moves an inch in the planned [economy] direction you are necessarily launched on the slippery path which will lead you in due course over the precipice.[49]

What is needed to ensure that government involvement in the market does not become authoritarian, said Keynes, is not so much a matter of economics but of morality. "What we need is the restoration of right moral thinking—a return to proper moral values in our moral philosophy. If only you could turn your crusade in that direction you would not look or feel quite so much like Don Quixote."[50]

WHEREAS KEYNES'S AND HAYEK'S disagreement in 1931 mostly revolved around the efficacy of a government interceding in a flailing economy, Friedman, taking Hayek's cue, concentrated upon the role of government itself. Hayek's fear of despotism by the back door chimed with Friedman's innate suspicion of big government.

Samuelson was well equipped to defend Keynesianism, given the appropriate battlefield, but Friedman's broadening of the argument to suggest that the institution of government itself impeded the efficient running of an economy put much of what Friedman said beyond Samuelson's reach. In the ensuing debate, two distinct, competing world views clashed, with Samuelson defending the world as it existed—a mixed economy made up of both private and state actors—and Friedman offering the prospect of a return to a libertarian Shangri-La. Samuelson pointed out that the free-market idyll Friedman yearned for had once existed in the United States.

Perhaps nineteenth-century America came as close as any economy ever has to that state of laissez faire which Carlyle called "anarchy plus the constable." The result was a century of rapid material progress and an environment of individual freedom. There were also periodic business crises, wasteful exhaustion of irreplaceable natural resources, extremes of poverty and wealth, corruption of government by vested interest groups, and at times the supplanting of self-regulating competition by monopoly.[51]

While Friedman disliked the behavior of the federal government, he drew the line at abolishing government altogether. "I wish the anarchists luck, since that's the way we ought to be moving now," he once observed. "But I believe we need government to enforce the rules of the game."[52]

Samuelson was less interested in realizing an ideal society than explaining how a sophisticated modern economy worked. Friedman was on a mission to derail what he thought of as a drift towards social democracy in America. He advocated a market-based system of government that minimized political discretion over the economy and replaced it with a rules-based regime that would maximize economic growth. And his main target was the unhindered creation of new money by the Federal Reserve. "A monetary rule [to limit the Federal Reserve's provision of new money] would insulate monetary policy both from arbitrary power of a small group of men not subject to control by the electorate and from the short-run pressures of partisan politics,"[53] he wrote.

Samuelson was rarely taken by surprise by the arguments Friedman employed. Like Friedman, he had been taught by prominent members of the Chicago School, who also held dear the notion of an ideal society underpinned by a vigorous free-market economy, and who were skeptical about the claims Keynesians made for their interventionist actions. Still, it was new for Samuelson to have to justify his positions. His smooth path to fame and fortune had entailed little confrontation or need for self-defense. Now, challenged by Friedman, he was expected to vindicate the existing order and defend the very edifice of representative democracy. For much of their clash, Samuelson could do little but sit back and watch, half in awe, half in horrified disbelief, as Friedman made his case and succeeded in persuading prominent conservative politicians to adopt idiosyncratic economic prescriptions.

As Friedman's campaigning gathered pace, Samuelson could hardly ignore his rival's many achievements. At first, as was the Keynesian way with dissenters, Samuelson ignored Friedman, or ridiculed his insurgent status. In the first edition of his *Economics* textbook, Friedman's name appears just once, and even then only in a footnote citing a paper he had written with Simon Kuznets. But as Friedman's long march gathered pace, Samuelson was obliged to credit him with a succession of triumphs.

Friedman, meanwhile, insisted that he had not deliberately conspired to undermine the existing order. "People have a tendency to attribute to me a long-term plan," he wrote. "I did no planning whatsoever. These things just happened in the order in which they happened to happen. And luck plays a very large role, a very large role indeed."[54]

6

To Intervene or
Not to Intervene

At the root of the Samuelson Friedman dispute was
whether governments could—and should—interfere
in the free market if an economy turns sour

Samuelson believed governments played an important role in shaping society for the good and that there was nothing wrong with a state managing its national economy through fiscal policy to improve the lives of its citizens. "It is a lucky accident that so much of economic life can be performed reasonably well by markets," he wrote. "But a long list of important cases arises where economics suggests that governments should intervene."[1]

The Keynesianism he described in his textbook *Economics: An Introductory Analysis*, by the mid-Sixties in its seventh edition, envisioned "a progressive full-employment economy in which the excesses of the business cycle are moderated. We want to control the 'mad dance of the dollar' as the business cycle passes from boom to crisis and slump."[2] Besides, he told *Newsweek* readers in 1968, "the New Economics really does work." He continued, "Wall Street knows it. Main Street, which has been enjoying 92 months of advancing sales, knows it. The accountants who chalk up record corporate profits know it. The children of the workingmen do not know it: but their mothers do, and so do the school nurses who measure the heights and weights of this generation and remember the bony structure of the last. . . .

Who does not know it? Of course, the exponents of orthodox finance deny the obvious."[3]

While in many respects he was a conservative economist, and an "exponent of orthodox finance," Friedman considered himself a radical freethinker, incapable of being categorized. Echoing his friend Hayek, who had famously written an essay entitled, "Why I Am Not a Conservative," Friedman declared, "I'm not a conservative. I don't want to keep things the way they are."[4] He was happy to be thought a libertarian, a respecter of the individual who was deeply suspicious of government activity. And it was often over the proper role of government in a free society, rather than economics per se, that Samuelson and Friedman argued.

When the pair first set out on their columns in 1968, Samuelson and the Keynesians were ascendant. An indication of how Keynesian ideas dominated the intellectual landscape can be gleaned from the contemporary histories of economic thought. For instance, William J. Barber, a professor of economics at Wesleyan, published *A History of Economic Thought* in 1967. While he gave due credit to "Classical Economics," with chapters on Adam Smith, Robert Malthus, David Ricardo, and John Stuart Mill, the book ends with the triumph of Keynes. There is no mention of the Austrian School, nor the Chicago School, nor von Mises, nor Hayek, nor Friedman.

In his textbook *Economics*, Samuelson suggested that the Chicago School, Austrian economics, and radical libertarian ideas about the preeminence of the market were of little contemporary relevance—and therefore of limited use to students of economics. In the first edition, in 1948, Samuelson had promised readers he would "include some of the burning issues you will live with all your lives,"[5] and he devoted a chapter to "Prices and Money," including a section on the subject of Friedman's special interest, "the money supply M and the way M has generally moved in relation to long-term prices."[6]

Other non-Keynesians were also given short shrift by Samuelson. In the first edition of his *Economics*, Samuelson mentions von Mises only in passing,[7] with Samuelson skeptically noting that "around 1920, Ludwig von Mises . . . set forth the challenging view that rational economic organization was logically impossible in the absence of free markets." Hayek, too, merits only a footnote.[8] Samuelson did, however, cite Friedman twice: once, en passant, as a footnote;[9] and a second time in a flick to Friedman's views when discussing what was to become the overarching subject of their disagreement: inflation, or the relationship between the speed of the growth of money in an economy and the change in prices.[10] As the Seventies progressed, price inflation became rampant in advanced economies and the central focus for political action. Events therefore played into the hands of Friedman, whose monetarist theories set out to explain both how rapidly rising prices came about and how to prevent them rising in the future. Samuelson had predicted the rising problem of inflation back in 1958. Asked what was the most pressing issue to be faced by the U.S. in the subsequent twenty years, he said, "The threat of inflation. . . . Inflation is itself a problem. But the legitimate and hysterical fears of inflation are—quite aside from the evil of inflation itself—likely, in their own right, to be problems. In short, I fear inflation. And I fear the fear of inflation."[11]

While Samuelson continued to revise his textbook, he found little space for Friedman's market theories. Keynesianism, then usually called "the New Economics," still ruled. Friedman took a wounded pride in being an outsider, considered somehow beyond the pale by the respectable mainstream. His maverick personality seemed to enjoy being set apart. "I was at odds with the reigning orthodoxy about both public policy and economic theory; about welfare-state and socialist views in public policy, and Keynesianism in economic theory," he wrote. "I recall well the Harvard graduate student who came to visit me, saying something like, 'I had to see for myself what that black magician from the Middle West was like.' "[12]

Back in 1966, *Time* magazine had published a cover story marking the arrival of "neo-Keynesianism," arguing that "because he was a creature of his times, Keynes was primarily interested in pulling a Depression-ridden world up to some form of prosperity and stability; today's economists are more concerned about making an already prospering economy grow still further," before quoting Friedman as saying, "We are all Keynesians now."[13]

The suggestion that Friedman, the champion of liberal economics, should concede that Keynesianism had triumphed was news. But, as with so much sensational journalism, it proved a story too good to check. Friedman, who had spoken to a *Time* reporter for the piece, was incensed at being misreported and wrote to the magazine's editor:

> You quote me as saying: "We are all Keynesians now." The quotation is correct, but taken out of context. As best I can recall it, the context was: "In one sense, we are all Keynesians now; in another, nobody is any longer a Keynesian." The second half is at least as important as the first.[14]

Samuelson wrote a letter of condolence to Friedman, saying he had been saved by his assistant from believing the explosive *Time* quote. "In the history of ideas, [Sir William] Harcourt's[15] statement 'We are all socialists now' is interpreted not as saying that he was a socialist, but as an ironic commentary on the times and its fashions," he wrote. "That is what economists inferred from the *Time* quote."[16] Many years later, Friedman told Samuelson that "one of the minor dividends for writing for *Newsweek* is that I have been freed from *Time* phone calls. In my experience, they have a very high record for unreliability."[17]

He later offered a less defensive explanation for how someone might conclude he had become a Keynesian. "We all use the Keynesian language and apparatus; none of us any longer accepts the initial Keynesian conclusions,"[18] by which he meant that all those who discussed macroeconomics were obliged to acknowledge Keynes's singular contribution to the discipline, whether they agreed with his remedies or not, as Keynes was largely responsible for persuading economists to take a macroeconomic view and look at the economic system as a whole, made up of interdependent parts. It was Hayek's "Austrian" rejection of macroeconomics per se, in favor of solely relying on microeconomic explanations, that led Hayek to say Friedman was in many important respects closer in thought to Keynes than to him. Asked which was the greater economist, Keynes or von Mises, Friedman did not hesitate to answer, "Keynes."[19]

The *Time* incident only served to confirm that Friedman's outsider status had become an essential part of his public persona. As one economist sympathetic to Friedman put it, "Until the 1970s, the economics profession overwhelmingly greeted Friedman's ideas with hostility."[20] Friedman and others of a similar persuasion were resigned to being pariahs. "Those of us who were deeply concerned about the danger to freedom and prosperity from the growth of government, from the triumph of welfare-state and Keynesian ideas, were a small beleaguered minority regarded as eccentrics by the great majority of our fellow intellectuals,"[21] Friedman wrote.

Friedman liked to quote a student who found that the Duke University library did not hold Friedman's books because "the Economics Department did not consider [his] work worthy of carrying."[22] The student demanded that either Friedman's books be included or the books on Karl Marx should be removed. According to Friedman, for fear of inviting bad publicity, Duke reluctantly agreed to add some Friedman tomes.

But while Keynesianism maintained its supremacy over economics taught in the Sixties, beneath the surface the discipline of economics was in flux. As Samuelson was aware, the tectonic plates of economic thought were shifting. He explained:

> The historian of the future, peering back to understand our age, could do worse than study carefully the successive editions of an economics textbook like mine. You will not find in the index of its first edition *Economics* (1948), "pollution" or "ecology." You will find back there the pressing concerns of the mid-century: eradication of mass unem-

ployment, moderation of the business cycle, macroeconomic control
of demand-pull inflation. . . .[23]

When Samuelson and Friedman first crossed swords in *Newsweek*, the economy was growing steadily, aided by spending on the Vietnam War; inflation was low and under control; and Americans were feeling prosperous as
never before. Samuelson was confident that Keynesian, or neo-Keynesian,
policies would continue unhindered. "We have eaten of the fruit of the Tree
of Knowledge and there is no going back. For better or worse," he wrote in
October 1966.[24] Laissez-faire was archaic and remained an irrelevant distraction. "Under laissez faire, everybody's business is nobody's business,"
Samuelson wrote in *Newsweek*. "In the good society, everybody's business is
everybody's business."[25] In practice, Samuelson's assertion meant that only
governments could save the nation from rapacious capitalism. And only
governments could protect citizens from violent threats, internal and external. He affected mild offense that conservatives should consider how a market was meant to work as all the economics anyone might ever need. "I've
never believed in Economics in One Lesson,"[26] he said.

Friedman and other libertarians, meanwhile, pitched free-market forces
as a cure-all for society's ills. They implied that avoiding public borrowing
and government spending was a civic virtue. All attempts by the state to
ameliorate the ills of society, however well intentioned, were dismissed as
socialistic and certain to inhibit the smooth operation of the free market,
thus slowing economic growth.

Friedman got close to suggesting that the market was a better indicator of what Americans wanted than elections. It was not so much that the
market trumped democracy as that the market reflected voters' true democratic intentions. "The Federal government is the engine of inflation—the
only one there is," he wrote. "But it has been the engine of inflation at the
behest of the American public, which wants the government to spend more
but not raise taxes—so encouraging resort to the hidden tax of inflation.

The public objects to inflation—but I have yet to hear any group object to a rise in the price of something it sells."[27] "Inflation is taxation without legislation,"[28] he wrote, borrowing from a chapter heading in Keynes's *A Tract on Monetary Reform*.

Samuelson saw the link between democracy and public spending as a red herring. "Experience with the political economy of social choice [will not] bear out the diagnosis that democracy by its nature must produce overlarge public spending," he wrote. "The economic principles of collective decision making and of competitive game theory demonstrate that there is as much an inherent tendency for governments to spend *too little* as too much."[29]

Friedman, in his inimitable finger-prodding style, made the case to *Newsweek* readers that free-market forces should reign supreme because it was the right of every citizen to be free from government interference. Rather than invoke economic theory, he instead conjured an ideal, ancient America in which the market was largely unchecked, before President Woodrow Wilson's World War I command economy and long before Franklin Roosevelt's 1933 administration used all elements of the government to free Americans from the scourge of the Great Depression.

Friedman wrote that between the Civil War and the First World War, "The U.S. came about as close to a laissez-faire, free-enterprise society as one could hope to observe in practice"[30] and the result was a rapid improvement in the wealth of individuals and the nation. This was because the government stepped back and allowed the market to rip. He described the free-enterprise system as "the most effective machine yet developed for eliminating poverty and raising the standard of life of the masses."[31]

Friedman omitted the business busts and bank failures[32] the American economy routinely suffered in the years before the federal government took closer control, or the human misery caused by the sudden loss of jobs, or the lack of enough jobs for everyone. He liked to press his arguments by pushing them to the extremes, with everything portrayed in black and white. It was as if nuance itself was a concession to his opponents' point of view. He

portrayed government spending not as if it had been mandated by a democratically elected Congress and president, but as something imposed against
the will of the people by an undemocratic, Soviet-like state. He even suggested that the primary duty of any state—to defend its borders and population from invaders—reeked of socialism, and that defense spending caused
private companies to become financially dependent on the state.

Taxation, which by its nature is compulsory, Friedman considered a
fiendish assault upon individual freedoms. In a feisty column titled, "Whose
Money Is It Anyway?"[33] Friedman explained that while citizens may assume
that money can be printed by the state and that entitlements were essentially
free, it was individual taxpayers, not the government, that ended up settling
the government's bills. "The Federal government has no widow's cruse[34] that
provides subsidies at no one's expense," he wrote. "Strictly speaking, there
are no Federal funds, only taxpayer funds."[35] The winner-takes-all nature
of democracy often meant the tyranny of the majority whereby those in a
minority who wanted less government and lower taxes were ignored.

He concluded that government spending was unfair to those who disagreed with the decision to spend, even if the demand for spending had
been sanctioned by democratically elected officials. Why should the government oblige individuals to pay taxes under penalty of the law if they did
not support what the government was spending the money on, Friedman
asked. "It is an act of compassion for one human being voluntarily to give of
his substance to another who is in need," wrote Friedman. "But is it an act
of compassion on A's part for him to force B to give assistance to C?"[36] For
Friedman, government actions on behalf of the majority plowed under the
individual rights—often the basic property rights—of the minority.

Friedman suggested it was the need to guarantee the freedom of individuals that inspired his devotion to the free market. While other market economists argued that only the operation of free-market forces could
ensure that an economy was at its most productive, for Friedman such efficacy was merely a bonus. "The preservation of liberty, not the promotion of

efficiency, is the primary justification for private property," he wrote. "Efficiency is a happy though not accidental by-product—and a most important by-product because liberty could not have survived if it had not also produced affluence."[37]

Samuelson found Friedman's equating definition of "freedom" with unfettered rights to private property to be unconvincing. "The rights of property shrink as the rights of man expand,"[38] he wrote. While some suffered because the government intervened in the market, an unfettered market had winners and losers, too, he argued. While the free market suggested that everyone was free to buy what they wanted, there was such a thing as rationing by price, which put many items well beyond the reach of those without the means. The children of those who could not afford good education, for instance, were deprived by the market setting too high a price. The "freedom" of individuals provided by the market was therefore only notional.

Yet free-market economists, like Friedman and Hayek, found the market system of settling on a price—a mutually agreed bargain between buyers and sellers—to be eternally virtuous. For them, prices were the way the market ensured that the maximum good was achieved through the consent of all parties. Samuelson saw prices merely as a means of rationing scarce goods, and he thought virtue had little to do with it. Indeed, the deliberate raising and lowering of prices was often a means of guiding human behavior rather than following it. Throwing Friedman's words back at him, Samuelson wrote, "Libertarians fail to realize that the price system is, and ought to be, a method of coercion."[39]

Americans may be skeptical of governments and suspicious of their elected officials, but Samuelson argued that representative democracy was essential for a fair and benign society. "We do not vote for social-security and welfare assistance out of love for Washington civil servants," he wrote. "Being human and realizing we are subject to the unknown perils of unemployment and destitution, we cannily opt for the mutual reinsurance of the modern welfare state, knowing that, but for the grace of God, the bell that tolls could be tolling for us."[40]

"Freedom" was a matter of establishing priorities, Samuelson explained. "In most actual situations we come to a point at which choices between goals must be made: do you want this kind of freedom and this kind of hunger, or that kind of freedom and that kind of hunger?"[41]

Samuelson believed that capitalist societies operated under an unwritten, unstated social contract, based on manners, traditions, conventions, and laws, that allowed people to live together peaceably. Social mobility was an important aspect of a market economy. "Capitalism is a hotel. Its penthouse suites are always filled, but not necessarily with the same people this decade as last. And its basement dungeons are also jam-packed; but not with the same faces and bodies."[42] The social contract between individuals meant pooling some individual rights so that the individual might enjoy broader freedoms. "Traffic lights coerce me and limit my freedom," Samuelson wrote. "Yet in the midst of a traffic jam on the unopen road, was I really 'free' before there were lights? And has the algebraic total of freedom, for me or the representative motorist or the group as a whole, been increased or decreased by the introduction of well engineered Stop Lights? Stop Lights, you know, are also Go Lights."[43]

Friedman rarely invoked his political heroes. But the tradition from which he emerged stemmed from a long list of big libertarian/conservative personalities who had challenged the sharp increase in state power that Keynesianism in practice demanded. The most extreme of these was Ayn Rand,[44] whose harrowing personal experience growing up in Russia under Soviet communism, which had attempted to purge the market from all aspects of Russian life, inspired her to adopt an absolutist position in which everything except the free market was an impingement on freedom. To Rand, even Hayek was a treacherous compromiser, and—Rand's behavior was as extreme as her politics—she once spat at Hayek at a party to show her disdain for his treachery.

Hayek agreed with Friedman that it was right to distrust government intervention. For more than twenty years, both supported Hayek's annual libertarian powwow arranged by the Mont Pèlerin Society. And, like Hayek, Friedman allied himself closely with the leading lights of the Chicago School—the Old School, which predated Friedman, was led by Frank Knight, Henry Simons, and Paul Douglas, as well as more recent members, such as Robert Lucas Jr.,[45] George Stigler, Gary Becker,[46] Robert Fogel,[47] and Theodore Schultz—and he had become the School's most dashing and well-known public intellectual.

Samuelson was mostly unimpressed by Friedman's ideological heroes. He thought little of "Ayn Rand's absurd religion of the selfish."[48] But as a distinguished graduate of Chicago's economics department, Samuelson was well placed to confront the theoretical basis of Friedman's thinking. And it was his intimate knowledge of the Chicago School that gave him the confidence to tweak Friedman's nose in argument by calling in evidence Friedman's home team.

Samuelson gave full credit to the Chicago School for keeping market forces at the center of economics, even though during the Great Depression free-market forces had failed to prevent—indeed, had contributed to—a worldwide humanitarian disaster. "From 1932–1945, faith in the market-pricing mechanism as the organizer of the economy sold at a discount," Samuelson wrote. "It was the priceless contribution of Frank Knight and the Chicago School to remind us of the market's merits."[49]

Samuelson was friends with the big personalities at Chicago and knew that they often disagreed with each other. "However homogenous modern economics might appear to an outsider, an insider can always point to the schismatic University of Chicago . . . for a refreshing departure from the new orthodoxy of the 'mixed economy,'"[50] Samuelson teased.

Samuelson had a particular regard for the intelligence and intellectual honesty of Knight, who felt that the free market was a poor mechanism for maximizing good in society—but that government intervention was likely to be even worse. "Knight was the founder of the Chicago School in economics," Samuelson wrote. "If he was Abraham, Henry Simons was Isaac and Milton Friedman is Jacob."[51] He continued, "If Dr. Friedman is one of those optimists who thinks that capitalism is the best of all possible worlds, Dr. Knight was one of those pessimists who is afraid that this is indeed the case."[52]

Samuelson readily agreed that market forces remained important to an economy, however much governments may intervene. He understood that there was a changing fashion in economic ideas and that the popularity of the market persisted, not least thanks to the evangelical activities of the Chicago School. "Make no mistake about it," wrote Samuelson in 1973, "rumors of the death of the market, like those of [Mark] Twain's[53] death, are greatly exaggerated. In Britain and Scandinavia, Socialist governments have in the last quarter of a century often been displaced from office. In America, too, the pendulum swings."[54]

Samuelson was happy to snipe at Friedman whenever the occasion allowed. And Friedman was never shy about complaining when he felt aggrieved. In 1971, in a lecture at DePaul University, Chicago, Samuelson said, "The truth is that every economic study of the demand for money concludes that there is a strong negative dependence upon the interest rate— that is everyone with the notable exception of Professor Milton Friedman, the sole scholar unable or unwilling to detect such an effect."[55] Affecting hurt, Friedman immediately sent Samuelson an article[56] he had written six years before which, he said, contradicted Samuelson's claim. Friedman told his old friend and rival, "I welcome criticism, constructive or destructive, but not flat misrepresentation of my views."[57] Samuelson replied:

I worded my remarks very carefully. (Never having regarded you as a defenseless fellow who can be bullied, I have always in my quoting of positions of yours made sure that I had evidence for them—and a jury will not consider that evidence refuted by your producing some other specimen of your writing or talking in which you may have said the opposite.) . . . The monetarism I attacked at DePaul is a straw man.[58]

While Friedman was invariably Samuelson's principal target for mockery, Stigler, too, often walked through Samuelson's crosshairs. He wrote:

My friend George Stigler points out certain defects of government action. By itself, that is like pointing out certain defects of marriages. What we need to know is, "What are the alternatives? Celibacy? Cold baths? Violent exercise?" Jesting aside, Professor Stigler obviously hopes that the market can undertake more tasks "efficiently" and "equitably." I, too, so hope.[59]

The difference between macro- and microeconomics formed a running theme in Samuelson's criticism of the free marketeers. While many market economists tended to argue from the particular to the general, using microeconomics and experience of business or the domestic household budget to point to wider truths about the operation of the economy in general, Samuelson believed there were important differences between household economics or business finances and the logic that underpinned economics, particularly macroeconomics. He wrote:

The most interesting and important thing about economics as a science is precisely that almost everything that is true for the individual is wrong for the society and almost everything that is true for the society as a whole is wrong for the individual. One individual can affect the price of hardly anything he buys. Yet, all individuals together make the price what it is."[60]

If Samuelson liked to tease Friedman, Friedman was not afraid of attacking the principles held dear by Samuelson's elite friends and neighbors in Cambridge, Massachusetts. Friedman enjoyed ribbing such well-meaning rich liberals, who put their devotion to the arts only second to their wish for the unfair society they presided over to become more equitable. For instance, he enjoyed questioning why taxpayers should fund two bodies that promoted and financed high-art performances, the Corporation for Public Broadcasting and the National Endowments for the Arts and for the Humanities. According to the evidence, he said, their activities were mostly enjoyed by the well-off and educated and were rarely watched by modestly schooled, poorly paid blue-collar Americans.

"What justification is there for imposing taxes on low income people to finance luxuries for high-income people?" asked Friedman. He answered his own question:

> Only the political power of the elite who find it easier to persuade legislators to spend other people's money than to pay for their luxuries themselves. Of course, we shall be told that it is all for the "benefit" of the poor suckers who pay the taxes—their tastes must be uplifted, though how their tastes can be uplifted by TV programs they do not watch or books they do not read has always been beyond my understanding.[61]

Samuelson, in turn, liked to question Friedman's narrow use of the word "freedom." It is not possible for individuals to cut themselves off from society, he argued, and the price of belonging to society was the obligation to pay for common services through taxation. Or, as he reminded *Newsweek* readers, Supreme Court Justice Oliver Wendell Holmes Jr. had once said, "Taxes are what we pay for civilized society."[62] Taxation, which to Friedman was an example of how the state coerced free individuals, was to Samuelson simply the means for a good citizen to pay her dues to society. "Anatole France said epigrammatically all that needs to be said about the coercion implicit in the libertarian economics of laissez faire," Samuelson wrote.

" 'How majestic is the equality of the Law, which permits both rich and poor alike to sleep under the bridges at night.' "[63]

Samuelson was impatient with libertarians like Friedman who described the coercion used by the state to ensure taxes were paid as an abuse of state power, as if the federal and state governments were necessarily authoritarian and wicked. "The whole matter of proper government policy involves issues of ethics, coercion, administration, incidence, and incentives that cannot begin to be resolved by semantic analysis of such terms as 'freedom,' 'coercion,' or 'individualism,' "[64] Samuelson wrote.

And even if "coercion" were the right word, Samuelson believed such compulsion to be way down the list of important issues for economists to be concerned about. "The notion that any form of coercion whatever is in itself so evil a thing as to outweigh all other evils is to set up freedom as a monstrous shibboleth,"[65] he wrote.

When Friedman accused governments of impinging upon personal freedoms, Samuelson countered by suggesting that, in a civilized society, individual freedoms had sometimes to be curtailed. "My privacy is your loneliness," he wrote. "My freedom to have privacy is your lack of freedom to have company. Your freedom to 'discriminate' is the denial of my freedom to 'participate.' "[66]

Samuelson believed that Friedman's advocacy of libertarian values and his belief in the absolute freedom of the market removed the restraints imposed by democratic checks and encouraged a sense of anarchy that would ultimately corrode society. If conservatives and libertarians believed that liberalism in its extreme form led to an authoritarian, Orwellian state, Samuelson countered by suggesting that a surfeit of libertarianism would inevitably lead to the opposite: a dystopia where individualism ran riot until anarchy reigned.

"The modern city is crowded. Individualism and anarchy will lead to friction. We now have to coordinate and cooperate," Samuelson wrote.

When we introduce the traffic light, we have by cooperation and coercion, although the arch individualist may not like the new order, created for ourselves greater freedom. The principle of unbridled freedom has been abandoned. It is now just a question of haggling about the terms.[67]

Samuelson's jibe about "haggling about the terms" was a conscious echo of the Keynes and Hayek debate, in which Keynes reminded Hayek that once absolute principles about the virtues of the market gave way to humanitarian refinements such as the provision of universal healthcare and unemployment insurance, as Hayek suggested was appropriate in *The Road to Serfdom*, the only question that remained was to draw the line exactly between the state and the market.

But Samuelson was not an advocate of government action per se. He recognized that too much government interference could be counterproductive to a well-ordered economy. "The moral is to render unto the market that which the market can handle," he wrote. "Just because government expenditures stem from the highest human motive is no reason for them to be undertaken unadvisedly—or inefficiently. Governments, like Casanova, too often never know when to stop."[68]

Friedman, however, believed that government action was a legal assault on an individual's wealth, based upon an impertinent belief by politicians and government employees that they knew best what was good for the rest of society. Like Hayek, Friedman thought the market, not civil servants, was the best means of reflecting people's desires. "There is no more egregious fallacy than the belief that order requires central direction," wrote Friedman. " 'Comprehensive policies' and attempts to have 'somebody' implement them with other people's money have generated many of our current problems and will continue to do so."[69]

Samuelson preferred the democratic process over the market. It was fairer, kinder, more civilized. "Democracy is the greatest system of mutual reinsurance ever invented. When we see a friend in the line for unemployment and compensation, we each say, 'There but for the grace of supply and demand go I,'" he wrote.'[70]

> Being human and realizing we are subject to the unknown perils of unemployment and destitutions, we cannily opt for the mutual reinsurances of the modern welfare state, knowing that, but for the grace of God, the bell that tolls could be tolling for us. Your typhoid is my typhoid and we are all, so to speak, citizens of the same Hiroshima.[71]

According to Samuelson, depending upon laissez-faire ideas to provide security against misfortune was wishful thinking. Nor had a truly free market ever existed. There was no lost Eden that Keynesians had despoiled. "Middle-class backlash and taxpayer revolts will not achieve restoration of . . . laissez faire," Samuelson wrote. "There is a science fiction of the right as well as of the left and center. Read it and enjoy. But don't bet your nest egg on wishful fantasies."[72] As he put it, in a reprimand to those who believed in free-market economics as if it were a religious faith, "Economics, not theology, is my beat."[73]

It was a conservative myth, Samuelson argued, that "self-made" businessmen were dashing, courageous characters inspired by the powerful forces of individualism to create wealth and stability for the rest of us. On the contrary, he said, it was society—a well-ordered, well-governed society—that always played the key role in providing the essential conditions for an entrepreneur's success.

Samuelson quoted the British liberal sociologist L. T. Hobhouse:[74]

> The organizer of industry who thinks he has "made" himself and his business has found a whole social system ready to his hand in skilled workers, machinery, a market, peace and order—a vast apparatus and

a pervasive atmosphere, the joint creation of millions of men and scores of generations. Take away the whole social factor and we have not Robinson Crusoe, with his salvage from the wreck and his acquired knowledge, but the native savage living on roots, berries and vermin.[75]

And, with the anticommunist witch hunt of the 1950s still fresh in the memory, Samuelson rejected out of hand that those who advocated the rational management of the economy by government were somehow "un-American" or were betraying a sacred doctrine of free enterprise laid down by the Founding Fathers. "The old-time religion of a budget balanced at a low level, and of the government leaving key economic decisions to the marketplace," he wrote, "is no more the ideology of most Americans than is [the prominent American Baptist evangelist] Billy Graham's version of religion the standard U.S. code."[76]

There were many things, wrote Samuelson, that were beyond the reach of free-market forces, which, it should be remembered, were merely a neutral mechanism of exchange rather than a moral means of organizing society. Sometimes governments were obliged to intervene. And when they did, it flowed from morality and humanitarian values rather than devotion to a certain brand of economics.

"Private enterprise is no substitute for government planning in dealing with ghettos and poverty,"[77] Samuelson wrote in 1968. When, a decade later, the president of the World Bank, Robert McNamara,[78] Lyndon Johnson's former defense secretary, admitted that the World Bank programs in Africa demonstrated the inability of free enterprise to cure poverty, Samuelson wrote, "I take my hat off to Robert McNamara for what has been his unique vision—his recognition that successful market forces alone can't be relied on to mitigate flagrant inequality and abject poverty."[79]

Samuelson hinted that unless government intervened in the market to increase economic growth, improve prosperity, and enrich people's lives, there would be a political price to pay. "Unless government motivates business by tax-and-expenditure programs, business cannot be expected to make even a dent in our urban problems," he wrote. "The business of business is business. Its customers are always right. And the consumer who is king is the electorate."[80]

Samuelson believed that at the core of the argument between him and Friedman were competing views of the role the individual should play in society. Friedman contended that, just as Adam Smith[81] had suggested in *The Wealth of Nations*, self-interest was the constant factor that ensured that society worked well for the maximum number. "As Adam Smith wrote over 200 years ago," Friedman wrote, "in the economic market, people who intend to serve only their own private interests are led by an invisible hand to serve public interests where there was no part of their intention to promote."[82]

But for Samuelson, Smith was a creature of his place and age— eighteenth-century Scotland during the Enlightenment. By the mid-twentieth century, Smith's notions about the role of self-interest and the application of the marketplace no longer applied. "Smith himself was what we today would call a pragmatist," Samuelson wrote. "He realized that monopoly elements ran through laissez faire."[83]

Smith's objection to government intervention, Samuelson contended, was due to the perennial incompetence of government servants, not because he was averse to civic involvement in government. Edinburgh in Smith's time was well run by a city government that ensured that individual freedoms were accompanied by individual obligations and duties. This was expressed most clearly in the city's expansion into the "New Town," a Georgian, privately funded model city laid out by urban planners to a strict, logical blueprint from which individuals were forbidden to depart.

"Knowing the caliber of George III's civil service," Samuelson wrote, "Smith believed the government would simply do more harm than good if it tried to cope with the evil of monopoly. Pragmatically, Smith would, if he were alive today, favor the [antimonopoly] Sherman Act[84] and stronger antitrust legislation, or even public utility regulation generally."[85]

In a gentle reprimand to Friedman and other conservatives who liked to invoke Smith, Samuelson continued, "One hundred per cent individualists skip these pragmatic lapses into good sense and concentrate on the purple passage in Adam Smith where he discerns an Invisible Hand that leads each selfish individual to contribute to the best public good."[86]

While Friedman, citing Smith, argued that everything in an economy was driven by—or should be driven by—individual self-interest, Samuelson suggested that for a nation to be truly civilized it would need more to guide it than the unhindered free market. "The pursuit of private profit will not keep carcinogens out of our rivers and atmosphere," he wrote. "Self-interest will not lead you and me to hire an army and navy to preserve the system that lets us be go-getters and private-utility maximizers."[87]

Besides, Samuelson suggested, it was not merely wrong to ignore the limits of the market's reach, it was immoral. Individuals in society needed to be defended from the many deleterious effects of the free market. And those who apologized for such antisocial side effects, stressing that market forces alone mattered, were not only woefully old-fashioned—"Those who take the time to investigate economics seriously, I mean modern economics, not that of your great-uncle Algernon . . ."[88]—but were living a dangerous daydream.

The profound difference between Samuelson and Friedman over the merit of the marketplace was an essentially philosophical matter that would never be bridged, however long they argued. But the differences between them were thrown into relief by a highly practical matter that engulfed the world as the Sixties came to an end: the rapid increase in the rate of price increases that roiled Western economies.

The modest inflation that had continued in the twenty years since the end of World War II before long turned to hyperinflation, a debilitating condition that, when it had taken place in Austria in the aftermath of World War I, had inspired Hayek to alert everyone to the dangers of Keynesianism. And as runaway inflation took hold in the developed world, threatening to undermine the fabric of society, rulers turned to their economists to ask what if anything could be done to stop it.

In offering advice in their columns to political leaders on how best to tackle rampant inflation, it was inevitable that Samuelson and Friedman would take opposite sides. And so the fight against inflation—its causes and its likely cures—became the central battlefield in their continuing war of economic ideas.

7

Money, Money, Money

Keynes said prosperity depends on keeping demand
for goods high. But Friedman harks back to a time when
economics was about money—and nothing but

The middle Sixties were busy years for Friedman as he juggled work on
several projects heading toward a single aim: to establish his reputation
as a major thinker in economics by refuting key parts of the Keynes inheri-
tance. If he did not openly state his ambition, everything he did was aimed
to achieve making an indelible mark on Keynes's theoretical legacy. It was
only in unpicking Keynes that Friedman sought to find new ground.

Friedman's brief sojourn in Cambridge, England, where he met and
debated with members of Keynes's Cambridge Circus, and his association
with Keynes's nemesis, Friedrich Hayek, gave him ammunition to help him
question the Keynesian hegemony. And while he would not be alone in his
efforts to point out flaws in Keynes's thinking, he made disproving Keynes
his top priority.

Friedman was well equipped for the task. He had a sharp intelligence,
an argumentative frame of mind, a stubbornness which kept him focused
on the job at hand, a skin thick enough to withstand the brickbats thrown
at him from the leaders of his discipline, and a knack for generating publicity. And to defeat Keynesianism, Friedman had a big idea: inflation was

caused solely by the velocity of money. Samuelson reminded George Garvy,[1] an archcritic of Friedman's monetarism and an authority on the velocity of money, that Thomas S. Kuhn[2] had written in *The Structure of Scientific Revolutions* his account of how paradigm shifts take place, that "it takes a theory to kill a theory."

One of Friedman's primary launching pads was an early work by Keynes, albeit a book that by the time of publication its author had discarded. Each summer in Cambridge, England, in the years immediately after World War I, Keynes gave lectures, which—he was the consummate self-marketing businessman—were published in book form the following fall. The summer of 1923 saw Keynes give talks that when collected became *A Tract on Monetary Reform*, in which the world's most famous economist critiqued the quantity theory of money, the notion that the amount of money in circulation and the speed at which it changed hands (the velocity of money) were directly linked to the price of goods and services. It was for Keynes only one more abandoned way station on the road to *The General Theory*. Nonetheless, Keynes biographer Robert Skidelsky[3] identifies *A Tract* as "the start of macroeconomics," the study of an economy as a whole—including inflation, growth, interest rates, and employment, and their relationships to each other—rather than microeconomics, the study of individual economic acts in isolation.

A Tract became an inspiration for counter-Keynesian revolutionaries like Friedman. "I am one of a small minority of professional economists who regard [*A Tract*], not the *General Theory*, as [Keynes's] best book on economics," wrote Friedman in 1989. "Even after sixty-five years, it is not only well worth reading but continues to have a major influence on economic policy."[4] Friedman's often-quoted one-liner that "Inflation is taxation without legislation" derives from the *Tract* chapter heading, "Inflation as a Method of Taxation."

Keynes asserted in *A Tract* that the general price level was directly linked to the amount and velocity of money in the system, which in turn reflected the extent of economic activity. If the money supply could be controlled—by banks rationing the supply of credit, say—inflation and growth could both be managed. Keynes makes a strong case in *A Tract* for the need to manage economies to iron out the vicissitudes of the business cycle, with its ebb and flow of money and concomitant rise and fall in prices.

The notion that an economy could and should be managed was—and to some conservative economists remains—a controversial notion. Managing an economy elevated the importance and power of public officials and economists, pitting their competence and judgment against the invisible hands of market forces. Friedman agreed with Keynes that an economy could be managed by government, and it was his belief that prices not only could but should be managed—by the central bank controlling the amount of new money entering the system—that caused many free marketeers, including Hayek, to sputter.

Austrian economists like Hayek believed such an approach would fail, as no one could know enough about the workings of the economy to manage it with any accuracy. In Hayek's view, the market was best left to right itself. He always complained that Friedman was closer to Keynes than Hayek was to either of them. "In one respect, Milton Friedman is still a Keynesian, not on monetary theory but on methodology," Hayek explained. By accepting the premises of macroeconomics—a branch of economics that Keynes had invented, "very much against his own intentions," according to Hayek—Friedman had made a serious intellectual error. He continued:

> Milton Friedman is one of the apostles of macroeconomics. His theory is based on the supposed regularities between statistical magnitudes. He's convinced and believes he has historically demonstrated that there is a simple relationship between the total quantity of money and the price level. . . . No one knows what the total quantity of money is, money has so many different meanings. . . . Aggregates, sums, averages, and statistics are no substitute for the detailed knowledge of

every single price and their relations to each other that guide economic activity. It is a mistaken attempt to overcome our limited knowledge.[5]

It was not just that Friedman had signed up to Keynes's macroeconomics rather than join the Austrian School, which relied solely on microeconomic activity, that caused Hayek offense. Friedman's belief that the money supply should be controlled by the central bank to keep prices in check put him firmly on the Keynesian side of the argument over whether governments should manage the economy. Hayek would never forgive him.

Keynes's *Tract* also anticipated a later fashion in economic thinking: the notion of "rational expectations," or the understanding that as economic actors wittingly anticipate a rise or fall in prices and other changes to the economic landscape when they make decisions, so the price of goods comes to reflect those expectations. In *A Tract*, Keynes describes how businessmen and consumers duck and weave to minimize the disruption of the change in prices, and that their attempt to dodge the worst effects of varying prices should be taken into account. If, say, an importer of oranges got wind of an impending shortage caused by a bad harvest or a lack of fruit pickers, they would anticipate the likely rise in the price of oranges and adjust their prices accordingly. As economists tend to exaggerate, simplify, and generalize, the notion of "rational expectations" before long led to an assumption that businessmen enjoy a total grasp of the economy and its likely direction and "price in" any imminent changes.

Economic actors expecting what was likely to happen in an economy led to that often-quoted remark—"In the long run we are all dead"[6]—which first appeared in *A Tract*. In linking prices to the quantity of money, Keynes noted, the quantity theory[7] assumed that if the quantity of money were doubled, prices would also, in the long run, double. But, he argued, before the quantity of money and the level of prices eventually came into alignment, those holding money or obtaining credit would anticipate the rise in prices and would likely deplete their cash holdings accordingly. Hence, until a new equilibrium was reached—in which the doubling of the amount of money in circulation resulted in the doubling of prices—prices would increase but would not double.

Keynes averred that the simple assumption that the quantity of money and prices were directly linked, therefore, was true but did not tell the whole story. The "velocity of circulation of money," rather than the amount of money, was key to understanding the relationship between the change in money and the change in prices. Rather like his later *General Theory* notion of the "multiplier"—which suggested that because over time money changes hands many times, any dollar spent had a "multiplier" effect as it passed from person to person—Keynes suggested in *A Tract* that it was not merely the quantity of money in circulation but the speed at which it changed hands that led to changes in prices. As economic activity sped up, so any "new" money—provided, say, through bank loans or the sale of government bonds—would appear to go further; as it slowed down, so prices, too, would level off.

Again, Keynes threw doubt on the value of waiting for an eventual equilibrium in the economy where prices remained constant. "Economists set themselves too easy, too useless a task if in tempestuous seasons they can only tell us that when the storm is long past the ocean is flat again."[8] The haphazard rise and fall of prices, he claimed, was wasteful and debilitating to businesses and sometimes even threatened social stability. Rather than watch idly by as such mayhem was unleashed, prices could be kept in check by the government controlling the supply of money through directing banks to tighten or loosen credit.

Samuelson agreed with Friedman about the value of Keynes's *Tract*. His "neoclassical synthesis," in which he tried to combine the best of classical economics and Keynesian notions, acknowledged the truth of much of what Keynes had written about money in *A Tract*. "I think nineteen-twenties Keynesianism—the Keynes of the *Tract on Monetary Reform*—that is what is needed in a well-run market economy. You lean against the wind and you try to do it intelligently,"[9] he said.

IN THE TWO DECADES before he began contributing to *Newsweek*, Fried-man opened several separate fronts in his campaign to counter Keynesian-ism. In 1956, an introduction by Friedman to a collection of learned articles[10] he edited for the University of Chicago Press marked an opening salvo.

Keynes's account of the causes and cure of the Great Depression had fast become the conventional wisdom among American economists after publication of *The General Theory* in 1936. In the thirty years that followed, Keynesian economists had tried to temper the business cycle to avoid high unemployment at the bottom of the cycle, as demand slumped, and to deter high inflation by slowing public spending at the top of the cycle, as too much money chased too few goods. Keynesian economists thought that by fiscal means alone—taxation and spending—they could manage the econ-omy to minimize its antisocial effects.

In *The General Theory*, Keynes had attempted to codify the link between the quantity and velocity of money and price movements and con-cluded that the variables were so many and so imponderable that, while the link between the money supply and inflation remained true in principle, the "extreme complexity" of the interrelationship made it a hard theory to apply in practice.[11] Taking their cue from *The General Theory*, Keynesians played down the value of the quantity theory of money and either ignored or derided it. Money, they said, didn't matter anymore. The main message of Friedman's collection of essays, however, was simple: money *did* matter. His own contribution to the collection was an exhaustively detailed and equation-ridden reiteration of the principles of the quantity theory, "The Quantity Theory of Money: A Restatement," which, he said, "fell into disre-pute after the crash of 1929 and the subsequent Great Depression and only recently has been slowly re-emerging into professional respectability."[12]

Friedman's decision to republish the long-forgotten pieces, he claimed, was "partly a symptom of this re-emergence and partly a continuance of an aberrant tradition" to be found at Chicago, where, he said, despite the rise of Keynesianism since 1936, "the quantity theory continued to be a central and vigorous part of the oral tradition." At Chicago, he said, where the theory was not merely kept alive by word of mouth but was revised and honed, it "differed sharply from the atrophied and rigid caricature that is so frequently described by the proponents of the new [Keynesian] income-expenditure approach."[13]

As Chicago's economics department's distinct approach was "not a rigid system, an unchangeable orthodoxy, but a way of looking at things," Friedman claimed that no one had codified the continued adherence to the quantity theory, which he described as "a theoretical approach that insisted that money does matter—that any interpretation of short-term movements in economic activity is likely to be seriously at fault if it neglects monetary changes and repercussions and if it leaves unexplained why people are willing to hold the particular nominal quantity of money in existence."

According to Friedman, Chicago economics luminaries Henry Simons and Lloyd Mints—as well as Frank Knight and Jacob Viner "at one remove"—had developed a more subtle version of the quantity theory, that they integrated with general price theory to make it a means of interpreting movements in economic activity and for developing policy prescriptions.

Although at this time Friedman made few bold claims for the quantity theory, the simple act of republishing articles that insisted on the pertinence of a notion that had been widely dismissed as fallacious by mainstream economists was a conspicuous act of defiance. Friedman's essay collection was largely met with silence from Keynesians, who felt Friedman was irrevocably stuck in the past.

Samuelson noted Friedman's efforts to rehabilitate the quantity theory not so much with alarm as with a wry smile. It was news to him that the quantity theory had been taught unofficially by word of mouth at Chicago, just as early Christians had learned the Bible by heart and recounted it to fellow Christians. Though Samuelson resisted public comment at the time, he later questioned whether there had ever been an "oral tradition" of the quantity theory at Chicago. "I was there, knew all the players well, and kept class notes,"[14] he recalled. He could not recall, nor find anything in his extensive lecture notes, to suggest that the quantity theory had been kept alive at Chicago.

But if Friedman's re-presentation of the quantity theory was based on a false memory, his attempt to revive it pointed the way forward. The next decade saw a hectic output from Friedman, all contributing towards a single counterrevolutionary thought: the quantity theory is still valid; money still matters.

The following year, 1957, Friedman's essay, *A Theory of the Consumption Function*, sought to overturn a key element of Keynes's *General Theory*, "the propensity to consume"—that is, the proportion of new income that people spend as opposed to save. Keynes had asserted that the greater an individual's income, the more likely she would save the new income rather than spend it. Conversely, as incomes declined, the propensity to save was less. His thinking was key to the Keynesian notion of the "multiplier," which suggested that every extra dollar added to a nation's income through public spending or tax cuts would be spent many times over, giving the economy a boost out of proportion to its cost. As Keynesians believed that to boost a sinking economy it was necessary to generate greater demand for goods—thereby promoting more business activity, investment, and jobs—they concluded it was best for governments to direct new stimulus money at the less-well-off, who, unlike the rich, would spend every last cent without delay.

To test Keynes's assumption, Friedman consulted five decades of data[15] about U.S. family budgets and concluded that, contrary to Keynes's contention, people made spending decisions not on their current income but on the state of their "permanent income," the amount of income a person expected to earn in the long run. So, he said, current income was no guide to whether a person saved or spent new income. Therefore, Friedman asserted, Keynes's assumptions about how quickly stimulus money—whether from tax cuts or government spending on public works—would be spent were wrong, which undermined the expected multiplier effect of a stimulus.[16]

In 1960, Friedman was asked to write an entry on money for the *Encyclopædia Britannica*,[17] which was revising its outdated 1929 fourteenth edition for a fifteenth edition, eventually published in 1974. To Friedman's surprise, he, not Samuelson, had been asked to revise the entry on Keynes. Friedman sent his entry to Samuelson for comment. "I don't want to question your beliefs about M [money] here," Samuelson wrote, but the entry was "not worthy of you." "You sketch the Keynesian alternative to the [quantity] theory in a way that will seem to a jury of reasonable economists who are well-informed on the subject as quite inadequate." He said readers would receive "a misleading impression of the macroeconomic model that is in the *General Theory*," by concentrating solely on what John Hicks—who reduced Keynes's complex reasoning to a simplified equation—had dubbed the "deep-depression version" of the theory.

The nub of Friedman's error, according to Samuelson, concerned one of the ways of measuring money in an economy. Exactly what money to measure, and how to obtain accurate measurements of money—essential prerequisites if a central bank were to intervene in the market with any confidence—would prove to be difficult, even for monetarists. Samuelson took Friedman to task for misrepresenting the value of one of the many ways of measuring money in the system, M1.[18] "To deny that M1 is infinite is not to believe that it is zero,"[19] he wrote.

On Samuelson's main charge, that he had misconstrued Keynes's account of monetary theory in *The General Theory*, Friedman replied, "There will of course be pieces in the *Encyclopedia* on the Keynesian theory" and that "my comments on the Keynesian theory were not intended to be in any way exhaustive but only to state the minimum necessary to make intelligible the developments that occurred in the quantity theory itself. I wanted to emphasize how much the present quantity theory approach does owe to the Keynesian inspiration. Apparently, I failed to do so." He said he would rewrite the offending pages, though, "I am not sure I shall be able to succeed."[20]

Friedman sent his rewrite to Samuelson, who considered it "an improvement [only] in one minor respect." In contention was a set of beliefs attributed to Keynes, which Samuelson suggested should simply be excised. "Attribute to 'some of Keynes's disciples' views like these," suggested Samuelson. "His disciples are a motley crew, and among them you can find a subset who believe in anything." He chided Friedman for not keeping up with "the post-Keynesian literature." He had shown Friedman's revised entry to Solow, Modigliani, Tobin, and others, and accepted that it was a "thankless task" to satisfy him and his Keynesian friends. But if the entry was to maintain its "objectivity and relevance," Friedman should try again. Like Keynes when remarking about Hayek's *Prices and Production* to Piero Sraffa[21]—"I can't help feeling that there is something interesting in it"[22]—Samuelson signed off with, "Like all moderns, I benefit enormously from reading your work closely."[23]

Friedman robustly defended his words, suggesting that "you and those who consulted are protesting much too much." "I read over the relevant parts of Keynes' *General Theory*," he wrote. "On this basis, I believe the views I attribute to him are correct." The question he had been trying to answer was, "why . . . the Keynesian revolution had such a drastic effect on beliefs about the role of money in the economy."[24]

When Samuelson gave a talk at DePaul University critical of Friedman's adherence to quantity of money theory, Friedman was quick to complain. "I welcome criticism, constructive or destructive, but not flat misrepresentation of my views,"[25] he wrote. Samuelson fired back. "The monetarism I attacked at DePaul is a straw man. But it is not one of my making," he replied. "Naturally I am pleased when I read an article of yours in which you show that you subscribe to a set of equations that Keynesians believed in in 1940. It gives hope that you will further develop them and expend them as Modigliani, [James] Tobin,[26] and others have done in the 30 years since then."[27]

Britannica published Friedman's essay on money, though it did not remain for long. Allan Meltzer,[28] an authority on monetary policy of the Fed, was asked to write a revised entry on money for the 1986 edition. Meltzer sent Friedman a copy of his essay and received back an "insightful, helpful, and courteous"[29] reply. For a while, the revised entry was published under both bylines.

Friedman knew he had little chance of persuading Keynesians about the virtues of the quantity theory. Asked years later to name his most interesting blunder, Friedman replied, "Attempt to sell Keynesians on my alternative monetary framework . . . I was naïve to think that by putting my ideas in Keynesian language I would make any dent on the Keynesians."[30]

Having dealt a blow against a key aspect of Keynes's *General Theory* in his *Theory of the Consumption Function,* in 1963 Friedman mounted his most powerful assault on Keynesian thinking thus far. Over the course of two decades, he and Anna Schwartz had compiled from many sources figures that told of the role of the quantity of money in the economic activity of the United States in the previous hundred years. They noted the amount of cash people held in their deposit accounts, the ratio of bank deposits to bank reserves, and looked not only at cash but other instruments that were used as cash. Friedman concluded that the data showed that the quantity of money in circulation and actions like the Federal Reserve increasing or decreasing the interest rate were intimately linked, and therefore the quantity theory continued to be valid.

Friedman and Schwartz began their epic investigation in the 1940s, but it was not until 1963 that they published their findings in *A Monetary History of the United States, 1867–1960.*[31] Their conclusions stood received wisdom on its head. Until their account, it was generally believed the Great Depression had been caused by factors such as a collapse in investor and consumer confidence and punishingly high interest rates. Friedman and Schwartz sought to prove otherwise.

In the final chapter of their magnum opus, the pair focused upon events between 1920 and 1940. In the decade after World War I, the American

economy boomed and Americans were caught up in the reckless extrava-
gance of the Roaring Twenties. But after years of nonstop boom, in 1929
the stock market collapsed, sending shock waves around the world. The
American economy ground to a halt. Banks ran out of cash and refused
to lend, and many of them closed their doors forever. Fortunes were lost.
Bankrupt investors died by suicide. For the duration of the Thirties, the
Great Depression held the world in an impoverished state, with millions
unable to find work.

What happened? And who was responsible? Keynes and others offered
a simple explanation, suggesting that the slump was the inevitable result of
too much money chasing too few goods, prompting a bubble in stock and
general prices that collapsed spectacularly between October 24 and October 29, 1929. Friedman and Schwartz came to a radically different conclusion. The Great Depression was not the result of overexuberance in the
market, they argued, but was instead precipitated by the failure of the Federal Reserve to pump enough dollars into the system through lending at low
interest rates to prevent the chronic lack of liquidity that ended up driving
so many banks to fail and businesses to go bust.

The pair noted that the Fed had raised the discount rate in 1920, then
again in 1931, two years after the Wall Street crash, then raised the reserve
requirement in 1937, which, along with other federal government measures,
caused the "Roosevelt Recession" of 1937. These three rate hikes, Friedman
and Schwartz observed, correlated exactly with the three sharpest declines
in money supply in nearly a century, and the rate hikes coincided, too, with
a dramatic collapse in industrial production, down 30, 24, and 34 percent
respectively. Friedman asserted that the Great Depression should more
accurately be renamed the Great Contraction, to reflect its true roots in the
money supply.

A Monetary History of the United States became an instant classic.
Friedman and Schwartz's approach was meticulously scientific: they took
the quantity theory of money, then looked at the changes in the supply of

money over time to see whether the changes were concurrent with events. The evident labor that Friedman and Schwartz had expended in archives trying to make sense of the empirical evidence—rather than rely, as Keynes had, on a hunch—convinced most economists and economic historians that the pair had succeeded in uncovering the true reasons for the Great Depression. By resurrecting the quantity theory of money, Friedman rehabilitated it as a valid tool with which to predict changes in an economy.

The Monetary History was a prime example of how Friedman and Samuelson sought explanations for economic phenomena in profoundly different ways. Samuelson, like Keynes, relied upon intuition. Samuelson's myriad of learned papers began with an informed surmise that was then tested through mathematical equations to prove its veracity. Friedman approached matters differently. He began with a plausible theory, then sought historical statistical evidence to test it.

Those without scientific training may imagine that Friedman's approach is more convincing as it tests notions against facts. But the methodology used by Samuelson and Keynes—conjecture followed by mathematical proof—is commonplace throughout the physical and social sciences. Many of the major breakthroughs in scientific thought—such as DNA being configured as a double helix, or the result of splitting of the atom, or the earth circling the sun, or how gravity works—are based upon deduction rather than laboratory work. Validation through experimentation often comes long after a problem has been solved logically. Samuelson was adamant that intuition, not long hours poring over data, was the key to discovery. He told Arthur Burns,[32] who had launched Friedman and Schwartz on their monetary research, that "regressions of the mind" were preferable to "regressions of the computer" when making economic forecasts. When asked, "How long do you think it will take before a computer will replace you?" Samuelson replied, "Not in a million years."[33]

Hardly had the ripples of *A Monetary History of the United States* subsided before Friedman launched his next sortie into the Keynesians. In 1967,

Friedman was invited to deliver, in Washington, D.C., on December 29, the presidential address[34] of the American Economic Association, the pre-eminent platform from which distinguished American economists[35] give keynote lectures. Borrowing freely from Keynes's *A Tract*, Friedman's talk, "The Role of Monetary Policy,"[36] would become the theoretical cornerstone of his emerging Friedmanite monetarism. Friedman's main proposition was that if the "velocity of money," which Keynes had identified in *A Tract*, was regulated so that prices were only allowed to rise at a low and steady pace, economic growth and prosperity would be maximized.

The AEA talk was an important step toward Friedman claiming a distinctive place in the history of economic thought. Although he relied on Keynes's *Tract*, at the AEA Friedman came to bury Keynes, not to praise him. He first took to task Keynes's account of the origins of the Great Depression, which assumed that the principal culprit was a lack of aggregate demand. "Keynes had dismissed the quantity of money theory," said Friedman, "because monetary policy was a string. You could pull on it to stop inflation but you could not push on it to halt recession. You could lead a horse to water but you could not make him drink." Keynes thought there were no investors left to take advantage of endless cheap credit when demand was on the floor.

The prolonged contraction of the Thirties was set in train, in Keynes's view, Friedman explained, "by a collapse of investment or by a shortage of investment opportunities or by stubborn thriftiness [which] could not, it was argued, have been stopped by monetary measures." By looking at events through a *General Theory* lens, Friedman argued, Keynes had offered at the same time an explanation for the presumed impotence of monetary policy to stem the Depression, a nonmonetary interpretation of the Depression, and an alternative to monetary policy for meeting the Depression. Keynes's remedy to recession, Friedman said, was fiscal policy. Government spending could make up for insufficient private investment. Tax reductions could undermine stubborn thriftiness.

Friedman conceded that the quantity-of-money theory was not so much out of fashion as barely considered by economists as an alternative to manipulating the economy through fiscal policy. Only "a few reactionary souls" were left remaining loyal to the quantity theory, Friedman said. "Money did not matter," he said. "Its only role was the minor one of keeping interest rates low." After World War II, when it was widely predicted there would be a resumption of the prewar Depression, this had led to the use of "cheap money" policies, in which governments kept interest rates low to maximize economic activity.

But, Friedman argued, by keeping rates unnaturally low, politicians and their tame economists were courting disaster. "They received a rude shock when these policies failed in country after country, when central bank after central bank was forced to give up the pretense that it could indefinitely keep 'the' rate of interest at a low level," he said. "Inflation, stimulated by cheap money policies, not the widely heralded postwar depression, turned out to be the order of the day." However, the inflation apparently stoked by Keynesian fiscal remedies suggested that the quantity of money did matter after all—the mishandling of monetary policy by Keynesian economists had caused prices to rise faster than necessary, he said. That realization was "the beginning of a revival of belief in the potency of monetary policy."

Friedman then called as evidence his research with Schwartz, which, he suggested, had caused a "reevaluation of the role money played from 1929 to 1933." He described how Keynes had concluded that the Great Depression had taken place despite aggressive expansionary policies by the monetary authorities that proved inadequate. But, said Friedman, Keynes's belief was misplaced because "recent studies [Friedman's own] demonstrated that the facts are precisely the reverse: the U.S. monetary authorities followed highly deflationary policies. The quantity of money in the United States fell by one-third in the course of the [Great Depression]."

The human disaster caused by the slump had therefore been wholly unnecessary, Friedman said. "The Federal Reserve System forced or permitted a sharp reduction in the monetary base, because it failed to exercise the responsibilities assigned to it in the Federal Reserve Act to provide liquidity to the banking system." He concluded that "the Great Contraction is tragic testimony to the power of monetary policy—not, as Keynes and so many of his contemporaries believed, evidence of its impotence."

Keynes's belief that fiscal policy should be used to invigorate a slumping economy was misplaced, said Friedman. Spending on public works and projects took far longer than expected to translate into increased economic activity, so to more quickly stimulate the economy, politicians had turned to tax cuts. It was now widely accepted by economists, he asserted, that the effect of money in the system had been underestimated and that "hardly an economist today accepts views that were the common coin some two decades ago." Whereas the chief role of money was traditionally considered to be to keep prices stable and maintain the price of the dollar steady in relation to the price of gold—"the gold standard"—the primary emphasis on monetary policy in the postwar world was to keep everyone in the nation employed, with the curbing of prices "a continuing but definitely secondary objective."

In a rare moment of caution, Friedman was not yet prepared to claim that monetary policy alone could achieve everything. As in the Twenties, he said, "we are in danger of assigning to monetary policy a larger role than it can perform, in danger of asking it to accomplish tasks that it cannot achieve."

He set out to describe what monetary policy could and what it could not accomplish, for fear it be considered a cure-all, not least because "the failure of cheap money policies was a major source of the reaction against simple-minded Keynesianism." He said monetary policy could not peg interest rates, except for very limited periods. And it could not keep employment high, except for a short time.

Since the 1940s, the Federal Reserve had been mandated by Congress to keep unemployment at a minimum by manipulating the interest rate.

(No such command was delivered to the Fed to keep inflation low or in check until 1977.)[37] Friedman described the process by which the Fed kept interest rates down: they bought government bonds on the open market, which raised the price of those securities, thereby lowering their yields— return on investment—which in turn drove interest rates down. But this trick could not be played ad infinitum. While increasing the amount of money in circulation by buying securities reduced interest rates for a while, "this is only the beginning of the process, not the end," said Friedman. Making money deliberately cheaper could increase spending and therefore demand for a while, but "one man's spending is another man's income." In less than a year, the rising incomes prompted by the Fed's measures would in turn increase the demand for loans and raise prices. Within "a year or two," the effects of keeping interest rates unnaturally low would "return interest rates to the level they would otherwise have had"—"the natural rate of interest"[38]—or even higher.

"Let the higher rate of monetary growth produce rising prices, and let the public come to expect that prices will continue to rise," he said. "Borrowers will then be willing to pay [the higher prices] and lenders will then demand higher interest rates."

In an aside, Friedman offered a glimpse into the problems he would later face when persuading politicians that control of the money supply was the key to a steady, prosperous economy. "Monetary policy cannot peg interest rates," he declared. That explains "why interest rates are such a misleading indicator of whether monetary policy is 'tight' or 'easy.' For that, it is far better to look at the rate of change of the quantity of money [the "velocity of money" Keynes described in *A Tract*]." But, as those who were to be converted to Friedman's way of thinking would soon discover, it was far easier to talk about the velocity of money than to measure it. This underlying issue made Friedman's monetarism a simple concept that, whether ultimately right or wrong, was hard to translate into policy.

Friedman addressed a key practical concern. If monetary growth tended to stimulate employment, and monetary contraction to cause job losses, he asked, "Why, then, cannot the monetary authority adopt a target for employment or unemployment—say 3 per cent unemployment; be tight when unemployment is less than the target; be easy when unemployment is higher than the target; and in this way peg unemployment at, say, 3 per cent?" The reason, he suggested, was again the lag between action and result.

He invoked the work of Knut Wicksell,[39] who contended that there was a "natural" rate of interest that was different from the "market" rate of interest, in which the "natural" rate was the rate that the market would settle upon if left to its own devices, and the "market" rate the rate set by monetary authorities. Those who regulated the supply of money "can make the market rate less than the natural rate only by inflation," he said, and "it can make the market rate higher than the natural rate only by deflation."

It was a short logical step for Friedman from the "natural rate" of interest to the "natural" rate of unemployment, or the rate that might exist if the monetary authorities and the government did not distort the free market by using fiscal policy to head off joblessness. At the "natural rate of unemployment," he said, "real wage rates are tending on the average to rise at a 'normal' secular rate." In these circumstances, "a lower level of unemployment is an indication that there is an excess demand for labor that will produce upward pressure on real wage rates," whereas "a higher level of unemployment is an indication that there is an excess supply of labor that will produce downward pressure on real wage rates."

For Friedman, even the "natural rate of unemployment" was not quite "natural" because of policies adopted by governments to maintain full employment. In the United States, the federal minimum wage, combined with other factors including the wage bargaining of labor unions who operated a monopoly through "closed shop" agreements with employers that allowed only union workers to be hired, "all make the natural rate of unemployment higher than it would otherwise be." (Samuelson agreed with Friedman about the minimum wage. He asked in the 1970 edition of his textbook: "What good does it do a black youth to know that an employer must pay him $2.00 an hour if the fact that he must be paid that amount is what keeps him from getting a job?"[40])

But the problem for policymakers as well as economists, Friedman candidly admitted, was that determining the "natural" rate was impossible. "Unfortunately, we have as yet devised no method to estimate accurately and readily the natural rate of either interest or unemployment," Friedman said. "And the 'natural' rate will itself change from time to time." Any attempt by a monetary authority to try to align its policies with the "natural" rate would be doomed to failure as "the 'market' rate will vary from the natural rate for all sorts of reasons other than monetary policy."[41]

In his address, Friedman also set out to disprove one of the most prominent established "truths" held dear by Keynesians: that there was a stable, measurable, inverse link between employment and inflation. As prices rose, so employers looked for economies and cut staff; when prices were held low, business activity increased and new jobs were created. By adjusting the interest rate, governments could reduce the level of unemployment. The jobs/prices relationship was established by William Phillips,[42] who, in "The Relation between Unemployment and the Rate of Change of Money Wage Rates in the United Kingdom, 1861–1957," published in 1960, interpreted the views of Keynes on the subject after researching a hundred years of data on wage inflation and unemployment in Britain.

In his lecture, Friedman offered his disproof of the Phillips Curve. While Phillips's analysis was "deservedly celebrated as an important and original contribution," it contained "a basic defect—the failure to distinguish between nominal wages and real wages, i.e., the amount of money that a worker was paid compared to the amount of goods and services those wages could buy when inflation was taken into account." While "there is always a temporary trade-off between inflation and unemployment, there is no permanent trade-off," said Friedman. How long before the natural rate of employment would reassert itself? His "personal judgment, based on some examination of the historical evidence [his work on the Great Depression]" suggested that the initial effects of a higher rate of inflation than anticipated lasted for between two and five years. A full adjustment to the new rate of inflation could take as long as a couple of decades.

Like Hayek, Friedman concluded that all attempts to trick the market into creating false prosperity were doomed.

> [While a monetary authority could] use this control over nominal quantities to peg a nominal quantity—the exchange rate, the price level, the nominal level of national income, the quantity of money by one or other definition—or to peg the rate of change in a nominal quantity—the rate of inflation or deflation, the rate of growth or decline in nominal national income, the rate of growth of the quantity of money, it cannot use its control over nominal quantities to peg a real quantity—the real rate of interest, the rate of unemployment, the level of real national income, the real quantity of money, the rate of growth of real national income, or the state of growth of the real quantity of money.

Friedman had no doubt that money was, of itself, a great invention that was every bit as responsible for the vast rise in economic growth and general prosperity in the previous two hundred years as the many technical inventions and machines that had transformed the economy. But money should be handled carefully. He warned that "when [money] gets out of order, it throws a monkey wrench into the operation of all the other machines."

In the past, he said, such instruments as the gold standard, by which currency prices were fixed to the price of gold, had provided monetary stability. But those days were fast disappearing. "There is scarce a country in the world that is prepared to let the gold standard reign unchecked—and there are persuasive reasons why countries should not do so," he said.

Control of the money supply could prevent market exuberance, such as existed immediately after World War II, when the rebuilding of war-torn Europe and anticipation of a booming world economy thanks to the arrival of peace and an end to arms spending led to a surge in economic activity. Not only could monetary policy help to hold in check such unpredictable forces, but it could tackle the consequences of Keynesian government spending. "If, as now, an explosive federal budget threatens unprecedented deficits, monetary policy can hold any inflationary dangers in check by a slower rate of monetary growth than would otherwise be desirable."

But there was a problem. Friedman reported that all attempts at ironing out the peaks and troughs of economic activity through monetary policy had gone awry because of the time lag between the Federal Reserve acting and the effect of the action on the economy months later. The monetary authorities, he said, "tend to determine their actions by today's conditions— but their actions will affect the economy only six or nine or twelve or fifteen months later. Hence they feel impelled to step on the brake, or the accelerator, as the case may be, too hard."

So, how *should* monetary policy be employed? Friedman confessed it was not clear, as the effects of increasing or decreasing the amount of money were so hard to measure. His recommendation for monetary authorities who wished to ensure a steady rate of price inflation was to provide a steady, small growth in the supply of money at somewhere between 3 and 5 percent per year. How he arrived at those figures he did not elucidate.

Friedman's solution to runaway inflation was to remove discretion from central bankers and install a system of fixed rules over monetary policy that he believed would provide certainty for businesses by keeping prices on an even, gently upward direction. "Steady monetary growth would provide a monetary climate favorable to the effective operation of those basic forces of enterprise, ingenuity, invention, hard work, and thrift that are the true springs of economic growth," he said. "That is the most that we can ask from monetary policy at our present stage of knowledge."[43]

As he was aware, Friedman's attempt to disprove the soundness of the

Phillips inflation/employment trade-off brought him into direct confrontation with Samuelson, who, with his MIT colleague Solow, had endorsed the validity of Phillips's research[44] and had dubbed the theory the Phillips Curve.[45] Samuelson and Solow concluded that the jobs/prices exchange was so reliable that it offered a menu of options for political leaders. If they wished to keep unemployment at a certain low level, it would cost a certain level of inflation. Their endorsement of the Phillips Curve came to be seen as "the high watermark of the Keynesian conceit, the West's counterpart to Soviet-style central planning: that the economy was a machine that could be fine-tuned by a wise, omniscient, and omnipotent government."[46]

According to the Curve, the trade-off worked on a sliding scale. For instance, to maintain unemployment at 3 percent, which they considered in practical terms full employment, annual prices would need to rise 5 percent.[47] But Samuelson and Solow were astute enough to provide a caveat: the relationship between employment and inflation may not hold up in the long term, as expectations about future price rises would begin to inflate wage demands, leading to higher general inflation.

Friedman concentrated his fire on Samuelson and Solow's proviso. He looked at post–World War II employment and inflation data and came to a different conclusion than that of Phillips. Instinctively, he did not like the Keynesian assumption that you could get something (low unemployment) for nothing (modest price inflation). That incompatibility was what Hayek had tried to prove to Keynes in 1931, to little effect. As Friedman's most famous catchphrase put it, "There's no such thing as a free lunch."[48]

Friedman was not alone in his skepticism about Phillips. At the London School of Economics, Edmund Phelps of Penn University was doing similar research independently of Friedman, and he, too, determined that the historical jobs and inflation figures did not back up Phillips's bold claim.[49] Both Friedman and Phelps suggested that as Wicksell had postulated a "natural rate of interest," there was a "natural rate of employment" that would reassert itself if governments stopped intervening in the market to keep unemployment artificially low.

Phelps and Friedman separately concluded that the trade-off between jobs and higher prices was only true in the short run, as eventually expectations about future price rises would lead to increasingly high inflation. "Participants in product and labor markets will learn to expect inflation," wrote Phelps, and "as a consequence of their rational, anticipatory behavior, the Phillips Curve will gradually shift, greater inflation will result than before, and the pattern will repeat as expectations are continually revised upwards." Phelps predicted that governments who relied on the Phillips Curve to maintain full employment were courting danger. Their actions would lead to a "wage/price spiral" followed by Weimar-like "hyper-inflation."

Some years later, having heard Friedman discuss his disproof of the Phillips Curve on a recording, Samuelson wrote that Friedman's remarks critical of the efficacy of the Curve were old news and had all been covered in his *Economics* textbook. "My book's discussion of the Phillips Curve problem makes all the points that you so properly made and many more," he wrote Friedman. "It discusses short run, long run, opposing views about natural rates of unemployment, about expectations, about variable leads and lags, and multi-dimensional relations, etc."[50]

Friedman's AEA lecture was well received.[51] But considering Friedman's many caveats about controlling the money supply, what practical use was monetary policy? In public pronouncements addressing the sharp rise in inflation from the 1960s onward, Friedman tended to simplify his message: money was the key. In 1962, in *Capitalism and Freedom,* he had declared that "history offers ample evidence that what determines the average level of prices and wages is the amount of money in the economy and not the greediness of businessmen or of workers."[52] But by 1970 he appeared to go further: "Inflation is always and everywhere a monetary phenomenon in the sense that it is and can be produced only by a more rapid increase in the quantity of money than in [economic] output."[53]

Friedman was on a roll. Whereas in the past, his wagging finger had been dismissed as the rebuke of a crank, his AEA address established him as a leader of a long overdue opposition to Keynesianism. Friedman was much in demand to pursue his assault on the New Economics and in 1978 he agreed to appear in a televised set-piece debate with the Keynesian Walter W. Heller, Kennedy's and Johnson's chairman of the Council of Economic Advisers, that was so well attended it spilled out of the lecture hall and took on the heightened atmosphere of a show trial.[54]

All Friedman now needed to prove his monetarist theories were correct was to persuade a government—any government, but the U.S. government was in his sights—to abandon Keynesianism and adopt his monetarist notions. To overturn the ruling order and replace its ideology with your own was a revolutionary ambition. His AEA address appeared to have caught the public imagination, though he had yet to win the battle of ideas. But finding a political leader who would embark citizens upon a risky economic experiment to display the worth of monetarism would prove far harder. Before long, however, Friedman would be heading for Washington, D.C., with the aim of putting his big idea to the ultimate test.

Hayek's persistent warnings to Friedman to avoid becoming too close to politicians went unheeded. Friedman was drawn to powerful people who could translate his ideas into action. He needed a result. So long as his monetarism remained untried, governments would continue to tinker with the economy through fiscal policy. Friedman had to find a Republican president he could work with. And who was open-minded enough to try something new.

The next president-in-waiting for the Republican Party, which in those days usually picked its candidates on a Buggins' turn basis, was Richard M. Nixon,[55] a man of fierce intelligence matched to a rat-like cunning. On Nixon's election in 1968, Friedman eagerly agreed to become an economic adviser to the new president. Here was a golden chance to turn the tide of

Keynesianism and apply the full rigor of monetarism to the American economy. Friedman felt he was on the threshold of success.

But soon he would discover that while bruising clashes over theoretical economics were always fought with gloves on, in the world of politics rivals arrived at a knife fight with a loaded pistol. And Friedman was to learn, too, that it was useful to embrace basic psychology when dealing with the imperfections of an image-obsessed president whose profound sense of what was right was easily jettisoned in favor of what was expedient.

8

Not So Fast

As Friedman's monetarist ideas gather momentum,
Samuelson hopes to stop the anti-Keynesian counter-
revolution in its tracks by cold, clear logic

Samuelson did not immediately respond to Friedman's American Economic Association lecture, though he was aware that in targeting the causes of inflation, Friedman was challenging Keynes's legacy. The American economy began to suffer from a lack of growth and inflation at the same time, an uncomfortable state of affairs that Keynesians had neither predicted, nor could easily explain.

It had long been assumed by Keynesians that inflation resulted from the increase in demand that economic growth provided. But they found it hard to explain why inflation persisted even when an economy went into recession. Explaining "stagflation"[1] —inflation during stagnation—was to provide the conditions for a crisis of confidence among Keynesians. Non-Keynesians had long warned that too much tinkering in the economy by governments would lead to uncomfortable distortions, and stagflation appeared to be the evidence they sought to prove that too much Keynesian management for too long undermined the natural self-regulation of a market economy.

Samuelson was at a loss to explain why stagflation had taken hold. "There's nothing in Keynesian economics that would allow you to solve stagflation,"[2] he admitted. For the first time, Keynesianism, which had dominated postwar economics in theory and practice, seemed vulnerable. "The failure to solve the ongoing problem of stagflation was the most important nail in the coffin of Keynesianism,"[3] Samuelson recalled.

He didn't blame an out-of-control money supply for stagflation but the contradictory demands of the electorate. "The fact that the modern mixed economy is a humane economy lies at the root of the stagflation problem," he wrote. Before Keynes, when an economy shed jobs during an economic downturn—which Samuelson described as one of "the cruelties of historic capitalism"[4]—the price of labor fell, which meant employers could afford to start hiring again, which in turn led to economic recovery. Since Keynes, market economies had become "mixed economies," with governments influencing markets to keep unemployment at a minimum. With the threat of unemployment removed, Labor demanded pay rises, which employers passed on to the consumer as price increases.

Samuelson's bitter childhood memories of the jobless Thirties made him reluctant to propose mass unemployment as a remedy to rising inflation—which he described as "the malaria of the modern mixed economy"[5]—even if it was an economically sound cure to rising prices. "I, with my vivid memories of the Great Depression, have a natural concern for those unskilled and minority workers who are called on to shoulder the burden of fighting creeping inflation by means of the nation's running a relatively slack labor market [i.e., a market in labor that had enough jobless that when they were hired it did not raise wages]."[6]

The novel circumstances of low growth and high inflation offered economists a renewed opportunity to explain how stagflation came about and how to cure it. Friedman proposed a simple explanation that, on the face of it, made sense, as Samuelson freely acknowledged. "Keynesianism, which worked so well in [Kennedy's romanticized presidency of] Camelot and brought forth a long epoch of price-level stability with good [quarterly growth] and nearly full employment, gave way to a new and quite different macro view after 1966," Samuelson explained. "A new paradigm, monistic monetarism, so the tale narrates, gave a better fit. And therefore King Keynes lost self-esteem and public esteem. The King is dead. Long live King Milton!"[7]

Samuelson had predicted in the early Sixties that burgeoning inflation might present new dangers to the apparently endless run of prosperity that America had enjoyed since the end of World War II. In his advice in early 1961 to John F. Kennedy, Samuelson had warned that the traditional trade-off between unemployment and price rises might have come to an end. He warned Kennedy that while America in the postwar period had enjoyed full employment and low prices simultaneously, it was premature to believe that high employment would not eventually lead to an increase in prices. In which case, he told the president, "new institutional programs, other than conventional fiscal and monetary policies, must be devised to meet this new challenge."[8]

By the end of the Sixties, Samuelson's dire warning had come true. Inflation and unemployment were increasing at the same time, as trade unions fought to catch up with rocketing prices. "If price increases could be held down to, say, less than 5 per cent per year, such a mild steady inflation need not cause too great concern," Samuelson declared in *Economics*. "[But] if each increase in price becomes the signal for an increase in wages and costs, which again sends prices up still further, we may be in the midst of a malignant, galloping, hyperinflation."[9]

In the decade 1958 to 1968, the U.S. Bureau of Labor Statistics consumer price index recorded a leap from nil inflation in early 1958 to nearly 5 percent by the end of 1968. That hike was just the start of an unprecedented period of compounding price rises that would continue unabated for more than a decade. Inflation leapt to a new high of 6.6 percent in December 1970, then from 4.9 percent in January 1971 to 11.7 percent the following month.

This record postwar rise in prices was outstripped toward the end of the Seventies when, from a low of 6.2 percent in February 1978, prices rose steadily until a peak was reached in June 1980 of 13.6 percent.[10] Such runaway inflation in the U.S., which alarmed both voters and governments the world over, demanded an explanation and a cure.

It was against this ugly price landscape that the long battle for monetarism was fought. At the core of the debate were competing theories about what caused inflation.

Samuelson described the cause of hyperinflation[11] in a *Newsweek* column:

> The escalation of the Vietnam war in 1965 produced classical demand-pull inflation—i.e., too much dollar spending chasing a limited supply of goods, with labor markets tight and order backlogs high as even overtime production could not produce as much as was wanted. By 1970, just as the demand-pull inflation was weakening in consequence of tight monetary and fiscal policies, the militant desire of union members to catch up to, and stay ahead of, the inflation led to upward cost-pressure on prices.[12]

Like most economists of the time, Samuelson believed inflation was either cost-push—as the cost of labor or raw materials increased, businesses passed on those costs to consumers—or demand-pull—too much demand was chasing too few goods, which drove up prices. In 1960, Samuelson hinted that there were problems with the Phillips Curve jobs/prices trade-off when he described cost-push inflation as "a force that operates year-in and year-out, whenever we are at high employment, to push up prices. . . . Instead of setting in only after you have reached over-full employment, the suspicion is dawning that it may be a problem that plagues us even when we haven't arrived at a satisfactory level of employment."[13]

Samuelson thought demand-pull inflation was a problem primarily for prosperous economies. As steady economic growth led to full employment, labor became scarce and allowed workers, in particular trade-union members, to win pay increases that restored the value of their wages when prices rose. Wage increases in turn drove prices up further because they increased the cost to producers of making goods. Similarly, as people found themselves better paid, with higher salaries and wages, sellers raised the price of goods because customers could bear higher prices, and some goods rose in price because they had become so in demand that they became scarce. If inflation was one of the disadvantages of governments maintaining full employment, argued Samuelson, never mind. It was a price worth paying to ensure that all Americans were in jobs and comfortably well-off.

For Samuelson, there was no easy cure for inflation. "Anyone with a good track record in analyzing the post-1950 developments in North America and Europe realizes that the only cure now known for creeping inflation is decidedly worse than the disease itself,"[14] he wrote. Americans—or more accurately their political leaders—faced hard choices. Inflation could be contained "by two kinds of fiscal restraints: either higher tax rates, or lower rates of government expenditure—or, of course, a combination."[15] And there was a third way, he said: the Federal Reserve could slow the economy by raising interest rates at the top of the business cycle. This would reduce business activity when inflation and employment were at their height.

Samuelson was in no doubt that galloping inflation was undesirable and should be tamed, but even though he had a number of theories about how that could be achieved, he was by no means certain which approach would work best. While hyperinflation was famously in evidence in Weimar Germany and post–World War I Austria, as had been experienced at first-hand by Hayek, it had not been addressed in a modern advanced Western economy. Samuelson feared the consequences if inflation were to resist all remedies. He warned:

If workers, farmers, and businessmen do not learn [that their welfare depends upon wage and price restraint], our economic system may be in for a bad time. In that case, whenever there is enough purchasing power [i.e., total aggregate demand] to bring the system near the full employment, there will tend to result a vicious upward spiral of prices and wages. Even more ominous is the possibility that prices may begin to shoot up long before full employment is reached.[16]

He believed that living with persistent, out-of-control inflation invited "dangerous consequences" and warned that governments would be pressed to act, perhaps by setting the price of wages and goods by law. Aside from the unfair burden placed on those living on fixed incomes, such as the elderly on fixed pensions and the poor who had no means of keeping with rising prices, he argued that inflation also raised the relative price of American goods for export, which increased America's balance-of-payments deficit.[17]

Of the available remedies for inflation, Samuelson favored raising taxes over the Federal Reserve raising interest rates to check growth. Higher borrowing costs would hit industries like housing and construction, and home buyers benefited from low mortgage rates. "If the Fed is left alone to do the job," he wrote, "experience shows that the resulting 'money crunch' will place a disproportionate burden on real-estate markets," which in 1966 had endangered savings-and-loan associations.

By raising taxes and maintaining high public spending, he believed, the poor and the disadvantaged would be protected from the ravages of rising prices. Besides, he argued, there was plenty for governments to usefully spend money on. "If the people give high priority to using economic resources to clean up our polluted rivers and atmosphere, the fact that we are . . . facing a problem of inflation should not stand in the way of their getting the program they want," he wrote. "If the people preponderantly desire that minimum standards of welfare be maintained and that the battle against poverty be vigorously pursued, neither war nor inflation provides legitimate economic obstacles to the attainment of these goals."[18]

Many politicians were anxious that voters would punish them for deploying taxes as a cure for inflation. But Samuelson insisted in 1968, the year after Friedman's AEA address, that "the United States is not today remotely near any limit of tax capacity" (i.e., taxpayers were not so overburdened by taxes that they could not pay more). "If the people desire more of government programs that they deem vital, there is vast scope in the 1968 economy for expansion of the public sector."[19] Indeed, he went further. Cutting government programs was both unnecessary and bad policy. And it offended his "credo for the good society."

> There is no such necessity and it is economic nonsense to postulate that there is. Compared with other Western societies and compared with our affluence and public needs, I find it easier to make the case that America today spends too little rather than too much on government.[20]

He concluded that it would be tragic if the federal government's campaigns against poverty and inequality at home and abroad were curtailed because of the "myth" of economic necessity.[21] Indeed, he considered that the inflation Americans were enduring at the end of the Sixties resulted from Congress not raising taxes sooner. "We are paying now—in rising prices, wage settlements outstripping productivity, balance-of-payments pressure [i.e., the need to export as much as was imported], soaring interest rates—for failure of Congress to raise taxes,"[22] he wrote.

And if the only way a tax cut could be agreed in Congress was by cutting social programs, Samuelson said he would rather live with inflation. But, if the right remedies were adopted, he did not think high inflation would become a permanent feature of modern life. "All experience shows that the rate of inflation of the next few years . . . crucially depends on the degree of excess in aggregate demand [i.e., both cost-push and demand-pull inflation] that is allowed to develop,"[23] he wrote.

In May 1970, *Newsweek* asked Samuelson and Friedman to discuss inflation, then running at 4 percent a year. Could we live with permanent inflation at that level? the editors asked. "I can live with one arm, but I would rather have two," was Friedman's reply. "The U.S. can live with any amount of inflation, provided it is permitted to be open and aboveboard and is not repressed by widespread wage and price controls. But the economy—and the social and political structure as well—will be far healthier if inflation is avoided." Samuelson, too, was sanguine about living with inflation. "We can do so without irreparable distortions and precipitous accelerations, provided a) that the other mixed economies experience about the same rate of creeping prices, and b) that we follow tax-and-money policies that will convince people that uncontrolled inflation is not in the cards."[24]

But a mere 4 percent inflation would appear moderate as the decade progressed. Before hyperinflation was defeated, it would approach three times that number, reaching a record 11.8 percent in 1975 before hitting a peak of 11.81 percent in 1981.

BUSY WITH OTHER THINGS, Samuelson might have left his textbook to answer the monetarist challenge Friedman had first launched in his AEA lecture. But Friedman was at the height of fashion and his new take on the old theory of money needed to be confronted before it gained too much traction.

Friedman knew Samuelson had little time for the quantity theory, as he had told him so many times, including in 1962, before the publication of *A Monetary History of the United States* and its attempt to demonstrate the key role money played in promoting and curbing growth. "As you know," Samuelson wrote Friedman, "my empirical and theoretical researches have not convinced me that the greatest emphasis is to be placed on the money supply as a causal determinant of economic activity."[25]

By 1969, however, Samuelson had decided it was time to act. He devoted much of an upcoming compendium[26] of writings on economics he was editing to detailed refutations of Friedman's monetarism. In his own essay on monetarism in the volume, Samuelson credited Friedman with successfully reviving interest in the quantity theory of money and reintroducing it to the mainstream debate in economics after a long period, coinciding with the rise of Keynesianism, in which the notion had not only been ignored but traduced as outdated and irrelevant. The quantity-of-money theory had so fallen into disrepute, wrote Samuelson, that many Keynesians, particularly in Britain, had concluded that "money does not matter."

"For centuries philosophers and economists have noted as no coincidence that vast increases in the supply of money have been accompanied by tremendous increases in the price level," Samuelson wrote. "Like many basic ideas, the Quantity Theory became so familiar and began to seem so simple that a later generation of economists became inclined to disparage its significance." He acknowledged Friedman's leading role in resurrecting a theory that had fallen into abeyance. "Prior to the 1970 edition of [my] textbook, the space given to monetarism was quite limited," he wrote. "The present discussion shows why this topic now deserves ample investigation."[27] Praising Friedman for "the brilliance of his analytical and empirical researches,"[28] Samuelson then published in his 1970 compendium two accounts by Friedman of his monetarist theories.[29]

The conclusion of Friedman's first essay, originally published in 1963 and written for Indian readers,[30] was less dogmatic than his later claim that there was a direct and sole link between the quantity of money and price rises. In the article, Friedman readily acknowledged that "the emphasis I have . . . been placing on the stock of money as the culprit [in the cause of inflation] is widely regarded as old-fashioned and out of date," a state of affairs he firmly placed at the foot of Keynesians. But in this early iteration of his monetarism, Friedman was prepared to acknowledge that there may be more than one explanation for inflation.

Friedman wrote that every time inflation occurred, two explanations were offered. One was that the amount of money in the economy had increased. The other was that special factors had contributed to the inflation: workers had pushed up wages; profiteers had gouged prices; the supply of goods from abroad had been interrupted, which pushed up prices; and so on. And he conceded that "these two separate explanations are not necessarily contradictory. The non-monetary factors may, on some occasions, be the cause of the monetary expansion."[31]

But, he concluded, "Whenever these or other factors have led to a substantially greater expansion in the stock of money than the current rate of increase in output, they have led to inflation. . . . I know of no exception to the proposition that there has been a one-to-one relation between substantial rises in prices and substantial rises in the stock of money."[32] In other words, money and inflation were directly linked, and when increases in the supply of money outstripped economic growth, inflation occurred.

Alongside the 1963 Friedman essay, Samuelson cited at length a 1958 paper by Friedman also linking inflation to the quantity of money.[33] The paper does, however, question which came first, the monetary growth or the rise in prices, a chicken-and-egg argument in which he conceded he might well have the order reversed. But he made a firm declaration that would underpin his subsequent arguments on inflation and how it might be controlled:

> It could be that a rise or fall in prices, occurring for whatever reasons, produces a corresponding rise or fall in the stock of money, so that the monetary changes are a passive consequence. Alternatively, it could be that changes in the stock of money produces changes in prices in the same direction, so that control of the stock of money would imply control of prices.[34]

It was a clear statement of faith: if the stock of money could be controlled, so inflation could be held in check. Despite the later simplifications of his monetarist faith, in his 1958 essay Friedman was prepared to acknowledge that "the relationship between changes in prices, while close, is not of course precise or mechanically rigid."[35] (That cautionary "of course" would later make a mockery of both his and his disciples' simplistic application of his monetarism.)

Friedman described how inflation could be curbed by a rise in the interest rate. It was a matter, he argued, of the relationship between what individuals were happy to hold in cash relative to their income. A higher interest rate encouraged people to invest in, say, government bonds, and keep less in cash, thereby removing it from the stock of money in circulation. Inflation and deflation had a similar effect.

> The rate of change of prices has no discernible effect in ordinary times when price changes are small—on the order of a few per cent a year. On the other hand, it has a clearly discernible and major effect when price change is rapid and long continued, as during extreme inflations or deflations. A rapid inflation produces a sizable decline in the desired ratio of cash balances to income; a rapid deflation [with prices falling], a sizable rise.[36]

As Friedman had observed from his extensive study of data,

> Over the [business] cycle, prices and output tend to move together— both tend to rise during expansions and to fall during contractions. Both are part of the cyclical process and anything, including a monetary change, that promotes a vigorous expansion is likely to promote a vigorous rise in both and conversely.[37]

As there was an increase in the money supply at either end of the business cycle—the naturally occurring ebb and flow of business activity with demand outstripping supply at the top of the cycle, and supply outpacing demand at the bottom—both during expansions and contractions, it was important to concentrate not on the raw money supply figures—the total in circulation at any time—but, as Keynes had argued in *A Tract on Monetary Reform*, on the rate of change of the quantity of money over time. He concluded, "On the average, the rate of change of the money supply shows well-marked cycles that match closely those in economic activity in general and precede the latter by a long interval." Then he ventured some hard-and-fast rules by which the money supply and inflation (or deflation) were related over time.

> On the average, the rate of change of the money supply has reached its peak nearly 16 months before the peak in general business and has reached its trough over 12 months before the trough in general business.[38]

He therefore determined that, while "this is conclusive evidence for the independent influence of monetary change . . . it means that it must take a long time for the influence of monetary changes to make themselves felt" as the "rate of change of the money supply may not be reflected in prices or economic activity for 12 to 16 months, on the average." This had profound implications for policy makers who, convinced of the need for monetary restraint, or loosening, sought to alter the supply of money to affect inflation. "Monetary action taken today may, on the basis of past experience, affect economic activity within 6 months or again perhaps not for over a year and 6 months."

This widely variable lag, which could be even longer or shorter as the event in question might be a statistical outlier—either shorter than six months or longer than eighteen months—meant that attempts to influence inflation through monetary means were at best haphazard. Not only did this lead "to misinterpretation and misconception about the effects of monetary policy, as well as to consequent mistakes in monetary policy," but, worse, for those like Friedman who believed the money supply to be the key to understanding the causes of inflation, "because the effects of monetary change do not occur instantaneously, monetary policy is regarded [by some economists] as ineffective."[39]

Friedman then speculated in the 1958 essay[40] on whether a steady, moderate inflation encouraged faster economic growth. There were two opposing views, he explained. One side suggested that moderate price rises were useful in allowing business to claw back "sticky" wage rates that otherwise hindered growth. As employers found it hard to cut wages, businesses had come to rely upon inflation to stealthily reduce the real value of wages over time. "Gently rising prices, it is argued, will tend to offset [the] upward pressure [on business costs] by permitting [nominal] money wages to rise without real wages doing so," he wrote. And because interest-rate rises to choke off inflation lag behind increases in costs, particularly labor costs, and the true interest rate is the actual interest rate minus the inflation rate, "productive enterprises find the cost of borrowing to be relatively low, and again have a greater incentive than otherwise to invest."[41]

Otherwise, inflation was a disincentive to businesses as "generally rising prices reduce the pressure on enterprises to be efficient, stimulate speculative relative to industrial activity, reduce the incentives for individuals to save,"[42] and inflation upset the relative price structure between goods as businesses were obliged to constantly alter prices to remain in line relative to other goods. Furthermore, he argued, if inflation becomes entrenched, unions tend to demand inflation-proof, or inflation index–linked pay raises to compensate for the rise in prices between wage rounds. Inflation then became "baked in" to an economy making it harder to cure. Economic growth would be inhibited if there was a need to resort to higher interest rates to check inflation.

Which view was correct? Was inflation useful or a curse? Friedman dodged the question, writing that "historical evidence on the relation between price changes is mixed and gives no clear support to any of these positions." His own conclusion? "Either rising prices or falling prices are consistent with rapid economic growth, provided that the price changes are fairly steady, moderate in size, and reasonably predictable. The mainsprings of growth are presumably to be sought elsewhere." What should be avoided, he declared, were "unpredictable and erratic changes of direction in prices" which were "as disturbing to economic growth as to economic stability." And that "past experience," which he failed to elaborate upon, "suggests that something like a 3 to 5 per cent per year increase in the stock of money is required for long-term price stability,"[43] though how he came to arrive at such precise figures he also omitted to explain.

How could a steady 3 to 5 percent increase in prices be achieved? As he had already argued, the time delay between attempting to alter the quantity of money in an economy and the resulting effect on prices was at best guesswork. "The available evidence casts grave doubts on the possibility of producing any fine adjustments in economic activity by fine adjustments in monetary policy," he declared.

Friedman warned of the "serious limitations to the possibility of a discretionary monetary policy [by the Federal Reserve] and much danger that such a policy may make matters worse rather than better." While the Federal Reserve had since 1951 "been distinctly superior to that followed during any earlier period since the establishment of the [Federal Reserve] System, mainly because it has avoided wide fluctuations in the rate or growth of the money supply," Friedman thought it offered too much opportunity for political interference.

He preferred "the much simpler policy of keeping the money supply growing at a predesignated rate month in and month out with allowance only for seasonal influences and with no attempt to adjust the rate of growth to monetary conditions."[44] Friedman was concerned by the intense political pressure on central banks and governments to intervene when an economy was suffering from hyperinflation or severe deflation. Voters always asked, What's the government doing about it? He warned that "yielding to these pressures may frequently do more harm than good." He concluded:

The goal of an extremely high degree of economic stability is certainly a splendid one; our ability to attain it, however, is limited; we can surely avoid extreme fluctuations; we do not know enough to avoid minor fluctuations; the attempt to do more than we can will itself be a disturbance that may increase rather than reduce instability.[45]

In light of the boldness of his later keynote address to the American Economic Association, Friedman in these earlier papers displayed a rare degree of caution. The benefits of running the economy according to the quantity theory of money expressed in his earlier essays were riddled with reservations and riders. He had allowed himself doubts and room for maneuver when suggesting how his monetarist notions could be applied by policy makers. Had Samuelson wanted to hold his rival up to ridicule, it would have been easy for him to have ignored Friedman's earlier ruminations and only assessed his American Economic Association lecture, for the certainty displayed in the AEA lecture made Friedman's arguments more vulnerable to disproof.[46] By revealing Friedman in all his complexity, Samuelson was prepared to give his nemesis the benefit of the doubt. Or to hang himself with his own rope.

Taking Friedman at his word, in his 1970 collection of essays[47] Samuelson set out to refute Friedman's trademark theory: that the quantity of money was the sole cause of inflation. His explication was a typical piece of Samuelson prose: witty, even lighthearted in its scathing dismissal of Friedman's logic. And throughout, Samuelson depicted the disagreement between monetarists and post-Keynesians, of which he counted himself one,[48] as a quasi-religious dispute. Like Hayek before him, Friedman had set himself up as an outsider banging on the firmly locked doors of evolved Keynesianism, which Samuelson described as "the ruling orthodoxy of American establishment economics."[49] And like the Keynes Hayek debate, the argument extended beyond economics into comparing a wider set of beliefs about politics and the role of government that lay behind the difference in views.

Samuelson's first point was a little grudging, pointing out that Friedman was merely rehashing the old quantity theory of money which had reigned supreme until Keynes had turned the world of classical economics upside down with his *General Theory* in 1936. Keynes had so fundamentally altered our understanding of macroeconomics that the importance given by old-school economists to the role of money had been made redundant. "By the end of the 1930s," Samuelson wrote, "after the so-called Keynesian revolution, courses and textbooks continued to be devoted to money. But in fact money had almost completely dropped out of them and the emphasis had shifted to analysis of [national] income determination in terms of such Keynesian concepts as the multiplier and the propensity to consume."[50]

There had been a postwar revival in interest in the role money played in an economy, Samuelson admitted, but Friedman was one among many who had facilitated its resuscitation. Others, such as Howard S. Ellis[51] of the University of California, had first reported "the rediscovery of money" in the postwar period. But Samuelson credited Friedman with "mountains of data, cogency of reasoning, and formidable powers of patient persuasion [that] have raised unto him a host of followers,"[52] making monetarism "a movement to reckon with." He thought the revival had been "fruitful," inasmuch as it had caused a shift away from "simpliste" Keynesianism "and made economists more willing to recognize that monetary policy is an important stabilization weapon, fully coordinate with fiscal policy as a macroeconomic control instrument."[53]

But, according to Samuelson, the importance of the revival in monetary theory had been overestimated. "Often, if a stock goes down too far in price, in reaction it may subsequently go up too far," he wrote. "There is [a] danger of this in the case of monetary theory. A crude monetarism is now stalking the land." He promised "a scientifically objective evaluation"[54] of how monetary doctrines had varied over the years.

While Samuelson said his appraisal of the current state of monetary theory was to be "scientific," he made clear from the start that his exposition would concentrate on the monetary-theory revival led by Friedman. "Undoubtedly the popularity of monetarism can be traced in large part to one man, namely Professor Milton Friedman of the University of Chicago," he wrote. He praised Friedman and Schwartz's *Monetary History of the United States, 1867–1960*, which he described as "the bible of the movement" and "a classic source of data and analysis to which all scholars will turn for years to come."[55]

Samuelson summarized Friedman's argument as follows:

It is the rate of growth of the money supply that is the prime determinant of the state of aggregate dollar demand [which Keynes had identified as the key engine of economic activity]. If the Federal Reserve will keep the money supply growing at a steady rate—say 4 to 5 percent by one or another definition of money supply, but the fact of steadiness being more important than the rate agreed upon—then it will be doing all a central bank can usefully do to cope with the problems of inflation, unemployment, and business instability. Fiscal policy as such has no independent, systematic effect upon aggregate dollar demand.[56]

While it was widely assumed by post-Keynesian economists that the rate of taxation and public spending by the agencies of government affected the rate of unemployment, he wrote, "crude monetarism" suggested that, so long as the rate of growth of the money supply was kept constant, such attempts by government to manage demand to promote growth were futile. Similarly, Samuelson pointed out that according to Friedman, "many people have wrongly inferred that fiscal deficits and surpluses have predictable expansionary and contracting effects upon the total of aggregate spending. But this is complete confusion. It is the changes in the rate of the money supply which alone have substantive effects. After we have controlled or allowed for monetary changes, fiscal policy has negligible independent potency."[57]

Samuelson noted that Friedman believed that close control of the money supply, combined with raising taxes resulting in lower interest rates, could curb inflation:

> Increasing taxation relative to public expenditure, although having no independent effect on aggregate demand, will tend to lower consumption and reduce interest rates. This contrived increase in thriftiness will move the mix of full-employment output in the direction of more rapid capital formation; it will speed up the rate of growth of productivity and real output, and will increase the rate of growth of real wages. If the trend of the money supply remains unchanged, this will tend toward a lower price level in the future or a less rapidly rising one.[58]

Samuelson disarmed those who believed that monetarism was somehow an antidote to Keynesianism by pointing out that Friedman was doing little more than agreeing with Keynes, who in *The General Theory* also suggested there was a direct link between an increase in the supply of money, at full employment, and a rise in prices. While Samuelson acknowledged that "when an author writes as much as did Keynes, it is inevitable that certain of his passages might seem to contradict others,"[59] he noted that Keynes believed that, if the long-term interest rate could be brought down low enough, monetary policy could play an effective role in curing depression and stagnation.[60]

Research in the Fifties and Sixties had traced how expanding the money supply through the open-market purchase of Treasury bills by the Fed[61] had its limitations. The intervention of the Fed tended to reduce interest rates, leading to a stimulation of investment that would otherwise not have taken place, as well as "an upward capitalization of the value of existing assets,"[62] which in turn promoted "a certain expansionary influence on consumer spending, and in a degree on business spending for investment."[63] But the newly created money could not be compared with new money "created by gold mining or money created by the printing press of national governments or the Fed and used to finance public expenditures in excess of tax receipts."[64] In many respects the action of the Fed was a zero-sum game, "taking from the system an almost equal quantum of money substitutes in the form of government securities."[65]

By buying its own assets, the Fed was "merely a dealer in secondhand assets, contriving transfer exchanges of one type of asset for another, and in the process affecting the interest rate structure that constitutes the terms of trade among them," whereas the creation of newly mined gold and the printing of money by the state left the community "permanently richer in its ownership of monetary wealth." "In money terms the community *feels* richer; in money terms the community *is* richer. And this [feeling of increased wealth] can be expected to reflect itself in a higher price level or a lower rate of unemployment or both,"[66] Samuelson averred.

Then Samuelson offered a post-Keynesian twist on one of Keynes's most quoted sayings, that it was rational to trade short-term benefits for long-term deficits because "in the long term we're all dead."[67] Because the reallocation of government debt by buying government bonds meant the repayment was delayed far into the future, which few could imagine, only those who lived forever would notice the cost of such an action. He wrote:

> Rejecting such a perpetual-life model as extreme and unrealistic, we must debit against an increase in money through open-market operations a partial offset in the form of retirement of some of the outstanding public debt.[68]

Samuelson drew attention to acts of economic behavior that contradicted Friedman's main contention: that the change in supply of money was the sole factor affecting inflation. First, changes in people's thriftiness or the propensity to spend would affect prices or production of goods and services, or both. Similarly, any spontaneous outburst of what Keynes called "animal spirits" among entrepreneurs or the emergence of new and exciting opportunities to invest would affect output as measured by the gross national product and therefore would alter prices. In a like manner, increases in public spending, reductions in taxation, even increases in public expenditure matched by raises in taxation, would affect output and therefore prices.

One of Friedman's key assumptions was that a rise in the quantity of money led, after a time lag, to rising prices. Yet Samuelson averred that the data showed that changes to the money supply did not precede the turndown in the business cycle, but followed it, as Friedman had hinted at in his 1958 essay. Only in recent years, Samuelson wrote, did the data suggest that it was an early indicator of a slowdown, but that was perhaps because "the Federal Reserve has been disregarding the advice of the monetarists and has tried to do some advance forecasting so that it can lean against the winds of recession before they begin to blow very hard."[69]

For all of Samuelson's attempts to complicate matters, Friedman was too well advanced in his practical campaign to have his notion tested to worry much about Samuelson's reservations. The proof of whether his monetarism held water would be in real life, applying Friedman's fixed input of new money to a real national economy with real citizens, and real inflation. With both sides of the argument at an impasse, observing real-life interventions was all that was left if the issue was to be resolved. So Keynesians and Friedmanites watched with amused fascination as Friedman set out to find a president, a prime minister, or a dictator who would agree to test his monetarist theory to destruction.

9

Tricky Dicky

Friedman thought he had found in Richard Nixon a president smart enough to apply his monetarist fix for Inflation. But Nixon was only interested in reelection

When asked to join John F. Kennedy's administration, Paul Samuelson had politely declined the invitation, preferring to keep a distance from government and concentrate upon maintaining the place he had carved for himself as America's most distinguished economist. But Milton Friedman had different ambitions. He was eager to see his radical views put into practice, and began to cultivate ambitious Republicans in the hope he could ride their coattails and influence the federal government's approach to the economy.

As a social and intellectual outsider, Friedman had come to accept that he was largely ignored by the mainstream, moderate Republican leadership based around East Coast business figures like Nelson Rockefeller, a scion of the New York construction family. Friedman was considered too dogmatic, too extreme, too dangerous by party leaders, who worried that his libertarian views would frighten away voters in the pivotal middle ground, where elections are traditionally decided.

But Friedman found a presidential candidate who did not care much what the East Coast Republican establishment thought. In the 1964 presidential race, Barry Goldwater, the maverick senator from Arizona, ran an insurgent campaign that condemned the mainstream Republican leadership for failing to advocate and apply genuinely conservative policies.

Friedman hoped that if Goldwater became president he would profoundly alter the way government was run. "I was impressed with Goldwater's firm adherence to basic principles, his courage in taking unpopular positions, his willingness to sacrifice what seemed like political expediency to stand up for what he thought was right,"[1] Friedman recalled.

Friedman's role in the Goldwater campaign at first was "writing such memoranda and discussing over the telephone various issues of policy as they came up."[2] Goldwater, shunned by traditional Republican thinkers, was in urgent need of intellectual backing to underpin his unconventional ideas, and Friedman was happy to provide it. Friedman and Goldwater enjoyed a warm and extensive correspondence in which they exchanged views on economics, but Goldwater was no economist, nor even political philosopher. He simply believed that central government was too large and too interfering. His prejudice against government was spun into a political philosophy in his personal manifesto, *The Conscience of a Conservative*, by L. Brent Bozell Jr.,[3] who largely shaped Goldwater's stated viewpoint in his own image. So it was with Goldwater's economic policy. From his rare meetings with Goldwater, but after a lively correspondence with him, Friedman found the Arizona senator refreshingly ignorant of economics, which allowed him to shape the candidate's economic policy to his own ends.

When asked by the *New York Times* magazine to flesh out Goldwater's thoughts on the economy, Friedman introduced his own notions about how the economy should be run. The long piece,[4] eloquent, accessible, and intellectually challenging, set about bringing together Goldwater's disparate thoughts into a coherent whole. It attempted to persuade ordinary Americans that Goldwater was not the reactionary, crusty, reckless Mountain State renegade portrayed by the liberal press and his ruthless Democratic rival, President Lyndon Johnson. Friedman stressed that although Goldwater did not believe in big government, he did not want to eliminate all federal government intervention in the economy; the candidate was not even recommending the balancing of the annual federal budget. But under President Goldwater, Friedman wrote, there would be a marked change in the use of fiscal stimuluses. A key element of Keynesian-influenced policy thinking—the automatic triggers of public spending intended to iron out the bottom of a business cycle—would be replaced by strict monetary discipline.

Drawing on his extensive research into the causes of the Great Depression, Friedman wrote, "erratic monetary policy has frequently introduced instability that the private economy has had to cope with, and, despite all the talk of using fiscal policy to stabilize the economy, the Government's own expenditures and receipts have been among the most unstable elements in the national economy—and in a direction increasing economic instability, not offsetting it."

By revising government priorities, "Goldwater would call first on monetary policy, which can react quickly yet gradually. In the past, monetary policy has all too often been restricted during much of a recession and so has made the recession deeper. Instead, the quantity of money and credit should increase at an encouraging rate." This practical application of Friedman's quantity-of-money ideas would provide a "stable money" rule aimed at ensuring a predictable, slow increase in the money supply, irrespective of quotidian economic conditions. A steady and predictable rise in inflation would result.

In the November 1964 presidential election, Goldwater was beaten by Johnson in the most resounding electoral defeat in America's history, with Johnson garnering 60 percent of the popular vote. But Friedman's efforts to change the direction of Republican economic policy did not end with Goldwater's candidacy. Whoever the next Republican presidential candidate was, Friedman was committed to convincing him of the merits of his monetarist policy. In the meantime, the prominence the Goldwater campaign conferred on Friedman's monetarist policy ideas had made an impact.

A growing number of intellectual conservatives and "sound money" Republican politicians adopted monetarism as their preferred policy. And some of the other pet notions Friedman urged on the Goldwater campaign—welfare reform, an end to conscription to the armed forces, and a return of political power to the states—also gained adherents.

It was not long before Friedman was given a second chance to influence federal government economic policy, when he agreed to join Richard Nixon's 1968 presidential campaign as chairman of an economics advisory group.

HAYEK HAD ALWAYS warned Friedman to avoid becoming too close to politicians, but Friedman needed a result. So long as his ideas remained untried, governments would continue to tinker with the economy through fiscal policy. Friedman had to find a Republican president he could work with.

On Nixon's election to the presidency in 1968, Friedman became one of his economic advisers. Here, Friedman felt, was a chance to turn the tide of Keynesianism and introduce rigor to monetary policy. But Friedman was soon to discover the failings of a politician whose compulsive wiliness did not respect political principle.

Friedman judged everyone by how smart they were and he was impressed by Nixon's brain. "I would rank [Senator Robert A. Taft of Ohio] with Richard Nixon as one of the intellectually ablest political figures with whom I have had close contact,"[5] he would later write. But Nixon was notoriously slippery. Friedman's first experience of Nixon's incessant deviousness came when the candidate summarily abandoned his principled preference for free trade—a fixture among all economic conservatives—in favor of imposing tariffs on imported textiles because Nixon believed his advocacy of targeted protectionism might win him a couple of the cotton-growing southern states at the general election. Friedman could only look on, appalled.

Friedman had to stick to Nixon—he was the candidate. And only he could become president and change economic policy. Amid chaos and recrimination among the Democrats and the intervention of a maverick southern racist, George Wallace, who split the Democratic vote, Nixon beat his rival Hubert Humphrey in the November 1968 election handily in the electoral college, though he only squeaked in by around half a million popular votes. Friedman found himself on a winning team with a full four-year term ahead of them.

In a meeting in January 1969, shortly before Nixon's inauguration, Friedman was given the chance to pitch ideas to the president-elect. He put to one side his monetarist theory and urged on Nixon another of his favorite ideas that directly challenged John Maynard Keynes's legacy: the dismantling of the Bretton Woods currency-fixing agreement that abandoned the gold standard in favor of fiat currencies, set up under Keynes's auspices in 1944 to moderate the wild swings in world currency prices that in the Thirties had caused economic turbulence. By agreeing to limit the range of prices within which currencies traded, Bretton Woods ensured that national economies stayed in step with each other and that no nation was tempted to devalue its currency to win a short-term advantage in pricing its goods more cheaply on the world market.

Friedman told Nixon that "the first few weeks of the administration . . . will offer a unique opportunity to set the dollar free and thereby eliminate for years to come balance of payments restraints on U.S. economic policy."[6] Friedman warned that if Nixon did not float the dollar immediately on taking office, such were the sensitivities around the management of currencies that he would "never again enjoy the freedom to make such an important move."[7] Samuelson took a more pragmatic line to floating the dollar. "It is not my position that governments should never intervene in foreign-exchange markets," he told *Newsweek* readers in 1978. "In practice, most interventions are stupid attempts to defend the indefensible [i.e., usually central banks intervene too late to do anything but protect untenably high currency prices]."[8]

Faced with firm opposition to allowing the dollar to trade freely on the market from Friedman's friend Arthur Burns, the president-elect's principal adviser, Nixon decided to ignore Friedman's advice and leave things as they were, at least for the time being. Before long, however, America's Bretton Woods partners began to balk at being dependent upon the U.S. for their currency policies.

Nixon appeared to ignore Friedman's suggestion to abandon Bretton Woods and let the dollar float free, nor did he appear to be much interested in Friedman's second suggestion: introduction of a negative income tax, which would combine welfare and tax assessments, with those with no or low incomes being given "rebates."

Despite these initial rebuffs, Friedman wholeheartedly welcomed the Nixon presidency and had earnest hopes for what could be achieved with a dynamic conservative in the White House. But he soon discovered that, as he put it, Nixon's "readiness to put his own political interests above the public interest"[9] would stand in the way of the adoption of coherent conservative solutions.

Nixon did not find a job for Friedman in his administration, but Friedman's views were well represented by others around the new president. Certain influential figures in the new administration were not only familiar with Friedman's monetarist theories and sympathetic to them, but most knew Friedman personally. Adherence to Friedman's views became something of a benchmark to journalists when assessing the ideological position of Nixon's appointments.

When the new chairman of Nixon's Council of Economic Advisers (CEA), Paul W. McCracken,[10] was asked whether he was a Friedmanite, he replied warily that he was "Friedmanesque." McCracken was suggesting a subtle difference, perhaps, noting that he acknowledged the logic behind Friedman's monetarist explanation for inflation but, crucially, that he believed the money supply was only one among a number of inflationary pressures.

When Arthur Burns was made chairman of the Federal Reserve in February 1970, Friedman may have hoped for a greater influence over economic policy. He had met Burns at Rutgers, and it was Burns who invited Friedman in 1937 to join the National Bureau of Economic Research to investigate the role of money in the business cycle. Burns turned out to be far more than a mere employer: he had become Friedman's main mentor. He encouraged him to believe that in concentrating on the quantity theory of money, he was on the right track. It was Burns's macroeconomic analysis that influenced the reasoning behind Friedman and Schwartz's *A Monetary History of the United States, 1867–1960*. And it was Burns, among others,[11] whom Friedman consulted when preparing his 1967 lecture to the American Economic Association.

But by the time the two men became colleagues advising Nixon's administration, Burns had become skeptical of Friedman's simpler monetarist ideas. As Herbert Stein,[12] whom Friedman proposed as a member of the CEA and who was its chairman from 1972 to 1974, explained, "Burns did not accept for monetary policy the primary responsibility for bringing about a non-inflationary expansion."[13] Although Friedman's monetarism was attractive to George Shultz, the new director of the Office of Management and Budget, who considered himself "a close friend, admirer and disciple of Milton Friedman,"[14] as well as to a majority of the Council of Economic Advisers,[15] Burns still considered the money supply only one component of inflation. And to counter inflation, Burns continued to prefer fiscal measures, such as cuts in public spending.

Although intrigued by Friedman's theories, Burns could not see how monetarism could be applied in practice. Even apparently simple questions about the quantity of money, and the velocity of money in the system, were hard to answer. For instance, what exactly did Friedman mean by money?

How could it be measured? And how could it be increased or decreased by the government with any accuracy? In testimony to Congress, Burns explained his dilemma: the data were wildly different, depending on exactly which way you tried to measure money. "Let me go to the month of February," he said. "We published a figure of 6.5 percent (for the growth of money supply). It might have been, using a different season correction, zero, or it might have been 10.6 percent. And that is not the end of the story. These figures are revised."[16]

Nixon was not much interested in economics, nor economic theory, but he knew one thing: bad news about the economy was a threat to his reelection. He had learned from bitter experience. Nixon blamed his predecessor Dwight Eisenhower for his defeat in the closely fought presidential race against John F. Kennedy in 1960. Ike had decided in the dying days of his presidency that, instead of conjuring a pre-election boom in the economy through tax breaks, which would have benefited his vice-president Nixon's chances of winning the White House, he should do the responsible thing and balance the federal government budget. On election day, the margin between Nixon and Kennedy was razor thin: Nixon won a plurality of the popular vote but was defeated in the electoral college. Nixon often grumbled that, had Ike not paid down the deficit and allowed a pre-election boom, he would have won the White House in 1960.

As president, Nixon was confronted with a number of economic issues made worse by the vast public spending on the Vietnam War and the "Great Society" measures to reduce poverty left by Johnson. There was rising inflation, and a balance-of-payments deficit made worse by a weakening dollar and the obligation in the Bretton Woods Agreement for the U.S. to sell gold to other nations at a low price.

Nixon was far more concerned about joblessness than inflation. He had inherited from Johnson full employment (3.3 percent unemployed), inflation at 5.3 percent, and interest rates at 4.25 percent, of which he considered low unemployment to be the most important. As he told Pete Peterson,[17]

Assistant to the President for International Economic Affairs, "I've never seen anybody beaten on inflation in the United States. I've seen many people beaten on unemployment."[18]

But in years three and four of Nixon's first term, inflation gathered pace and became a toxic political issue. Labor unions started demanding inflation-proof pay deals. A strike of 1.5 million United Auto Workers at General Motors, which began in September 1971, lasted sixty-seven days and won a pay increase of 30 percent over three years, along with "cost of living" increases, to compensate for inflation. Nixon was rattled when, in the midterm elections of November 1970, Democrats increased their majority in the House and retained a majority in the Senate. As his favorability numbers headed below 50 percent, Nixon planned a big gesture to show voters he was doing something to control rising prices. Here was a golden chance for Friedman's theories on monetarism to be tried in practice. But while, according to one White House insider, "Keynesian management of the economy was fading [and] acceptance of the key role of money was rising,"[19] Friedman's monetarism did not figure in Nixon's thinking.

This became evident early in January 1971 when, in his State of the Union address, Nixon announced "a full employment budget,"[20] a budget designed to be in balance if the economy were operating at its peak potential. "By spending as if we were at full employment, we will help to bring about full employment."[21] He went on:

> With the stimulus and the discipline of a full employment budget, with the commitment of the independent Federal Reserve System to provide fully for the monetary needs of a growing economy, and with a much greater effort on the part of labor and management to make their wage and price decisions in the light of the national interest and their own self-interest—then for the worker, the farmer, the consumer, for Americans everywhere we shall gain the goal of a new

prosperity: more jobs, more income, more profits, without inflation and without war.[22]

Friedman, distressed to find himself shut out of the decision making, was taken by surprise when, in an interview immediately after the State of the Union, Nixon declared, "Now I am a Keynesian." (Friedman wrote to J. K. Galbraith, "You must be as chagrined as I am to have Nixon for your disciple.")[23] Nixon said that while he remained committed to market solutions in theory, he felt that free enterprise was no longer doing its job. "We do not live in a world in which the market works anymore,"[24] he told two of his top economic advisers. In an attempt to appease conservative Republicans who thought the reference to Keynes was evidence the president had switched ideological sides, the president's aides said he was simply acknowledging that a recession would cause a budget deficit that should not be exacerbated by raising taxes; he was not advocating a full-scale intervention in the economy to "correct" a slump. But it was clear despite the denials that Nixon was determined to spend what was necessary to remain in the White House.

In June 1971, following up on his State of the Union demand that the Fed "provide fully for the monetary needs of a growing economy," Nixon asked Friedman, who was still no more than an informal adviser to the president, to lobby Burns to sharply increase the money supply through lower interest rates to boost economic activity. Friedman argued strongly against the move, telling the president flatly that increasing the money supply was certain to increase inflation. "Nixon agreed," Friedman recalled, "but said that it would first promote economic growth and assure that the economy was expanding before the 1972 election." Friedman asked Nixon whether he thought it was worth winning the election if the cost was "major inflation." "We'll worry about that when it happens,"[25] Nixon replied.

Nixon was not done. In August 1971, he called a summit of top economic advisers— Burns, John Connally,[26] his new Treasury Secretary, and Paul Volcker,[27] his Undersecretary of the Treasury for Monetary Affairs, who would soon succeed Burns as chairman of the Federal Reserve—to Camp David to discuss a wide package of new economic measures—named by the press "The Nixon Shock"—ostensibly to bring inflation down. Again, Friedman was conspicuously left out.

The pressing problem for Nixon was that the Vietnam War, a widening trade deficit, growing labor problems, and a 10 percent increase in the money supply had left the dollar profoundly weakened, undermining the basis of Bretton Woods, which depended upon a strong dollar. Bretton Woods obliged the United States to sell gold to other nations at $35 an ounce, and, as the dollar continued to weaken, an alarming drain on U.S. gold reserves began that suggested that the vast stock of ingots stored in Fort Knox[28] would soon run out[29] as nations dumped their stocks of diminishing dollars and sheltered their assets in gold bought from the U.S. at a bargain price. In May 1971, West Germany withdrew from Bretton Woods rather than devalue the mark. In July, Switzerland traded $50 million in dollars for gold. And in early August, France sent a warship to New York Harbor to take delivery of its purchase of $191 million in gold held in the vault of the New York Federal Reserve Bank. Nixon finally agreed with Friedman that Keynes's Bretton Woods agreement should be brought to a swift end.

Friedman and other market economists had always favored a free-floating dollar, one that would allow the market rather than the administration to settle on the price of the nation's currency. Nixon's August 1971 declaration effectively killed off Bretton Woods by allowing the U.S. monetary authorities to end their promise to exchange dollars for gold. In March 1973, Nixon formally ended Bretton Woods, leaving the dollar to float freely on the open market. As a means of addressing the balance-of-payments deficit, caused by Americans buying more from abroad than they sold in exports, Nixon also announced in August 1971 the immediate imposition of a 10 percent tariff on all imports.

Nixon had been warned that ending Bretton Woods and allowing the dollar to float might cause the dollar to drop in price, or devalue, which patriotic Americans were likely to perceive as weakness. So, as a deliberate distraction, Nixon added a policy intended to reassure voters he was addressing one of their main concerns: rapidly rising prices. With inflation on the agenda, Friedman was optimistic that his monetarist ideas to halt inflation might be tried. But Friedman's proposals were not discussed at Camp David in 1971, nor was any mention made of the money supply. Always with an eye on his reelection, the president was more interested in conspicuous, direct action on rising prices.

Nixon's chosen policy was a ninety-day freeze on all wages and prices with immediate effect, to be followed by the permanent federal government control of all wages and prices. Other nations[30] suffering from a similarly damaging hike in prices of goods and labor were also resorting to a freeze on prices and wages by law, not so much to cure inflation as to buy them time to show voters they were doing something bold and practical to halt the wage-price spiral. The Democratic Congress had passed legislation to introduce price controls in 1970 in the hope that Nixon would take up the measure, but he was reluctant to use the powers given to him. His experience of price controls at firsthand, working in the wartime Office of Price Administration in 1942 that had legally curbed prices, did not give him confidence that his price controls would work. "The difficulty with wage-price controls and a wage board, as you well know, is that the God damned things will not work," he told Shultz. "They didn't work even at the end of World War II. They will never work in peacetime."[31]

Nixon also feared that controls might "lead to a terrible smothering [of] this whole free economy of ours"[32] and that the process was little more than "a socialist scheme, a scheme to socialize America."[33] But Nixon said that Burns, Connally, and Volcker[34] had pressed him to introduce wage and price controls and he saw the policy as a great vote-winning stunt. So Nixon introduced the price curbs, although he knew they would fail. "In principle,

[Nixon] was strongly opposed to wage and price controls," recalled Friedman. "But as we all know, Nixon had the capacity of rising above principle if politics demanded it."[35]

Friedman was appalled by what he was witnessing. As a free trader, he disliked all tariffs that restrained trade. And his reading of the U.S. inflation figures suggested that inflation was lower than at any time since 1967 and that there was no need therefore to counter inflationary pressures.[36] He believed Nixon was indulging in politics and introducing wage and price controls, even though he knew they would not work, to disguise his decision to float the dollar. "I am strongly opposed to both guidelines and controls," Friedman wrote. "They have been tried many times and have never yet worked. In failing, they have just distorted the economy and spread misinformation about the causes of inflation. Inflation is made in Washington and nowhere else."[37] His later judgment? That Nixon's price and wage controls "did far more harm to the country than any of the later actions that led to [Nixon's] resignation."[38] Samuelson, too, put little faith in the efficacy of price controls, but thought that sometimes they could prove useful.

But in the immediate aftermath of Nixon's new economic policy, it was Friedman, not Samuelson, who let off a tirade against Nixon in *Newsweek*[39] for tampering with free-market forces. Under the heading "Why the Freeze is a Mistake," Friedman described Nixon's prices and wages controls as "one of those 'very plausible schemes,' to quote what Edmund Burke said in a different connection, 'with very pleasing commencements, [that] have often shameful and lamentable conclusions.'" Freezing prices and wages to cut inflation was like fixing a boat's rudder, making it impossible to steer, he suggested. "How will it end? Sooner or later, and the sooner the better, it will end as all previous attempts to freeze prices and wages have ended, from the time of the Roman emperor Diocletian to the present," wrote Friedman, "in utter failure and the emergence into the open of the suppressed inflation."[40] And he blamed Burns for stoking inflation by increasing the supply of money by 10 percent in six months at Nixon's urging.

The super-self-confident Friedman wasn't afraid to tell the most powerful man in the world he had gone wrong. In the Oval Office in September
1971, a month after the crisis summit at Camp David and the imposition of
price controls, Nixon told Friedman he knew his wage and price freeze was
bad policy and that he would get rid of it as soon as possible. Then, pointing to the man charged with administering the controls, George Shultz,
Nixon said, "Don't blame George for this monstrosity." To which Friedman
sharply replied, "I don't blame George. I blame you, Mr. President."[41]

In the October 18 issue of *Newsweek*, Friedman continued his cataclys-
mic theme. "Under cover of the price controls, inflationary pressures will
accumulate, the controls will collapse, inflation will burst out anew, perhaps
sometime in 1973, and the reaction to the inflation will produce a severe
recession," he wrote. If there was a resulting stampede for higher wages and
prices, to catch up for the loss of increases during the freeze, hyperinflation
was likely to take root, Friedman argued.

Friedman was offended by Nixon interfering with the free working of
the price mechanism, in which the "natural" price was arrived at and supply
and demand were matched as the market "cleared." He had warned fifteen
years before that "even open hyperinflations [periods of high inflation] are
less damaging to output than suppressed inflations in which a wide range of
prices are held well below the levels that would clear the market."

In the October 18 *Newsweek* column Friedman argued that there were
only two remedies for hyperinflation, neither of which he found palatable:
"The re-imposition of controls, this time far more widespread, detailed and
stringent; or sharply deflationary monetary and fiscal measures. The first
would at best be a temporary expedient that would severely strain the economic and social structure; the second would produce a recession."[42] Friedman was accurately predicting the acute political dilemma that would face
Nixon's successor Jimmy Carter when confronting roaring inflation later
in the decade.

For his part, Samuelson, who was proud to be on Nixon's hit list of political enemies,[43] was sympathetic to the intentions of those who hoped price and wage controls would work, but he did not believe that they would. When asked in December 1970 whether controls should be introduced, he had replied, "I'd save outright wage-price controls for a greater emergency," concluding that "on the present evidence, I cannot favor price-controls."[44] The following year, when Nixon introduced his price curbs, Samuelson did not think circumstances had changed enough to warrant the controls and he made fun of those on the left, like J. K. Galbraith, who demanded price controls in the face of evidence from a dozen countries showing that such measures did not work—or only worked for a short time before collapsing.

But, as we saw in the last chapter, Samuelson disagreed with Friedman on the reasons for the stagflation—i.e., rising prices, stagnant growth, and rising unemployment—that was slowly emerging not only in the United States but across much of the rest of the developed world. He blamed the "cost-push" hyperinflation on "exogenous factors," such as a worldwide rash of crop failures, and "overheated" economies with high inflation. He took a sideswipe at dogmatists like Friedman who offered an oversimplified explanation and an apparently easy solution to checking inflation. "Hayekians [say] the free market plus control on the supply of money is the only way to deal with stagflation," he wrote. "But a majority of their colleagues will read in the evidence of the modern world greater costs and less benefits from such policies than are dreamed of in these philosophies."[45]

IN SEPTEMBER 1971, Friedman and Samuelson were invited, as the best-known economists in America, to appear before the Joint Economic Committee of Congress in the grandeur of a Senate Committee room on Capitol Hill to offer their views on Nixon's new economic policy. The hearing was a rare occasion when the two old friends and rivals sat side by side and engaged in direct debate in front of television cameras. And although the result was as inconclusive as the original Keynes Hayek debate, it exposed the clear divisions between Friedman and Samuelson not only on matters of economic policy but in their contrasting philosophies and their very different temperaments.

Conservative politicians like to blame trade unions for rising prices by exerting monopoly power over the labor market that first drives up wages, then general prices. But if union bashers were hoping for some backing from Friedman at his Committee appearance, they were in for a disappointment. Whatever is wrong with unions, Friedman told the congressmen, it is not that they produce inflation. "I am rather unaccustomed to defending trade unions," he told the committee. "They do a great deal of harm, in my opinion, in denying opportunities to people who have low incomes; that is to say, through their restrictive measures. But the one thing I do not think they are guilty of is producing inflation." He cited a recent General Motors pay deal in which a high wage demand from its unions was met because "earlier contracts were made under the expectation of much smaller inflation." Wages catching up with rising prices was inevitable and it was the unions' job to ensure their members' wages kept up with prices. Samuelson agreed, but warned the committee of the consequences of such deals. "If everybody wants to catch up all the time to the previous situation, then you are going to have an egg-chicken-egg situation which will perpetuate the rate of inflation,"[46] he said.

While praising Nixon's proposed cuts in public spending on health, education, and urban renewal, although he did not believe the president would ensure that the Democratic-held Congress would make such cuts, Friedman was unequivocal in his opposition to the federal government intervening in the labor market and consumer prices. "I strongly oppose the wage-price freeze and the more limited control of wages and prices that will doubtless succeed the freeze," he testified. "These are purely cosmetic measures that do not affect the basic sources of inflation. Those basic sources are government monetary and fiscal policy." He went on:

Insofar as wage and price controls have any effect, they distort the economic structure and do harm. Insofar as they are evaded, they do little economic harm but they add yet another mite to the weakening in the respect for law that is at the bottom of some of our social problems.[47]

Samuelson told the committee he did not agree with Friedman's pessimism about Nixon's price controls, which, he said, would "on balance . . . do something to moderate the rate of price and wage inflation this year and next."[48] And while evidence from other countries suggested that controls were often no more than a short-term fix, it was his view that "American society and the American economy will not stand for a permanent incomes policy [a deliberately planned year-by-year wage growth target agreed by the federal government and labor, as existed in many western European countries]" and that "I do not think you can roll back prices and wages by King Canute's edicts."[49] He conceded that the August 1971 emergency measures would likely contribute to some economic growth and that they would also likely check wage and price inflation by slowing the cycle of price rises followed by demands for higher wages. "The ultimate targets and guidelines cannot hope to roll back prices and wages or stabilize prices, but can hope to moderate the price-wage creep,"[50] he wrote in a statement to the committee.

While agreeing with Friedman that controls were not guaranteed to cut wages or prices, Samuelson could not resist publicly tweaking Friedman's nose for ruling out such measures in any circumstances. "I have often done thought experiments in place of counting sheep, asking myself, what if I were Professor Friedman?" he said. "Would a 7 per cent open rate of inflation [i.e., an inflation rate arrived at without intervention by government] cause me to come out in favor of an incomes policy? And in my first pass at this problem, my answer is always no. Then I try 8 percent and I still get no. By this time, I fall asleep at night."[51]

Friedman believed the price controls program would be counterproductive and stoke the flames of inflation rather than put them out, as businesses and labor unions sought to "catch up" when the controls were lifted, and as Congress and politicians believed that they did not now have to concern themselves with rising prices. He predicted that if the controls were imposed for too long, they would break down, as similar measures had elsewhere. "The controls can contain the pressure perhaps for a time in terms of keeping stated prices down," he said. "But if you have such pressure building up, you will almost surely have a collapse of the controls." If that happened, he warned, "you would have to once again contemplate a very sharp stepping on the brakes of monetary and fiscal expansion in order to offset that inflation."[52]

Samuelson took a swipe at Friedman's dogmatic approach to public spending and taxes. Nixon's August measures had hinted at cutting both government spending and taxes, but Friedman's motive for cutting public spending was political, not economic, Samuelson argued. "Professor Friedman has said that, in season and out of season, it is always time to cut expenditures and taxes," he said. "This is not for macroeconomic reasons but for deep philosophical and other reasons. I do not share in that judgment. I think we have tremendous public needs and we have a need to tax in order to finance those."[53]

Friedman's response to Samuelson's charge was suitably humorous, avoiding the big picture argument and concentrating instead on Samuelson's suggestion that Friedman's predictions were always too pessimistic. "I cannot justify or excuse Paul Samuelson's masochistic instincts," Friedman told the committee, "but I would like to correct his statement about my predictions. It so happens that his statement is false."

Friedman explained his reasoning behind his advocacy of public spending cuts and tax reductions:

I think that talk about tax cuts being pro-business or not is demagogy. Business does not pay any taxes, it can't. Only people pay taxes. The question is if you impose a tax that the corporation writes the check

for, who pays it? Either the employees of that corporation or the customers of that corporation or the stockholders of that corporation.
People pay. The corporation as such has no tax paying capacity.[54]

In the final minutes of giving evidence, Samuelson and Friedman took
each other on in a face-to-face exchange. Or, rather, Samuelson interrupted
Friedman in full flow when answering a question on what should be the
right level of taxes to be levied on private companies. Samuelson had floated
the idea that, "as the price of consensus," profits should be controlled by law
as a quid pro quo for labor unions agreeing to hold down wages. As freezing profits would be practically very difficult if not impossible to achieve,
he believed corporation taxes should be hiked instead, which would in turn
reduce profits.

Friedman profoundly disagreed. "I believe that corporation taxes are
now too high. They ought to be lower. It just seems to me again it is a—"

And he did not get to finish his sentence, as Samuelson interjected:
"You understand that I do not believe that, organized labor does not believe
that, and the lower income classes generally do not act as if they believe that
[corporation taxes are too high]."[55]

To what extent did Nixon advance Friedman's cause? He may have
ignored Friedman's thesis about the money supply and inflation, and he
took no notice of Friedman's opposition to price and wage controls. But
Friedman's influence on Nixon's administration was considerable. He could
claim two concrete achievements: persuading Nixon to free the dollar to
find its own price; and, in January 1973, an end to the military draft, one of
Friedman's abiding ambitions.

But while sympathetic to Friedman's monetarist ideas, Nixon and
members of his administration readily abandoned the free market by erect-
ing mandatory wage and price controls and imposing trade tariffs. "Being

'Friedmanesque,' [Nixon's] economists put much more weight on the money supply as cause of the inflation," Stein would later recall. "They did not, however, feel sufficiently confident of this position to go against the combination of conventional wisdom—both Republican and Keynesian."[56]

Stein continued his assessment of Friedman's influence on Nixon's actions by pointing out the central flaw in the practical application of Friedman's theories: how exactly to move from an economy with a variable money supply to one with a steady, fixed, predictable supply of money at or around 2 percent a year. Stein wrote:

> The idea of a "Friedmanesque" policy of stable monetary growth ran into a number of difficulties. The policy may be the most appropriate one for keeping an economy stable when it is in a position where it should be kept stable. But the problem of 1969 was not to stabilize the economy; it was to reduce the on-going inflation. That called for a reduction in the rate of monetary growth, but the "stable money" rule provided no guidance about the speed with which monetary growth should be decelerated.[57]

Ultimately, Nixon proved a disappointment to Friedman. "I was a strong supporter of Nixon in 1968," he recalled. "In retrospect, I must confess that I question whether the support was justified." He then listed how Nixon had disappointed him:

> Few presidents have come closer to expressing a philosophy compatible with my own; and few if any have had a higher IQ; yet performance belied the rhetoric and ability. The most extreme, but by no means the only, example is wage and price controls.
>
> Though Nixon supposedly was for a smaller and less intrusive government, federal-government spending came to about the same percentage of national income at the end of his term as at the beginning.

On reexamining the evidence, I was shocked to find that the explosion in federal regulatory activity had its start in the Nixon administration. . . . The number of pages in the Federal Register, a record of all government regulations, went from 20,000 in 1968 to 46,000 in 1974, the year Nixon resigned.[58]

Friedman listed some of the new government agencies Nixon had introduced: the Environmental Protection Agency (EPA); the Occupational Safety and Health Administration (OSHA); the Consumer Product Safety Commission (CPSC); the Legal Services Commission (LSC), the Department of Energy (DOE); and the Economic Employment Opportunity Commission (EEOC).

Friedman's dislike of regulation per se stemmed from his belief that economic growth could only improve if businesses were not stymied by rules and legal obligations. Like many other Friedman causes, deregulation became a common conservative argument against the busybodies and do-gooders he accused of hog-tying the market with excessive and expensive rules. Even Samuelson would concede that "safety regulations and pollution controls do lower productivity as conventionally reported, but longer lives and purer air are part of what an affluent society will rationally want."[59] But Samuelson thought of such regulations as countering the market failure in which the costs of pollution or unsafe working practices were never fully borne by the perpetrators.

In 2002, Friedman looked back on his first brush with government with a jaundiced eye, describing Nixon as "the most socialist of the presidents of the United States in the 20th century," because "you had the biggest increase in government regulation and control of industry during the Nixon administration than you had in the whole postwar period."[60]

10

The Chicago Boys

Friedman's trip to Sweden to accept his Nobel Prize is
overshadowed by advice he had given the general who
overthrew the elected socialist president of Chile

Nixon's administration may have been a missed opportunity to put mon-etarist ideas into practice, but before long Friedman found another president who urgently needed help curing runaway inflation. Between 1955 and 1964, the University of Chicago had welcomed graduate students in economics from the Catholic University of Chile, funded by the U.S. Agency for International Development, who on their return to Chile called themselves "The Chicago Boys." Some attended Friedman's "Workshop in Money and Banking" course.

In 1970, Chile elected a Marxist, Salvador Allende,[1] as president, despite efforts by Nixon and covert actions by the CIA[2] to ensure his defeat. By 1972, a combination of poor economic management and a punitive trade embargo imposed by Nixon to "make the economy scream,"[3] caused the annual rate of inflation to reach 200 percent, the fiscal deficit to run at 13 percent of GDP, and real wages to fall by 25 percent. There were short-ages of essential items, including food. In September 1973, with help from the CIA,[4] Allende was deposed in a military coup, led by General Augusto Pinochet.[5] Allende and 4,000 of his supporters were murdered, 1,500 of them by torture and summary execution. The Chilean economy went into free fall; by April 1974, inflation was running at between 10 and 20 percent per month. Drawing on what they had learned from Friedman and others, the Chicago Boys drew up a plan for recovery and presented it to Pinochet.

Friedman was in no doubt that helping the Chileans was the right thing to do. He told journalist Sidney Blumenthal:

> Allende brought the coup on himself, but not necessarily through his inflationary policies. It was because he was trying to turn the coun-try into a standard Communist totalitarian state. He was aware of the danger of a coup, but he thought he was going to be able to carry through this plan. . . . Why should I have had qualms about going down there? I'm not going down to help the government. I'm going down to say what I believe. If they're willing to have me, that's that. The military hadn't overthrown a democracy. It had overthrown a regime headed toward Communist dictatorship. Between the two evils, I have no doubt the military junta is the lesser evil.[6]

In March 1974, Friedman and Arnold C. Harberger,[7] the point man between the University of Chicago and the Catholic University of Chile, visited Santiago to encourage their former pupils with a series of seminars and public talks that were also attended by junta officials and members of the military. Friedman was pleased to report that "thanks to their train-ing, our students were almost the only economists in Chile who had not been involved with or favorable to the Allende government."[8] Friedman met with Pinochet in private in the presidential palace and recommended that Chile undergo "shock treatment"[9] to restrict the growth of the money sup-ply. Pinochet told Friedman he was sympathetic to the idea, "but was clearly distressed at the possible temporary unemployment that might be caused."[10]

Pinochet asked Friedman to send him a summary of his recommen-dations for fixing the Chilean economy, which the economist did on his return to Chicago. Friedman thanked Pinochet "for the warm hospitality that was showered on us" before itemizing an eight-point plan to produce "an economic miracle" that involved a severe and immediate restriction of the money supply. The plan included cutting public spending by 25 percent in six months, which Friedman said would cause "severe transitional difficulties" in which thousands of government workers would be fired.[11] As Friedman would later recall, "That six-day visit and my prior role as a professor turned out to have consequences [both for Friedman and Chile] that we never anticipated and that we had to deal with for the next decade."[12]

ONE MORNING IN 1970, Samuelson was woken before dawn by a telephone call asking, "How does it feel to win the Nobel Prize?" "It's nice to have hard work rewarded," he replied. "My daughter said that was a very vain thing to have said," Samuelson recalled. "I said no, actually it was the case."[13]

Neither Samuelson nor Friedman was overmodest about their achievements. But to win a Nobel Prize was special, even for those who wear their geniuses conspicuously. By any measure, Samuelson was likely to win the accolade. As America's foremost economist, with a full roster of important technical publications, and a textbook that had become the foremost worldwide macroeconomics manual for undergraduates, it would have been strange if he had not. The Nobel for economics was one year old, with only two previous recipients, a Norwegian and a Dutchman, who shared the 1969 award. The Nobel committee might have chosen any number of reasons for Samuelson to be awarded the second Nobel Memorial Prize in Economic Sciences, but they decided to focus on the way "he formalized economics research using mathematics," noting that now "his work influences practically all branches of modern economics."[14]

Rose Friedman recalled that when the first Nobel for economics was mooted, "two names appeared in every newspaper story or conversation about the coming award—Paul Samuelson and Milton Friedman." When there was speculation about who would win the second economics Nobel, Rose Friedman recalled, "the two names most often mentioned remained the same."[15] Nonetheless, when Samuelson won it, it took him by surprise. "I certainly did not expect to get the Nobel Prize in the second year of it," he said. In light of Harvard's decision not to offer Samuelson a position commensurate with his ability, because of the institutional anti-Semitism in the economics faculty at that time, it was especially pleasing to Samuelson that the Nobel committee gave him the award because of his *Foundations of Economic Analysis*, the publication of the PhD thesis he had written at Harvard.

Friedman opened his *Newsweek* column in November 1970 with a paean of praise to his old friend and opponent. "The readers of this space know Paul Samuelson as a witty, informed and often acerbic commentator on current affairs, as a 'liberal' supporter of the economic policies of the Kennedy and Johnson years, and as a critic of current Nixon economic policy," he wrote. Samuelson was "a brilliant and original mathematical economist," who had "helped to reshape and improve the theoretical foundations of our subject." Moreover, "Samuelson has been the leader in creating a great center of economic study and research at MIT, raising a run-of-the-mill department to one of the premier departments in the world."

Privately, Samuelson wrote to Friedman, "Thanks for the nice note and kind column. When your time comes, you'll find words from old friends count most," before remarking on the personal taxation implications of the Nobel Prize stipend. "Anyone in the 70 percent bracket who is sure to get the prize is best off getting it late."[16] [In 2020 dollars, each sole winner of a Nobel Prize was awarded $1.1 million and a gold medal priced at $10,000.]

Only the previous month, the University of Chicago alumni affairs department had canvassed Friedman for his view of Samuelson, whom they were considering giving a "professional achievement award." Friedman's effusive reply said that "Samuelson is clearly one of the leading economists of the world" and had made "important scientific contributions that are clearly embedded in our present economic doctrine."[17]

Samuelson and his wife Marion flew to Stockholm in 1970 for a lavish formal banquet and, as was customary, he delivered a grateful speech of acceptance. "The dream of any scholar has for me come true by virtue of this award," he told the audience of Swedish dignitaries. He listed the many teachers, colleagues, and pupils who had influenced him,[18] suggesting that he was only one part of a long line who had led to his winning the award. "One of the pleasing things about science is that we do all climb towards the heavens on the shoulders of our predecessors,"[19] he said. "In honoring me, the Committee of the Royal Academy of Sciences is in fact saying a good word for all of those of my generation who have been laboring in the same vineyard."

Samuelson heaped praise on the author and Soviet dissident Alexander Solzhenitsyn, that year's winner of the Nobel for Literature, who was afraid to go to Stockholm to accept the award lest the communist authorities declare him an undesirable and deny him reentry to his beloved Russia. "If Alexander Solzhenitsyn had been here to speak from the heart, from his heart, all of us would be the better for it, you and me, all mankind and I dare to think *every* country under the sun without a single exception," Samuelson said. "His spirit hovers over our celebration here tonight."

The following day Samuelson gave a lecture titled, "Maximum Principles in Analytical Economics,"[20] a text strewn with complex equations, which gave no quarter to those who knew little economics or mathematics. When explaining his "Revealed Preference" theory, he spoke about how consumers came to choose to buy a product, and he could not resist a drive-by shot at the Austrian School, whose leading members were Hayek and von Mises, the latter now teaching at New York University and about to enter his tenth decade:

> Austrian economists would insist that people acted to maximize their utility, but when challenged as to what that was, they found them-

selves replying circularly that however people behaved, they would presumably not have done so unless it maximized their satisfaction. Just as we can cancel two from the ratio of even numbers, so one could use Occam's Razor to cut utility completely from the argument, ending one up with the fatuity: people do what they do.

And it was largely to Americans that he directed his final remark, which reflected on his lifelong contest with Friedman over the future of economics. He quoted the American economist and archcritic of capitalism Thorstein Veblen:[21] "There is no reason why theoretical economics should be a monopoly of the reactionaries." "All my life I have tried to take this warning to heart," Samuelson said, "and I dare call it to your favorable attention."

Four years after Samuelson's Nobel in 1970, Friedrich Hayek was awarded the seventh Nobel Prize for economics, but his nomination was considered so controversial he was obliged to share the award with Gunnar Myrdal, a left-leaning Swedish economist and sociologist known for his work on exposing racial problems in America. Samuelson was pleased for Hayek. "In my judgment his was a worthy choice," said Samuelson. "And yet in the 1974 senior common rooms of Harvard and MIT, the majority of the inhabitants there seemed not to even know the name of this new laureate."[22]

SIX YEARS ELAPSED between Samuelson and Friedman being awarded the economics Nobel. Rose Friedman suspected foul play. "When my husband was passed over for the next five years, it seemed obvious to me as it did to many colleagues that there was something in addition to contribution to economic science that was being weighed on the scale,"[23] she recalled. *Newsweek* piled in behind Friedman: "If his peers were voting, Friedman would long since have had the prize—and by all accounts, Sweden's Royal Academy has delayed the honor only because of his penchant for controversy and right-wing political activism."[24]

Just as Samuelson had said he felt he deserved the Nobel, so Friedman was lacking in grace when discussing his impending honor. On the morning of October 14, 1976, he was approached in a parking lot in Detroit by a broadcast reporter who asked, "Do you regard this as the high point of your career?" Friedman replied, "I care more what my successors fifty years from now will think about my professional work than I do about the judgement of seven people from Sweden who happen to be serving on the Nobel Committee." The American press relished pointing out Friedman's gaffe. He had responded with "characteristic gall," and his "brutally candid" reaction was "pure Friedman, arrogant to the last where many other men would have tried to be humble."[25]

Rose Friedman leapt to the defense of her husband's good name. "No one would ever call my husband humble," she said, "but only someone who did not know him or deliberately wished to misrepresent him would describe him either as 'arrogant' or with 'characteristic gall.' "[26] Rose Friedman could be as prickly as her husband. When asked whether she was proud of him winning the Nobel, she snapped, "I have always been proud of my husband, and it didn't take the Nobel Prize to persuade me."

In the words of the citation, Friedman won the Nobel "for his achievements in the fields of consumption analysis, monetary history and theory, and for his demonstration of the complexity of stabilization policy." The official announcement continued:

> Milton Friedman's name is chiefly associated with the renaissance of the role of money in inflation and the consequent renewed understanding of the instrument of monetary policy. He has given us the terms "money matters," or even "only money matters," with the emergence of monetarism as a Chicago school. This strong emphasis on the role of money should be seen in the light of how economists—usually advocates of a narrow interpretation of Keynesian theory—have, for a long time, almost entirely ignored the significance of money and mon-

etary policy when analyzing business cycles and inflation. As far back as the beginning of the fifties, Friedman was a pioneer in the well-founded reaction to the earlier post-Keynesian one-sidedness. And he succeeded—mainly thanks to his independence and brilliance—in initiating a very lively and fruitful scientific debate which has been going on for more than a decade. . . .

The widespread debate on Friedman's theories also led to a review of monetary policies pursued by central banks—in the first place, in the United States. It is very rare for an economist to wield such influence, directly and indirectly, not only on the direction of scientific research but also on actual policies.

But the fulsome tribute to Friedman's achievements disguised a controversy that had taken place behind closed doors as the Nobel committee hotly debated whether Friedman's work as a *Newsweek* columnist and as a chief economic adviser to Barry Goldwater undermined his scholarly status—charges that might as easily have been laid at the door of Samuelson based on his work for Kennedy.

When news of the divisions in the committee leaked out, Rose Friedman blamed the row on the liberal views and ignorance of economics of the general Nobel committee, who had to endorse Friedman's award. "Approval by the broader committee is a mere formality—but this time it was apparently not," she wrote. Friedman's economics was well regarded by both sides of the political divide, "from the extreme right to the extreme left," she wrote, but "the non-economists on the committee knew only of his more publicized role as a political gadfly out of sympathy with the dominant socialist philosophy of our time." It was hard not to conclude that, as with the Hayek Nobel, the Swedish Academy tended to tilt leftward and was harder on conservative nominees than on liberals.

Samuelson was quick to congratulate Friedman and wrote a fulsome tribute to his genius in *Newsweek,* describing the award as "fitting recognition of his scientific contributions and his scholarly leadership." After commending his genius as "the architect of much that is best in our conservative tradition and not merely the expositor of that viewpoint," Samuelson celebrated Friedman the human being. "What I have failed to convey is Milton Friedman's bounce and gaiety, his rapier intelligence, his unfailing courtesy in debate. The world admires him for his achievements. His intimates love him for himself."[27] Friedman soon wrote to Samuelson, "Your wire and your column were among the most valuable dividends of the award."[28]

Friedman's Nobel was welcomed by the *Financial Times*, whose editorial writers declared that he was "unquestionably the most influential economist of our day." And a testament to Friedman's moral rectitude emerged from an unlikely source: Steve Rattner,[29] an economics correspondent for the *New York Times*. "Throughout the long years of advocating laissez-faire principles and monetary economics, even his critics agreed that he never sacrificed his intellectual integrity," he wrote. "He turned down a number of government posts partly because he did not believe that he would be able to maintain his principles."[30]

On reflection, Friedman thought his initial reaction to the award too sharp and that he should have thought more carefully before speaking. "I do not mean to denigrate the Nobel Committee," he said. "They have been doing a very conscientious and good job on the whole. But at the same time, what really matters to a scientist is the long-run effect of his work on his science."[31] Appearing on NBC's *Meet the Press*, Friedman tried to explain why he had appeared to diminish the members of the Nobel panel who chose him. "The jury I would like to have judge my work is the economics profession not today, primarily, but twenty-five or fifty years from now," he said, "and the real pinnacle of the work would be the embodying in the whole body of economic analysis of some of the work I had done."[32]

In a talk at the Hoover Institution the following January, Friedman continued his criticism of Nobel Prizes—indeed, all prizes—per se. "The whole system of Nobel awards may well do more harm than good," he said.

"It causes the public at large to attribute to the opinion of people who receive this particular award an importance that is utterly unjustified." As for the members of the committee who judged him, whom, he acknowledged, were "eminent, able scholars who did their best," he continued:

> Is it desirable in any discipline that a few scholars who have made their mark in that discipline should have the power to decide the kind of work that is prestigious, on which other scholars ought to concentrate if they want their work to be recognized as important? Is it desirable to have that much centralization of power effectively directing the course or research in basic fields? The effect is not restricted to economics; it is the same for physics, chemistry, or any other area.[33]

IN DECEMBER 1976, the Friedmans flew to Stockholm to receive the prize and were alarmed to discover that their presence in Sweden triggered street demonstrations over the assistance Friedman had given to Pinochet's military junta in Chile. The threats of the protesters were deemed so grave that the Friedmans were accompanied everywhere by armed bodyguards.

The protests put under close scrutiny the circumstances of Friedman's visit to Chile in 1975 and what had transpired in his conversation with Pinochet. Friedman's colleague who accompanied him to Santiago, Arnold Harberger, wrote to the president of the Nobel Foundation to try to put the record straight. "We were not there as consultants to the government and neither of us had any official connection with the present government of Chile," he wrote. "Our visit to Chile did not and does not in any way connote approval of the present Chilean government, much less of its repression of individual liberty and its imposition of restraint on free and open discussion and debate." Friedman had turned down two honorary degrees from Chile, "precisely because he felt that acceptance of such honors from universities receiving government funds could be interpreted as implying political approval." Harberger said Friedman had given a lecture that condemned the assault upon political freedom by the coup "and expressed the hope that in the near future Chileans would once again enjoy a full measure of political and intellectual liberty."[34]

Shortly after the announcement of Friedman's Nobel, a sharp exchange of letters was published in the *New York Times*. Four Nobel laureates— Linus Pauling (1954 Nobel in Chemistry), and George Wald, David Baltimore, and S. E. Luria (Nobelists in Physiology or Medicine, 1967, 1975, and 1969)—wrote to protest at Friedman's prize, citing his consultancy work in Chile. Friedman's written response was robust. Despite having written a letter of economic recommendations to Pinochet, Friedman declared that he "was not then and never have been an economic adviser to the Chilean junta," and he asked his Nobelist critics why they had not objected when he gave lectures in the Soviet Union and communist Yugoslavia. By employing a double standard, "you did an injustice to me personally," he wrote. Two of the Nobelists wrote to reiterate their accusation: "Your identification with the shock treatment policies, reinforced by your trip to Chile, associated you with the economic policies and repressive action, that are inseparable aspects of the Chilean junta regime."

Friedman wrote again, complaining that the Nobel winners had dared criticize the nature of the economic advice he had tendered when they were not competent in economics to make such a judgment. He rightly insisted that the policy Chile had pursued on his advice had been effective: inflation was cured and a general recovery was well underway.[35] Jobs were being created and there were signs of growth. "The economic policy, which I commend, can be separated from the political situation, which I deplore," he wrote. "Your support of a political test for recognition of scientific achievement flies counter to the traditions of freedom of speech, freedom of thought, and academic freedom that the intellectual community has defended for many centuries,"[36] he said.

While protesters chanted abuse outside the banquet hall as he spoke,

Friedman's acceptance speech on December 10, 1976, attempted to lighten the mood, drawing attention to what he called a potential "conflict of interest" in his being honored. He said:

> My monetary studies have led me to the conclusion that central banks
> could profitably be replaced by computers geared to provide a steady
> rate of growth in the quantity of money. Fortunately for me person-
> ally, and for a select group of fellow economists, that conclusion has
> had no practical impact . . . else there would have been no Central
> Bank of Sweden to have established the award I am honored to receive.
> Should I draw the moral that sometimes to fail is to succeed?

He described how the prize had already affected him. "Not only is there no free lunch, there is no free prize," he said. "The announcement of an award converts its recipient into an instant expert on all and sundry, and unleashes hordes of ravenous newsmen and photographers from journals and T.V. stations around the world. I myself have been asked my opinion on everything from a cure for the common cold to the market value of a letter signed by John F. Kennedy."[37] In fact, though flattered by the attention, Friedman felt the award had come too late to be of much use to his career. "By the time I received it, I was too old for it to have much of an effect,"[38] he would later comment.

As if to defy those who criticized his remedies for inflation offered to Pinochet, Friedman chose as the subject of his Nobel memorial lecture, "Inflation and Unemployment,"[39] in which, dressed incongruously in white tie and tails, he again buried the Phillips Curve and explained the "natural rate of unemployment." He noted that in the three decades after World War II, "it seemed to take larger and larger doses of inflation to keep down the level of unemployment. Stagflation reared its ugly head." But he observed that "the natural-rate hypothesis in its present form has not proved rich enough to explain a more recent development—a move from stagflation to slumpflation [a rare combination of recession accompanied by high inflation]."

It would have seemed natural at such a conspicuous lecture telling of the rise of hyperinflation that Friedman would have pronounced clearly his flagship theory, that "inflation is always and everywhere a monetary phenomenon in the sense that it is and can be produced only by a more rapid increase in the quantity of money than in output."[40] But he chose a simpler message for such a wide audience. "I wrote my lecture primarily to make the point that economics was or could be a positive science like physics or chemistry, [a "positive science" being evidence- and data-based rather than philosophically founded],"[41] he said.

CERTAINLY, by the time of his Nobel, Friedman had left a distinct mark in the history of economic theory. According to his Chicago colleague George J. Stigler, "Friedman loomed over macroeconomics between 1960 and 1975, although he was outside of and hostile toward the dominant Keynesian approach. . . . I used to say that he controlled Cambridge universities and Yale. They were devoting much of their efforts to seeking to refute what he had most recently written."[42] With Friedmanites dominating the economic dialogue, Samuelson was asked point blank whether Keynes was dead. "Yes," he replied. "So are Newton and Einstein."[43]

There is no better way of understanding the rising weight of Friedman's influence over economic thought than to see how Samuelson was obliged to alter his *Economics* textbook to acknowledge Friedman's influence in reviving interest in classical economics. In the 1955 edition, Samuelson recorded that "today few economists regard federal reserve monetary policy as a panacea for controlling the business cycle."[44]

Having ignored Friedman in his textbook for more than a decade, Samuelson found room in the fifth edition in 1961 to mention his old friend twice. In the section on "The Quantity Theory of Money and Prices,"[45] Samuelson described the notion that prices were directly reflected by the velocity of money in an economy as "crude" but "useful to describe periods of hyper-inflation." He wrote that while "few people are still alive who subscribe to the crude quantity of money theory," he felt it worth exploring "since there has been something of a revival of interest in the quantity theory by a number of competent American economists in recent years." Among the "competent" economists named was Friedman.

By 1973, while still dismissing monetarism as "an extreme view," Samuelson accepted that "both fiscal and monetary policies matter much."[46] In 1985, Samuelson had gone further, crediting for the first time Friedman's unique brand of economics, which in his *Economics* textbook he dubbed "Chicago Libertarianism,"[47] to which the Austrian School of von Mises and Hayek was pinned. And by 1995 he was acknowledging that "fiscal policy is no longer a major tool of stabilization policy in the United States. Over the foreseeable future, stabilization policy will be performed by Federal Reserve monetary policy."[48]

He also conceded that the quantity theory of money had some virtue. "Since galloping inflation can put an intolerable strain on a democratic society, it is well to preach the crude quantity of money theory in season and out of season," Samuelson wrote, "because its message is so urgently needed in those disorganized times when its message is in season." He wrote:

> What is generally agreed upon today is that action by the government to affect the supply of money, its availability to investor borrowers, and the interest cost of such borrowings can have important effects on the total of consumption + investment + government spending, and thus on prices and wage levels.[49]

And by 2005, Friedman and Hayek were given a section of their own: "Guardians of Economic Freedom." Friedman was credited with launching "the monetarist revolution." In a fulsome and ungrudging tribute to his old friend, Samuelson wrote that around the world there had been a swing towards free market ideas:

> No one within the economist guild has been more important, both as an architect and as an expositor of this shift, than Milton Friedman. His classic book, *Capitalism and Freedom* (1962), argues why a rational thinker might, along with advocating free international trade and maximal deregulation, deplore the minimum wage, state licensing of surgeons, and prohibition of drugs like heroin and cocaine. All thoughtful economists should study his arguments carefully.[50]

Friedman was credited in Samuelson's *Economics* for other achievements, too. One of Friedman's favorite topics was the inadequacy of the welfare system: he considered it a triumph of well-meaning intentions over obvious, proven failure. Samuelson had insisted in the 1970 edition of his textbook that "the modern welfare state has been both humane and solvent."[51] A decade later, however, after Friedman had dismissed many antipoverty programs as ill-conceived and counterproductive, Samuelson conceded that some welfare programs were "indeed costly" and "often inefficient"[52] and he gave space to explain Friedman's substitute for welfare payments: a negative income tax.[53] By 1995, Samuelson was posing the question Friedman had asked decades earlier: "Have antipoverty programs helped . . . [or] produced counterproductive responses?"[54] And by 2004, Samuelson included a section describing the "Twilight of the Welfare State,"[55] in which he accurately summarized Friedman's views.

> Critics of government say that the state is overly intrusive; governments create monopoly; government failures are just as pervasive as market failures; high taxes distort the allocation of resources; social security threatens to overload workers in the decades ahead; environmental

regulation dulls the spirit of enterprise; government attempts to stabilize the economy must fail at best and increase inflation at worst. In
short, for some government is the problem rather than the solution.[56]

While Samuelson liked to portray Friedman as a lone wolf and an outsider, he could hardly deny that many of his old friend's pet concerns had
changed economics and caused politicians to think twice about spending
money to boost a flagging economy. "Right at this moment there are people
all over the land—I could put dots on the map—who are trying to prove
Milton wrong," he said. "At some point, somebody else is trying to prove
he's right. That's what I call influence."[57] And over time, notwithstanding
the failure in practice of Friedman's monetarism, such was the potency of
Friedman's antigovernment arguments that political leaders were obliged to
abandon spending on public programs and projects as a method of stimulating the economy. Instead, tax cuts became the policy instrument of choice.

11

Fed Up

Friedman's monetarism is given a second chance when
a new president, Jimmy Carter, assigns to the Federal
Reserve the task of bringing inflation to heel

By the time Jimmy Carter, a highly intelligent former U.S. Navy submariner and peanut farmer from Georgia, faced Nixon's accidental successor, Gerald Ford, in the election of November 1976, the main issues of concern to voters were not so much Nixon's Watergate disgrace and resignation[1] but high unemployment and high inflation. By 1975, prices were rising at 6.9 percent a year and joblessness had reached, at its peak, 8.2 percent, the highest unemployment rate recorded since World War II. The 1976 election year saw a small improvement—with unemployment at 7.8 percent and inflation at 4.9 percent—but not enough to save Ford from defeat.

Having won the White House, Carter was tasked with fixing the broken economy that had helped put him there. But after a series of missteps, by 1978 Carter was deep in an economic crisis, with inflation running at 9 percent and joblessness at 6 percent. The dollar was weak on foreign markets and only intervention by the Federal Reserve kept the currency steady. Inflation appeared to be baked into the system, with a widespread expectation it would continue at a high rate, driving high wage demands and more price increases.

Carter's approval rating in the polls continued to slide.[2] Samuelson thought Carter had wished the bad economic news on himself. If he was to stand any chance of being reelected, the president needed to do something dramatic to break the cycle of inflation. Samuelson suspected Carter would engineer a recession to purge inflation from the economy. "The fear of inflation is my No.1 Concern," Samuelson told *Newsweek* readers, "concern lest that fear stampede us into trying to contrive a 'preventive recession.'"[3] And that is exactly what transpired. On November 1, 1978, in an effort to stem the decline in price of the American dollar, Carter held a press conference announcing an increase in interest rates to 9.5 percent, a move that many, including Samuelson, thought would provoke a recession.[4] Writing in *Newsweek* a year later, Samuelson sourced the recession, by then in full flood, to Carter's interest-rate hike a year earlier. "Carter promised the world a U.S. recession on November 1, 1978,"[5] he wrote.

In the three months preceding June 1979, inflation was running at a chilling 13 percent. On July 15, 1979, Carter broadcast to the nation a frank assessment of where America stood. It proved to be a political disaster. Instead of inspiring Americans with hope, Carter filled them with despair, describing "a crisis of confidence" in the country that amounted to "a fundamental threat to American democracy" that was "threatening to destroy the social and the political fabric of America."[6] He blamed the economic turmoil Americans were enduring on the deliberate 18 percent hike in oil prices imposed by the oil-producing countries in December 1978, with a further 14.5 percent increase due in 1979. His remedy was a plan to make America energy-independent as fast as possible.

But as rational and accurate as Carter's words were, their effect proved devastating. Americans were not used to being told the unvarnished truth by their presidents; they preferred stirring calls to arms, and invocations of the greatness of the national character. In his speech, Carter had urged Americans on: "Whenever you have a chance, say something good about our country." Yet the effect of his own words was the opposite. In the presidential election of November 1976, Carter had beaten Gerry Ford by 50.1 percent to 48 percent. By the end of July 1979, the president's approval rating dipped below 30 percent to 28 percent,[7] only four points higher than Nixon's lack of popularity (24 percent approval) at the height of Watergate.

The day after what became known as his "malaise" broadcast, Carter invited all his Cabinet and top White House staff to tender their resignations. This included Carter's pick to replace Burns as chairman of the Federal Reserve, G. William Miller.[8] On July 24, Carter interviewed in the Oval Office one man thought likely to bring some fresh thinking at the Fed, Paul Volcker.[9] Volcker, already a member of the Fed board, was an unusual government servant. Standing at a towering six foot seven, this bald, softly spoken, cheap-cigar-puffing fifty-seven-year-old banker had been in and out of the private and public sectors, including a stint as president of the Federal Reserve Bank of New York, where, like Friedman, he had been an advocate of ending one of Keynes's lasting legacies: the linking of the dollar to the price of gold.

The job interview in the Oval Office did not appear to go well. Miller, the outgoing Fed chairman, was present, which inhibited Volcker from answering candidly Carter's pointed questions. "I was sitting alongside the president, who sat in a wing chair," Volcker told friends that evening. "I said that I attached great importance to the independence of the Federal Reserve and that I also favored a more restrictive monetary policy. And just for emphasis I pointed at Miller, who was sitting in a chair next to me, and added that I wanted a tighter policy than him."[10] Carter remained silent. The audition had lasted less than an hour. Volcker was convinced the president would pick someone else.

The following morning at 7:30, Carter called Volcker and offered him the job. Perhaps it was Volcker's record as an unwavering Democratic voter that tipped the president's hand. It seems that Carter, who showed no interest in economic theory, had not, by choosing Volcker, intended to give more prominence to the monetary causes of inflation. But Volcker's appointment signaled a change of direction at the Fed and a new seriousness about trying to check inflation. As the *New York Times* noted, "Volcker, a skilled market technician . . . and monetary diplomat . . . [will] be more rigorous in the application of orthodox monetary policies than . . . Mr. Miller."[11]

It now fell to Volcker to square the circle of Congress's demands for the Federal Reserve to achieve two important goals simultaneously: to provide the best conditions for the U.S. economy to provide full employment and for the Fed to keep inflation in check. Since the debunking of the Phillips Curve, which had suggested there was a predictable trade-off between unemployment and inflation, the Fed had seen employment hold steady while inflation soared. How would Volcker cure inflation without taking measures, such as raising interest rates, that would slow the economy and cause unemployment to rise? For those who followed the Fed's decisions closely, there was evidence that Volcker was prepared to take tough decisions based on monetary measures: twice, in March and April of 1979, Volcker had been in the minority on the Fed board when he voted to raise interest rates to temper the hyperinflationary trend.

For Friedman, Volcker's appointment presented the best chance yet of translating his ideas about the link between money supply and inflation into action. But there was a hitch. Although Volcker was sympathetic to the quantity theory of money—he had studied economics at Princeton, Harvard, and the LSE—he did not ascribe to money the central importance Friedman claimed.

Volcker had listened carefully in 1957 when, on a tour of state reserve banks to promote his monetarist theories, Friedman paid a visit to the Federal Reserve Bank of New York. While there, the economist explained the implications of his research into how poor management of the money supply had led to the Great Depression. In the intervening twenty years, Volcker remained unmoved by Friedman's bold assertion that the quantity of money was the sole cause of inflation. "Milton was convinced he had found the gospel truth," Volcker recalled. "I was skeptical of anyone so confident—whether from Chicago or Cambridge."[12]

Despite Volcker's evident skepticism, Friedman saw the appointment of Volcker as a benefit: a fellow spirit with a knowledge of his monetarist notions had risen to the most important economic position in the land. Friedman was among the first to write a letter of congratulation to Volcker, urging him on to monetary continence. He wrote:

> My condolences to you on your "promotion.". . . The years 1930–1933 aside, and perhaps also 1920 and 1921, there has never been both a greater need and greater opportunity for the [Federal Reserve] to render service to the nation by courageous and steady policy of monetary restrained, experienced gradually and moderately. As you know, I do not believe that the System can rise to that challenge without major changes in its method of operation. My very best wishes to you for success in pushing those changes and those results.[13]

Volcker replied:

> I don't know whether I have simply been elected the fall guy in most difficult circumstances, but some of the broad directions of necessary change seem clear enough. . . . I am perfectly confident you will find plenty to criticize but I also suspect you know I will not be unhappy to have you preaching the doctrines of monetary rectitude as we move ahead. . . . In any event, the test will come soon enough, and we will, as always, be following your comments with interest.[14]

Volcker could not agree with Friedman that "inflation is always and everywhere a monetary phenomenon," because, like Samuelson and others, he believed other factors were also at work. Volcker's understanding of how best to cure inflation was based in part on the quantity-of-money theory he had learned at Princeton in 1945–1949, where he was taught by, among others, prominent German economists Oskar Morgenstern[15] and Friedrich A. Lutz.[16] In his senior thesis, Volcker wrote, "A swollen money supply presented a grave inflationary threat to the economy. There was a need to bring this money supply under control if the disastrous effects of a sharp price rise were to be avoided."[17] He also acknowledged that it was not just inflation but the anticipation of future inflationary trends by consumers and businesses that contributed to the rise in prices.

Monetarism was only one of several economics fads Volcker had to contend with. A movement, emanating from Chicago, argued that market forces accurately reflected the "rational expectations" of those who took part in financial transactions. Without going along with the whole "rational expectations" logic, Volcker was convinced that broad market psychology had to be taken into account when the Fed made decisions. "I am impressed myself by . . . the degree to which inflationary psychology has really changed," he told the Fed board at his first meeting as chairman. "It's not that we didn't have it before, but I think people are acting on that expectation . . . much more firmly than they used to. . . . The dollar externally obviously adds to the dilemma. . . . Nobody knows what is going to happen to the dollar, but I do think it's fair to say that the psychology is extremely tender."[18]

As the British chancellor of the exchequer at the time, Denis Healey,[19] explained, the world of money trading and finance was in large part operated by young Turks, often untrained in economics, who were vulnerable to passing crazes. "The financial markets were advised by clever young men who were particularly susceptible to changes in academic fashion," recalled Healey. "These advisers were mainly converts to the monetarist theories popularized by Milton Friedman; they began worrying about the monetary statistics, believing that inflation depended wholly on the money supply."[20] According to Healey, what ensued was a false and unnecessary intellectual battle in the financial industry and in finance ministries between Keynesian diehards and monetarist nonbelievers. "I have never met a private or central banker who believed the monetarist mumbo-jumbo," wrote Healey. "But no banker could afford to ignore monetarism so long as the markets took it seriously. So a conflict developed in [the British Treasury] between unreconstructed Keynesians and unbelieving monetarists."[21]

As many of the young economists and traders on Wall Street were fired up by Friedman's one-cause theory of inflation, and as their decisions to buy and sell resulted in part from "rational expectations" of whether Volcker would adhere to Friedman's prescriptions, Volcker was obliged to take Friedman seriously.

Volcker had confronted the logic behind the Friedmanite fashion for attributing all inflation to the quantity of money three years before, in September 1976, in his presidential address[22] to the American Economic Association. Drawing upon his experience as a member of the Fed's Open Market Committee (FOMC), the committee that sets interest rates, Volcker explained how the system then operated.

In response to the rise of the Friedmanite monetarists, who had revived "one of the oldest propositions in the history of economic thought . . . that in the long run . . . an excess supply of money contributes not to real income or wealth, but simply to inflation,"[23] the Committee had adopted, under a compulsory order from Congress, what he called "practical monetarism" and the regular publication of the Fed's monetary targets. He considered publishing targets to be "useful. It has assisted in communicating our intentions both to the political authorities and to the marketplace." The committee's monthly meeting considered "numerical 'tolerance' ranges for key monetary aggregates for the period immediately ahead" along with a similar range for the federal funds rate, "taking into account the evidence we have about the interest rate-money supply relationship."

Declaring that "sorting out what is true and valid from what is fashionable is never easy," Volcker confessed to "a certain intellectual conservatism." He acknowledged that monetarism had "helped bring a distinctly different flavor to much macroeconomic policy making and analysis in recent years." The return of such thinking accompanied a general understanding that there were "real limitations on the possibilities for manipulating the mix of fiscal and monetary policies to achieve our objectives" which undermined the "faith in our ability to make short-term adjustments—to 'fine tune' the economy."

The decision, prompted by Congress, for the Fed to publish monetary goals was welcome, Volcker added, so long as the Fed retained "the right to change the targets in the light of emerging developments," though he stressed that "there was no general agreement on which monetary aggregate is most relevant," even among monetarists. But, he noted, mere "recognition of the broad relevance and desirability of longer term monetary targets also has left unresolved important tactical issues as to just how these targets should be achieved." What is more, the "forecast errors [in the estimates of money circulating in the economy] are large, no matter what procedure is used, particularly over periods of one to three months."

In brief, Volcker argued that even if everyone were to agree on the importance of money and on which money aggregate target to adopt, the choice remained moot as to how to proceed as there was no way of knowing how to influence future money supply growth. His conclusion? "These uncertainties are likely to make precise monetary control elusive under any set of procedures." Attempts to change the money supply were so treacherous, he said, that "attempts to respond immediately by shifting reserve availability and allowing the money market abruptly to tighten or ease could . . . easily result in whip-sawing of the market."

He observed that even among monetarists, not counting Friedman, there was little appetite for trying to find a way of controlling the money supply in the short run. "Few, if any, still seriously push the need or practicality of keeping monetary growth rates on track month by month," he said. In any case, the practicalities of guiding monetary growth should not distract from trying to assess whether such actions were necessary or important. "Concentration on the problems of chasing aggregate targets should not cause us to neglect their limitations," he said. His recent experience assessing a range of urgent financial crises—which he listed as "thrift institutions and the mortgage market, Penn Central and commercial paper, Herstatt and the Eurodollar market, New York City and the municipal bond market, and the rising level of commercial bank loan losses"—suggested to him that the explanation for economic problems that had to be addressed by the Federal Reserve banks had no monetary basis. "Perhaps answers to questions like these can be traced back in some ultimate sense to the behavior of money. But I doubt it," he said, clearly indicating that he was under no illusion that monetarism was a magic bullet.

Then he challenged Friedman's simple assertion that "inflation is always and everywhere a purely monetary phenomenon." Volcker agreed that, on the face of it, money was linked to inflation. He agreed that "pressures to increase the money supply to serve some presumed short-term objective are a basic source of inflationary pressure," and that "excessive monetary expansion is a sufficient condition for inflation," and "no important inflation can be sustained without money rising substantially faster than real income [i.e., incomes adjusted for inflation]." He agreed that "there is always some rate of monetary growth (perhaps zero) that will in principle achieve price stability. But still, I don't think we can draw much comfort from those principles as a full explanation of where we are and a guide as to how to proceed."

He took as an example the acceleration in inflation since the 1960s. The rise in prices in the 1970s, for instance, was driven by "the oil situation, some crop failures, the spread of unions into some new areas, and shortages in particular industries that ran up against capacity pressures before the economy as a whole reached full employment." Rather than invoke monetary changes to explain the persistent high inflation, "we have to ask ourselves about the nature of the economic, social, and political forces and attitudes that seem to have aggravated the difficulties of reconciling full employment with price stability."

Then came a warning. For central bankers to strictly limit the money supply according to some automatic formula, as Friedman advocated, might end up as an affront to democracy. Central banks could always resist inflationary pressures by simply refusing to provide enough funds to finance them, but such an approach would conflict with the goals of economic growth and full employment that were important national goals. "In a democracy," Volcker wrote, "the risk would be not just the political life of a particular government, but the democratic way of government itself."

A theory that suggested that chronic inflation was only caused by money supply changes, as promoted by Friedman, Volcker said, was not only inadequate, but got in the way of searching for true remedies for rampant inflation, which he felt was caused by a number of factors beyond the quantity of money. Friedman's oversimplified claims for the money supply were just that, too simple to be useful, he said. He understood how such a simple explanation had become popular. A simple, unified view of economic policy was "a comforting thing: a kind of security blanket in an uncertain world," he said. But the world was in truth a complex and confusing place and simplified explanations rarely made sense. Eventually, said Volcker, the simple doctrine comes up against complex and harsh reality.

Volcker would return to spelling out his reservations about Friedman's simple monetarism in the *Journal of Monetary Economics* two years later, in 1980. In a paper titled "The Role of Monetary Targets in an Age of Inflation,"[24] which drew upon his experience at the Federal Reserve using the monetary targets the Fed had drawn up, Volcker spelled out his differences with Friedman. He agreed that "inflation cannot proceed for long without sufficiently rapid monetary growth to accommodate it" and that "by the same token, inflation cannot be eliminated for any significant period without a corresponding elimination of monetary excesses,"[25] but the supply of money was not the only factor contributing to inflation. "I believe there are in fact a variety of non-monetary . . . factors that can affect the rate of inflation in the short—and not so short—run . . . My own support of the use of monetary 'targets' does not start from a 'monetarist' perspective."

He flatly denied Friedman's universal assertion about the causal link between money and inflation. Those, like Friedman, who believed the money supply was the answer to everything were mistaken. Again, while acknowledging that "in the longer run, a general parallelism between monetary performance and price performance is unmistakable," drawing on recent experience of money in the American economy,[26] Volcker pointed out the practical difficulties in measuring money or the velocity of money in a system, and of identifying which measure, if any, predicted the inflation rate with any certainty. "The definition of money itself is not free from ambiguity and fuzziness," he wrote, and changes in the velocity of money were often "seemingly inexplicable."

While the Federal Reserve, with the benefit of monetary targets, had "adopted a middle course" between hard-core monetarists and mainstream economists like Samuelson, who deemed monetarism a red herring, holding the middle ground in an argument "does not in itself guarantee the wisdom of the action." But Volcker was certain that money alone could not be the key to dampening inflation.

He wrote that inflation is difficult to eliminate because of forces deeply embedded in the structure of the national economy, the nation's social policies, and American political life. Although Volcker had in 1971 been a strong proponent of Nixon uncoupling the dollar from the 1944 Bretton Woods agreement, he hoped the Fed's publication of monetary targets would in some measure reinstate the sort of certainty that Keynes had sought and established at Bretton Woods for the market in currencies. The role in stabilizing expectations about future prices was once the function of the gold standard, the doctrine of the annually balanced budget, and fixed exchange rates. He expected that the announcement of monetary targeting would signal that the Federal Reserve was taking seriously its responsibility to curb inflation.

As Volcker would write in his memoir, "One thing was clear to me at the time. If all the difficulties growing out of inflation were going to be dealt with at all, it would have to be through monetary policy. It was not just that other policies [such as fiscal measures] seemed to be caught in a sort of political paralysis, but that no other approach could be successful without a convincing demonstration that monetary restraint would be maintained."[27]

THE FEDERAL RESERVE is above all a maker of weather for the U.S. economy. The smallest change in policy, or the gentlest hint from a Fed chairman, can send markets reeling. On August 6, 1979, as Volcker took up the reins at the Federal Reserve amid widespread voter alarm about stagflation and inflation at 11.09 percent, he pondered his first move. Volcker had let it be known he believed money mattered, even if he did not think that only money mattered. But would he bring about the radical change in monetary policy that he felt was needed? Expectations had built up that he would swiftly move in a monetarist direction, which would entail a large hike in interest rates to stem the flow of new money into the system.

Backed by monetarists on the Board led by Lawrence Roos, president of the Federal Reserve Bank of St. Louis, a monetarist bastion, and with inflation now running at 11.3 percent, Volcker launched the Fed on a new approach to tackling inflation through greater emphasis on monetary restraint, a policy ratified by the Federal Reserve Board at their second meeting, on September 19. But what would Volcker do? The markets, economists, and commentators all avidly awaited his first move.

Volcker ordered an increase in the "federal funds rate," the overnight interest rate on loans of reserves between commercial banks, and doubled the discount rate on loans of reserves to commercial banks from 5.75 to 11 percent. Using the Fed's federal funds rate as its guide, commercial banks set their prime rates far higher, causing widespread pain to businesses and consumers. And there was a further catch. Any change to interest rates, with their profound effect on the value of the dollar and the extent of business activity, is best achieved through unanimous decision. But Volcker's rates hike had divided the Fed Board, with eight members in favor and four against. Such was the expectation that Volcker would sharply tighten money that when he finally announced his hike in interest rates the news was greeted by the business press not as a first step towards monetary restraint but as a U-turn away from that goal. Journalists were quick to question Volcker's resolve. With a third of the board resistant to the Fed chair's approach, some commentators saw the tweak to 11 percent not so much as the beginning of a new monetary policy but as the first and last gasp in Volcker's brief monetarist experiment.

"The vote left uncertain whether Paul A. Volcker . . . could continue to command a majority for his high rate policies," reported the *New York Times*. "The split was seen as indicating a fundamental division within the Board over whether inflation remains a more pressing problem than recession."[28] Evidence that Volcker might not be in control of events sent the price of gold soaring. As Volcker acknowledged, "The split vote spelled hesitation and left the impression that this would be the board's last move to tighten money. The whole maneuver was therefore counterproductive in seeming to send a message that inflation could not be, or would not be, dealt with very strongly."[29] Volcker's first tentative step had turned out to be a disaster. As he explained, "I realized that we had this credibility problem worse than I thought."[30]

Spooked by what was seen as his display of weakness the previous week, Volcker decided he had to do something even more bold and to do it without delay. The following day, Volcker assigned two members of the Fed staff, Stephen Axilrod and Peter Sternlight, to explore how to best change the institution's focus from unemployment to inflation. Their confidential report, delivered a week later, declared: "The Federal Open Market Committee . . . would seek to hold increases in the monetary base and other reserve aggregates to amounts just sufficient to meet monetary targets and to help restrain growth in bank credit, recognizing that such a procedure could result in wider fluctuations in the shortest term money market rates [interest rates]."

Under the new policy, instead of fixing interest rates with a view to boosting or calming the market, the Fed would primarily attempt to influence specific monetary targets. Already the Fed was obliged under law to report its monetary estimates, however inaccurate, and these were now to become "targets," even when they were nothing of the kind.[31]

At a hastily arranged press conference on October 6 in the Eccles Building, with the October inflation figure at 12.83 percent, Volcker announced a complete shift from interest rate targets to monetary targets. "By emphasizing the supply of reserves and constraining the growth of the money supply through the reserve mechanism, we think we can get firmer control over the growth in money supply in a shorter period of time," Volcker told reporters. "But the other side of the coin is, in supplying the reserve in that manner, the daily [short-term interest] rate in the market . . . is apt to fluctuate over a wider range than had been the practice in recent years."[32] Shifting from emphasis on controlling the federal funds rate to controlling bank reserves entailed limiting the amount banks could lend by raising the discount rate—the interest rate at which the Fed lends funds to banks—by 1 percent and demanding that banks permanently maintain larger reserves, money that could therefore not be lent to borrowers. In turn, banks were given leeway to set interest rates as they thought fit.

Volcker was aware he was setting out on a mighty gamble:

I was as skeptical of the extreme claims of [Friedman's monetarist school] about the virtues of constant money growth as I had been about the efficacy of floating exchange rates in escaping our external constraints. But shorn of some of those extreme claims, the [quantity of money] approaches . . . seemed worth looking at again.[33]

He hoped the new emphasis on monetary targets would undermine the widespread assumption that prices were sure to rise, which fed into expectations of future inflation that set the bar for wage demands and purchasing decisions. As he explained:

> More focus on the money supply . . . would be a way of telling the public that we meant business. People don't need an advanced course in economics to understand that inflation has something to do with too much money. If we could get out the message that when we say we're going to control money, we mean we're going to deal with inflation, then we would have a chance of affecting people's behavior.[34]

Volcker had always thought that the public held the commonsense view that inflation was caused by too much money chasing too few goods. So a good way to explain what needed to be done to stop inflation was by saying that money should be made more scarce by raising interest rates.[35] He could not, however, resist a sideswipe at the "oversimplification" of monetarist notions by Friedman and his disciples.

So in short order the Fed moved from concerning itself with unemployment, inflation, and the general health of the economy to chasing imprecise monetary targets. There were two profound problems in this approach. The first was the conundrum of which monetary measure the Fed should use and whether that measure could be controlled adequately to slow quantity of money. Was it M1, which logged cash in circulation and checking accounts, M2, or M3, which included savings accounts and other liquid sources of money, or a combination of all three? Even Friedman was a little vague about which measure was the right one to target. "Long-run considerations call for a gradual reduction in the rate of monetary growth to a level consistent with zero inflation (about 0 to 2 per cent per year for M1, 3–5 per cent for M2),"[36] he wrote.

The second drawback was the cost to businesses and mortgage holders of a capricious interest rate. As many of Friedman's critics had pointed out, it was easier to reduce inflation by monetarist means in theory than it was in practice. Attempting to hold the quantity of money steady meant erratic and often exaggerated changes in the short-term interest rates set by the Fed, sometimes plunging, sometimes soaring. The erratic interest rate moves gave the impression the Fed didn't know what it was doing. As Healey recalled, "Volcker used to complain bitterly as chairman of the Fed that he was expected to drive the economic automobile with no instrument except the throttle—the steering wheel and the brakes were in other, less responsible hands."[37] Before long, Volcker's new quasi-monetarist approach set off uncertainty about the direction the interest rate would move next, which rattled the markets. He wrote:

> In theory, and as it turned out in practice and in spades, concentrating on direct control of bank reserves and the money supply would produce much more volatile interest rates, and in the short run, before inflation came under control and confidence was restored, the whole level of interest rates would rise.[38]

At what point should Volcker be concerned that the high interest rates needed to damp down the money supply were ruining the economy by choking the free flow of credit? He explained his predicament:

> With the best staff in the world and all the computing power we could give them there could never be any certainty about just the right level of the federal funds rate to keep the money supply on the right path and to regulate economic activity. The art of central banking lies in

large part in approaching the right answer from a sense of experience and successive approximation. But it is also a psychological fact of life that the risks almost always seem greater in raising interest rates than in lowering them. After all, no one likes to risk recession, and that is when the political flak ordinarily hits.[39]

To ensure he would survive the inevitable political heat, Volcker needed Carter to endorse his new policy direction. But the president remained unconvinced that Volcker's monetarist plan would work. His Council of Economic Advisers, too, was skeptical and preferred to stick to the old ways, if necessary agreeing the hiking of interest rates by a massive 2 percent to show the Fed's intent. Samuelson thought the president had wished the harsh Fed policy on himself. "Carter promised the world a U.S. recession on November 1, 1978," he wrote in *Newsweek*. "On October 6 [1979], the occasion of Paul Volcker's 'midnight massacre,' the President's I.O.U. was presented for payment."[40] But although the prospect of continuing high, erratic interest rates was sure to be painful for Americans to endure, Carter did not urge Volcker to change course.

"It was significant to me that the president did not ask to see me directly," recalled Volcker. "My reading of the situation was that while the president would strongly prefer that we not move in the way we proposed, with all its uncertainties, he was not going to insist on that judgment in an unfamiliar field over the opinion of his newly appointed Federal Reserve chairman."[41] Instead, "the president, when questioned, was remarkably supportive of what we had done."[42]

By March 1980 the extent of the damage being done to the economy by Volcker's shift from interest rates to reserves was evident. Interest rates were now at an eye-watering 15.28 percent and the economy was heading into a nosedive. Samuelson's prediction of a man-made recession was coming true. Volcker could not understand why things had gone so wrong so quickly. "Through all the interest rate increases in the previous six months, the economy had continued to grow," he recalled. "Now the bottom just fell out, literally within a matter of days."[43]

At a grand White House ceremony on March 14, 1980, Carter and Volcker announced consumer credit controls that would curb the amount individuals could borrow. (It was thought restraints on business borrowing, which accounted for the bulk of total credit growth, would prove too hard to police, as businesses would use bond and commercial paper transactions to dodge the controls.) The medicine appeared to work. Inflation peaked at 16.32 percent the following month, April, then headed south, hitting 14.26 percent in May, 12.71 percent in June, and 12.19 percent in July. To Volcker's surprise, the money supply also dropped precipitously. Over the course of three months, under the policy of shadowing the monetary targets, the federal funds rate dived from 20 percent to 8 percent before the money supply began to rapidly increase again.

With the November 1980 presidential election looming, which would decide Carter's fate, Volcker was under pressure not to make the stumbling, erratic economy any worse. High and rising interest rates were hampering business activity and causing Americans to either cut consumption or take on crippling debt. Yet he soon found himself obliged to increase interest rates again, even though the money supply figures were well below the Fed's targets and thus suggested that interest rate cuts were in order. As the general election approached, inflation remained stuck in double digits at 14.21 percent.

Samuelson had long condemned the logic of the new Fed policy. "Yes, inflation is an evil," he had written a decade before, "but curing it by engineering a slowdown in real growth and a contrived increase in unemployment is a still greater evil. . . . There will result so great an increase in unemployment among ghetto youths as the result of a general slowdown as to cause riots and violence."[44] He saw one benefit in the Fed inviting an unnecessary recession. "I much prefer for the country a recession contrived by Fed chairman Paul Volcker and President Carter rather than one created by blind Mother Nature," Samuelson wrote in *Newsweek* in December 1979, as the Volcker measures began to bite. "What man does, man can undo. Acts of God and the King's enemies are harder to diagnose and reverse."[45] But he was doubtful Volcker's policy would work. "What is so frustrating about the present phase of mini-recession is the patent fact that the United States economy is not yet showing any signs that the rate of inflation is abating,"[46] Samuelson told his *Newsweek* readers.

All this mayhem was watched from the sidelines by Friedman. At last his monetarist theories were close to being implemented, yet in the name of monetary targets Volcker was presiding over high interest rates and economic disaster. Friedman was furious his take on monetarism had been rejected by Volcker in favor of monetarism lite, and he was even more angry that it was in the name of monetarism that Volcker had caused the economy to head into recession. Friedman had long believed that for monetarism to work, the Fed should be deprived of all discretion over the money supply, leaving the creation of new money in the hands of a computer algorithm that could not be swayed by personal whim of the Fed chairman, by unexpected events, or by public opinion.

Reflecting on Volcker's motives years after the event, Friedman reiterated his belief that Volcker's apparent conversion to monetarist thinking was a cover for a more conventional though unpopular approach to curbing inflation: the sharp hiking of interest rates. "What [Volcker] really wanted to do was to have the interest rate go up very high, to reflect the amount of inflation," recalled Friedman. "But he could do it better by professing that he wasn't controlling it and that he was controlling the quantity of money, and the right policy at that time was to limit what was happening to the quantity of money, and that meant the interest rate shot way up."[47] Friedman believed Volcker's professed devotion to the quantity-of-money theory was window dressing. As Friedman put it, "The Fed has given lip service to changing its procedures, but it has repeatedly failed to put its money where its mouth is."[48]

Samuelson observed that Volcker's deliberate crashing of the economy to purge inflation had been cheered on by "conservative economists" who wanted to choke off steeply rising prices by throwing Americans out of work—what he had described as "a little bloodletting at the expense of the unemployed."[49] He wrote:

> I've quoted conservative economist friends who have said at Washington meetings: "If you're contriving a teensy-weensy recession for us, please don't bother. It won't do the job. What's needed is a believable declaration that Washington will countenance whatever degree of unemployment is needed to bring us back on the path to price stability, and a demonstrated willingness to stick to that resolution no matter how politically unpopular the short-run joblessness, production cutbacks and dips in profit might be."[50]

Samuelson did not believe the Volcker approach would produce miracles. "Though a recession will not cure inflation," Samuelson wrote, "some slowdown will help keep it from getting worse and will improve the inflation rate a bit."

If Volcker did not believe in monetarism, why did he use the language of monetarism when he deliberately crashed the economy? Princeton economics professor Alan S. Blinder[51] explains it like this:

> Volcker was determined to vanquish inflation and knew that disinflation would require excruciatingly high interest rates. He could not imagine going to Congress, puffing on his cigar, and arguing that the country needed a 21 per cent prime rate. Monetarists provided the

political heat shield the Fed needed. When people complained about high interest rates, Fed officials could (and did) hide behind monetarist dogma. . . . The marriage of the Fed and monetarism was one of convenience, not devotion.[52]

Friedman was so irritated by Volcker's sleight of hand he decided to publicly distance himself from the Fed's actions. In June 1980, Volcker and Friedman were invited to address a monetary conference in New Orleans held by the American Bankers Association. With Volcker's conspicuously tall frame hunched prominently in the audience, Friedman mounted a spirited attack from the podium on Volcker and the Federal Reserve.

The Fed's monetary targets were, Friedman said, a "particularly egregious example of the contrast between talk and action." Although Volcker had paid "lip service" to controlled, steady money supply growth, many in the Fed had been "manipulating interest rates" in a way that made nonsense of true monetarism. The Fed was making the same mistake it made in 1931, when a too-tight monetary policy exacerbated the Great Depression. In 1979, rather than easing the money supply, as Friedman believed necessary, thereby allowing the stalling economy to recover, Volcker's Fed had imposed an "incredibly restrictive" monetary policy that starved the economy of funds, making the recession far worse.[53]

The carefully calibrated ambush was Friedman at his most invidious, a brutal ad hominem assault on a friend and colleague, with the amiable Volcker mugged in front of an audience of top bankers and economists. Yet Friedman appeared to have little concern for the human cost of his harsh words. As ever, he remained true to his big idea, which he thought was being not so much maligned as—worse—ignored.

How should Volcker respond to Friedman's public rebuke? Reporters, eager to extend the embarrassing clash between two big beasts of the financial jungle, the chairman of the Fed and the self-ordained high priest of monetarism, invited Volcker to strike back. But rather than engage with Friedman in a public spat, Volcker's large frame absorbed the blows. Nodding his head sagely, Volcker simply whispered, "Oh, Milton!"[54] and left it at that. Samuelson was amused at Friedman's chastisement of Volcker. "I am not one loath to criticize the Federal Reserve," he wrote. "There is no other activity that so much adds to an economist's professional and self-esteem."[55]

Friedman returned to the attack on Volcker in July 1980, pointing to the sharp rise in unemployment that, he claimed, was the direct result of the rapid decline in monetary growth. He believed "the Fed's targets for monetary growth have been reasonable." But "the problem is with the failure to achieve them. If a private enterprise's actual production deviated from plan as frequently and by as much, heads would roll. The Fed should be held to at least as high standards." His conclusion? "The Fed's failure has condemned us to a more severe recession than we need have suffered."[56]

In September 1980, in the light of Carter's initiative to boost industrial productivity by government incentives, *Newsweek*'s editors published a special "productivity edition" and invited Samuelson and Friedman to respond to identical questions. Whereas Samuelson thought Carter's measures "part election-year placebo and part a desirable new effort to promote capital," Friedman thought them an "assemblage of all the things that are wrong with past governmental measures allegedly directed at improving productivity and employment."

When it came to fiscal policy, the differences between them were already well established. Friedman believed that "fiscal fine-tuning has long had the perverse effect of increasing instability and uncertainty and thereby inhibiting growth," and that "government deficits have absorbed capital funds that would otherwise have gone into productive private investment. High marginal tax rates have diverted enterprise and ingenuity from the promotion of productive efficiency to the creation of tax shelters."

Samuelson, however, blamed "political infighting" for producing "a high-consuming, low-investing society." He wrote:

1) We run budget deficits to cure unemployment and stagnation.

2) Then we use tight interest-rate policies to mop up inflation.

3) Results: consumption is encouraged, capital formation is discouraged.[57]

FRIEDMAN SUFFERED conspicuous indignity at being ignored by Volcker, but on other fronts he and his ideas had been making steady progress. In 1980, Friedman appeared as the star of his own television series. The chief executive of the Philadelphia public television station WQLN had been eager to counter *The Age of Uncertainty*, a series of shows about economics presented by the arch-Keynesian J. K. Galbraith, with a series celebrating conservative economics. Although many at PBS thought Friedman "a fascist, an extreme right-winger,"[58] liberals in public broadcasting could not resist the argument that the network should offer its viewers a balance of opinions. In 1977, Friedman had readily agreed to what became a mammoth project, with lectures, discussions with the public, a tour of the world to provide the right background for his arguments, and a book, *Free to Choose*, which would sell more than a million copies.

More popular in tone than *Capitalism and Freedom*, *Free to Choose*—billed on the cover as "the controversial best seller"—brought together Friedman's libertarian arguments against government, his "cure for inflation," and his plea for parents to be given vouchers for schools. By this time, all the caveats about the causes and cures of inflation that Friedman had mentioned in his 1967 AEA lecture were abandoned in favor of simple language. "Substantial inflation is always and everywhere a monetary phenomenon,"[59] he declared. "Just as an excessive increase in the quantity of money is the one and only important cause of inflation, so a reduction in the rate of monetary growth is the one and only cure for inflation."[60]

The series was broadcast, and the book published, in 1980, which would prove to be the high-water mark of Friedman's influence. While he was able to write, in a final chapter headed "The Tide is Turning," that "the failure of Western governments to achieve their proclaimed objectives has produced a widespread reaction against big government,"[61] and that "the tide toward Fabian socialism and New Deal liberalism has crested,"[62] he was reluctant to say that his counterrevolution had succeeded in full. Even at the high point of his popularity, he remained pessimistic about the permanence of the shift in public opinion towards conservative solutions. "The reaction may prove short lived and be followed, after a brief interval, by a resumption of the trend toward ever bigger government,"[63] he said.

12

No Hollywood Ending

Friedman's monetarism is given another chance
by Ronald Reagan, the most conservative postwar
president. But Volcker remains in charge at the Fed

In November 1980, Jimmy Carter was roundly defeated in the presidential election. While contemporary observers tended to blame his downfall on a bungled rescue of American hostages held in Tehran by Islamist revolutionaries, just as important to Carter's defeat were the high interest rates imposed by Paul Volcker at the Fed. As Hayek had predicted, "The politician, acting on a modified Keynesian maxim that in the long run we are all out of office, does not care if his successful cure of unemployment is bound to produce more unemployment in the future. The politicians who will be blamed for it will not be those who created the inflation, but those who stopped it."[1]

The ailing U.S. economy was only one of the many reasons voters felt they wanted a fresh start. They chose as president Ronald Reagan, a former movie star and California governor. He knew something about economics, albeit a pre-Keynesian version. As a young man in Illinois, as the Great Depression was about to engulf America, Reagan had studied classical economics and sociology at Eureka College, attaining a C grade. Like Friedman, Reagan had established his conservative credentials by lending his support to the maverick 1964 Goldwater campaign in a masterly televised speech, "A Time for Choosing,"[2] which set out his ultraconservative agenda. The broadcast established him as Goldwater's obvious successor. The 1980 election won, a meeting of Reagan's coordinating committee on economic policy was promptly called in Los Angeles to discuss a vague program of action that would become known as Reaganomics. Among those attending were Friedman, George Shultz, Arthur Burns, and Alan Greenspan.

On his return to Washington, D.C., from the meeting, an obviously agitated Burns called Volcker and asked to see him in his office at the Fed as soon as possible. Volcker recalled that Burns "had gotten so red at the end of the conversation that I thought he was going to have a stroke."

"Milton wants to abolish the Fed," Burns told Volcker. "He wants to replace you with a computer."

"It's a metaphor, Arthur," said Volcker. "This battle over the Fed's independence is nothing new."[3]

Irritated by Volcker's failure to follow his exact monetarist strictures, Friedman had repeated at the Reagan policy powwow that it was important to remove the human element from the control of the money supply, because humans were too easily blown off course by events. Friedman's solution to this human error, suggested only half in jest, was that the Fed— and the Fed chairman—should be replaced by a computer algorithm that could funnel new money into the economy without discretion. Samuelson saw it this way: "He wanted a machine that spit out M0 basic currency [one of the many measures of money in an economy[4]] at a rate exactly equal to the real rate of growth of the system. And he thought that would stabilize things."[5]

When Burns raised the alarm with Volcker about Friedman's suggestion, it was a heads-up to Volcker that, with a conservative Republican in the White House, life was about to become more uncomfortable. His friend and sometime nemesis Friedman, who had nagged from the sidelines, hoped to become an important figure in the Reagan administration, which would soon pit Friedman's ideas directly against Volcker's actions.

Friedman had worked closely with Reagan when he was governor of California, from 1967 to 1975. At Friedman's encouragement, Reagan had championed a state constitutional amendment to limit how much the state government in Sacramento could spend each year. With Reagan in the White House, Friedman felt he was in a good position to profoundly influence, if not steer, the new administration's economic policy. During the campaign, Friedman had criticized Reagan for backing federal bailouts of Chrysler motors[6] and the City of New York, as well as for condoning import quotas on cars and steel.[7] Nonetheless, he was invited by Shultz, the chair of Reagan's thirteen-person pre-election Economic Policy Coordinating Committee, to join Reagan's economic team and draw up a list of recommendations for the incoming administration's new economic strategy. Friedman was also invited to join the President's Economic Policy Advisory Board (PEPAB).[8]

Friedman soon discovered, however, that PEBAB was little more than a genial talking shop at which Reagan liked to chew the fat with chums about which conservative economic policies to pursue. What was said in the meetings, however, rarely led to concrete action. As Reagan aide Martin Anderson recalled,

> What [the old friends who made up PEBAB] did for [Reagan] more than anything else was to reassure him that the course he was following was right. It was they who pressed him to resist any tax increases; it was they who strongly urged more and more cuts in federal spending; it was they who strongly pushed for more deregulation.[9]

Friedman had convinced Reagan of the virtues of monetarism, which, though the policy would have to be executed by the independent Federal

Reserve under Volcker, became the official economic orthodoxy of the new administration. As Friedman recalled,

> Reagan was very knowledgeable about monetary policy, recognized the key role of monetary growth, and was fully aware that the initial impact of a disinflationary policy would be a recession, and perhaps a fairly serious one, as indeed it was. He was prepared to take the heat on that for the long-term advantage of bringing down inflation.[10]

Over the next two years, Reagan fully supported Volcker in his efforts to defeat stagflation by hiking interest rates sharply, thereby deliberately sparking the recession of 1981 and 1982. Volcker's anti-inflation gambit eventually paid off. Inflation fell precipitously and hyperinflation was brought under control. But Friedman played little part in the defeat of inflation. Shut out from the Fed's decisions, he remained resentful that Volcker had not wholeheartedly embraced the true monetarist faith. Friedman confessed to being "highly critical of the erratic way that the Fed operated, letting monetary growth vary widely in brief periods."[11] And for Friedman, Volcker's betrayal was not merely intellectual. He could rarely resist making ad hominem assaults upon the Fed chairman.

Chief among Friedman's complaints was that Volcker did not take a close enough grip on the money supply, and by concentrating upon interest rates, allowed it to swing between extremes. Friedman acknowledged that the tools the Fed used to influence the money supply were inadequate, and was quick to suggest ways to keep closer control over it. He disparaged Volcker's erratic attempts at monetary control as like "driving a car with a highly defective steering gear. [Volcker] is driving down a road with walls on both sides. [He] can go down the middle of the road on the average only by first bouncing off one wall and then off the opposite wall. Not very good for the car or the passengers or by-standers, but one way to get down the road."[12] "[The years 1979–1982] have seen the most erratic ups and downs in monetary growth in our history," he complained. "They've also seen the most erratic ups and downs in interest rates. They've also seen the most erratic ups and downs in the economy. Those are all related."[13]

Friedman warned that hyperinflation could return. In response to a remark by Volcker in April 1983 that "if the inflation outlook is as good as I think it is, long-term interest rates are far too high," in *Newsweek* Friedman accused the Fed chairman of chutzpah, which, quoting Leo Rosten,[14] he described as "that quality enshrined in a man who, having killed his mother and father, throws himself on the mercy of the court because he is an orphan."[15] Friedman insisted that the Federal Reserve allowed the surge in the money supply to occur and could have prevented the surge if it had wanted. And he warned that continuing to preside over monetary growth at similar rates would lead to an upsurge in inflation in 1984 or 1985 at the very latest and higher long-term interest rates much sooner. As ever, Friedman was quick to blame Volcker. "Past experience gives little reason to put much confidence in the judgments of [the Fed chairman]," he sniped.

By mouthing monetarist phrases while ignoring the pure, strict monetarism that Friedman extolled, Friedman was anxious that Volcker's faux monetarism would give true Friedmanite monetarism a bad name. In assessing Volcker's "monetarist experiment" between 1979 and 1982, when the Fed switched from inflationary targets to monetary goals, Friedman declared, "Though the Federal Reserve System's rhetoric was 'monetarist,' the actual policy that it followed was anti-monetarist." Volcker did not do enough. "A monetarist policy involves not only targeting monetary aggregates, but also—as a major and central element—achieving a steady and predictable rate of growth in whatever monetary aggregate is targeted," Friedman wrote. "The wide gyrations in monetary growth rates . . . rapidly disillusioned any naive agents who initially accepted the Fed's rhetoric as a guarantee of steady and predictable monetary growth."[16]

Friedman summed up what he believed to be Volcker's betrayal many years later:

The so-called monetarist experiment was in 1979 when Volcker announced that he was going to take the quantity of money and not the interest rate as his guide. But he didn't do it. If you look at the monetary aggregates, they were more variable during the Volcker period than at any previous time in history. So he did not follow a monetarist course.[17]

Nevertheless, Volcker's brand of monetarism—real or imagined— achieved considerable success in its stated aim of purging inflation from the U.S. economy. And Volcker, not Friedman, was given full credit for the achievement.

Meanwhile, another economic fad engulfed the Reagan administration, one Friedman had little to do with: supply-side economics.[18] From 1975 on, supply-side arguments were all the rage among conservative economists and commentators, boosted by publication in 1978 of Jude Wanniski's supply-side primer *The Way the World Works*, while monetarism was deemed old-hat. As Samuelson wryly observed, economists were always subject to the latest fashion: "Economists are said to disagree too much, but in ways that are too much alike: If eight sleep in the same bed, you can be sure that, like Eskimos, when they turn over, they'll all turn over together."[19]

As the name "supply-side economics" suggests, its adherents were countering Keynes's remedy of reviving a sluggish economy by deliberately boosting aggregate demand, though Keynes had anticipated the truth at the idea's kernel in his 1936 *General Theory*: "Supply creates its own demand in the sense that the aggregate demand price is equal to the aggregate supply price for all levels of output and employment." Supply-siders asserted that an increase in the supply of goods and services would provide an inflation-proof way of boosting an economy. One way of bolstering demand advocated by Keynes was to cut taxes, allowing individuals to spend more and thereby increase demand. The logic of supply-side economics was in many ways similar to Keynes's tax-cutting remedy and in turn was merely a variation on Say's Law,[20] which states, "A product is no sooner created, than it, from that instant, affords a market for other products to the full extent of its own value." Put another way, aggregate production creates an equal quantity of aggregate demand and the act of making goods in itself prompts demand for those goods.[21] Supply-siders set out to grow the economy by making conditions right for an increase in the supply of goods and services by removing regulations and cutting taxes, thereby achieving a more productive economy without risk of inflation. Or at least that is what the theory's followers believed. And they were never more excited than when imagining the magical qualities of drastically reducing personal taxation. Samuelson was disparaging about supply-side economists. "Hard-headed Republicans would not run their own private businesses on the basis of such hoped-for miracles [that by making the goods that demand would surely follow],"[22] he told *Newsweek* readers. "One should never believe in a miracle beforehand. It is hard enough to do so after the fact."[23]

The conservative hero of the hour was Arthur Laffer,[24] who, over lunch in 1974 with Wanniski, Donald Rumsfeld (then Gerald Ford's chief of staff), and Rumsfeld's deputy Dick Cheney, had drawn a bell curve on a table napkin[25] to demonstrate that raising the tax rate did not automatically raise tax revenue, as taxpayers amended their behavior in face of higher tax rates. Rather than raising taxes to produce higher revenue, there was a tax rate "sweet spot" on the curve where taxes were lower but total taxation revenue was higher.

As Herbert Stein, who coined the term "supply-side economics," explained:

> According to supply-side economics, a large across-the-board equal cut of income tax rates would not reduce but would raise the revenues and so would not increase the deficit but would reduce it. This wonderful consequence would be produced by a large increase in the taxable income base—large enough so that the revenue would

be larger even though the tax rates were lower. The large increase in the taxable income base would come about mainly because of a large increase in the total national output and income, resulting in turn from an increase in the quantity of labor and capital supplied when tax rates were reduced and the after-tax return for working and saving was increased.[26]

Stein believed there was intentional sleight of hand in switching attention to tax cutting from what he called "the old time religion of cutting government expenditures."

[The Republicans] needed to show that there could be a big tax cut without a big expenditure cut and without an increase in the deficit. The basic supply-side proposition provided them with a way to show that.[27]

By the seventh edition of his *Economics* textbook, Samuelson had conceded there might be some merit in Laffer's contention that cutting taxes may increase revenue. "To the extent that a tax cut succeeds in stimulating business, our progressive tax system will collect extra revenues out of the higher income levels," he wrote. "Hence a tax cut may in the long run imply little (or even no) loss in federal revenues, and hence no substantial increase in the long run public debt."[28] In 1992, in the fourteenth edition of his primer, Samuelson corrected that assumption, writing that the "Laffer-curve prediction that revenues would rise following the tax cuts has proven false."[29]

Samuelson had made a deadly cameo appearance in the debate about the virtues of the Laffer Curve when, in 1971, he gave a lecture at a conference in Chicago titled "Why They are Laughing at Laffer." "In one of my writings I referred to him as Dr. Arthur Laffer, thinking naturally that he was a Stanford PhD," wrote Samuelson. "Somebody in Washington, perhaps it was Joseph Pechman,[30] subsequently kidded me for pinning on him the indignity of being a doctor when he was not one. I explicitly corrected myself and said, 'I mean Mr. Laffer.' Subsequently various notes were passed up to me at the head table saying that he was Dr. Laffer and so I corrected myself once again." Two hours later, Samuelson was contacted by Emile Despres,[31] an economics professor at Stanford, who said, "Stop picking on Art Laffer. He's a nice boy and it is only a formality that stands between him and his PhD degree."[32]

In their rush to hire a rising conservative star and award him tenure in 1970, lest he go elsewhere, Chicago's economics department had failed to check Laffer's claim that he held a doctorate in economics from Stanford. But Laffer had not completed his PhD thesis,[33] a damning fact that was to cast a shadow over Laffer's standing among economists attempting to assess supply-side economics and over the academic integrity of the Chicago School. Laffer was driven from the Chicago faculty in shame. "It was horrible," Laffer recalled. "I knew there was no way on God's earth that I could make it in the profession. So I went other routes—the press, the political process, consulting."[34]

Samuelson personally liked Laffer, and knew him as his daughter Jane's teacher at Stanford, so he was in two minds about trashing the young man's theory. "The only moral problem I ever faced was whether for someone of my position in the profession to come out strongly in criticism of the work of a 30-year-old would do irreparable damage to his reputation," Samuelson wrote. "I decided on this that national policy was involved; and, further, that in the case that his forecasts proved to be right (as I doubted but could not rule out) the laugh would strongly be on me, a risk a responsible commentator ought to be prepared to take."[35]

The switch to supply-side thinking among conservative economists eventually moved the spotlight off Friedman and his pursuit of monetarism. During the Reagan years, Friedman's contribution to monetarist theory and its role in bringing about the end of stagflation was eclipsed in the minds of lawmakers, commentators, and economists by arguments about whether Reagan's deep income tax cuts—the highest rate of income tax was reduced from 70 to 50 percent in 1981 and from 50 to 38.5 percent in 1986[36]—were successful in fostering economic growth.

Even if he did not sign up to the larger assumptions of supply-side economics, Friedman approved of slashing income tax per se. And like Laffer, he believed that cutting income tax would increase rather than diminish federal tax revenues. "The personal-income tax costs taxpayers far more than it yields to the government," he wrote. "However . . . with a top rate of 25 per cent, net taxable income reported would go up by more than enough to offset the arithmetical loss of 13 per cent."[37]

For Friedman, supply-side-sponsored tax cutting offered another benefit. Even if they did not pay for themselves, tax cuts would not prove inflationary if they were accompanied by adequate cuts in public spending, he argued. If the size of government was reduced by cutting taxes, that was one more nail in the coffin of Keynes's big government legacy. He wrote:

An equal cut in taxes and in spending is neutral in the short run—involving simply a shift from government spending to private spending. In the long run, it is a stimulus—but to output, not inflation. Since that part of private spending that is invested adds to productive capacity and hence to the future supply of goods, it will tend to reduce inflation.

Samuelson thought Friedman had misrepresented the facts about government spending and inflation over many years. "The real goods and services consumed by government—by all levels of government—are lower than they were five years ago when the inflation began," he wrote in 1973. Rather than endlessly increasing, as conservatives alleged, public spending in recent years had not even kept up with inflation, meaning that in real terms it had decreased. "Not only has the public share of GNP dropped in percentage terms," he wrote, "its money magnitude has not even kept up with the rising prices of public goods and services."[38] He was also sharply critical of cutting taxes as a means of shaming legislators into cutting government expenditure. "To conservatives this is a no-lose deal. If productivity and capital formation pick up, fine. Even if they do not, you have scaled down the scope of government. If some poor people get hurt, who said life is fair?"[39]

For those who fell in behind the logic of the Laffer Curve, tax cuts seemed to be a magic bullet that would solve the discrepancy between taxation and spending without inflicting too much pain. Friedman warned that it would be spending cuts rather than tax cuts that would truly boost economic growth. While some who advocated cutting tax rates claimed the lower rates would yield higher revenue, the ultimate aim should be not to raise revenue but to lower revenue and lower public spending. If a tax cut led to higher revenue, that was simply evidence that the rates had not been cut enough.[40]

And Friedman, always eager to promote his notion that inflation is everywhere and always solely a factor of monetary growth, predicted what the main problem with Reagan's tax cuts would be: contrary to the beliefs of supply siders, federal spending would *not* likely be cut to compensate for the loss of tax revenue. Whether the cuts would be inflationary depended on whether the resulting deficit would be covered by increased government borrowing or by cutting public spending. He wrote:

> The deficit is definitely inflationary only if it is financed by creating new money—in which case the excess of government spending over tax receipts is not balanced by a private shortfall. But the deficit need not be so financed. If it is, that is a failure of monetary policy, not of fiscal policy.[41]

In the event, the Reagan tax cuts—making income tax lower than at any time since the 1920s—were not matched by cuts in spending: on the contrary. Above all, his ambition to bring the Cold War to an end by outspending the Soviet Union on defense made balancing the budget impossible. Therefore, despite the promise of the Laffer Curve and "trickle-down economics," in which the taxes saved by the rich were claimed to eventually benefit those further down the economic food chain, Reagan's tax cuts did not increase revenue but led to a ballooning of the federal deficit—funded by borrowing, or printing money. Before long, with federal tax revenues slumping by 6 percent in real terms—a reduction of at least $200 billion in 2012 dollars over the first four years—Reagan agreed that taxes should be slyly increased. Following the much-heralded tax cuts of 1981, taxes were raised in 1982, 1983, and 1984. Further tax cuts by Reagan in 1986 were met by tax increases in 1987.[42]

Friedman's monetarist argument about deficits fitted snugly with his general antipathy towards government action, particularly government acts that cost taxpayer dollars. As he explained:

> Deficits are bad primarily because they foster excessive government spending—the chief culprit, in my opinion, in producing both inflation and slow economic growth. If spending is financed by creating money to meet deficits, the link between spending and inflation is direct. If spending is financed by borrowing or taxes, the link is indirect but nonetheless real. Both borrowing and taxes crowd out private spending, absorbing resources that might otherwise be used for private consumption or productive capital investment.[43]

Friedman's strictures on the federal deficit anticipated the many attempts by successive conservative presidents to make a dash for growth by slashing taxes without Congress in turn cutting public spending. The soaring deficits that resulted from this disconnect became the focus of the conservative economics narrative, particularly after the financial freeze of 2008, when Republicans blamed Democrats for failing to bring spending on expensive public programs in line with shrinking tax revenues.[44] Demands for Congress to approve a "balanced budget," in which the tax yield would match spending dollar for dollar,[45] were before long to become an article of faith for conservatives, even if such a state was only achieved once, under a Democratic president, Bill Clinton.[46]

Friedman, as ever, had his own take on the evil of deficits and the "balanced budget" remedy.

> The political appeal of a "balanced budget" has often been counterproductive. Big spenders have pushed through government programs leading to higher deficits. Fiscal conservatives, having lost that battle, have responded by supporting an increase in taxes to narrow the deficit. The fiscal conservatives have been turned out of office, partly for having the courage to raise taxes. The big spenders have been re-elected, partly for their irresponsibility in raising spending. They have then set off on another spending spree and launched yet another cycle of higher spending, bigger deficits, higher taxes.

It was that scenario, he wrote, that had persuaded him many years before to favor tax cuts under almost any circumstances. If tax cuts threatened bigger deficits, to achieve a balanced budget politicians would be encouraged to balance the budget by cutting government spending rather than raising taxes.[47]

The removal of the spotlight from monetarism to cutting taxes and balancing the federal budget was, for Friedman, something of a welcome distraction. Efforts by Volcker at the Fed to harness the money supply—and therefore, according to Friedman, to anticipate economic growth—were proving hopeless. Even which measure of money needed to be controlled continued to be hotly debated. Friedman held to his preferred measure, M1, an amalgam of physical currency and coin, demand deposits, travelers' checks, other checkable deposits and negotiable order of withdrawal (NOW) accounts. But M1 was proving a poor indicator of future growth.[48]

After three years of Volcker's monetarism, the U.S. economy was deep in recession, unemployment was over 10 percent and rising, yet the monetarist remedy was not to expand the money supply but to constrict it further. After a switchback ride in which interest rates rose precipitously, then plunged, in the fall of 1982 Volcker made a momentous decision: the Fed would abandon its quasi-monetarist experiment and resume managing interest rates, not as a means to control inflation by limiting the velocity of the money supply but according to the likely effect it would have in spurring or depressing economic growth.

In a crisis meeting with the Federal Open Market Committee on October 5, 1982, Volcker officially pulled the plug on monetarism and, in the face of three dyed-in-the-wool monetarists on the FOMC, cut the discount rate that reduced the price of money: the exact opposite of what Friedman's monetarism recommended. As Volcker recalled, "There didn't seem to be the relationship between money growth and the economic numbers you would have expected."[49]

To keep the market from thinking the Fed had abandoned its quest to keep inflation in check, Volcker's announcement arrived disguised as a technical change in the way M1 was measured, but the upshot was clear: monetarism no longer guided the Fed's actions. Reagan's White House, itself at odds over economic policy, made no effort to question Volcker's decision. They, too, had abandoned monetarism as a noble but failed experiment.

Friedman was profoundly irritated by the decision to ditch monetarism, even of a bastard sort, but before long his judgment was called into question, even by monetarists. While the stock market had surged after the Fed announcement, Friedman warned that there would be a high price to pay for Volcker's abandonment of monetarist logic. He predicted that the effect of the Fed increasing the money supply by slashing interest rates would be inflation in double digits. And in 1983 he predicted that the slowdown in growth that year of M3—the broadest measure of money in circulation, including cash, checking accounts, travelers' checks, and "liquid" financial products such as certificates of deposit[50]—would lead to a recession the following year.

To Friedman's embarrassment, however, neither prophecy came true. Inflation declined further and the 1984 recession did not happen. Friedman was, for once, lost for words. "I was wrong, absolutely wrong," he admitted. "And I have no good explanation as to why I was wrong."[51] As William Poole,[52] a former chief executive of the monetarist redoubt the Federal Reserve Bank of St. Louis, put it, "Those of us who have developed strong theories tried to fit the world into the theory rather than the other way round."[53]

Despite the public failure of Volcker's monetarism, Friedman insisted that his version of monetarism remained true. He doubled down on his belief that controlling the money supply was the key to managing inflation. "I don't feel there has been any repudiation of the theory," he said. "If we have been wrong about some things, they have to be corrected."[54] But Friedman's credibility among conservative economists and politicians had been severely damaged. Fed governor J. Charles Partee[55] saw in the end of monetarism in practice not so much a failure of an economic theory but a human tragedy for Friedman, by now in his early seventies. "I feel sorry for him," Partee said. "He's an old man now. He spent his life on this theory. Now it's destroyed."[56]

The failure of Friedman's monetary theories in practice came as no surprise to Hayek. He always professed to be uncomfortable finding fault with Friedman: "I don't like criticizing Milton Friedman, not only because he is an old friend but that outside of monetary theory we are in complete agreement."[57] Yet in 1983, as the Fed complained that it had no means of accurately measuring or managing the quantity of money in the U.S. economy, Hayek asked, "Has monetary policy ever done any good? I don't think it has. I think it has done only harm." He continued:

It is true that the price level is determined from the quantity of money. But we never know what the quantity of money in this sense is. I think the rule ought to be that whoever issues the money must adapt the quantity so that the price level will remain stable. But to believe there is a measurable magnitude that you can keep constant with beneficial effects is completely wrong.[58]

Hayek had identified the fatal flaw with monetarism. Even if what Friedman contended was true, it was hard to identify which measure of money to control and how it could be adjusted. As Hayek had explained in 1980:

> The problem is that in its crude form [monetarism] provides no adequate measure of what is the supply of money and that not only the supply of all kinds of money but also the demand for them determines its value. This, however, does not alter the fact that its value can be controlled and can be adequately restricted only by limiting the basic cash supplied under the existing system by the central bank.
>
> Since this is a government institution, all inflation is made by government and nobody else can do anything about it. It does, however, make impracticable the Friedmanite plan of fixing by law the rate at which the quantity of money may and should increase. This would probably produce the greatest financial panic of history. [59]

Friedman's monetarism had been tried, but found wanting. For the rest of his life he would complain that his single-cause-of-inflation theory was correct, but that Volcker had not given it a chance to be put into practice.

Despite his defeat on the arcane dispute about which form of monetarism the Fed ought to follow, Friedman did not feel the same disappointment about Reagan that he had about Nixon. Although his "high hopes that 1980 would mark a decisive turn toward smaller government were frustrated," Reagan had at least backed Volcker in breaking the back of inflation in the economy, even if he had allowed Friedmanite monetarism to be ignored. And Friedman was heartened that, by confronting the Soviet Union and challenging them to an arms race they could not afford, Reagan had contributed to the collapse of Marxism-Leninism.[60]

The collapse of communism in Russia, and in its East European satellites, between 1989 and 1991 would mark a clear victory for the free market. Friedman, who had visited the Soviet Union with Rose in 1962, was elated by the end of Soviet tyranny, for it marked the triumph of capitalism and the free market over an all-embracing, powerful state. Counterrevolutionaries in the Soviet bloc had long been inspired by the ideas of libertarian thinkers like Hayek and Friedman and had avidly consumed their books. One observer reported that "the one name that you hear more than any other throughout Central and Eastern Europe is Friedrich Hayek. Underground, or samizdat, editions and rare English copies of *The Road to Serfdom* are widely read."[61]

Friedman's writing on the overweening power of the state was a key factor behind the collapse of communism spearheaded by Lech Wałęsa's[62] Solidarity workers' revolt in Poland. Friedman's best-selling books had been declared subversive under the fierce communist assault upon freedom of thought, but being forbidden only made their free-enterprise message more attractive. Readership behind the Iron Curtain had boomed. Friedman had Lenin on the run.

When the collapse of the Berlin Wall in 1989 signaled the last gasp of the oppressive Marxist-Leninist experiment in purging markets, Friedman found himself a hero of the capitalist-loving counterrevolutionaries who took charge. When he had toured Czechoslovakia, Hungary, and Poland in the mid-eighties, while exploring whether to update the Free to Choose series, he was warmly welcomed as a seer. He was amused to see a *Christian Science Monitor* cartoon headed, "Historic Event: Statue of Milton Friedman is erected in Poland in place of Whatsisname [Lenin]." The grateful embrace of Friedman's ideas by those trapped behind communist lines was one of the highest points of the economist's career.

The "major theme" of Friedman's benchmark book *Capitalism and Free-*

dom was that "competitive capitalism" was not only "a system of economic freedom [but a] necessary condition for political freedom."[63] He argued in the book, "I know of no example in time or place of a society that has been marked by a large measure of political freedom, and that has not also used something comparable to a free market to organize the bulk of economic activity."[64] And later he could not resist pointing out that Reagan's robust opposition to communist tyranny was "in sharp contrast to the favorable comments on the Soviet Union at about the same time by such prominent intellectuals as John Kenneth Galbraith and Paul Samuelson."[65] As he had argued in *Capitalism and Freedom*, "The great tragedy of the drive to centralization, as of the drive to extend the scope of government in general, is that it is mostly led by men of good will who will be the first to rue its consequences."[66]

By 1982, monetarism was dead in the United States, an awkward footnote in the history of economic thought, forgotten except for a few true believers. Across the Atlantic, however, Friedman was held in high esteem by Margaret Thatcher, leader of the Conservative Party since 1975. Like Reagan, she had abandoned the consensus politics that British conservatives had followed since the end of World War II. Thatcher believed inflation a far more pressing problem than unemployment and she was determined as prime minister to purge the British economy of runaway price rises. And, unlike Reagan, she was the mistress of all she surveyed. She could insist that her chancellor of the exchequer and the governor of the government-run Bank of England, the U.K.'s central bank, should adopt monetarism as their lodestar. She befriended Friedman and offered him a second chance to prove that his brand of monetarism could cure inflation.

13

End of the Line

Samuelson struggles with describing the Soviet economy
in his *Economics*. And after eighteen years, Samuelson
and Friedman stop writing for *Newsweek*

For a libertarian like Friedman, who believed that total political freedom could only be guaranteed by free-market capitalism, the notion of
"socialism" was an anathema. He fell into the category described by Samuelson as someone for whom "the term 'socialist' is frequently used as a
disparaging stereotype to discredit anyone who believes in social security,
progressive taxation, bank-deposit insurance, some other social improvement, or free love."[1,2] Friedman thought that the burgeoning government
sector that had emerged since World War II as successive governments used
Keynesian measures was stultifying the U.S. economy and that capitalism
would only thrive in the U.S. if free-market forces were left to do their work.
"The experience of recent years . . . raises a doubt whether private ingenuity
can continue to overcome the deadening effects of government control if we
continue to grant ever more power to government,"[3] he wrote.

Be that as it may, Samuelson had set himself the task, through his textbook, of describing not only the way capitalism was supposed to work, but
how it worked in practice. He also felt he should explain in his textbook
the "socialistic" or "social democratic" alternatives to unbridled capitalism

that had been adopted in many countries, including in Britain. For libertarians, even to describe dispassionately how socialism may or may not work in practice was to condone it.[4] But Samuelson was careful to insist that "as a science, economics can concern itself only with the best means of attaining given ends; it cannot prescribe the ends themselves."[5] The problem with Friedman, Samuelson said, was that "[he] thought of himself as a man of science but was in fact more full of passion than he knew."[6]

Samuelson deemed the capitalist system operating in the U.S. imperfect and capable of improvement, but, as Winston Churchill had said about democracy, it remained "the worst form of government except all those other forms that have been tried from time to time."[7] Samuelson's statements, like "There is nothing sacred about the results achieved by a free market system; no, not even if it worked completely without friction and under the most perfectly competitive conditions imaginable," caused many conservatives to doubt the sincerity of Samuelson's devotion to the American way.

From the very first edition of his *Economics* primer in 1948, Samuelson had struggled to make sense of the Soviet command economy. One major problem was that the workings of the Soviet system were kept well hidden from public view and the data issued by the Soviet government were unreliable when they were not downright lies.[8] Still Samuelson tried to fathom what was going on in a society that had notionally abolished the free market from all aspects of daily life and replaced it with a top-down, heavily planned command economy that ignored the material desires of the Russian people. For Friedman, the conspicuously empty shelves of nonexistent consumer goods in GUM, Moscow's flagship department store, were evidence of an economy incapable of serving its population, who were kept incarcerated in their own country lest they emigrate with their skills to a capitalist country.

For Samuelson, the failure of the Soviets to make their economy work for its citizens was as much a failure of management as the failure of the Soviet socialist system itself. He did not rule out that a command economy might in the right circumstances work, though he was careful not to suggest that it would lead to a democratic society. Conspicuous by its absence, however, was any attempt to evaluate the critical importance in the Soviet system of the "black market"—illicit trade in goods and services—that enabled wealthier Russians to circumvent material shortages. Samuelson's attempts to explain communism in practice was colored by the Red Scare that had subsumed so much American political debate in the 1950s, with many academics and idealists considered by many conservatives to be inappropriately sympathetic to America's ideological nemesis. Hence Friedman's pointed snipe at the tacit support for socialism given by "prominent intellectuals" such as Samuelson and Galbraith.[9]

Friedman thought liberal intellectuals too stupid to understand the complexities of the market. "I think a major reason why intellectuals tend to move towards collectivism is that the collectivist answer is a simple one," he told *Reason* magazine in 1974:

> If there's something wrong it's because of some no-good bum, some devil, evil and wicked—that's a very simple story to tell. You don't have to be very smart to write it and you don't have to be very smart to accept it. On the other hand, the individualistic or libertarian argument is a sophisticated and subtle one. If there's something wrong with society, if there's a real social evil, maybe you will make better progress by letting people voluntarily try to eliminate the evil. Therefore, I think, there is in advance a tendency for intellectuals to be attracted to sell the collectivist idea.[10]

Samuelson tried to meet the criticism that he was somehow a fellow traveler who gave communism the benefit of the doubt. By the fifth edition of his *Economics*, in 1961, he was careful to point out the cost to individual Soviet citizens of being deprived of access to the free market. He gave examples of the industrial inefficiency that followed from a centrally based planning authority, one unable to rely upon prices to determine what citizens wanted. The lack of freedom of choice in stores was one subject guaranteed to make any American flinch. "If the local store or commissary had shoes not exactly your size, you were glad to take them a little large rather than do without," Samuelson wrote.

Because a communist economy was incapable of the endless innovation that consumers in the West demanded, and there were no Soviet entrepreneurs to provide attractive new products for the home, Soviet planners turned to America to see what ordinary people wanted. Therefore, "that rare comrade who gets a car—and he is very rare indeed—will find it resembling our cars of the past," he wrote. Statistical goals imposed by Moscow—with "carrots of reward and kicks or imprisonments as penalties" to those who failed to meet them—led to devious manipulation of the data by plant managers. "Stories have been well told where, for example, a transportation enterprise would move carloads of water back and forth in order to be able to say it had accomplished the target to so many ton-miles."

Nonetheless, Samuelson asserted that, while "it is a mistake to think that everyone is miserable [in the Soviet Union], [and that] it is undoubtedly true that few citizens of the West would trade their degree of economic comfort and political freedom for life in the Soviets, it is also true that a Soviet citizen thinks that he is living in a paradise in comparison with life in Communist China." But Samuelson had not been careful enough. A prominent graph in *Economics* comparing the likely future size of U.S. and Soviet economies suggested that, in certain circumstances, Soviet communism could overtake the U.S. in the mid-Nineties. The suggestion was laughable. But Samuelson recovered by declaring which side he believed was right. "It is only too easy to gloss over the tremendous dynamic vitality of our mixed free enterprise system, which, with all its faults, has given the world a century of progress such as [a socialized economy like the Soviet Union] might find it impossible to equal."[11]

By the eleventh edition of *Economics*, published in 1980, Samuelson had amended his textbook so that it reflected the many attempts, by progressive communist leaders in Yugoslavia, Poland, Hungary, Czechoslovakia, and elsewhere, to temper the harshness of the communist system with free-market forces. He adapted his contentious economic growth graph to show that, even in the best-case scenario, the Soviet Union would not overtake the U.S. economy until 2010 at the earliest.

In the final words of the final chapter of the eleventh edition, Samuelson addressed Friedman's contention that political freedoms can only be assured through absolute economic freedom. First, he questioned whether American citizens truly enjoyed the political freedoms that were meant to accompany economic freedom. He invoked the concern of "the younger generation," who doubted that genuine freedom was enjoyed by those who did not prosper under America's market economy:

> What matters it to them that monopoly be less prevalent in 1980 than in 1900—if it still is too much prevalent, and if no great diminution has taken place since 1945.
>
> What to them that the poor are less numerous and less poor than they used to be—if still there persist stubborn inequalities of economic opportunity, and no strong reductions in inequality of income since 1945?
>
> In their eyes, how can a system be deemed satisfactory that still countenances discrimination by race, sex, religion, and ethnic affiliation?

To weigh such concerns against those like Friedman who believed political and economic freedoms to be inextricable, Samuelson paraphrased the arguments against government measures to make Americans more materially equal made by Hayek, Friedman, and their ilk, who, he said, hankered after "the laissez faire dreamworld":

In seeking a better division of the pie, you will reduce the size of the
pie by creating distorting inefficiencies. But more important, personal
and property freedoms are one and inseparable. Only in the Herbert
Spencer[12] laissez faire society that you find so repellent will people be
free to speak their minds and choose their rulers.

And Samuelson offered a graph to disprove Hayek's contention in *The
Road to Serfdom* that creeping government intervention led inevitably to the
diminution of freedom. He plotted Britain's political and economic freedoms enjoyed in 1850—the rule of law, the right of all propertied men
to vote, the freedom of speech, the freedom to publish—and the present
day against the political and economic record of other countries. While
the totalitarian regimes of Hitler's Germany, 1931–1945, and the military
dictatorship in Chile, 1973–1990, clearly enjoyed economic freedom at the
expense of political freedom, Samuelson showed that social-democratic
countries like Norway in the postwar period enjoyed both political and economic freedoms simultaneously. He concluded, "One can try to have the
best of both worlds: Some programmed improvement of the workings of
the market economy, and still those best things of life that aren't measured
in the gross national product—freedom to criticize, freedom to change, and
freedom to do one's own thing."

While Friedman wanted to return as much power to the individual as
possible, even he could not get around the fact that in many respects the
U.S. economy, with its vast public sector, was not so much a free-market
economy as a mixed economy—and likely to be permanently so. The federal
and state governments wielded huge discretionary budgets that, particularly
when Keynesianism was in the ascendant, had been used to manage the
economy. Social programs including pensions, Medicare, and safety nets
for the poor could not be cut without inviting great political anguish. There
was an elaborate system of government regulations, levies, subsidies, and

tariffs imposed, often at the urging of private businesses, in the face of free-market thinking.

The U.S. private sector was a poor example of unbridled capitalism, with legal monopoly corporations imposing higher prices than a free market would deliver, and a system of government that allowed businesses, through expensive lobbying of Congress, to alter laws to improve their profitability.[13] Even Friedman's trademark policy—insisting that the Federal Reserve provide a steady, slow increase in the supply of money to keep inflation low and predictable—acknowledged as appropriate the role of an unelected government body in creating economic stability.

BY 1981, writing for *Newsweek* had become a chore for Samuelson. The original reason for his agreement to venture into journalism was that the magazine was read by millions around the world. He was handsomely paid for his efforts. Beginning at $750 a column in 1968, or $5,756 in 2020 dollars, by December 1974 Elliott was able to write to him that "the mills of *Newsweek's* Wage-Price Control Board grind slowly," but that from the first day of the new year, he would be given a 15 percent increase, bringing his annual fee to $23,000, or $170,383 in 2020 dollars. In addition, from 1976 onwards, Samuelson's and Friedman's appearances at *Newsweek* marketing events provided a further $1,000 per turn. Fourteen years on, however, Samuelson had no need for publicity, nor for money—his textbook had many years before made him a multimillionaire—nor did he need an outlet to express his views. His fame and reputation meant that any serious publication would happily offer a platform for his views.

Then came an incident that caused him to consider how much he needed *Newsweek*. In 1974, Samuelson had written to *Newsweek's* editor in chief, Oz Elliott, asking for clarification about the ground rules of his column and its contents. "I had thought that it appeared under my by-line and that I alone was essentially responsible for its contents (profanity and treason aside)." He recounted an incident in which two *Newsweek* editors had held out a column by him that discussed *Time on the Cross: The Economics of American Negro Slavery* by economists Robert Fogel and Stanley L. Engerman, because the book had been reviewed in the magazine three weeks before. They asked for a replacement column. "I in turn could not have been nicer in my reaction," Samuelson told Elliott. "I set to work Saturday morning and wrote an entirely new column." But he was unhappy about the decision.

His column had "embodied what earlier and lay notices could not do, namely, my benefiting from reading some hundreds of pages of the Fogel-Engerman selection and analysis of data," he wrote. "Without displaying a prickly concern for the niceties, I'd still like some statement of the guidelines. If making even a little fuss inhibits my getting suggestions in the future about possible topics and feedbacks on earlier columns, then I have not succeeded in putting the matter in the low-keyed way I had aimed for."[14] The *Newsweek* managing editor, who had been involved in the decision to hold out the original column, intercepted the letter to Elliott, who was "traveling in Asia," and offered an explanation. "Your notion that you are essentially responsible for the content of the column is correct," he wrote. "I certainly have no desire to alter what has plainly has [*sic*] been a very fruitful mode of operation, both for you and the magazine,"[15] before reiterating his belief that the original column was unsuitable.

Journalism, however, is a fickle master and often so concerned with logging an account of the immediate past that it has little time for inherited memory. Seven years later, in 1981, Samuelson reviewed his old friend and somewhat rival J. K. Galbraith's memoirs, *A Life in Our Times*. Samuelson on Galbraith would seem to be a perfect "get" for a news magazine, and one which readers would consider a perfect match of subject and author. But the new chief editor at *Newsweek*, Lester Bernstein, thought differently.

He repeated the calumny that had so upset Samuelson in 1974. "I've been unable to reach you to let you know I dropped the piece on Galbraith's memoirs this week because we reviewed the book rather thoroughly three weeks ago . . . and I didn't feel we could justify dealing with it again." Samuelson was incensed. "It had been my understanding that columns that appeared under my name did so under my responsibility," he wrote to Bernstein. "It is now necessary to terminate my *Newsweek* affiliation." He did not rescind his decision.

Samuelson's departure led to an anguished letter from *Newsweek*'s owner and a personal friend, Katharine Graham. "I am truly sorry to lose your column for *Newsweek*—and over such a sad misunderstanding," she wrote. "It has added immeasurable stature and intellectual content to the magazine. We will miss it and so will *Newsweek*'s readers." Bernstein left the magazine the following year.

BY 1983, Friedman, too, became irritated by his treatment at *Newsweek* and wrote to the editor in chief, William Broyles Jr.,[16] to complain. In the past, because of a shortage of space, his columns had on rare occasions been held over and published the following week. Now such delays were commonplace. "My column has appeared on time less frequently than it has been postponed," he wrote. "I have always tried to make my columns as topical as possible. I cannot do that if I do not know whether the column will appear next week, two weeks later, or three weeks later. I do not write columns for cold storage." Then came a threat. "My activities with *Newsweek* have been a source of great satisfaction to me. I have been very pleased with the relationship we have had," he wrote. "I would not like to see it terminate, but quite frankly it is not worth continuing unless that can be done under conditions that are satisfactory to both you and me."[17]

Column writing suited Friedman. As a natural gadfly, the short, sharp

jab at a subject proved to be his perfect format. He relished the task and happily paid testament to the magazine's editors "for offering me so effective a
forum for communicating with the public."

> The task has been challenging and highly rewarding. . . . It has pro-
> duced a stream of reactions from readers—sometimes flattering, some-
> times abusive, but always instructive. I have learned in the process how
> easy it is to be misunderstood or—to say the same thing—how hard
> it is to be crystal clear. I have learned also how numerous are the per-
> spectives from which any issue may be viewed. There is no such thing
> as a purely economic issue.[18]

Friedman admitted to "mixed feelings" when in early 1984 a new *Newsweek* editor in chief, Richard M. Smith, ended Friedman's columns—along
with the columns of Samuelson's replacement, Lester Thurow,[19] who would
become dean of the MIT Sloan School of Management at about the same
time. "I must candidly say I regret its termination,"[20] Friedman wrote to
Smith. Friedman was immediately offered columns in the conservative *Wall
Street Journal* and in Rupert Murdoch's conservative papers in the U.S. and
Britain, but he decided to take a break from deadline journalism. From then
on, like Samuelson, he would write occasional columns[21] as and when the
mood took him.

14

The Grocer's Daughter

Friedman's U.S. monetarist experiment ended in tears.
But in London, Thatcher gave his ideas another chance.
And, unlike Volcker, she was a true believer

British monetarism didn't start with Margaret Thatcher. James Callaghan's Labour Government, which preceded Thatcher's election victory in 1979, was dogged by debt and inflation. By 1975, inflation in the U.K. had reached 26 percent and basic hourly wages were up 32 percent year on year. Callaghan's chancellor of the exchequer, Denis Healey, found the old Keynesian tools did not work as well as they had in the past. As he explained:

> The fundamental concept of demand management had become unreliable. Keynes believed that a government could maintain full employment of a country's productive capacity without creating inflation, by reducing the demand for output, through adjusting taxes or government spending. But it had become impossible to discover with any accuracy how much additional demand the government should inject into the economy so as to produce full employment.
>
> It was equally impossible to know how many people would use the money you did inject by cutting taxes or increasing public spend-

ing. Or it might go into higher wages or profits, creating more inflation rather than more jobs. It might be used to buy foreign rather than
British goods, so worsening the balance of payments and creating jobs
abroad instead of in Britain. Or it might be saved instead of spent.[1]

Like Richard Nixon and others around the world, to counter inflation
Callaghan and Healey imposed an incomes policy to limit wage raises,
trusting in their influence within the trade-union movement that financed
Labour to curb high pay demands. For Healey, it was a no-brainer. "Whatever governments may claim, none can avoid having some sort of pay policy,
if only because they themselves employ millions of men and women." For a
country like Britain with a large public sector, enacting a pay policy was an
obvious choice. Within a year, the measure appeared to be working. From
a high of 26.9 percent in August 1975, inflation halved to 12.9 percent by
July 1976. But Healey was aware of trouble ahead. "Adopting a pay policy is
rather like jumping out of a second-floor window," he wrote. "No one in his
senses would do it unless the stairs were on fire. But in postwar Britain the
stairs have always been on fire."[2]

Callaghan's son-in-law, Peter Jay,[3] was economics editor of *The Times*,
London, and, like many younger voices in his trade and within the financial sector, had been an early adopter of monetarism. He had even given
a lecture to economists praising its virtues.[4] Jay found a ready disciple for
his monetarist reasoning in his *Times* editor, William Rees-Mogg, who was
always looking to propagate the latest in American conservative thinking.
Taking Friedman at his most literal, and reducing monetarism to a simplistic truism, Rees-Mogg set out to show there was a direct one-to-one cor-
relation between increases in the money supply and increases in prices. The
headline of his piece said it all: "How a 9.4% Excess Money Supply Gave
Britain 9.4% inflation."[5]

Support from *The Times* was a significant catch for Friedman. But far
more important to the clash between a defensive Keynesianism and a floun-

dering, almost mystical monetarism, was that, over long country walks at Callaghan's farm, Jay had persuaded the prime minister that the days of Britain living on borrowed cash from abroad was inflationary and that financial continence could be regained.

Callaghan took Jay's lessons to heart. In September 1976, at the Labour Party conference in Blackpool, he delivered a speech that would mark the end of Keynesianism as the principal guiding tool of economic policy in Britain. Jay himself had written the key passage in Callaghan's address. It read:

> Britain has lived for too long on borrowed time, borrowed money, borrowed ideas. . . . For too long this country has been ready to settle for borrowing money abroad to maintain our standards of life, instead of grappling with the fundamental problems of British industry. . . . The cozy world we were told would go on for ever, where full employment would be guaranteed by a stroke of the Chancellor's pen, cutting taxes, deficit spending, that cozy world is gone.
>
> We used to think that you could spend your way out of a recession, and increase employment by cutting taxes and boosting Government spending. I tell you in all candor that that option no longer exists, and that in so far as it ever did exist, it only worked on each occasion since the war by injecting a bigger dose of inflation into the economy, followed by a higher level of unemployment as the next step.[6]

Callaghan's stark message was not heeded. Union leaders could not contain grassroots pressure for higher pay. And as Labour's incomes policy started to flounder, as union leaders ignored their government's requests to temper their wage demands, and inflation began to return, Healey found himself bombarded with advice from commentators and financial analysts to embrace the simple solution offered by Friedman.

Friedman had established a profile in Britain as a mad American professor with way-out views on economics. He had become a celebrity on British television, like an Archie Bunker with brains, whose every appearance was guaranteed to create controversy. At a dinner thrown by Queen Elizabeth for Ronald Reagan on the royal yacht *Britannia* anchored off Santa Barbara in 1983, the monarch had warmly greeted Friedman with, "I know you. Philip [her husband, the Duke of Edinburgh] is always watching you on the telly."[7]

In a BBC television interview, Friedman banged the drum for the free market—"If you take off this straitjacket that you have fastened on yourselves, give people an incentive, you would be amazed at the results which could be achieved"—and warned that Britain faced the "collapse of democracy and freedom, the substitution of a command economy for the free economy, of totalitarian society," unless it abandoned the welfare state. He noticed Callaghan's tip to monetarism at Blackpool and said he had been heartened by the prime minister's apparent conversion. "If that is more than words, if it means a fundamental change in the direction of policy, then I will have to revise my probabilities," he said.

In short order, then, Friedman's monetarism had become the official policy of the United Kingdom. It remained unclear to many Keynesian economics professors that they had just suffered a massive defeat. The complacency emanating from academia was hard for some to comprehend. Ian Gilmour, who in 1979 became a prominent member of Thatcher's government and a relentless critic from within of its monetarist policies, believed that mainstream Keynesian economists had failed to mount a sturdy enough response to Friedman's theory. "Most academic economists pursued their recondite studies undisturbed," Gilmour later wrote. "In the resulting near-vacuum, the monetarists prospered like Jehovah's Witnesses when the Churches slumber. And important conversions were made in Fleet Street, in the City, and in the Conservative Party."[8]

Healey, who faced a barrage of monetarist advice, immediately grasped the key problem with putting monetarism into practice. "No one has yet found an adequate definition of money, no one knows how to control it, and no one except Friedman himself is certain exactly how the control of money supply will influence inflation, which is supposed to be its only purpose," Healey wrote. "Moreover, the monetary statistics are as unreliable as all the others."[9] Healey found that to appease the head of steam behind monetarism in the City of London, which set the weather of the British economy, there was little alternative but, like Volcker across the Atlantic, to pay prominent lip service to the money supply.

Like Volcker, Healey started publishing monetary forecasts that, because they were largely meaningless, had until then been kept secret. "Because I managed to keep the growth of £M3 (then the favored measure of money in the UK) averaging ten percent throughout my five years, I kept the markets quiet," he wrote. Friedman, however, remained unimpressed by Healey's efforts, telling NBC's *Meet the Press* in October 1976, "Britain is on the verge of collapse."[10] He told a newspaper a week later, "I fear very much that the odds are at least 50-50 that within the next five years British freedom and democracy, as we have seen it, will be destroyed."[11]

While Labour governed, the focus was on their economic policies. But Gilmour noticed a change taking place in the Conservative Party, too. Monetarism was on the march. The most successful democratic party in the Western world had triumphed from century to century because, like many British people, it was ignorant and distrustful of concepts and ideologies. "The dominant traits in the Conservative intellectual tradition, to be found in Halifax, Hume, Burke, Coleridge, Disraeli and Salisbury, are skepticism, a sense of the limitations of human reason, a rejection of abstraction or abstract doctrines, a distrust of systems and a belief instead in the importance of experience and of 'circumstance,'" Gilmour wrote. "For Conservatives to embrace monetarism was contrary to all of them."[12]

Traditional Conservative institutional skepticism, which had served the party so well for so long, was about to make way for a devotion to ideas that affronted many old-school Tories. The defeat of the moderate Tory Edward Heath at the hands of the similarly moderate Labour leader and former prime minister Harold Wilson in the general election of February 1974, followed later by a more resounding defeat in October 1974, set off soul searching within the Conservative Party. Some questioned the unwritten settlement followed by all postwar Conservative premiers—Winston Churchill, Anthony Eden, Harold Macmillan, Alec Douglas-Home, and Heath—that the clear message of the landslide victory of Clement Attlee's Labour Party in 1945 should be respected and the voters' demand for a welfare state, including a government-run healthcare system, should not be contradicted.

The postwar consensus between the parties had proved hugely beneficial to the Tories. Although it seemed the electorate wanted benign intervention from Westminster to ease their lives, they appeared to trust Conservatives more than Labour to run the system. After Attlee lost the 1951 election, Labour had struggled to win back the confidence of the British people, with huge defeats in the elections of 1955 and 1959. Meanwhile "one nation" conservatism, which embraced all the people rather than merely the better off, inspired by the Victorian Conservative prime minister Benjamin Disraeli, had proved hugely popular. Macmillan, prime minister at the general election of 1959, even boasted of the achievements of the mixed economy in a slogan that rang true to voters: "You've never had it so good."

Dogged by sex scandals and weak leadership, the Tories found themselves in Opposition between 1964 and 1970, but, on winning the 1970 election, Heath's government soon ran into the sand. It attempted to break out of the boom-and-bust of the business cycle with a daring, even reckless bid for faster growth. Public expenditure was boosted and restrictions on business relaxed. But the consequence was roaring inflation, met by trade-union demands for higher pay.

Like Nixon, Carter, and Callaghan, Heath imposed a mandatory wages policy, but the unions were not prepared to moderate their claims. In the fall of 1973, in pursuit of a 35 percent increase in wages, a punishing and bitter overtime ban by the National Union of Mineworkers cut supplies to power stations and brought the nation to an abrupt halt. Without the ability to move coal supplies from mines to factories and power plants, Heath imposed a three-day working week on all except essential industries. Television stations were shut down at 10:30 p.m. to save electricity. Heath's days as prime minister were numbered.

As were his days as Conservative leader. A group of MPs who blamed Heath's economic policies for the mayhem gathered around the Centre for Policy Studies (CPS), a free-market think tank set up by a former minister for social services, Keith Joseph,[13] and Margaret Thatcher, a former minister of education. The Centre was run by Alfred Sherman,[14] a maverick dogmatist who had fought for the antifascist Republicans in the Spanish Civil War.

In the six months between Heath's twin defeats of 1974, Joseph had tied his colors to the monetarist mast in a mea culpa speech at Preston—penned by Sherman, the *Financial Times* economics commentator Sam Brittan, and another prominent CPS member, Alan Walters[15]—whose title, echoing Friedman, questioned the postwar Conservative orthodoxy that blamed inflation on the unions. It read: "Inflation is Caused by Governments."[16]

"I begin by accepting my full share of the collective responsibility," Joseph said. Incomes policies, like the one which led to Heath's defeat, Joseph dismissed as "like trying to stop water coming out of a leaky hose without turning off the tap. If you stop one hole it will find two others."

Then, with a flourish, Joseph declared himself a true believer in Friedmanite monetarism. It sounded like a religious conversion. "I once believed that much of our inflation, particularly recently, was a product of rocketing world prices," said Joseph. But he had been wrong all along, duped by wicked Keynesians. "In more specifically economic terms, our inflation has been the result of the creation of new money—and the consequent deficit financing—out of proportion to the additional goods and services available." Heath was unimpressed and dismissed Joseph's defection as "a good man fallen amongst monetarists. They've robbed him of all his judgment. Not that he ever had much in the first place."[17]

Joseph's newfound rationale was pure Friedman. He quipped that "when the money supply grows too quickly, inflation results." At first you may not feel the full benefits of the monetarist medicine; in fact the opposite would be the case. But in time the economy would be restored to natural good health, he said. He, like Friedman, could not promise results overnight, but in "a year or two" everything would be fine.

Joseph broke with an ancient shibboleth at the core of the postwar consensus; that Keynesian economics was needed to ward off a return of the chronic unemployment that had cursed Britain's jobless Twenties and Thirties. Unlike the U.S. economy, which boomed during the 1920s, Britain suffered mass unemployment from the end of World War I in 1918, thanks to the Conservative government's "sound money" policy, which fixed the price of the pound sterling too high. British goods became uncompetitive on the world market, throwing millions of Britons out of work. The failure of the Tories to remedy such a vast human tragedy was to cast a long shadow over British politics for the next fifty years. It prompted at the end of World War II in 1945 the defeat of the war leader Winston Churchill and a landslide electoral victory for Clement Attlee's progressive Labour Party. Attlee's "cradle to grave" welfare state proved so popular that the Tories were obliged to adopt it as their own. The notion of "sound money" fell into disfavor. "To us, as to all post-war governments, sound money may have seemed out-of-date," Joseph explained. "We were dominated by the fear of unemployment. We were haunted by the fear of long-term mass unemployment, the grim, hopeless dole queues and towns which died."

Without evident irony, Joseph invoked the ghost of Keynes to justify his embrace of Friedman's monetarism:

From what Keynes wrote, it seems likely that he would have disowned most of the allegedly Keynesian remedies urged on us in his name and which have caused so much harm. His thesis was that even when there was large-scale medium and long-term involuntary unemployment, the proper way of dealing with it would not necessarily be to increase the money supply or demand. [The opposite was in fact the case; the deliberate stoking of aggregate demand by the government and the disregard of conventional concerns about the money supply lay at the heart of Keynes's revolutionary *General Theory*.]

The cure for unemployment was to modify the rate of increase in the supply of money and rely on the free market to provide an optimum equilibrium for prosperity. "If we can in fact gradually start moderating the trend rate of growth of money supply—which entails also moderating the budget deficit—then the balance of payments deficit, and after a lag, the rate of inflation will start to ease. In due course, and without any artificial stimulus or reflation, spontaneous in-built correctives will begin to make themselves felt."[18] And thus, without mentioning Friedman by name, Joseph set the Conservative Party on a Friedmanite monetarist course.

While Volcker in Washington, D.C., kept Friedman and his monetarist ideas at arm's length, in London Friedman's stock began to rise. The British government enjoyed the absolute obedience of its central bank, the Bank of England, an arrangement envied by American presidents. When Heath's failed incomes policy led to his removal from Downing Street, Friedman was given a boost by the election in 1975 of Margaret Thatcher to lead the Conservatives. The woman who became the Leader of the Opposition would almost certainly become the next prime minister of Britain.

The election to replace Heath as Tory leader was, like so much of British Conservative politics in those days, a shambles that owed more to the arcane workings of a St. James's gentlemen's club than a modern political party. A bastion of male chauvinism, the Tories had little intention of electing a woman to lead them. There was a short line of eminently suitable gray men ready to allow their names to be put forward to replace Heath. But Heath wasn't budging and remained on the ticket. And one by one the frontrunners began to drop out.

First, the leader of the coup, the twitching, conspicuously hyperanxious Joseph, in a speech also penned by Alfred Sherman, sank his chances by suggesting that the poor deserved their plight.[19] Then for a while the back-bench MPs' leader, Sir Edward du Cann,[20] headed the list, until his financial dealings were considered a scandal waiting to be exposed. A little too late, Heath abandoned the race and encouraged his bumbling sidekick Willie Whitelaw[21] to set off in pursuit of Thatcher, who by then had established a firm lead. The satirical magazine *Private Eye*'s cover pictured Whitelaw in a pinafore, his hands plunged deep in a soapy bowl of dishes, saying: "If it's a woman you want, I'm your man."

It was too late to stop the Thatcher bandwagon. When the final tally was counted, she was the last man standing. In the excitement of electing a woman leader, few Conservatives, either in Parliament or around the country, realized they had also voted to abandon the postwar consensus for a set of beliefs that had remained dormant since before World War II. "A number of Conservatives had never liked the mixed economy, which they regarded as a long step towards a socialist state," recalled Gilmour. "The contention of Friedman that government intervention was invariably self-defeating was, therefore, in tune with their prejudices."[22]

Heath took a less charitable view. He spoke for all Keynesians when he wrote:

> The Conservative Party had rightly criticized socialists for their attachment to doctrinal, impractical ideas. The purpose of politics is to bring benefit to one's country, not to experiment with academic theories.
>
> Monetarism, the idea that inflation is a purely monetary phenomenon, the product of nothing more than an increase in the money supply, is perhaps the most deceptively simplistic of all economic theories. As such, it was always likely to be especially attractive to those whose understanding of economics was limited.[23]

Thatcher's devotion to Friedmanite monetarism was not intellectual; it was visceral. "There is no better course for understanding free-market economics than life in a corner shop," the grocer's daughter from Grantham, Lincolnshire, would later reflect. "I was thus inoculated against the conventional economic wisdom of post-war Britain." She wrote:

> Primarily under the influence of Keynes, but also of socialism, the emphasis during these years was on the ability of government to improve economic conditions by direct and constant intervention. . . . Whereas a household which spent beyond its income was on the road to ruin, this was (according to the New Economics) for states the path to prosperity and full employment. . . . Before I ever read a page of Milton Friedman . . . I just knew that these assertions could not be true. Thrift was a virtue and profligacy a vice.[24]

While Joseph had encouraged Thatcher to read Hayek's *Road to Serfdom* and Friedman's *Free to Choose*, her conversion to Friedman's monetarism was a short step from an existing devotion to the free-market ideas of her hero Enoch Powell.[25] The intellectually brilliant, high flying Conservative MP's career was cut short in 1968 by his lurid suggestion in a speech in Birmingham that nonwhite immigration would lead to bloodshed on Britain's streets. Quoting Virgil's *Aeneid*[26] (Powell was a classics professor), "I am filled with foreboding. Like the Roman, I seem to see 'the River Tiber foaming with much blood,' "[27] Powell became for many a pariah within the mainstream Conservative Party, but an inspiration for some on the far right.

Powell's reputation as an unswerving free-market advocate had been cemented in November 1956 when, as financial secretary to the Treasury, he had resigned over the issue of sound money. Along with the chancellor, Peter Thorneycroft,[28] and Treasury minister Nigel Birch,[29] Powell resigned from the government rather than increase government spending without imposing commensurate new taxation, which he and the others considered inflationary. Their argument was simple, old-school monetarism.

Thatcher, whose ambition to become a minister meant that her admiration for the renegade Powell had to be kept well hidden, considered Powell's 1969 collection of reactionary speeches, *Freedom and Reality*,[30] "My Bible." When elected Conservative leader, her prior restraint about promoting Powell's sound money views gave way to the championing of the doctrine he held dear.

In 1976, she penned a glowing introduction to a CPS publication of Joseph's Stockton Lecture given that year, titled "Monetarism is Not Enough,"[31] in which her political guru lavishly praised monetarism. "If we desire a monetary framework within which steady growth and high levels of employment can be achieved," he said, "we have no alternative but to maintain a stable money supply eschewing the use of demand creation as a short cut to growth and full employment."

In his invocation of a sound money policy to purge inflation and restore the economy, Joseph invoked the notion of a free-market Eden in which everything would end up at a perfect equilibrium that provides endless prosperity. Quoting himself, from a lecture in 1974, Joseph claimed that getting the money supply right provided a solid foundation on which the rest of the economy was built. Monetarism would unleash pent-up free-market forces, liberate the economy, and make it more efficient.

"Monetary control is a pre-essential for everything else we need and want to do," he had said. "An opportunity to tackle the real problems— labor shortage in one place, unemployment in another; exaggerated expectations; inefficiencies, frictions and distortions; hard-core unemployment; the hundreds of thousands who need training or retraining or persuading to move if they are to have steady, satisfactory jobs; unstable world prices."

Thatcher, a research chemist by trade, agreed entirely with Joseph's thinking. Like Ronald Reagan, she was that unusual thing, a book-reading conservative interested in ideas for their own sake. She enjoyed political theory and found it inspirational. She liked nothing better than a good argument and was aggressive and persistent in pursuit of her goals. When she grasped Friedman's argument that, when it came to inflation, only the money supply mattered, she was delighted by its simplicity. She promptly adopted the defeat of inflation by monetary means as her principal economic policy.

Unlike her predecessors, Thatcher made clear that her Conservative Party would stick unswervingly to a specific set of beliefs—there was so much at stake she would not tolerate dissent. To this end, she provided members of her shadow cabinet with a reading list, drawn up by Sherman and Joseph, that included Hayek, Friedman, and other conservative or libertarian heroes.

In 1977, with a general election looming, Thatcher asked Joseph to compile a new economic policy that would owe nothing to Heath. Published in the pamphlet "The Right Approach to the Economy," it advocated "strict control by the Government of the rate of growth of the money supply."

When the Conservatives won a majority of the Commons in May 1979, making Thatcher prime minister, she appointed Geoffrey Howe,[32] an obedient and competent barrister, to carry out changes to the Treasury's approach to reducing inflation. A hurriedly arranged budget introduced a number of reforms—a reduction in direct taxation on individuals; a switch from income taxes to indirect taxes on goods and services, known as Value Added Tax—that laid the foundations for the introduction of monetarism in Britain.

Friedman was ecstatic at Thatcher's victory. It would allow his monetarism to be given a second chance, this time with a single-minded, stubborn individual who, armed with a considerable majority, had complete control of all aspects of government. And if reducing the size of the state and the application of monetarism succeeded in Britain, the Federal Reserve might have second thoughts about the policy. Heath observed from the sidelines "an administration that talked of the market as some sort of deity which must never be affronted."[33] Samuelson visited Britain early in 1980, when Thatcher's monetarist experiment had barely started. He reported to *Newsweek* readers, "British price inflation still rages, despite pedantic allegiance to a naïve monetarism."[34]

In June 1980, much to the alarm of her senior colleagues, Thatcher invited Friedman to address the economic ministers[35] in her Cabinet, leaving them alone with Friedman so he could put them straight on policy. "The meeting generated an interesting and spirited discussion," recalled Friedman, "especially after Mrs. Thatcher left, asking me to instruct some of the 'wets'[36] in her cabinet." While in London, Friedman also addressed a key Commons economics committee, saying he welcomed the chance to explain monetarism to British lawmakers because its realization in Britain would have "an important effect" on economic policy in the United States. He declared:

> I strongly approve of the general outlines of the monetary strategy outlined by the Government: taking monetary growth as the major intermediate target; stating in advance targets for a number of years ahead; setting targets that require a steady and gradual reduction in monetary growth; and stressing the Government's intentions of strictly adhering to those targets.[37]

He believed targets set for the growth of £M3 in March to be "of the right order of magnitude, and were set to decline at about the right rate." He said Britain's approach was in stark contrast to that of the United States, which offered a particularly "egregious example" of central bankers paying lip service to monetary targets without following appropriate constraints. Few had made decisions that matched their profession of faith in sound money. Most had instead tried to control monetary aggregates, interest rates, and foreign exchange rates, "in the process introducing excessive variability into all three." Friedman blamed the failure to obey the strictures of monetarism on "bureaucratic inertia."

But he warned that the British government's policy since the Budget of 1981 of sharply reducing public borrowing [reducing the PSBR, or the public sector borrowing requirement to pay for services] as a means of suppressing monetary growth was inappropriate, as there was "no necessary relation between the size of the PSBR and monetary growth." Government spending, not government borrowing, was the key indicator, and government expenditure should be reduced.

The best means of controlling the money supply, Friedman argued, was control of the "monetary base," the purchase and sale of government bonds by the Bank of England to clearing banks. "Control of the monetary base should be exercised through open market operations primarily in short-term debt, which, with a single reserve asset, would no longer be close to a perfect substitute for base money," he wrote. "The Bank should decide in advance each week how much to buy or sell, not the price at which it will buy or sell. It should permit interest rates to be determined entirely by the market." The price of sterling, too, should not be maintained by government intervention but left to the free market.

As for the inevitable economic downturn as money tightened, "Unemployment and excess capacity are an unfortunate side effect of reducing inflation, not a cure—just as staying in bed is a side effect of an appendicitis operation, not a cure for appendicitis." What was causing the contraction? "The slowing of [public] spending in response to the slowing of monetary growth and the inevitable lags in the absorption of slower spending by wages and prices."[38]

So much for the theory. In practice, the experience of British monetarism was unrelentingly horrible. Mass unemployment, which Joseph had once dismissed as a bogus scourge inspired by liberal guilt—"We found it hard to avoid the feeling that somehow the lean and tight-lipped mufflered men in the 1930s dole queue were at least partly our fault"[39]—returned with a vengeance.

In the first two years of Thatcher's government, unemployment rose from 5.5 percent to 11 percent—that is, from 1 million to 2.3 million. Around 3 million would remain unemployed for the rest of the 1980s. In the summer of 1981, there was widespread civil unrest on Britain's streets, with violent rioting in the cities of London, Manchester, and Liverpool.

The deleterious effect of monetarism on the British economy was evident. As one Bank of England official put it, "In the summer of 1980 you only had to look out of the window to see that monetary policy was too tight."[40]

Industrial output fell 6 percent, the largest one-year drop in output since 1921. Interest rates leapt from 12 percent under Healey to a high of 17 percent in November 1979 under Howe, where they remained for eight months. A balance-of-payments crisis was provoked by the high price of sterling caused by high interest rates, making British exports more expensive than their competitors' while making imports cheaper.

Friedman had warned that imposing monetarism would be painful. "If you cut down the rate in the money supply, you will go through a period of unemployment, slow growth, pain, in return for which you will come out after an interval into a period in which you'll have rapid economic growth without inflation," he wrote.[41]

Heath, meanwhile, had warned that monetarism would prove too painful to introduce. "I was convinced that a further, more severe, dose of monetarism from a Conservative government would bring misery to many Britons, and deep unpopularity for the party," he wrote. "Common sense suggested that a more judicious mix of economic policy should be used."[42]

But few in Thatcher's government had expected things to go so wrong so quickly. Whitelaw, Thatcher's Home Secretary, whose job it was to contain the street protests with squads of riot police, was openly alarmed that a Conservative government had brought the country to the edge of chaos and anarchy. And, to add insult to injury, the new economic policy missed all the monetary targets it had set itself.

Heath, sidelined to the backbenches, was scathing. He wrote:

The main reason for the government's failure was that monetarism is self-defeating. The unemployment created by the crude application of tight monetary policy after 1979 meant that public spending could not be brought down. Benefits had to be paid for, and many people who could have been paying taxes were forced instead to look to the state for help. Similarly, companies which would have been paying corporation tax went bankrupt. . . . [43]

The decimation of manufacturing industry, which lost over one-sixth of its capacity between the second quarter of 1979 and the first quarter of 1981, meant that, when recovery eventually came, there was sure to be a balance of payments crisis. . . . The 1981 budget . . . further reduced demand during the depths of the worst recession since the 1930s.[44]

What was to be done?

The whole subject of monetarism had grown so toxic that a secret report to discover what was going wrong at the Treasury was hastily commissioned by Thatcher from the monetarist economist Jürg Niehans[45] of Bern University, who was invited to look at the books and offer a remedy. Niehans was paid by the privately funded CPS, not the Treasury, so that the damning conclusion that monetarism was being too tightly applied would not have to be published, as all taxpayer-funded reports were. Monetary policy in Britain, Niehans concluded, "appears to have been more abrupt than even the most ardent monetarists advocated,"[46] and because the money supply was too tight, it should be allowed to rise without delay.

In the March 1981 budget, with inflation at 13 percent, Howe quietly forgot about monetary targets, cut government borrowing by £3 billion, and froze income tax allowances, which in the light of the record high inflation amounted to an increase of £4 billion in personal taxes. By raising taxes in the middle of a recession, Howe's budget ran counter to all conventional economic wisdom.

Thatcher recalled the choice her government faced:

> If you believed, as [our critics] did, that increased government borrow-
> ing was the way to get out of recession, then our approach was inex-
> plicable. If, on the other hand, you thought, as we did, that the way
> to get industry moving again was above all to get down interest rates,
> then you had to reduce government borrowing. . . . I doubt that there
> has ever been a clearer test of two fundamentally different approaches
> to economic management.[47]

While Howe was announcing the details of his budget in the Commons, previously loyal Conservative MPs walked out of the chamber in
disgust. A group of 364 prominent economists, including a future governor
of the Bank of England and two Nobel Prize winners in economics, wrote a
letter to *The Times* (London) claiming that the budget had "no basis in economic theory or supporting evidence" and that it threatened Britain's "social
and political stability."[48] Thatcher shrugged.

Friedman tried to persuade Thatcher to abandon the monetary target
of £M3 in favor of "monetary base control," which would limit the monthly
extension of new government debt, but this approach was dismissed by both
the Bank of England and the Treasury as certain to cause volatile interest
rates that would disrupt the economy, just as had happened in the U.S. To
all intents and purposes, by the summer of 1981, monetarism in the U.K.
was dead.

Nonetheless, in September that year, Thatcher fired all those who
objected to her monetarist policies, among them Gilmour, who declared:

"It does no harm to throw the occasional man overboard, but it does not do much good if you are steering full speed ahead for the rocks."[49]

The purge of the "wets" was merely vindictive. Gilmour and the other opponents of monetarism in the cabinet had argued that the application of Friedman's untried economic dogma was causing mayhem in the British economy and should stop. And that is exactly what happened. Because none of the monetary targets Howe had set could be met, from the 1981 budget onward monetarism in Britain was abandoned. From then on, it would be interest rates and the price of the pound sterling, not the money supply, that were the key targets on which to base policy.

A monetarist rump in the government, who believed that monetarism had never been given a chance, ensured that some lip service continued to be made to monetarist goals, and from 1981 to 1985, while monetary targets were retained, they were repeatedly readjusted upward to match the largely meaningless Treasury estimates of monetary measures. John Fforde, an executive director of the Bank of England and a persistent skeptic about the use of money-supply figures, was able officially to report that "except in some grave emergency, or in the initial phase of a novel strategy, the abandonment of judgment in favor of some simple, rigid, quantitative rule about the money supply does not reliably deliver acceptable results."[50]

In June 1983, Howe was replaced by Nigel Lawson,[51] who continued the retreat from monetarism, abandoning the goal of eliminating inflation in favor of keeping it low—below 5 percent—and maintaining a steady exchange rate and a rising gross domestic product.

In October 1983, Lawson delivered the annual chancellor's address to prominent members of the financial community at the Mansion House in the City of London, and acknowledged that "monetary targets have not been, nor have ever intended to be, a form of automatic pilot. Over the years we have adjusted the targets themselves; and we have always sought to take account of shifts in the demand for money."[52]

In October 1985, Lawson formally announced that the targeting of

£M3 was suspended for the rest of the year. And in the March 1986 budget, the target for £M3 was set for a single year, not the three or four years ahead that Howe had introduced. The Treasury and Civil Service Select Committee of the House of Commons, in its report on the 1986 Budget, noted that "skepticism at the continued use of £M3 as a target aggregate stems in part from the fact that the authorities now seem to have virtually no control over it."[53]

In October 1986, the governor of the Bank of England, Robin Leigh-Pemberton, declared, in a lecture at Loughborough University, "It cannot be said that our experience with our chosen framework for operating monetary policy has been satisfactory," and he questioned the wisdom of continuing to target £M3 and other broad monetary aggregates.[54] The following financial year, 1987–1988, the targeting of £M3 was abandoned for good.

Having been sidelined by Volcker in Washington, D.C., now Friedman's monetarism was closed down in London, too. It was the killer blow. Never again would there be a chance to convert two such vast economies as the U.S. and the U.K. The opportunity to leave an indelible mark on the world, through economies with a low, steady level of inflation brought about by a steady increase in the money supply, was spent.

Friedman could hardly complain that the British did not have the power and the personality to make monetarism work. Unlike in the U.S. system, Thatcher had enjoyed total power. She kept monetarist theoreticians Alan Walters and Brian Griffiths[55] as private advisers, mainly to intimidate her chancellors into sticking to her economic priorities. She had wanted the theory to work, but when it didn't, she did not spare a moment to shed a tear. She abandoned Friedman to his fate and moved on.[56]

Still there was a lingering desire within Conservative Central Office to suggest that Britain's brush with monetarism had been a triumph, rather than a disaster. Thatcher found it hard to admit that she was ever at fault, so her party managers were obliged through a fanciful fiction to explain why, despite the abandonment of monetarism in 1981, she had been right all along.

The Campaign Guide for 1987, intended to keep all Conservative candidates singing from the same hymn sheet, reported that the "green paper" on monetarism, published by the government in 1980, "explicitly stated that to assess underlying monetary conditions properly it was necessary to take account of the evidence of all the various monetary indicators. It was never envisaged that any one indicator or target would convey so much information about future inflation that it could be mechanically followed to the exclusion of all other evidence."

The Guide claimed that it was seen "as early as the summer of 1980" that the chosen narrow measure of sterling M3 had "ceased to be a good indicator of the growth of nominal GDP or inflation"[57] and needed to be changed. M1 was tried, but found wanting. Since 1984, "more emphasis has been put on a yet narrower measure of money—M0." But even that had its limitations. "The Chancellor [Lawson] therefore decided that there should be no formal target for broad money in 1987–8, though it will be taken into account."

Even in 1989, the year before Thatcher was ousted by her senior colleagues, *The Campaign Guide*[58] would describe monetarism as the basis of Thatcher's "economic miracle."

> Sterling M3 was the Government's original choice as the key indicator of money supply. Throughout the 1970s M3 had shown a fairly close relationship to the role of inflation, increases in M3 being followed about two years later by a surge in inflation. [But M3] has become a less reliable indicator of inflationary trends. For these reasons the Government has, since 1987, given greater emphasis to M4 [M3 plus mortgage lending] as a wider and less erratic measure.[59]

The guide admitted that the government had "set no target range for M4, though its movements will continue to be taken into account," and that the exchange rate of the pound was also monitored for its effect on the money supply.

Thus, Friedman's simple dogma, which appeared to make sense to a number of financial journalists, market analysts, and a clique in the Conservative leadership in the mid-Seventies, ended its British life as an apologia postscript to a decade of unnecessary mass unemployment and painful lost opportunities.

15

Beating bin Laden
with Cheap Money

The terrorist attacks of September 11, 2001, aimed
to wreck the Western economies. But Fed chair
Greenspan found a way to keep capitalism afloat

Friedman had little respect for George H. W. Bush, an aristocratic New England WASP posing as a Texan. The former CIA chief's whole demeanor—his height, his unflappability, his large extended family, his aristocratic drawl, his seaside redoubt in Kennebunkport, Maine—was totally at odds with Friedman's quick-brained, meritocratic persona. Most offensive of all to Friedman, however, was that Bush did not sign up to Reaganomics, the mixture of monetarist, trickle-down, and supply-side economics championed by Reagan and those around him.

Friedman was unforgiving. "I believe that Reagan made a mistake when he chose Bush as his vice-presidential candidate," he wrote. "Indeed, I regard it as the worst decision not only of his campaign but of his presidency."[1] He recalled that "while Vice-President George Bush was almost always one of the entourage that accompanied Reagan to [PEPAB] meetings, I do not recall his ever making a comment of substance."[2]

Bush did not disguise his skepticism about Friedman's approach to the economy. At Carnegie Mellon University on April 10, 1980, during the presidential primaries in which he lost to Reagan, Bush had directed his fire at the whole edifice of Reaganomics. "What I'm saying is that it just isn't going to work," Bush declared. "And it's very interesting who invented this type of what I call a voodoo economic policy is Art Laffer, a California economist. . . ."[3] The phrase "voodoo economics" quickly caught on and pithily encapsulated the wackiness of the untried, outsider ideas brought to the Reagan administration by maverick economists like Friedman.

Bush's speech was written by his press secretary, Pete Teeley, who came up with "voodoo economics" after reading a newspaper editorial suggesting that Reagan's economic team were little more than witch doctors, conjuring up crazy solutions from the ether. The utterance was enough to ensure Friedman's lasting contempt for the man who would become Reagan's vice president, then the forty-first president, and, as such, would come to decide whether to resume the Fed's abandoned monetarist experiment.

Friedman mounted a sneering assault upon Bush's lack of knowledge of economics and apparent lack of ethics. While "Bush may have strong principles in some areas like foreign policy," Friedman wrote, "he clearly has none on economic policy." Bush may have dismissed Reaganomics as "voodoo economics" when running against Reagan, said Friedman, but "when Mr. Reagan nonetheless chose him as his running mate, Mr. Bush changed his tune and praised Reaganomics as the road to prosperity." He continued:

> His conversion continued through the 1988 campaign, with his "read my lips" promise of "no new taxes." Once elected, Mr. Bush, with the cooperation and encouragement of the Democratic Congress and some of his White House appointees, reversed course and followed a policy that can only be described as Reaganomics in reverse.[4]

Friedman relished listing the failures of President Bush's economic policy. Under Bush, who was obliged to work with a Democratic Congress, government spending rose sharply, as did the federal deficit. Welfare payments were raised, along with more regulations that hampered businesses.

(Friedman cited both the Clean Air Act and the Americans with Disabilities Act as abuses of government power.) To his credit, Bush also presided over an extension of free trade, including the negotiation of NAFTA (North American Free Trade Agreement).

For Friedman, Bush 41 presided over a negation. "If Reaganomics brought exuberant expansion, why should we be surprised that reverse Reaganomics brings stagnation?" asked Friedman. His verdict: "Thanks to the continued control of the House by the Democrats, government spending and taxing was reduced much less than Reagan hoped, but there was a start that would have accelerated with the end of the cold war, if Bush had not reversed Reaganomics."[5]

Bush 41 turned out to be a one-term president, losing to Bill Clinton in the 1992 election. Clinton promised a triangulation of American politics, to find a "third way" that broke free of the traditional left-right battle lines. Surprisingly, the return of a Democrat to the White House represented an unlikely extension of Friedman's influence. With Clinton's declaration that "big government does not have all the answers. The era of big government has ended,"[6] Friedmanite ideas had, apparently, even caused the Democrats to change their free-spending ways. But it would take a defeat for Clinton, not victory, before genuine change took place. After spending the first two years largely occupied with his wife Hillary Rodham Clinton's failed attempt to introduce universal health care, Clinton suffered a rout at the 1994 midterm elections, with Democrats losing the House to the Republicans for the first time since 1952. In a self-styled "Republican Revolution," the new House Speaker, Newt Gingrich, was determined to make headway with his radical conservative agenda, even if it meant threatening a government shutdown.

The result was an economic policy in many ways closer to the ideas of Friedman than of Samuelson. Gingrich had offered voters a "Contract with America," in which he promised smaller government, lower taxes, supply-side measures to improve entrepreneurship, and welfare reform. Although

Friedman did not sign off on all of Gingrich's proposals, and monetarism was conspicuously missing from Gingrich's to-do list, many of its aims stemmed from the general change in public attitudes that Friedman had championed.

Under the odd and largely unhappy partnership of Clinton and Gingrich: the federal budget deficit was reduced—falling from 47.8 percent of GDP in 1993 to 31.4 percent in 2001; federal spending fell from 20.7 percent of GDP in 1993 to 17.6 percent in 2000; the budget deficit of $290 billion was turned into a budget surplus of $128 billion—largely through "peace dividend" cuts to defense spending, since the demise of the Soviet Union brought an abrupt end to the expensive Cold War. Other Clinton/Gingrich measures included: welfare reform; free-trade deals, including the signing of the North American free-trade deal NAFTA; higher taxes on fuel, higher earners, and Social Security payments; and deregulation of financial services—all while maintaining robust public spending on education and entitlements.

Friedman had always thought tax cuts and the size of government went hand in hand. As such, cutting taxes was always a good idea because it put pressure on lawmakers to curb their big-spending habits. He said:

> I am in favor of cutting taxes under any circumstances and for any excuse, for any reason, whenever it's possible. The big problem is not taxes; the big problem is spending. The question is, "How do you hold down government spending?" . . . The only effective way, I think, to hold it down, is to hold down the amount of income the government has. The way to do that is to cut taxes.[7]

The tenor of the Republican House majority's demands on the Clinton administration was that free-market solutions should get more emphasis. Few conservatives could claim to have encouraged and articulated the antigovernment opinion that led to the Republican midterm victory more than Friedman. The decision to play hardball with the executive was Gingrich's, but the growth of the small-government movement over the course of decades was undoubtedly due to the proselytizing of Friedman. According to Friedman, "During the 1990s, you had the combination that is best for holding down spending. A Democrat in the White House and Republicans controlling Congress. That's what produced the [federal budget] surpluses at the end of the Clinton era, and during the whole of that era there was a trend for spending to come down."[8]

But the "Republican Revolution" ended in farce. Tom DeLay, the new House Speaker, complained that "big government had been feeding at the public trough too long,"[9] and Gingrich set about bringing it down to size, even engineering the shutdown of the federal government by failing to agree on a budget to show his seriousness. But Gingrich's victory was short-lived. His self-regard and pomposity kicked in and hubris struck. His complaint, in the midst of the government closure, that his assigned seat on Air Force One—taking him and other political leaders to Israeli leader Yitzhak Rabin's funeral—was too far to the back of the plane for one of his status revealed a personal vanity that sat badly with his claims to be a no-frills reformer. "It was pitiful," recalled DeLay. "Newt had been careless to say such a thing, and now the whole moral tone of the shutdown had been lost. What had been a noble battle for fiscal sanity began to look like the tirade of a spoiled child."[10] Friedman could only look on in disbelief as the best chance to turn back the scale of the burgeoning state was lost to Gingrich's egotism.

If Friedman's role on the sidelines of the sputtering "Republican Revolution" was scantly recognized, he was optimistic that his arguments in favor of a smaller government sector were gradually winning the day. Throughout the world he had noticed a trend for lawmakers to cut governments down to size, particularly in former communist states. "Creeping socialism . . . is a lot better than galloping socialism. That's a turn of the tide,"[11] he said. And he was optimistic, too, that the trend would continue.

"What I foresee is government growing smaller as a fraction of the national income because the national income grows, while government more or less stagnates,"[12] he said.

ON DECEMBER 8, 1995, Samuelson wrote to Friedman out of the blue, reminding him that "it was just 62 years ago . . . that we first met. I was a lowly sophomore and you were already spottable as a scholar of destiny." It was an endearing piece of sentimentality, stressing that the many things the two men shared were more important than their differences. "I hope it will be said of us that, though we disagreed on much, we understood wherein our logical and empirical differences were based and that we were pretty good at preserving the amiability, friendship, and respect throughout,"[13] Samuelson wrote.

In his reply, Friedman said that he and Rose "were very touched" by Samuelson's note and that he agreed about the early years together in Chicago. "Those were truly great days," he said. "However," Friedman continued, "I do have one correction to make. It must have been either 63 or 61 years ago that we first met; I suspect 63 years."[14]

IF THE FORMER Soviet states and Eastern European satellites treated Friedman as a seer, it was harder going in the United States. The hotly disputed presidential election of 2000 delivered a second Bush to the White House. But while his father, George H. W. Bush, was an unapologetic old-school elitist, with patrician ideas about the government's responsibility for the well-being of its citizens, George W. was a drawling, smirking Texan playboy with political ambitions. He had successfully navigated the Bush family's transformation from the confluence of two prominent Connecticut Republican dynasties—the Walkers and the Bushes—to that of a Texan oil baron family more suited to the Republicanism of the age. Unlike his father,

George W. had promised on the campaign trail to cut taxes, and cut taxes he did: $1.35 trillion over the rest of the decade, with an initial rebate in his first budget of $400 billion. But such drastic action had consequences. By July 2001, tax receipts were way down as the stock market tanked, prompting the Federal Reserve chief, Alan Greenspan,[15] to slash interest rates to avoid the economy from crashing into recession.

But Bush's problems with the economy were soon overshadowed by an event that was to shake the world: the September 11, 2001, attacks by Al Qaeda terrorists on the World Trade Center in New York and on the Pentagon in Washington, D.C. The shock to the world economy, that terror could so easily strike at the hearts of America's financial and political sectors, presented a new problem to economists: how to steady the nerves of a financial system that depended on confidence to deliver prosperity. As Greenspan described it, "For a full year and a half after September 11, 2001, we were in limbo. The economy managed to expand, but its growth was uncertain and weak. Businesses and investors felt besieged."[16]

For his part, Friedman had total confidence that the Western system of values would survive such violent assaults from its Islamist opponents. "The forces in favor of liberalization are infinitely more powerful than those who act in the opposite direction," he said. "Threats, we have already known! But none has hindered this development, as free societies have managed to achieve a reasonable level of economic efficiency that protects them from such 'bad weather.'"[17]

Greenspan's solution to the shock of the attacks—to keep interest rates low for as long as was needed—raised new arguments about the role of money in the economy while resurrecting old disputes about how money should be treated. Greenspan's response to the uncertainty caused by the terror attacks was to "maintain our program of aggressively lowering short-term interest rates," which came on top of seven cuts to interest rates by the Fed "to mitigate the impact of the dot-com bust and the general stock market decline."[18]

Greenspan went on to cut the rate five more times, so by October 2002 it had reached a meager 1.25 percent, lower than at any time since Eisenhower was in the White House, and, for Greenspan, "a figure most of us would have considered unfathomably low a decade before." The economy seemed to be turned on its head and the old certainties were certain no more. Greenspan explained:

> As officials whose entire careers had been devoted to fighting inflation, we found the experience of making such cuts decidedly strange. Yet the economy was clearly in the grip of disinflation, in which market forces combine to hold down wages and prices and cause inflation expectations, and hence long-term interest rates, to recede.

And that was just the beginning. The whole world appeared to be in the grip of disinflation, a widespread slowdown in the rate of rising prices, that presaged a condition economists of all persuasions agreed would be even more disastrous: deflation, or the persistent reduction in prices across the board. The traditional means of heading off deflation was to flood the system with new borrowing. "I'd always assumed that if deflation seemed imminent, we could start up the printing presses and create as many dollars as would be necessary to stop a deflationary spiral," recalled Greenspan. "Now I was not sure."[19]

Flooding the system with cheap money was one of the few instruments left to Greenspan, though the Fed chair knew the truth of Keynes's economic adage, "You cannot push on a string"[20]—in other words, you can offer cheap money to banks and entrepreneurs, but, if investors see no opportunities and therefore do not wish to borrow, or banks are reluctant to lend, there is nothing a government can do to force them.

Acutely aware that by cutting interest rates further he risked "a bubble, an inflationary boom of some sort," which would have to be addressed at some time, in June 2003 Greenspan cut rates again, to 1 percent. Friedman thought he understood why Greenspan was so eager to keep interest rates low. "Greenspan is looking back at the 1930s in the U.S. and the 1990s in Japan. He's saying. 'If I make a mistake, I'd rather err on the side of being too expansive than too contractionary.' "[21] Seventy years after the events that Friedman had studied so closely, in which the government had held money too tight, leading to bank failures and bringing on the Great Depression, an eternal question surfaced about the role the money supply can play in saving an economy from recession.

The conundrum was not new. As Samuelson had written in the first edition of *Economics* in 1948,

> By increasing the volume of their government securities and loans and by lowering Member Bank legal reserve requirements, the Reserve Banks can encourage an increase in the supply of money and bank deposits. They can encourage but, without taking drastic action, they cannot compel. For in the middle of a deep depression, just when we want Reserve policy to be most effective, the Member Banks are likely to be timid about buying new investments or making loans.[22]

Alongside persistent, record-low interest rates, George W. Bush presided over a mounting federal deficit, a subject that would become the main topic of debate in Congress in the early years of the new century. Bush had inherited a burgeoning budget surplus from Clinton—$237 billion in 2000, $127 billion in 2001—but government spending soon outstripped tax revenues as Bush fulfilled his campaign promises to introduce deep tax cuts, to increase defense spending, and to introduce an expensive Medicare drugs bill. Within a year, by the end of 2002, the budget deficit had soared to $158 billion. Then, in response to the 9/11 terrorist attacks, Bush went to war on two fronts, in Afghanistan, in pursuit of Al Qaeda, and in Iraq, ostensibly to destroy Saddam Hussein's "weapons of mass destruction."

The fiscal continence that once represented the Republican view of deficits was replaced by a more carefree attitude toward government debt. For some Republicans, borrowing itself was to be avoided at all costs. Deficits represented a simple failure of America to live within its means, which was an aberration. Just as domestic households could not live on borrowing forever, so nations, in normal times, should balance the books as a matter of public virtue. But one Republican president after another had believed that deficits were allowable in pursuit of reducing taxes. As George W. Bush's vice president Dick Cheney readily acknowledged in 2002, Reagan's carefree approach to the nation's finances had shown that "deficits don't matter."[23] Now Bush was radically increasing the nation's debt and Republicans were left struggling to justify his behavior.

As always, Friedman thought the lawmakers should use the expanding deficit as an excuse to cut public spending. "During the whole of [the Nineties] there was a trend for spending to come down," he explained. "Then the Republicans come in, and they've been in the desert, and so you have a burst of spending in the first Bush term."[24] He thought that to reduce federal government borrowing, lawmakers should introduce legal limits on the amount a government could spend. "What we should consider . . . is a Tax and Spending Limitation Amendment, an amendment to hold down total spending," he said. "I don't think it needs to be in the form of a Balanced Budget Amendment, but that's one form it can take."[25]

Friedman had little expectation that Bush II would adopt his ideas. His final verdict on the George W. presidency was mixed. "I have to give the Bush administration very high marks on having produced a major tax reduction. I have to give him very high marks on the talk that emanates from the Bush administration. But in terms of practice on the economic front, you have to say that they're a disappointment."[26]

Samuelson, for his part, was more anxious that the controversy surrounding Bush's tax cuts, which overwhelmingly benefited rich Americans, meant that, in the event of an economic downturn, taxes would not be used as Keynes had recommended, as a stimulus to a flagging economy. "The legacy that Bush leaves us with is terrible because people today confuse his giveaways to the rich with tax reductions that can have a meaningful effect on economic growth,"[27] he said. The supply-side logic behind the tax cuts, to inspire entrepreneurs to work harder, was a myth. "Giving tax cuts to the Fortune 500 companies and their shamelessly overpaid executives is not going to make them suddenly dynamic,"[28] he said. He continued:

> The system of corporate governance that has allowed CEOs to earn 400 times the median wage of their employees—two decades ago it used to be 40—has undermined any case for tax cuts to the upper brackets. Corporate pay based on quarterly earnings instead of long-term growth, combined with golden parachutes even if executives fail, undermines productivity. Tax cuts for this group, then, is literally counterproductive.[29]

If Friedman hesitated to endorse Greenspan's emergency measures, Greenspan remained an unashamed admirer of Friedman. "His views have had as much, if not more, impact on the way we think about monetary policy and many other important economic issues as those of any person in the last half of the twentieth century," he said. But he had not embraced monetarism as Fed policy, because he, too, was flummoxed to find a measure of money that was appropriate to curb prices. He told Friedman:

> We recognize that inflation is fundamentally a monetary phenomenon, and ultimately determined by the growth of the stock of money, not by nominal or real interest rates. In current circumstances, however, determining which financial data should be aggregated to provide an appropriate empirical proxy for the money stock that tracks income and spending represents a severe challenge for monetary analysts.[30]

Nonetheless, when Greenspan retired from the Fed in 2006, Friedman was flattering about his record overall. "The rate of growth in the money supply has been more stable under the Greenspan administration than in almost any previous administration," he said. "I think by comparison with earlier Feds, Alan stands out as having done an absolutely first rate job."[31] He declared that "Greenspan's great achievement is to have demonstrated that it is possible to maintain stable prices."[32]

Friedman had long advocated a rules-based approach to monetary growth, but Greenspan had used his own discretion, to impressive effect. "I have long favored the use of strict rules to control the amount of money created," Friedman wrote. "Alan says I am wrong and that discretion is preferable, indeed essential. Now that his 18-year stint as chairman of the Fed is finished, I must confess that his performance has persuaded me that he is right—in his own case."[33] But Friedman still believed the human element at the Fed was a danger in the future if a weak Fed chairman bowed to political pressure to increase the money supply. "Alan Greenspan may be splendid, but who knows who the next one will be? Money is too important to be left to central bankers."[34]

Samuelson took a more critical view of Greenspan and bemoaned the absence of morality behind his actions. "The trouble is that he had been an Ayn Rander," said Samuelson, referring to Greenspan's early devotion to the absolutist free marketeer Rand, the patron saint of unbridled, selfish capitalism. "You can take the boy out of the cult, but you can't take the cult out of the boy. He actually had instruction, probably pinned on the wall: 'Nothing from this office should go forth which discredits the capitalist system. Greed is good.'"[35] And although "at bottom Greenspan was an okay character. That's different from Rand and [Arthur] Burns—both despicable human beings," Greenspan had displayed recklessness when, "after 1996 [and] clear signs of a stock bubble he (rashly?) refused to engage in any preventative against-the-winds policies. . . . He had no reason to believe that after the bubble burst he could effectively take corrective action. No surprise then that as Enron and new financial-engineering monsters were clearly bubbling-bubbling, he took no notice or action. When he left office, his successors were left holding a fretting baby."[36]

The George W. Bush administration was to prove Friedman's last plausible chance to make a lasting change to the way the money supply in the United States was managed. In response to, above all, the apparently endless wars in Afghanistan and Iraq, the American people chose as their next president a Democrat, Barack Obama, a lawyer with little interest or knowledge of economics. Although the new chairman at the Fed was an unavowed admirer of Friedman, the election of Barack Obama, a Democrat, in 2008 coincided with a step change in the way the country's economy was shaped by the federal government. Friedman's ideas, like Friedman himself, were old hat and, when the world economy was shaken by a sudden freeze in credit and the prospect of devastating bank failures, it was Keynesians like Samuelson to whom the federal government turned for advice.

16

All Going Swimmingly

Bernanke, chairman of the Fed, thought the economy
had reached a state of permanent, inflation-free
prosperity. But he failed to see trouble ahead

Friedman was to be pleasantly surprised by "the next one" at the Fed, Ben
Bernanke,[1] who in February 2006 succeeded Greenspan. On paper at
least, Bernanke was more to Friedman's liking and more sympathetic to his
views. A professor of economics and chair of the economics department at
Princeton, Bernanke's special interest was the role of government in affecting the business cycle, a core dispute between Keynes and Hayek carried
on by their followers over the intervening seventy years. Bernanke was also
an expert on how to curb inflation and, more recently pertinent, on how to
cure deflation. Above all, he was an authority on the causes and effects of the
Great Depression, and an admirer of Friedman and Schwartz's research on
its monetary causes. On his office wall at the Fed, Bernanke hung a photo-
graph of the four Fed bankers who had kept the supply of money too tight
in 1931, provoking and prolonging the slump. For once, Friedman had a
devotee at the Federal Reserve.

In November 2002, Bernanke had been the guest speaker at an event
to mark Friedman's ninetieth birthday. He told the audience he had first
read Friedman and Schwartz's *Monetary History of the United States* when

studying for his doctorate at MIT, Samuelson's bastion. "Friedman and Schwartz's analysis leaves many lessons," he concluded. "The best thing that central bankers can do for the world is to avoid such crises by providing the economy with, in Milton Friedman's words, a 'stable monetary background'—for example as reflected in low and stable inflation." Then, in an extraordinary mea culpa on behalf of the Federal Reserve Board, Bernanke accepted the blame for inducing the Great Depression by making money too tight. Looking directly at Friedman, he said, "Regarding the Great Depression: you're right, we did it. We're very sorry. But thanks to you, we won't do it again."[2]

Later the same month, Bernanke addressed the problem of tackling deflation in an economy where interest rates were at or near zero. "Once the nominal interest rate is at zero," he explained, "no further downward adjustment in the rate can occur, since lenders generally will not accept a negative nominal interest rate when it is possible instead to hold cash." When the short-term interest rate reached zero, it had been suggested that central banks would "run out of ammunition" and would be powerless to affect events through manipulating interest rates.

However, Bernanke argued that, notwithstanding Keynes's notion that "you cannot push on a string," a central bank still retained "considerable power to expand aggregate demand[3] and economic activity even when its accustomed policy rate is at zero." This included the wholesale printing of money through credit swaps—the Fed buying back its own debt and relending at a lower rate—a policy that would become known as "quantitative easing." He reassured Friedman and the other economists in his audience that "the Federal Reserve and other economic policymakers would be far from helpless in the face of deflation, even should the federal funds rate hit its zero bound."[4]

In his office at the Fed, Bernanke kept a signed copy of Samuelson's *Economics* textbook and considered him "a titan of economics." But Samuelson was skeptical about Bernanke. As intelligent and accomplished as he was—

he scored 1590 out of 1600 in his SAT test and taught himself calculus as a boy because his school did not teach it—Samuelson felt Bernanke did not have an intuitive understanding of events that would have given him a more rounded view of the Great Depression, the subject of his PhD thesis. Samuelson went to the trouble of looking up Bernanke's dissertation. "I realized that when you're writing in the 1980s, and there's a mindset that's almost universal, you miss a lot of the nuances of what actually happened during the Depression,"[5] Samuelson said. "[Bernanke, born in 1953,] did not have a feel for what it was like. If you were born after 1950, you really don't have the feel of that Great Depression in your bones. Being a bright boy at MIT [like Bernanke], it's not really a substitute for that."[6]

Like many younger Americans, Bernanke's failure to grasp the full horror of the decade of unemployment during the slump had, in Samuelson's view, caused him to play down the importance of unemployment when deciding Fed policy. Samuelson believed that short memories about the mass unemployment of the Thirties and the sacrifices made by ordinary Americans during World War II had made more tolerable the joblessness inherent in policies proposed by Friedman and others. "There has been a 1980–2003 swing to the right among voters, whose swing away from 'altruism' is somewhat proportional to the time elapsed since the Great Depression and since the U.S. government's effective organization for World War II's 'good' war,"[7] Samuelson explained.

FRIEDMAN DIED of a heart attack at his home in San Francisco on November 16, 2006. He had enjoyed good health for most of his ninety-four years. In 1972, he suffered from angina and underwent open heart bypass surgery at the Mayo Clinic. Then, after suffering a heart attack in New Orleans in 1984, he was flown to Stanford Hospital, where a second heart bypass was performed. Despite those two major operations, he continued to play tennis every week and to ski. In the last five years of his life, Friedman was

conscious of slowing up, incapable of the innovative, combative, counterin-
tuitive thinking that had animated earlier years. In 2001, in reply to Samuelson, who had sent him his most recent piece of work, Friedman wrote,
"I was interested in skimming through the pages and seeing what you have
done but I have nothing to add or subtract. More power to you that you
are still capable of this kind of work. I am afraid I am not."[8] The following
month, when discussing in an interchange of letters with Samuelson how
Edward Teller,[9] a Hoover Institution fellow, had casually accused J. Robert
Oppenheimer[10] of disloyalty to the United States, Friedman said he now
rarely attended the lunches at the Hoover that were once famous for his
feisty contributions to their debates.

In his condolence letter to Rose Friedman, Samuelson expressed his
profound sense of loss. "When the news came of Milton's death, I felt as
if my universe had changed," he wrote. "Ever since autumn of 1932, when
Milton came to the Midway, I was aware of the high IQ person who followed his own logic to wherever it cogently led. Whenever my path led elsewhere, I found it expedient to ponder every word and equation of Milton
Friedman's, the highest compliment." He continued:

> Milton Friedman, more than any other twentieth century scholar, has
> moved the academic economists rightward toward free market liber-
> tarianism. By contrast, John Kenneth Galbraith has cut almost no ice
> with our fraternity. While Friedrich Hayek has had considerable influ-
> ence with the lay public, Hayek's persuasiveness with us academics
> cannot compare with Milton's.[11]

And Samuelson added a personal note. His wife Marion had died of
cancer in 1978, age sixty-two. He wrote:

> Rose, I know what it is to lose a mate. Happily, the passage of time
> does not dull the emotion of bereavement. Rather, by some mysterious

alchemy, time serves to accentuate the good recollections. Your friends and progeny have been blessed by Milton and his memories.

FRIEDMAN ARGUED his corner to the last. The day after his death saw publication of a column that would be his final salvo, "Money Matters," in the *Wall Street Journal*. Based on a research paper he was in the process of writing that compared three periods of economic boom—the U.S. in the 1920s, Japan in the 1980s, and the U.S. in the 1990s—in the column he attempted to show the pivotal role played by the money supply in determining national income and stock prices. Asked shortly before he died whether he had succeeded as much as he had hoped, Friedman replied, "I think on the whole I've done very well. I haven't won all of them, by any means. You shouldn't win all of them. But on the whole I feel pretty good."[12]

Although central bankers, not computer programs, regulated the supply of new money, Friedman took credit for inspiring them to keep the supply of money growing at a steady rate. They "finally learnt that the cure for deflation is printing enough money and the cure for inflation is not printing too much money,"[13] he said. The result, over the previous twenty years, had been "a golden period. It's a period in which you had declining inflation but a fairly steady rate, a steady level. You had only three recessions, all of them brief, all of them mild. I don't believe you can find another 20-year period in American history."[14]

The *New York Times* described Friedman as "the grandmaster of free-market economic theory in the postwar era and a prime force in the movement of nations toward less government and greater reliance on individual responsibility" and "one of the 20th century's leading economic scholars, on a par with giants like John Maynard Keynes and Paul Samuelson."[15] Sam Brittan, in the *Financial Times*, paid tribute to Friedman's bluntness and nerve. "Part of his appeal lay in his willingness to come out with home truths that had occurred to many other people who had not dared to utter them," wrote Brittan. "Friedman would then go on, however, to defend these maxims against the massed forces of economic correctness."[16]

A most generous and candid tribute to Friedman was made by Lawrence Summers, [17] Clinton's former Treasury secretary and Samuelson's nephew and tennis partner. "He was the devil figure in my youth," Summers wrote. "Only with time have I come to have large amounts of grudging respect. And with time, increasingly ungrudging respect." Now, with Friedman gone, Summers was prepared to go further. "If Keynes was the most influential economist of the first half of the 20th century, Friedman was the most influential of the second half," he wrote. "Republican Richard Nixon once pointed out that 'We are all Keynesians now.' Equally, any honest Democrat will admit that we are all Friedmanites now. We are because he won so many of his arguments with the conventional wisdoms of his time."[18]

In a piece in the *New York Times*, Summers wrote that "as an undergraduate in the early 1970s, I was taught that everyone other than Milton Friedman and a few other dissidents knew that fiscal policy was of primary importance for stabilizing economies, that the Phillips Curve could be exploited to increase employment if only society would tolerate some increase in inflation, and that economists would soon be able to take economic fluctuations through finely calibrated policies." He noted that "Friedman's heresies had become the orthodoxy," with "total agreement" now among politicians and economists that "monetary policy can shape an economy more than budgetary policy can; extended high inflation will not lead to prosperity and can lead to lower living standards; policy makers cannot fine-tune their economies as they fluctuate." He concluded: "I feel that I have lost a hero—a man whose success demonstrates that great ideas convincingly advanced can change the lives of people around the world."[19]

Samuelson wrote to Summers:

For a period after an important scholar dies, the doctrine of *nihil nisi bonum* [say nothing unless it is good] properly applies. Tom Sawyer enjoyed attending his own funeral. Milton (in that heaven he did not believe in) must be relishing his many headlines. Knowing him for 74 (long) years, I believe his major motivation was to persuade modern societies to take the libertarian view. . . . As memories of the Great Depression faded, . . . Friedman inside academia speeded our profession to catch up with self-centered electorates.

Samuelson took Summers to task for conceding that monetary rather than fiscal methods had been proven by Friedman to be the most appropriate way of tackling inflation. He continued:

> Your clause that caught my eye was: "monetary policy can shape an economy more than budgetary policy." Who proved that (and what does it mean)? Lucas? Barro?[20] Friedman himself? Martin Feldstein?[21] What set of 2006 macro equations deduces that as a cogent theorem? . . .
>
> For your eyes only, reading every published word by Milton Friedman, I had to grade him low as a *macro* economist. As a micro economist he was stubbornly old-fashioned, sticking with [Alfred] Marshall's *partial equilibrium* that lacked *micro* foundations. (A. M. knew that.) . . . Such ad hominem stuff matters little. We'll not see his like again for many a moon.
>
> Please do not quote from this letter. The time is not yet ripe for the doctrine of *nihil nisus verum* [nothing but the truth] to come into season.[22]

When asked to comment in public on Friedman's legacy, Samuelson was suitably gracious about his old sparring partner's achievements. "No one in the 20th century has had the ideological influence that Milton Friedman has had in moving the economics profession from the Great Depression-era do-goodism towards a friendliness toward, and appreciation of, the free market," Samuelson told the *Wall Street Journal*. "We've lost a giant in economics."[23] And he told the *New York Times*, "Friedman thought of himself as a man of science, but was in fact more full of passion than he knew."[24] Samuelson was to reserve a more damning assessment of Friedman's life and career for a more fitting time.

On the death of Rose Friedman, on August 18, 2009, Samuelson wrote a letter of condolence to Friedman's children, David Friedman and Janet Martel, both living in California, and "the entire Friedman Family." "Milton's abilities were self-evident from the beginning," he wrote. "For two-thirds of a century, despite the differences in our value judgments, we were able to maintain civil discourse. I think that was a tribute to both of us."[25] David Friedman replied, "It is indeed a good thing when people can disagree and get along in a peaceable and even friendly fashion." But he took Samuelson to task for writing in his condolence letter that he and Milton Friedman enjoyed "differences in value judgments." "People on all sides of the political spectrum are too willing to attribute differences in policy preferences to differences in values," he wrote. "The implicit assumption is that one's positive views about the effect of different policies are so obviously true that the only reason to disagree with one's conclusions is disagreement about what effects are good or bad."

He raised Samuelson's objection to Friedman's controversial view that licensing medical doctors, rather than certifying them for competence, was little more than an inhibition on trade.

> I suppose it is logically possible that the reason you disagree is that you put a higher value than he did on the welfare of physicians and a lower value on that of their patients, and so are in favor of restricting the supply of physicians in order to raise the price they can charge for their services, but that does not strike me as likely. If not, then in that example at least the disagreement is over economics, not values. I suspect that the same would be true in many other cases, although probably not all.[26]

17

Capitalism Teeters

The financial freeze of 2008 proved a severe test for the competing
ideas of Samuelson and Friedman. Then along came COVID-19

Had he lived one more year, Milton Friedman would have witnessed
a financial catastrophe that tested the limit of his theories about
the Fed providing enough money in times of tight liquidity: the financial
freeze of 2007–8. In 2002, Ben Bernanke had been confident—even perhaps complacent—that the U.S. financial and banking structure was secure.
"A particularly important protective factor in the current environment is
the strength of our financial system," he declared. "Our banking system
remains healthy and well regulated, and firm and household balance sheets
are for the most part in good shape."[1]

But the system harbored a peril that before long would trigger a world
economic catastrophe of such magnitude that Bernanke, an expert on the
slump of the 1930s, rated it as "the worst financial crisis in global history,
including the Great Depression."[2] Few realized either at the time or since
then how close to the abyss America had come. In the darkest days of the
financial freeze, September and October 2008, Bernanke believed that of
the thirteen "most important financial institutions in the United States,
twelve were at risk of failure within a period of a week or two."[3]

When Bernanke had raised a glass to Friedman at his ninetieth birthday with the words, "Regarding the Great Depression: You're right, we did it. We're very sorry. But thanks to you, we won't do it again,"[4] perhaps he assumed that the days of financial crashes were over and that the years he dubbed "Great Moderation" had rounded off the edges of booms and busts. Yet, far from the U.S. economy being stuck in a comfortably settled rut, the financial industry—the very powerhouse of American capitalism—was teetering on the cliff edge of collapse and chaos. Similarly, while the great division between conservative and Keynesian economists had lain dormant for some decades, it was about to erupt anew, with the rediscovery of Keynes as a pilot in times of economic peril. And the financial freeze once again put to the test the competing ideas that Friedman and Samuelson—as successors in the duel between Hayek and Keynes—had battled over for so long.

The origin of the financial freeze, according to Bernanke,[5] was the endless cheap credit that stemmed from the Federal Reserve's decision after the shock of 9/11 to hold interest rates low to encourage business activity. The abundance of cheap money led to a housing boom in the U.S., fueled by a rapid expansion of mortgage lending, often to borrowers whose credit record would not in normal times have passed muster. Such was the rush to enroll new customers that mortgage companies waived cash deposits on properties and appeared to ignore whether the borrower could afford the loan repayments. In addition, the abandonment during the Clinton years of longstanding regulations on the banking sector—at the behest of Greenspan and Republican lawmakers—meant that bad practices among lenders and bundlers of bad debt went unchecked. As Bernanke explained, "Regulators did not do enough to prevent poor lending, in part because many of the worst loans were made by firms subject to little or no federal regulation."[6] And financial companies deliberately made new investment products complex, hiding bad loans among good to ensure that the extent of the risk was hard for buyers of debt to sound out.

Through the first decade of the new century, the U.S. economy avoided a post-9/11 recession and even enjoyed a mild boom, fueled by the relentless rise of property prices. But when, in early 2007, house prices began to fall and mortgage delinquencies started to rise, financial institutions began to curb lending and investors fled from funds containing dubious mortgage-based securities.

That summer, it emerged that the giant mortgage lenders Fannie Mae and Freddie Mac, which between them guaranteed more than half of America's $12 trillion mortgages, were in serious trouble. As mortgage borrowers, watching the price of their properties plummet, began to default on repayments, Fannie and Freddie's shares tumbled. The pair began hemorrhaging cash and in November 2007 Fannie posted losses of $1.4 billion and Freddie recorded a $2 billion loss.

In July 2007, IndyMac, a California bank, suffered a run on its assets by customers anxious that the bank was insolvent. They were right. Indy-Mac closed its doors and went bust. At the time there were few calls for the federal government to intervene. But if the demise of IndyMac did not set off alarms about the impending financial tempest, before long the scale of the threat to the world's financial system became clear. In August 2007, the French bank BNP Paribas suddenly suspended withdrawals from three of its investment funds, because "the complete evaporation of liquidity in certain market segments of the U.S. securitization market has made it impossible to value certain assets fairly."[7] In other words, the bank was honest enough to confess that it did not know whether it was the holder of good or bad debt.

The unease at BNP Paribas was evident in other big banks around the world, who also were awash with bad paper. They had also abandoned the traditional restraint of bankers by "leveraging," that is, borrowing and lending at many more times the amount of assets they had lodged in their vaults. By the time some banks had diagnosed the extent of their problem, it was too late. "The banks were so highly leveraged, they didn't have the capital to keep themselves going," recalled British prime minister Gordon Brown. "We were running capitalism without capital."[8]

In March 2008, the financial behemoth Bear Sterns, America's fifth-largest investment bank, whose ledgers contained tens of billions of dollars' worth of flaky "subprime" loans, teetered on the edge of bankruptcy and its investors rushed to cash out before their holdings proved worthless. A hastily negotiated sale to JPMorgan, its old rival, was agreed, but with one important proviso. The sale was conditional upon the Fed agreeing to underwrite $30 billion of Bear Sterns mortgage securities of dubious quality. This stipulation demanded a radical change of thinking in Washington, D.C. With scant public debate, Bernanke agreed that the Fed should intervene directly in the market, arguing that if Bear Sterns demurred, its collapse would set off a chain of catastrophic bankruptcies. The phrase on everyone's lips was: Bear Sterns is "too big to fail." But what of other banks facing similar liquidity crises?

Samuelson considered the continuing turmoil at Fannie and Freddie an omen, telling his nephew, Larry Summers—at the time president of Harvard, but before long to join the Obama administration as director of the National Economic Council—that, after accepting an emergency loan of $25 billion from the Treasury on July 22, 2008, the two great mortgage lenders were effectively owned by the government and that both were "toast." He could not resist a sideswipe at Friedman's heirs, the "inflation targetters," writing to Summers:

> You correctly doubt that the many hidden and admitted losses that resulted from a burst real estate bubble impinging on the new dynamite of Frankenstein financial engineering can heal themselves by private initiative.
>
> Before we are out of the mess, the Federal purse—the Treasury and the Federal Reserve Board—is going to lose amounts that dwarf previous real estate failures and anything that happened after 1939.
>
> Accordingly, I thought your stance, approving the Bear Stearns caper but worrying that Freddie and Fannie executives and sharehold-

ers were left to revert to their bad old ways or bad new ways, was strange. Strange and harmful if believed in. Freddie and Fannie are from now on the on-stage dummies run by [Treasury Secretary Hank] Paulson[9]-Bernanke ventriloquists. . . . It's tough-donuts time for fervent inflation targetters.[10]

Summers replied:

I agree with you the situation is grave, the government will have to do much more. . . . No time for moral hazard speeches. . . . But what about Fannie and Freddie? No time to shrink or restrict them. But when Paulson and Bernanke run them, why should it be done for sake of current management and shareholders? . . . By the way I am still young and naïve, but Fannie Freddie were worst special interest corruption I saw in 8 years in government. So I stay with my view of: do what is necessary for housing market now but no need to bail out the shareholders.[11]

Samuelson wrote:

Maybe naively, I deem Fannie-Freddie shareholders to be *already* toast. *De facto*, if not *de jure*, they are now both government agencies. . . . By the end they will eat up a lot of government money.[12]

The prospect of Fannie and Freddie going bankrupt was too much for Paulson, who on September 7, 2008—two weeks after Samuelson's letter to Summers—took the mortgage giants into federal government ownership. "Fannie Mae and Freddie Mac are so large and so interwoven in our financial system that a failure of either of them would cause great turmoil in our financial markets,"[13] Paulson declared. Again, the federal government stepped in to prevent a large financial company's failure because it was too big to fail. How many more companies would end up in government hands?

When, two weeks later, on September 15, Lehman Brothers filed for bankruptcy, there was a fair expectation that the Fed would step in to save the company, as it had done Bear Sterns and Fannie and Freddie. Like other financial companies, in recent years Lehman had made a decent profit flipping federal government money, borrowing it short-term and relending it to borrowers for higher returns. But its $600 billion in assets matched by the $572 billion it had lent to borrowers left it highly vulnerable. Its shareholder equity would be wiped out if its assets fell only 5 percent, which in such a volatile market was likely. And that, along with the desertion of its short-term lenders, is exactly what happened. At first the Treasury and the Fed tried to find a private buyer for Lehman. But when none was forthcoming, they decided to allow the company to go bust and face the consequences. Lehman duly filed for Chapter 11 bankruptcy.

It was a gamble. If Lehman was allowed to go broke, was any big financial institution safe from extinction? Would a domino effect leave America with an even smaller number of very big banks? Would the contagion bring about a widespread financial collapse? The immediate result was panic among senior financial industry executives, quickly followed by paralysis.

The day after Lehman's demise, AIG, the world's largest insurance company, filed for bankruptcy. Startled at the news, the Fed agreed to buy the giant insurer: an immediate loan of $85 billion was exchanged for 80 percent of AIG's equity. Once again, the free market had stalled and the federal government felt it could not stand idly by. Bernanke and Paulson now found themselves in the invidious position of having to pick winners and losers among some of America's largest companies. The free market was conspicuously failing.

Financial institutions, wary of being caught with bad loans, abruptly stopped lending to each other. Credit markets froze and financial businesses

ground to a halt. With the federal government scrabbling to do the right
thing and with no end of the crisis in sight, the stock market plunged. It was
not exactly 1929 all over again, but the financial freeze of 2008 was to prove
as profound in its effect on the U.S. and world economy. "Declining stock
values, a teetering financial system, and difficulties in obtaining credit triggered a remarkably rapid and deep contraction in global economic activity
and employment,"[14] explained Bernanke.

On September 18, Bernanke and Paulson asked Congress to provide
a $700 billion emergency bank bailout fund to buy up "troubled assets."
"If we don't do this, we may not have an economy on Monday," Paulson
told them. On September 29, lawmakers, many of whom were ideologi-
cally reluctant to see the free market sidelined, voted against making funds
available for the Troubled Asset Relief Program (TARP). It was a final act
of impotent defiance by myopic lawmakers. The market response to their
dissent was swift and brutal. As soon as the vote was lost, the Dow Jones
plunged 770 points, the largest single-day fall in prices in Wall Street's history. Legislators who had devoted their careers to the belief that the market
is always right looked on in horror as that same market passed judgment
on their actions. Chastened by the market verdict, Congress revisited their
TARP decision on October 3 and voted a second time, this time agreeing to
fund the program in full.

The Fed was making other, less visible moves to head off a collapse of
the financial markets. Armed with Friedman's rebuke to the Fed for its failure to blunt the Great Depression by increasing the money supply, Bernanke
hosed cash at the system, slashing the price of short-term borrowing from
5¼ percent in September 2007 to 2 percent by the spring of 2008. And
when this proved inadequate, in December 2008 the Fed reduced interest
rates to zero and let it be known there was little prospect of raising them
again for a very long time. The Federal Reserve became the lender of last
resort to banks and financial institutions it deemed creditworthy, stepping

in to guarantee short-term loans between banks that otherwise may have been considered too risky.

It was not enough. The truth of Keynes's adage "You cannot push on a string" soon became evident. It proved easier to make limitless amounts of cash cheaply available than it was to find good uses for it. As Bernanke explained, "Conventional monetary policy alone is not adequate to provide all the support that the economy needs."[15]

In its dying days, the Bush administration prepared the Economic Stimulus Act of 2008 that would, when passed by Congress in the early weeks of Barack Obama's presidency, provide nearly a trillion dollars to stimulate the economy directly through government spending on infrastructure, tax breaks, and other Keynesian antirecession devices. "Shovel ready" public works projects, such as already planned roadworks and new bridges, were identified so the vast sums soon would be passed on to contractors, architects, and so on, to boost the economy.

But would the Keynesian stimulus work? Samuelson's concern—and that of many in the Obama administration—was that the sum Congress provided of around $800 billion [$958 billion in 2020 dollars] would not be enough. "It is in the right ball park," he said, but "in the end it may take more."[16]

Nothing would be quite the same again. More than thirty years before, Samuelson had predicted that another Great Depression was impossible. Having learned the lessons of the slump, and having designed the macroeconomic tools to manipulate the economy, he was sure that a similar tragedy could not be replicated. "The basic reason why the Great Depression was not inevitable, and why anything really like that depression is improbable now, is that in those days governments all over the world hewed to the lines of orthodox finance," Samuelson had written in 1974. "As things got bad, they tightened their own belts and forced the populace to do likewise. . . . We live in the age *after* Keynes, and there is no going back to Herbert Hooverism."[17] But by denigrating over many decades government intervention of any sort, Milton Friedman and others had invited the return of do-nothing Hooverism. And if in 2008 a second Great Depression had been narrowly avoided by a return to Keynes-like policies, the financial freeze served to upset the cozy assumption held by Bernanke and others that the bad old days of bank runs and serial bankruptcies had been replaced by the sunlit certainty of the Great Moderation. The events of 2008 undermined the logic of the rational-expectations school who argued that those who operate the markets know enough to avoid catastrophe. Why had there been no "rational expectation" of a financial freeze?

Instead, America was to endure a painful, decade-long haul out of the ditch. Recovery was woefully slow. Friedman's championing of the free market had been hugely successful in his lifetime, but the financial freeze shook the commonly held belief that free-market forces, left to their own devices, would act to ensure the perpetual prosperity, full employment, and growth that Americans demanded. The same tone-deaf legislators who had voted down TARP led the charge against any federal government action that would hasten a recovery. There was talk that bailing out companies presented a "moral hazard" that would encourage recklessness among financiers confident in the knowledge that the government would step in and save them at the last moment.

But the principle that the government should keep out of the way and let the market do its worst had been shaken to destruction. In the heat of the crisis, no respected economist could be found to argue that it would be better to watch the economy fall off a cliff and wait for the market to provide a solution.[18] Friedman's perennial prescription, to give the market time to cure itself, was not found wanting; it wasn't even considered. Events happened so quickly, there was no time. The cost to businesses and the human devastation of letting the chips fall was not thought a politically viable solution. And with joblessness soon reaching 8 percent and rising, it was unthinkable that the government would watch, helpless, from the sidelines as mass unemployment on the scale of the Great Depression returned.

And what of Friedman's—and Hayek's—warning that flooding the economy with cheap money would inevitably stoke inflation? While Samuelson conceded that the stimulus would likely lead to higher prices, he argued it was acceptable. "If, optimistically, we are back at 4 percent unemployment by 2012, the price level will be higher than it is today, probably rising at 2 percent a year, culminating in 8 percent," he said. "I think that is worth it, because deflation is the greater worry. Given the circumstances, we should err on the side of over-stimulus. Nobody in their right mind would try to roll back that level of inflation if it avoids deflation and leaves us with an intact, self-sustaining economy again."[19] Bernanke agreed, concluding that when the dust had settled and the economy had been made secure, the Fed could manage the inflationary pressures by slowly reducing the supply of money as soon as an upward swing in prices became evident.

Samuelson thought the financial freeze had sparked "the worst experience America or the world has faced since the end of World War II," but that, like Bernanke, the precedent for gauging when a full recovery would have been achieved, "even with very large deficit spending by the government," was the Great Depression. He saw little prospect for recovery before "the second half of 2012" or even by 2014, "the time frame it took Roosevelt from his inauguration in March 1933 to the eve of World War II."[20]

The main problem in determining when recovery would take place in 2008 was the sophistication and complexity of the modern economy. By 2008, it was beyond the understanding of even those who were its top managers. "There have been ups and downs and economic bubbles since the cavemen," Samuelson said.

What makes this meltdown different is that we have built such an elaborate house of cards on the fiendish financial schemes of "bril-

liant" MIT and Wharton School graduates that it will take a great deal
of time to unwind the mess and rebuild confidence in the financial
system. They created instruments so complex that no CEO understood them. They so lacked transparency that the meltdown came as
a surprise. [21]

Samuelson was admiring of "brilliant MIT graduate" Bernanke's performance and wrote "a fan letter" to praise him for his "flexibility in adapting
to the new 2007+ scene."[22]

The treatment applied in the 2008 financial crisis was in part Keynesian, but also in part a vindication of Friedman's money-supply notions. The
lesson of his work on the Great Depression with Schwartz was that central
banks can head off liquidity problems that affect an economy in recession
by flooding it with money. When Japan suffered a lengthy liquidity crisis in
the 1990s, Friedman's solution was:

> The Bank of Japan can buy government bonds on the open market,
> paying for them with either currency or deposits at the Bank of Japan,
> what economists call high-powered money. Most of the proceeds will
> end up in commercial banks, adding to their reserves and enabling
> them to expand their liabilities by loans and open market purchases.
> But whether they do so or not, the money supply will increase. . . .
> Higher monetary growth will have the same effect as always. After a
> year or so, the economy will expand more rapidly; output will grow,
> and after another delay, inflation will increase moderately.[23]

The Bank of Japan had duly adopted a policy of quantitative easing
(QE), buying government securities and other financial assets on the open
market. The effect was to increase the price of those securities and assets,
thereby reducing the interest that they paid to investors.

Bernanke also deployed QE, increasing the Fed's pre–Great Recession holdings of $800 billion in Treasury notes to a peak of $2.1 trillion in June 2010. When in November 2010 this proved inadequate, the Fed launched a second round of security buying, known as QE2, followed by a third round, QE3, in November 2012. While some conservative economists questioned whether Friedman would have approved of quantitative easing, for Bernanke the lesson of Friedman's Great Depression research was clear. The Fed chair was not going to be found guilty of starving the economy of funds. Despite the wailing and gnashing of teeth from conservative politicians, and the noticeable silence from conservative economists, quantitative easing had proved its worth during the financial freeze, heading off a full-scale Depression. What is more, and contrary to all warnings from conservative Cassandras, the pumping of such vast amounts of borrowed cash into the economy did not result in a surge in inflation.

But if Friedman's view of the money supply during a recession appeared justified, the experience of 2008 and its aftermath proved above all that Samuelson's neoclassical synthesis was on target. In good times, the general principles of a market economy were useful. But when an economy started heading into recession, Keynesian remedies still had an important part to play. Samuelson and Friedman had both seen the same history unfold before them, from the mass unemployment and the business and bank failures of the Great Depression, through the decades of prosperity when governments eagerly used Keynesian demand management to iron out the peaks and troughs of the business cycle, to the rise of stubborn stagflation, the half-hearted experiments in Friedman's monetarism, and the arrival of supply-side economics and rational expectations. When years of near-zero interest rates led to a catastrophic financial freeze, the George W. Bush Treasury team and Bernanke's Federal Reserve did not reach for Friedman or Hayek: they found relief in old-fashioned Keynesian remedies.

"What then is it that, since 2007, has caused Wall Street capitalism's own suicide?" asked Samuelson the following year. "At the bottom of this worst financial mess in a century is this: Milton Friedman-Friedrich Hayek

libertarian laissez-faire capitalism, permitted to run wild without regulation. This is the root source of today's travails. Both of these men are dead,
but their poisoned legacies live on."[24] For Samuelson, the financial freeze
and its cure were the ultimate vindication of a lifetime as "an incurable
centrist." "I am old enough to have seen the cycle come full circle," he said.
"Today we see how utterly mistaken was the Milton Friedman notion that a
market system can regulate itself."[25]

Back in 1970, when stagflation first began to take hold, Samuelson had
insisted that "for a modern 'mixed economy' in the post-Keynesian era, fiscal and monetary policies can definitely prevent chronic slumps, can offset
automation or under-consumption, can insure that resources find paying
work opportunities."[26] And in 2009, a year after the financial freeze gripped
the world economy, Samuelson could still say with confidence, "You can't
do better than the 1965 Hicks/Hansen version of the Keynesian system,
which is pretty clear cut on how a central bank can, by diddling its discount
rate up and down judiciously, lead toward a period of great moderation
rather than the terrible ups and downs of the 20th century."[27]

SAMUELSON HAD a long memory. That is why it was rash to invite a ven-
detta from him. There was a postscript to the 1941 snub Harvard had aimed
at Samuelson when an anti-Semitic professor in its economics department
failed to offer him a suitable post on his achieving his PhD. The more distinguished Samuelson's career became, the more valuable his cache of papers
was to a research university. In November 2006, Samuelson asked the Harvard Archive about lodging his voluminous files of personal and academic
papers with the university. He reminded Harvard that they held Joseph
Schumpeter's papers, but that the archives of Nobelists Franco Modigliani
and Robert Solow were to be found at the impressive library facilities at
Duke University, in Durham, North Carolina. "When one stays preoccu-

pied with doing new research," he wrote, "little time is left to plan optimally autobiographical and archival matters. However, those tasks do need to be attended to."[28] He suggested a meeting. The director of Harvard's University Library responded suitably: "I cannot tell you how honored we are at the prospect of housing your papers." There was, however, an unmistakable sense of entitlement in the letter. "Your strong ties to the University warrant our stewardship," he wrote, "and your contributions to the discipline, as well as to the development of several generations of economists, further warrant Harvard's preservation of your collected material. . . . Your papers would add luster to the collection."[29]

But back in 1992, Samuelson had received an approach from Duke, whose archive contained the papers not only of Modigliani but of Burns, Alex Leijonhufvud,[30] Walter Lippmann, Robert E. Lucas, the founder of the Austrian School Carl Menger, Don Patinkin,[31] the William Volker Fund, and much of Hayek's collection, and it would receive, on her death, the papers of Anna Schwartz. The director of Duke's Rare Book, Manuscript and Special Collections Library, Robert L. Byrd, met with Samuelson when he was leaning toward lodging his papers at MIT. Byrd stressed that Duke's archive provided "a different kind of setting, one which focuses on the history of economics as a field of study rather than the history of a particular academic institution."[32]

In 2005, Byrd sent the terms of the finding aid for the Modigliani papers to Samuelson to give an indication of how his collection would be treated. "It is my understanding that your own papers are being placed at the MIT Archives," he wrote. "If however, that is not the case . . . please let me know."[33] Later that year, when Samuelson intimated he was considering Duke, Byrd wrote again, expressing gratitude and humility at the prospect of Duke winning such a valuable prize. He was "delighted to learn" Samuelson was thinking of Duke, he wrote, and listed the reasons Duke would be the perfect home for his archive. "It would of course be an honor for us to serve as the archival repository for your papers," he wrote. "I sincerely believe that by placing the collection here, you will increase its impact and benefit scholars who wish to study your contributions and accomplishments."[34]

The following month, Samuelson wrote to Byrd, "I am leaning towards using the Duke archive for my various materials. . . . What I find attractive is Duke's concentration in these matters and my brainchildren would rest happily until eternity in the neighborhood of so many other brainchildren."[35] And so it was that Duke, not MIT, nor Harvard, became the final resting place for Samuelson's papers.

For his part, Friedman left his archive to the Hoover Institution, the conservative bastion in a sea of progressives on Stanford's campus that had welcomed him as a towering figure in conservative/libertarian economics after his retirement from Chicago.

PAUL SAMUELSON died at his home in Belmont, Massachusetts, on December 13, 2009, aged ninety-four. He had been suffering from high blood pressure for years and had been prescribed antihypertensives and anti-cholesterol medication. He was survived by his wife of twenty-eight years, Risha Eckaus, as well as four sons, two daughters, a stepdaughter, and fifteen grandchildren. A private funeral was followed by a public memorial service. In lieu of flowers, the family asked well-wishers to give a donation to the Massachusetts Audubon Society.

Obituaries praised Samuelson's breadth of knowledge, his many breakthroughs in macroeconomic theory, his success at MIT, his mathematical approach to economic problems, his *Economics* textbook, and above all his championing of the neoclassical synthesis. "Samuelson reshaped academic thinking about nearly every economic subject," declared the *New York Times*, which noted that "a historian could well tell the story of 20th-century public debate over economic policy in America through the jousting between Mr. Samuelson and Milton Friedman."[36] The paper's principal economics commentator, Paul Krugman, wrote, "Most economists would love to have written even one seminal paper—a paper that fundamentally changes the way people think about some issue. Samuelson wrote dozens."[37] The conservative *Wall Street Journal* acknowledged Samuelson as a "Titan of economics," while *The Economist* pronounced him "the last of the great general economists."[38]

The *Daily Telegraph*, London, wrote that "Samuelson made such diverse contributions to his field—ranging from welfare economics, theories of consumption, prices, capital accumulation, economic growth, public goods, finance and international trade—that it is hard to think of a debate to which he did not make a trenchant contribution," and that his textbook "effectively gave the world a common language with which the complexities of world markets can be discussed and understood." The paper noted that "Samuelson frequently crossed swords with the monetarist Milton Friedman," but that "in 2008, when the world slipped into the steepest downturn since the Great Depression, it was Samuelson's prescriptions, rather than Friedman's, that carried the day."[39]

NEITHER MAN was alive to witness the next catastrophic threat to the world's prosperity: the emergence in China in November 2019 of the coronavirus COVID-19, a highly contagious pneumonia-like disease that often proved fatal, particularly to the elderly or patients with debilitating conditions. Using the authoritarian powers vested in it as the sole legitimate political force in a one-party communist state, the Chinese government imposed a strict curfew on the citizens of Wuhan, Hubei, a city of 11 million. No one was allowed to enter or leave the city and people were told to remain at home or, if an essential worker, wear face masks and other protective clothing to prevent the disease's spread. But the Chinese lockdown came too late.

According to official Chinese figures,[40] there were sixty COVID-19 cases in Hubei on December 20, which rose to 266 cases by December 31. The numbers of patients infected roughly doubled every seven days.

With international air travel continuing, within a month the virus spread fast, killing hundreds of Italians in Milan and Turin.[41] Democratic governments were alarmed to discover that to allow a breathing space for their inadequate health services, they were obliged to impose restrictions on their citizens every bit as severe as those inflicted by the communist leadership in Beijing. Travel bans and the compulsory wearing of face masks were imposed, but the disease continued to spread. By the end of March 2020, the United States boasted the highest number of COVID cases. By the end of July, the global death toll had reached nearly 200,000, nearly a quarter of them in the U.S.

The dilemma for governments was whether to try to prevent the disease from spreading further and deliberately collapsing a large portion of the economy, or whether to risk the deaths of vast numbers by doing little or nothing. The virus was so virulent, there was little time for governments to debate the implications of their anti-COVID measures, even though imposing a total stay-at-home order meant a severe curtailment of economic activities. Those who were able to work from home did so, and those who could not were confined to their homes without work. Essential workers, in hospitals and care facilities, were obliged to continue to work, even when there was not enough personal protection equipment and clothing to protect them from catching the virus, or to prevent it spreading further. The result was a precipitous decline in economic activity worldwide. The financial freeze of 2008 was until 2020 deemed the worst economic disaster since the Great Depression of the 1930s. That record was soon overtaken by COVID. Even the ruinous world wars of 1914–18 and 1939–45 affected only part of the globe; COVID threatened the whole world.

In the United States by the end of July, over four million Americans had contracted COVID, of whom 136,484 had died. The stock market fell by 35 percent, and credit markets froze. Commercial activities like international aviation, tourism, hospitality, and personal services like barber shops and dentists were closed. The federal government's response, in so much as there was one, was to borrow money and give it to citizens to bolster demand. There was no time for a traditional Keynesian stimulus through infrastructure construction. Instead checks for $1,200 were sent to all Americans. The Republican Treasury Secretary Steve Mnuchin[42] said one in five Americans would be thrown out of work because of COVID—twice the number as during the 2008 financial freeze. A temporary $600 per week boost in unemployment pay was introduced and by March 21, 2020, 48.8 million[43] Americans had signed on for unemployment pay. Businesses large and small were offered federal government grants or loans to tide them over until a COVID vaccine was discovered, though that breakthrough was not expected until sometime in 2021. As in the aftermath of the 2008 financial freeze, Congress was divided over what to do to offset the virus's assault on the American economy, with Republicans reluctant to take action and Democrats willing to do more but inhibited by their opponents in Congress and a federal government led by an out-of-touch, self-obsessed president who showed little sign he had grasped the severity of the tragedy unfolding on his watch. Despite the lessons of 2008, the threat of a return to Hooverism was real.

Across the Atlantic, the British government was taking a similarly interventionist approach. With the country in lockdown, the government agreed to pay 80 percent of workers' wages per month across the board, up to £2,500 [$3,200]. Loans and grants were made available to faltering companies, big and small, as well as to the self-employed. As the Nobel-winning Chicago School economist Robert Lucas wrote during the 2008 financial freeze, "I guess everyone is a Keynesian in a foxhole," a remark that served to confirm the validity of Samuelson's neoclassical synthesis. In America in 2020, the scale of the government aid was hotly debated and widely deemed not enough to save much of the economy. Many businesses would never recover. Many workers would never get their old jobs back.

While both Keynesians and Friedmanites could claim that the remedy of pumping liquidity into the economy was true to their masters' wishes, the COVID crisis dealt a severe blow to Friedman's desire for smaller government and the removal of government from interference in the marketplace. The federal government was now in total control of the market, and decided which businesses were allowed to operate, which lived, which died. The universal response to COVID among responsible governments was that only "big government" was capable of providing the wherewithal to limit, then overcome, the pandemic. Countries with small or incompetent governments—usually presiding over countries with small or broken economies—could not cope with the medical disaster that overtook them. Even in the United States, where the notion of "big government" had long been besmirched by conservatives quoting Friedman as their inspiration, there was little argument among federal government ranks that the temporary closure of large parts of the economy was the only responsible action. While there were small rebellions from Tea Party types about the effects of the lockdown on businesses, it rarely extended beyond rallies to protest the mandatory wearing of masks in public when "social distancing"—leaving a gap of six feet between one person and the next—was not possible. Would Friedman have worn a mask? It is hard to imagine that Rose would have allowed him to risk his life on such a slender principle.

The COVID pandemic showed not only that big government was necessary but that it was both the lender of last resort and the only means of keeping the tens of millions suddenly made unemployed[44] from starving. In the 1930s, the Hoover administration stood idly by as Americans joined dole lines and scrabbled for food. His successor, Franklin Roosevelt,[45] tried a raft of New Deal initiatives to return people to work, even though many measures impinged upon the basic right to run a business.[46] And in 1936, Keynes's *General Theory* provided an intellectual justification for vast government borrowing to spend on public works to provide jobs. In 2020, the pandemic slowed economic growth more dramatically than any time since the Great Depression, with the U.S. domestic economy plunging 5 percent annually between January and March and a record 33.4 percent between April and June.[47] In response to this natural disaster, the dwindling rump of "Austrian" (Hayekian) economists offered little alternative to central government intervention to step into the breach and few could be found to recommend that on principle the virus should be allowed to do its worst, leaving the market to pick up the pieces. As in 2008, conservatives were instead left on the sidelines complaining about the creeping influence of government diktats—the demand to wear protective face masks, the compulsory closure of businesses where the virus could spread, the extension of government regulations on everything from the distance people should stand from each other to where to sit in a restaurant—and the vast increase in government borrowing and the speed of its repayment, while doing little of consequence to counter the Keynesian rescue going on about them.

WHAT WERE THE lasting legacies of Samuelson and Friedman? When Friedman was asked point blank whether he had altered the shape of economics, his response was, "Very hard to say."[48] His many achievements are more evident in politics than in economics. His ability to enthuse others in the virtues of the free market was exceptional, but he was a one-man band, and while his libertarian, antigovernment arguments steamed on beyond his death, his efforts to return economies to "sound" economics fell on stony ground. Nonetheless, his singular achievement was to wrench the federal government away from attempting to manage the economy through fiscal measures. The Keynesian "New Economics" was beaten by stagflation and by Friedman. But successive Fed chiefs and Treasury secretaries complained that interest rates and monetary policy alone were insufficient instruments to juggle the price of the floating dollar, inflation, unemployment, and the rate of economic growth. Some of Friedman's theoretical economics, such as his work on the consumption function, continues to be admired. But few have continued to hanker after Friedman's flagship idea, doctrinaire monetarism, which is remembered, if remembered at all, as an arcane, otiose footnote in the history of economic thought.

While Friedman's son David became a libertarian economist, after winning a BA in chemistry and physics from Harvard, and an MA and a doctorate in theoretical physics from Chicago,[49] Friedman left behind no band of Friedmanite economists; there is no Chicago equivalent to Keynes's fiercely devoted disciples, the Cambridge Circus. Nor did he found a Friedmanite school of economics. He was unique. A maverick to the last.

Some economists resented the time wasted having to prove that Friedman's monetarism was little but a distraction. Fellow Brooklynite and Nobelist Robert Solow, among Samuelson's closest colleagues at MIT, pronounced in 2013 a damning verdict on Friedman's life's work. "I'm glad there is no Milton Friedman anywhere on the political-economy spectrum today," he wrote. "I think that Milton Friedmans are bad for economics and bad for society."

He continued:

> Fruitless debates with talented (near-)extremists waste a lot of everyone's time that could have been spent more constructively, either in research or in arguing about policy issues in a more pragmatic way. I suppose that such debates also help to clarify implicit assumptions and shady arguments, but I think that is a small benefit compared with the cost in sheer hassle.[50]

Friedman fared better in the success of his idiosyncratic policy recommendations. His plea to end punitive income taxes has largely been realized. In the three decades 1950–1980, the federal income tax rate had never dipped below 70 percent. By 2021, it had fallen to 40.8 percent.[51] Friedman could also claim a victory in the abolition of compulsory military service, though, after the horrors endured by those conscripted to fight the Vietnam

War, the draft would likely have ended anyway. His attempt to wrest public education out of the hands of politicians proved partially successful, with the idea picked up by both sides of the political divide, from Bill Clinton to Margaret Thatcher, often in the shape of taxpayer-funded charter schools. But public schools remain overwhelmingly underfunded and overadministered by government officials. Doctors continue to operate a closed shop through the strict system of professional licensing, rather than the simple certification Friedman sought. The Department of Energy, which Friedman wished to abolish, continues to operate. His advice to successive Republican presidents and congressmen to allow hard drugs like heroin and cocaine to be sold legally fell on deaf ears. An outsider all his life, Friedman remains an outsider in death.

Friedman's continuing influence on American politics, however, became evident in 2009 in the rise of the Tea Party, an anti–big government, anti-taxation, angry grassroots movement born of the Bush/Obama/Bernanke stimulus that purged the Republican Party of moderates and laid the foundations for the election of Donald Trump[52] as president in 2016. Could there have been a President Trump without Friedman? Perhaps. But Friedman's long libertarian march over several decades paved the way and helped deliver in Trump a president as wayward, self-serving, intellectually inconsistent, and focused solely on reelection as any since Nixon.

At the heart of Trump's rise was the disenchantment of older blue-collar workers, or former workers, who had been made redundant by the end of the smokestack industries—coal, steel, shipbuilding—in large part due to imports enjoying the advantage of cheap foreign labor. The worldwide free trade that Friedman had so eagerly championed, and President Clinton eagerly executed—with NAFTA in 1994 providing a free trade area between Mexico, Canada, and the United States, and the translation of GATT (the General Agreement on Tariffs and Trade) into the WTO (World Trade Organization) in 1995—may have benefited the U.S. economy in general, but many in U.S. manufacturing found their jobs lost to poorly paid, often Asian, workers operating without benefit of the health and safety regulations and other protections that American workers enjoyed. Free trade divided Americans down the middle, and those whose livelihoods had been lost to its consequences found in Trump an articulate ally who promised to renegotiate trade deals that were bad for Americans.

Samuelson, who approved of globalization and the benefits it brought to the countries involved, had drawn attention to the dark side of the removal of protective tariffs for American workers. In 1972 he had given a talk— "International Trade for a Rich Country"[53]—which became a popular part of his speaking repertory. In it he pointed out that "free trade need not help everybody everywhere" and that "a rich place can lose net when a poor one newly gains comparative advantage in activities in which previously the rich country had enjoyed comparative advantage." It was an economic truth given prominence by Trump[54] in his 2016 insurgent presidential campaign that promised a renegotiation of America's trade deals and the introduction of selective tariffs to protect home markets.

Friedman's novel plan for a negative income tax to replace traditional welfare payments attracted support from across the political spectrum, including from Samuelson, who praised it as "an idea whose time has come."[55] The idea morphed into the "universal basic income" in which the state would provide a minimum wage to everyone as a right. The COVID-19 pandemic saw governments around the world adopting similar schemes, at least temporarily, though the prospect of a world economy dependent upon robots rather than humans made more likely permanent direct state funding of those not needed for work.

Friedman's long march was always as much political as economic. And he was at pains to stress that, like Hayek, he did not consider himself a conservative but a libertarian. Among the principal themes of his campaigning was the championing of the intellectual case arguing for a sharp diminution of state powers across the board. While stressing that he had little time for anarchy or anarchists, from Barry Goldwater's presidential run in 1964 through Ronald Reagan's eight-year term and beyond, Friedman led the charge against the overweening state and welcomed every small victory as the big government programs implicit in Keynes's remedy for a nation's good health were slowly turned back. Reagan said in his first inaugural address that government was not the solution to America's problems, it *was* the problem, though it is unlikely that he or Friedman could have envisioned the overnight rise of the populist Tea Party, born out of the vast public borrowing to offset the collapse in economic activity following the financial freeze of 2007. While Friedman may in principle have supported the rise of the angry blue-collar white right, who felt they had been ignored by successive governments of both stripes, it is a shame we did not get to hear his pithy judgment on the vast ragbag tribe of anti-government hyper-activists who adulated Trump.

The small government movement, for which Friedman provided the intellectual justification, fired the imagination of Republicans for five decades and successfully altered the party from one of traditional middle-of-the-road conservatism to one of unabashed libertarianism. Friedman could count on that conversion of Republicanism to his central cause as a great success. After the presidency of George H. W. Bush, no Republican could become the party's presidential champion unless they agreed a checklist of beliefs that echoed Friedman's small government strictures. Yet in 2020 the movement ate its own tail when on January 6, 2021, a mob of Trump supporters stormed the Capitol building in Washington, DC, laying waste to offices, artefacts, documents, monuments, and the fabric of the building, causing the evacuation of lawmakers in fear of their lives, and culminating in an invasion of the Senate chamber itself. Five people died as a result of the mayhem. Most disturbing, some protestors made up a lynch mob, declaring that they intended to kidnap lawmakers and summarily execute Vice President Mike Pence and Leader of the House Nancy Pelosi. Whether the violent protest was intended as a full-scale insurrection to overthrow the government, or merely an attempt to frustrate the constitution, or whether it was merely an overzealous demonstration of solidarity with the roundly defeated president, who had urged the protesters to storm the Capitol, remains uncertain. But the scale and avidity of the protesters proved to be the culmination of the long march of Friedman's arguments condemning the burgeoning role of the federal government in favor of states' rights or little or no government at all. There is little doubt that Friedman would have roundly condemned the insurgents' use of force and been appalled at their denial of any facts that did not suit them, but he could hardly deny that the well-spring of the arguments that inspired the fatal failed comedic coup was his own clearly articulated and persuasive thoughts.

IF FRIEDMAN'S LEGACY is best found in politics rather than economics, Samuelson's mark on economics and society is less conspicuous but none-theless indelible. Opinion is divided over whether Samuelson left a distinct Samuelsonian school of economics. His myriad technical papers, which flowed from him with such facility, would have been a towering achievement for any academic economist. His application of mathematics to economics transformed the discipline from something akin to a branch of philosophy to a true social science.

Samuelson left a personal dynasty of sorts, with a brother, Robert Summers,[56] a sister-in-law, Anita Summers,[57] a brother-in-law, Kenneth Arrow,[58] and a nephew, Larry Summers, all distinguished economists. His most lasting accomplishment, however, is found in the generations of young economists around the world who have learned economics from his textbook, which has made him Keynes's most effective proselytizer. Samuelson's neoclassical synthesis remains the most widely acknowledged guide to how macroeconomics can be made to avoid catastrophe. In the debate over government intervention in the economy begun by Keynes and Hayek in 1931, Samuelson could claim his mélange of the two traditions to be the true winner.

As he reached into his nineties, Samuelson maintained a full daily schedule. "That's what I would like to do until the end of time," he said, "to go on scribbling my articles [in his office] on the third floor of [MIT's] Sloan Building, in between playing tennis and drinking coffee at my other study in the Concord Avenue branch of Burger King."[59] But he made time to reflect on his lifelong rivalry with Friedman:

> Despite his I.Q. potential, he was neither an early nor a prolific writer. He was a weird temperament, whose gut ideologies ruled over his logic, coherence, and empirical inferences. . . . Charisma and high polemical speediness explains why his influence exceeded Hayek or Mises in turning post-1965 economists rightward. . . . Had Milton never blown his horn, the rightward shift would have happened anyway— but not so quickly.[60]

Samuelson tried to make sense of the fact that he and Friedman had so much in common yet they had taken very different roads to the top. It was, he thought, a function of their personalities. They had adopted differing views about the biggest event in their shared history, the Great Depression. "If young Milton had ever been touched by the vague socialism and do-goodism of his boyhood background," Samuelson wrote, "all that evaporated under the strong acids of economic law."[61] And while Samuelson had chosen an apparently effortless path to fame and fortune, Friedman had a constant need to challenge those ahead of him. "Had he swum with the tide, all would have been quick," Samuelson wrote. "But here was a libertarian immune to compromise, opposed to state power, skeptical of both politicians and bureaucrats, unmoved by good intentions."[62]

Samuelson's final verdict, however, was that, for all of Friedman's ultra-confidence, his certainty of purpose had led him up a blind alley. "Milton

Friedman never made a mistake in his whole life. That's remarkable, isn't it?" Samuelson asked one of his last interviewers. He went on:

> [Friedman] is as bright a guy as you would ever meet. But I don't think he realizes the tremendous amount of mistakes he made in his life. I don't think anybody has read every line of Milton Friedman's work in the world except me. . . . Most of my jokes about Milton Friedman are actually deep truths. Sometimes I say he's got such a high IQ that he has no protection against himself. He looks at his work and he is satisfied with it. However, I think that it is a tragedy when somebody really takes the wrong train in life.[63]

Acknowledgments

Writing this book has taken me from coast to coast of the United States. I am grateful to the archivists in the Hoover Institution, where Milton Friedman's papers are lodged, and to the librarians at the David M. Rubenstein Rare Book & Manuscript Library at Duke University, which is home to Samuelson's archive. Both showed me great courtesy and encouragement. I am particularly indebted to Sara Seten Berghausen and Elizabeth B. Dunn and the other archivists at Duke, and Eric Thomas Wakin, Carol A. Leadenham, Jean McElwee Cannon, Sarah Patton and Jenny Mayfield at the Hoover.

The germ of this book was my account of the duel between John Maynard Keynes and Friedrich Hayek in 1931, which both set the battle lines between left and right in economics and established the sour tone of the debate ever since. Forty years after Keynes and Hayek reached an uneasy truce, the argument was still going on, but with two new champions, Paul Samuelson, from MIT, and Milton Friedman, from the University of Chicago. For this story of the lifelong friendship and disagreements between these two towering figures, I am indebted to many of the same people who helped me with *Keynes Hayek*. Among the most important are Vicky Chick of University College, London, whose knowledge and enthusiasm for Keynes and the Keynesians is contagious, and Bruce Caldwell, Research Professor of Economics at Duke University and Hayek's official biographer, who held my hand through Keynes Hayek and smoothed my path to study the Samuelson archive at Duke.

I owe a great debt to my friend and mentor Edmund Phelps, Nobel Prize winner in Economics, 2006, who has offered constant encouragement in my getting to grips with this long and complicated tale. As someone who, coincidentally with Friedman, exposed the flawed logic of the Phillips Curve—the supposed direct trade-off between unemployment and inflation—Ned played an important part in prompting the unraveling of Keynes's remarkable legacy. Ned invited me to become a Visiting Scholar at his pioneering Center on Capitalism and Society at Columbia University and has involved me in his mind-stretching annual conferences on topical aspects of economic thought, for which I am most grateful.

Three dear chums with vast knowledge of economics read through this book at a final stage and I cannot thank them enough for their keen eye for an ambiguity, a confusion, or a missed dimension. They are James Ledbetter, Peter V. Rajsingh, and Tom Sharpe QC. *Samuelson Friedman* is a much better book thanks to their intelligent, astute observations. But I should stress that all errors in the text are mine and mine alone. Grateful thanks are due, too, to John Aslet for his research.

A special thank you is due to Paul Samuelson's stepdaughter, Jane Samuelson; his son, William Samuelson; and Milton Friedman's daughter, Janet Martel, for allowing me to quote from their fathers' correspondence and works. I am also grateful to Friedman's son David Friedman for putting me straight on some of his father's views. Thanks, too, to Samuelson's longtime literary collaborator Janice Murray.

I am grateful to the University of Chicago Press for allowing me to quote from *Two Lucky People*, the memoirs of Rose and Milton Friedman, and to McGraw-Hill , for permission to quote from Samuelson's *Readings in Economics, Sixth Edition.* Grateful thanks to Sony/ATV Music Publishing/ Famous Music for permission to quote from the Harry Ruby and Bert Kalmar song "I'm Against It."

This is the third of my books edited by Brendan Curry at W. W. Norton. I cannot imagine a more sympathetic editor, whose light touch on the tiller has kept me from straying into arcana. Brendan has sat on my shoulder throughout the writing and editing process and his contributions have been invaluable. I am grateful, too, to his talented colleagues, in particular Bee Holekamp, Nancy Green, Rebecca Homiski, Anna Oler, and Beth Steidle.

This is also the third book I have written under the wise guidance of my literary agent Rafe Sagalyn. Once again, he has effortlessly kept me focused on the essential story. There is a magic that binds authors and agents, and Rafe and I hit it off from the start, when, cold calling him without prior introduction, he instantly grasped what I had in mind for a book and found me a publisher within a few days. The result was *Keynes Hayek*. He immediately understood, too, the charms of *Samuelson Friedman*.

And I cannot end a list of thanks without mentioning the endless help and support given by my wife Louise Nicholson. For some years now she has listened with patience to my scattered thoughts on Samuelson, Friedman, Keynes, Hayek, Volcker, Greenspan, Bernanke, and the rest, and she has calmed my troubled brow when the going was hard. This book—and all the others—could not have been written without her love.

Nicholas Wapshott
New York City
July 2020

Notes

CHAPTER 1: THE LAND OF OZ

1. William Vincent Astor (November 15, 1891–February 3, 1959).
2. Italianate mansion (1851) by Sir Charles Barry, near Taplow, Buckinghamshire.
3. William Waldorf "Bill" Astor II, 3rd Viscount Astor (August 13, 1907–March 7, 1966).
4. Waldorf Astor, 2nd Viscount Astor (May 19, 1879–September 30, 1952). Owner of the London *Times*.
5. Nancy Witcher Langhorne Astor, Viscountess Astor (May 19, 1879–May 2, 1964), the first woman member of Parliament to take her seat.
6. By 1958, Cliveden was enjoying a brief period of calm. Within three years, however, the house would find itself again in the headlines, as the place where Conservative government ministers romped with their prostitute mistresses, in a scandal known as the Profumo Affair. John Profumo, secretary of state for war in Harold Macmillan's government, had an affair with prostitute Christine Keeler. He at first denied the affair in the Commons before admitting he had lied, leading to his resignation. The scandal, and similar events, shook Macmillan's government to the core and contributed to the Conservatives' 1964 general election defeat.
7. John Jacob "Jack" Astor IV (July 13, 1864–April 15, 1912).
8. *A Night to Remember* (1958), British movie directed by Roy Ward Baker, starring Kenneth More, Honor Blackman, Kenneth Griffith, Alec McCowen, David McCallum, Michael Bryant.
9. Benjamin Crowninshield "Ben" Bradlee (August 26, 1921–October 21, 2014), *Washington Post* reporter, Washington bureau chief of *Newsweek*, and managing editor of the *Washington Post*.
10. David Halberstam (April 10, 1934–April 23, 2007), *New York Times* journalist whose reporting from Vietnam won him a Pulitzer Prize in 1964.
11. Norton Winfred Simon (February 5, 1907–June 2, 1993), Californian industrialist and philanthropist whose substantial art collection became the Norton Simon Museum in Pasadena, California.
12. Osborn "Oz" Elliott (October 25, 1924–September 28, 2008), editor of *Newsweek*, 1961–1976. Under his leadership, the magazine's weekly circulation doubled to three million.
13. Philip Leslie "Phil" Graham (July 18, 1915–August 3, 1963), publisher (from 1946 until his

death) and co-owner (from 1948) of the *Washington Post*, married to Katharine Graham, daughter of Eugene Meyer.

14. Ben Bradlee, *A Good Life* (Touchstone, New York, 1995), p. 249.

15. Walter Lippmann (September 23, 1889–December 14, 1974), often described as "the most influential American journalist of the 20th century." Author of the influential book *Public Opinion*.

16. Emmet John Hughes (December 26, 1920–September 18, 1982), a foreign-bureau chief and article editor for Time-Life and a speechwriter for Eisenhower.

17. Henry Stuart Hazlitt (November 28, 1894–July 9, 1993), conservative economics writer with a libertarian bent.

18. Henry Christopher Wallich (June 10, 1914–September 15, 1988), professor of economics at Yale and a member of Eisenhower's Council of Economic Advisers before joining the Federal Reserve Board in 1974.

19. John Maynard Keynes, Lord Keynes (June 5, 1883–April 21, 1946), a Cambridge University mathematician turned economist whose book *The General Theory of Employment, Interest and Money* (1936) overhauled macroeconomics and encouraged governments to borrow and spend to avoid recessions.

20. Lyndon Baines Johnson (August 27, 1908–January 22, 1973), a Texan Democrat who served as the thirty-seventh vice-president of the United States under President John F. Kennedy, from 1961 until Kennedy's assassination in November 1963, and then as the thirty-sixth president of the United States, from 1963 to 1969.

21. John Kenneth Galbraith (October 15, 1908–April 29, 2006).

22. *The Affluent Society* (1958) described how the U.S. private sector had become more prosperous since World War II but the public sector lacked adequate social and physical infrastructure, which caused intolerable income disparities; the book anticipated President Lyndon Johnson's "War on Poverty."

23. John Fitzgerald "Jack" Kennedy (May 29, 1917–November 22, 1963), the thirty-fifth president of the United States, from January 1961 until his assassination in November 1963.

24. The brief, glamorous presidency of John F. Kennedy was widely likened to the idyllic world of King Arthur's Camelot, portrayed in 1960 in an eponymous Lerner and Loewe musical, then a 1967 movie starring Richard Harris and Vanessa Redgrave.

25. Paul Anthony Samuelson (May 15, 1915–December 13, 2009), the first American to win the Nobel Memorial Prize in Economic Sciences. The author of the definitive economics textbook, named simply *Economics*. The *New York Times* dubbed him the "foremost academic economist of the 20th century."

26. Interview with Samuelson, *New York Times*, October 31, 1993.

27. Arthur Meier Schlesinger Jr., born Arthur Bancroft Schlesinger (October 15, 1917–February 28, 2007), historian, social critic, and public intellectual.

28. John Kenneth Galbraith, *A Life in Our Times: Memoirs* (Ballantine, New York, 1982), pp. 389–90.

29. Richard Parker, *John Kenneth Galbraith: His Life, His Politics, His Economics* (Farrar, Straus and Giroux, New York, 2005), p. 416.

30. Letter from Elliott to Samuelson, May 17, 1966. Duke Samuelson archive.

31. Milton Friedman (July 31, 1912–November 16, 2006), conservative economist who advised presidents Nixon and Reagan and British prime minister Thatcher. Described by *The Economist* as "the most influential economist of the second half of the 20th century . . . possibly of all of it."

32. *Oriental Economist,* November 1976, pp. 17–18.

33. Ibid.

34. George Joseph Stigler (January 17, 1911–December 1, 1991), Chicago School economist who won the 1982 Nobel Prize in Economic Sciences.

35. Milton Friedman and Rose D. Friedman, *Two Lucky People: Memoirs* (University of Chicago Press, Chicago, 1998), p. 357.

36. *New York Times,* September 4, 1966.

37. Friedrich Hayek, known as F. A. Hayek (May 8, 1899–March 23, 1992), an Austrian-born and later British economist and philosopher, key figure in the Austrian School, who defended classical liberal economics from the Keynesians. Notable for moving to London from Vienna to better challenge the revolutionary ideas about macroeconomics emanating from Keynes from 1931 onward. The 1974 Nobel laureate in economics.

38. Since America had entered World War II in 1941, the U.S. economy had been managed by the federal government under both Democratic and Republican administrations. But by the end of the Sixties, the relentless use of taxpayer dollars and public borrowing to maintain economic growth had reached an impasse, with rampant inflation and a sharp slowing of growth.

39. Friedman and Friedman, *Two Lucky People,* p. 357.

40. Letter from Samuelson to Friedman, December 8, 1995; *Two Lucky People,* p. 357n.

CHAPTER 2: BORN AGAIN IN A CHICAGO CLASSROOM

1. Interview with Samuelson by William A. Barnett, University of Kansas, December 23, 2003.

2. Massachusetts Institute of Technology (MIT) 150 Oral History project, July 19, 2007. https://infinitehistory.mit.edu/video/paul-samuelson.

3. As first cousins, they were obliged to move from Chicago, where the marriage of first cousins was illegal, first to Wisconsin, then Indiana, where it wasn't.

4. MIT 150 Oral History project, July 19, 2007. https://infinitehistory.mit.edu/video/paul-samuelson.

5. Ibid.

6. MIT150 Oral History project. https://infinitehistory.mit.edu/video/paul-samuelson.

7. Karen Ilse Horn, *Roads to Wisdom, Conversations with Ten Nobel Laureates in Economics* (Edward Elgar, Cheltenham, England, 2009), p. 43.

8. MIT150 Oral History project. https://infinitehistory.mit.edu/video/paul-samuelson.

9. Ibid.

10. His father owned a set of Harvard Classics—the most important books in the Western canon—included one of the founding works of economics, Adam Smith's *Wealth of Nations*, but young Samuelson failed to read it.

11. Thomas Robert Malthus (February 13, 1766–December 29, 1834), English cleric who studied the influence of demographics on economics.

12. MIT 150 Oral History project. https://infinitehistory.mit.edu/video/paul-samuelson.

13. Aaron Director (September 21, 1901–September 11, 2004), a professor at the University of Chicago Law School who played a central role in the founding of the Chicago School of economics. Director influenced some prominent jurists, including Robert Bork, Richard Posner, Antonin Scalia, and William Rehnquist. He was an early patron of Friedrich Hayek and was instrumental in having Hayek's *Road to Serfdom* published in the U.S.

14. The Chicago School of economics at the University of Chicago has championed a neoclassical school of economic thought, which, during the Keynesian hegemony, countered the new orthodoxy with traditional market-based arguments. School members included Gary Becker, Ronald Coase, Eugene Fama, Robert Fogel, Milton Friedman, Lars Peter Hansen, Friedrich Hayek, Frank Knight, Robert E. Lucas, Richard Posner, Theodore Schultz, D. Gale Johnson, and George Stigler.

15. Frank Hyneman Knight (November 7, 1885–April 15, 1972), one of the founders of the Chicago School of economics, who taught Nobel economics laureates Friedman, George Stigler, and James M. Buchanan.

16. Jacob Viner (May 3, 1892–September 12, 1970), Canadian economist who cofounded the Chicago School of economics. Viner was more skeptical of the virtue of the free market and is therefore often not considered a member of the Chicago School.

17. Henry Calvert Simons (October 9, 1899–June 19, 1946), University of Chicago economist and early exponent of monetarist theory.

18. Paul Howard Douglas (March 26, 1892–September 24, 1976), professor of economics at the University of Chicago and other schools, who served as a Democratic senator from Illinois from 1949 to 1967.

19. Roger E. Backhouse, *Founder of Modern Economics: Paul A. Samuelson*, vol. 1: *Becoming Samuelson, 1915–1948* (Oxford University Press, Oxford, 2017), p. 103.

20. Samuelson credited the inspiration for his model to Alvin Harvey Hansen (August 23, 1887–June 6, 1975), known as "the American Keynes," a Harvard professor of economics who advised the Roosevelt administration on the application of Keynesian ideas to government and who helped create the Council of Economic Advisers and the Social Security system.

21. Theodore Shultz, chairman of the Chicago economics department, tried to persuade Samuelson to stay, saying, "We'll have two leading minds of different philosophical bent—you and Milton Friedman—and that will be fruitful." But Samuelson decided to go, saying that as a centrist he would feel obliged to adopt leftist opinions he did not agree with, simply to "fruitfully" counter Friedman's right-wing views.

22. MIT Oral History project. https://infinitehistory.mit.edu/video/paul-samuelson.

23. Obituary of Samuelson, *New York Times*, December 14, 2009.

24. Horn, *Roads to Wisdom*, p. 47.

25. David C. Colander and Harry Landreth, *The Coming of Keynesianism to America: Conversation with the Founders of Keynesian Economics* (Edward Elgar, Cheltenham, U.K., and Northampton, Mass., 1996).

26. Friedman was to go further, suggesting that "all of the progress that the US has made over the last couple of centuries has come from unemployment. It has come from figuring out

how to produce more goods with fewer workers, thereby releasing labor to be more productive in other areas. It has never come about through permanent unemployment, but temporary unemployment, in the process of shifting people from one area to another." Interview with Friedman, *Wall Street Journal*, July 22, 2006.

27. Interview with Samuelson by William A. Barnett, University of Kansas, December 23, 2003, p. 156.

28. Wassily Wassilyevich Leontief (August 5, 1906–February 5, 1999), American economist, born in Austro-Hungary, winner of the 1973 Nobel Prize for Economics.

29. Joseph Alois Schumpeter (February 8, 1883–January 8, 1950), Austrian-born American economist and political scientist who served as finance minister of Austria in 1919. Associated with the term "creative destruction" in which markets gradually restore themselves after a crash.

30. Gottfried von Haberler (July 20, 1900–May 6, 1995), an American economist born in Austria.

31. Alvin Harvey Hansen, professor of economics at Harvard, helped create the Council of Economic Advisers and the Social Security system. Best known for introducing Keynesian economics in the United States in the 1930s and popularizing the ideas in Keynes's *The General Theory*.

32. MIT Oral History project, July 19, 2007. https://infinitehistory.mit.edu/video/paul-samuelson.

33. Paul A. Samuelson and William A. Barnett (eds.), *Inside the Economist's Mind: The History of Modern Economic Thought, as Explained by Those Who Produced It* (Wiley-Blackwell, Hoboken, N.J., 2005), p. 11.

34. Samuelson told Karen Ilse Horn, as recounted in her *Roads to Wisdom, Conversations with Ten Nobel Laureates in Economics*, p. 49, that had he stayed at Chicago, "I would have missed out on the monopolistic competition revolution, which they didn't believe in. I would have missed out on the Keynesian revolution that they didn't believe in. I would have missed out on mathematization of economics, although some of that did even take place at the University of Chicago."

35. Harold Hitchings Burbank (July 3, 1887–February 6, 1951), Harvard professor of economics from 1927, David A. Wells professor of political economy from 1931, department chairman, economics, 1927–1938.

36. Samuelson conversation with William A. Barnett, *Inside the Economist's Mind: Conversations with Eminent Economists*, ed. Paul A. Samuelson and William A. Barnett (John Wiley & Sons, Hoboken, NJ, 2009), p. 156.

37. Edwin Bidwell Wilson (April 25, 1879–December 28, 1964), Yale and Harvard mathematician and polymath.

38. MIT Oral History project. https://infinitehistory.mit.edu/video/paul-samuelson.

39. Ibid.

40. Ibid.

41. Lorie Tarshis (March 22, 1911–October 4, 1993). For a full account of the incident, see http://community.middlebury.edu/~colander/articles/Political%20Influence%20on%20the%20Textbook%20Keynesian%20Revolution.pdf.

42. William Frank Buckley Jr. (christened William Francis Buckley but known as William Frank) (November 24, 1925–February 27, 2008). American conservative journalist, editor, and commentator, founder in 1955 of *National Review* magazine, and host of the combative television interview show *Firing Line.*

43. Karl Taylor Compton (September 14, 1887–June 22, 1954), physicist and president of the Massachusetts Institute of Technology, 1930–1948.

44. Quoted in Samuelson, "On the Prowl in an Enchanted Forest," *New York Times,* October 12, 1986.

45. Samuelson, Nobel Economists Lecture Series, Trinity University, San Antonio, February 1985.

46. David Warsh, "The Rivals: Paul Samuelson and Milton Friedman arrive at the University of Chicago in 1932," *Economic Principals* blog, July 12, 2015. http://www.economicprincipals .com/issues/2015.07.12/1758.html.

47. Ibid.

48. Adlai Ewing Stevenson II (February 5, 1900–July 14, 1965), governor of Illinois, 1949–1953; Democratic candidate for president in 1952 and 1956; U.S. ambassador to the United Nations, 1961–1965.

49. William Averell Harriman (November 15, 1891–July 26, 1986), secretary of commerce under President Harry S. Truman, governor of New York, 1955–1958; candidate for the Democratic presidential nomination in 1952 and 1956; U.S. ambassador to the Soviet Union; and U.S. ambassador to Britain.

50. MIT 150 Oral History project. https://infinitehistory.mit.edu/video/paul-samuelson.

51. Walt Whitman Rostow, aka Walt Rostow or W. W. Rostow (October 7, 1916–February 13, 2003), American economist and political theorist who helped formulate U.S. anticommunist foreign policy in Southeast Asia in the 1960s, and a strong proponent of U.S. involvement in the Vietnam War.

52. Interview with Samuelson by William A. Barnett, University of Kansas, December 23, 2003, in *Macroeconomic Dynamics,* 8, 2004, p. 533.

53. Joseph Pechman, interview with Samuelson, Council of Economic Advisers Oral History August 1, 1964.

54. Ibid.

55. Quoted in *New York Times* obituary of Samuelson, December 14, 2009.

56. MIT 150 Oral History project. https://infinitehistory.mit.edu/video/paul-samuelson

57. Samuelson said at a talk at Claremont Graduate University, Calif., in January 1991 that he had been advised to float the dollar by Nicholas Kaldor, the Cambridge economist. Nicholas Kaldor, Baron Kaldor (May 12, 1908–September 30, 1986), born Káldor Miklós, Cambridge economist, acolyte of Keynes, and special adviser to the British prime minister Harold Wilson, 1964–1970. It was Kaldor who, while at the London School of Economics in 1931, had, on Lionel Robbins's instruction, helped Hayek with his use of English in the duel-by-learned-journal against Keynes.

58. MIT Oral History project. https://infinitehistory.mit.edu/video/paul-samuelson. file:/// Users/nicholaswapshott/Downloads/Paul%20A.%20Samuelson.pdf.

59. Lawrence Henry "Larry" Summers (November 30, 1954–), whose father, Robert Summers,

(who changed his name from Samuelson to Summers) is Paul Samuelson's brother. President Emeritus and Charles W. Eliot University Professor of Harvard University. Former chief economist of the World Bank (1991–1993); Undersecretary of the Treasury for International Affairs (1993–1995); Deputy Secretary of the Treasury (1995–1999); Secretary of the Treasury (1999–2001); President of Harvard University (2001–2006) Director of the National Economic Council (2009–2010).

60. MIT memorial service for Samuelson, April 10, 2010. http://news.mit.edu/2010/samuelson -memorial-0412.

61. Samuelson personal correspondence, 2004. Quoted in Michael Szenberg, Michael Ramratttan, and Aron A. Gottesman, eds., *Samuelsonian Economics and the Twenty-First Century* (New York, Oxford University Press, 2006), p. xxv.

62. The post was eventually taken by the Keynesian economist Walter Heller (August 27, 1915– June 15, 1987), who is credited with suggesting to Lyndon Johnson that he wage a "war on poverty."

CHAPTER 3: PARADISE LOST

1. Friedman's biographical note for the Nobel Prize committee. http://www.nobelprize.org/ nobel_prizes/economic-sciences/laureates/1976/friedman-bio.html.

2. John B. Taylor interview with Friedman. http://web.stanford.edu/~johntayl/Online paperscombinedbyyear/2001/An_Interview_with_Milton_Friedman.pdf.

3. Interview with Friedman for the WGBH economics series *Commanding Heights*, 2002. https://www.pbs.org/wgbh/commandingheights/shared/minitext/int_miltonfriedman.html.

4. Aaron Director inspired a generation of conservative jurists, including Robert Bork, Richard Posner, Antonin Scalia, and Chief Justice William Rehnquist.

5. Friedman's biographical note for the Nobel Prize committee. http://www.nobelprize.org/ nobel_prizes/economic-sciences/laureates/1976/friedman-bio.html.

6. David Friedman (born February 12, 1945), American economist, physicist, legal scholar, and anarcho-capitalist theorist, followed his parents into economics, sharing their belief in free markets and libertarian thinking. He wrote *The Machinery of Freedom* (1973), which advocates an anarcho-capitalist society.

7. Friedman left the shoe store job abruptly after receiving just a seventy-five-cent commission for a twelve-hour day.

8. Warsh, "The Rivals," *Economic Principals* blog, July 12, 2015. http://www.economicprincipals .com/issues/2015.07.12/1758.html.

9. Harold Hotelling (September 29, 1895–December 26, 1973) was a mathematical statistician and an economic theorist He was Associate Professor of Mathematics at Stanford University 1927–1931, a member of the faculty of Columbia University 1931–1946, and Professor of Mathematical Statistics at the University of North Carolina at Chapel Hill from 1946 until his death. Known for Hotelling's Law, Hotelling's Dilemma, Hotelling's Rule in economics, and Hotelling's T-squared distribution in statistics.

10. Wesley Clair Mitchell (August 5, 1874–October 29, 1948), American economist known for his empirical work on business cycles who led the National Bureau of Economic Research in its first decades.

11. John Maurice Clark (November 30, 1884– June 27, 1963), American economist who was a pioneer in developing the notion of "workable competition" and the theoretical basis of Keynesian economic notions, including the concept of the multiplier.

12. Lloyd W. Mints (February 20, 1888–January 3, 1989), American economist and early monetarist whose quantity theory of money ideas were central to the Chicago School.

13. Wilson Allen Wallis (November 5, 1912–October 12, 1998), American economist and statistician, chancellor of the University of Rochester and undersecretary of State for Economic Affairs, who advised presidents Eisenhower, Richard Nixon, Gerald Ford, and Ronald Reagan on economic policy.

14. Henry Schultz (September 4, 1893–November 26, 1938), American economist, statistician, and one of the founders of econometrics.

15. Arthur Cecil Pigou (November 18, 1877–March 7, 1959), English economist, Professor of Political Economy at the University of Cambridge 1908–1943.

16. Frank William Taussig (December 28, 1859–November 11, 1940), American economist credited with creating the foundations of modern trade theory.

17. Simon Smith Kuznets (April 30, 1901–July 8, 1985), American economist and the 1971 Nobel laureate in economics.

18. Friedman was never one to waste an opportunity to publish. Just as he had turned his work for the National Resources Committee into a book, so his work on professional incomes became a book, coauthored with Kuznets, *Income from Independent Professional Practice* (National Bureau of Economic Research, New York, 1945). As Friedman wrote in his biography for the Nobel Committee, "That book was finished by 1940, but its publication was delayed until after the war because of controversy among some Bureau directors about our conclusion that the medical profession's monopoly powers had raised substantially the incomes of physicians relative to that of dentists."

19. Warsh, "The Rivals," *Economic Principals* blog, July 12, 2015. http://www.economicprincipals .com/issues/2015.07.12/1758.html.

20. Friedman and Friedman, *Two Lucky People,* p. 59.

21. Ibid., pp. 58–59.

22. Ibid., p. 58.

23. Walter A. Morton (1899–1982), economics professor at the University of Wisconsin-Madison 1926–1969, an expert on tariffs, taxes, unemployment insurance, and British finance in the 1930s.

24. Carl Sumner Shoup (October 26, 1902–March 23, 2000), American economist who contributed to formulating the tax codes of Canada, the United States, Japan, Europe, and South and Central America in the 1930s, '40s, and '50s. McVicknar Professor Emeritus of Columbia University.

25. Ruth Prince Mack (November 6, 1903–December 30, 2002). A member of the National Bureau of Economic Research staff in New York City from the 1940s through the 1960s. On the faculty of Columbia University, the New School for Social Research, New York, and the Baruch School of Business and Public Administration, City University of New York.

26. Meanwhile, Rose Friedman worked part-time at the Bureau of Home Economics.

27. Keynes's solution was neither price controls nor additional taxation but "forced savings," taxation that would be levied but returned after war's end. Hayek agreed with Keynes, but suggested that the savings should be invested in the stock market.

28. Friedman and Friedman, *Two Lucky People,* pp. 112–13.

29. Ibid., p. 123.

30. John B. Taylor interview with Samuelson. http://web.stanford.edu/~johntayl/Online paperscombinedbyyear/2001/An_Interview_with_Milton_Friedman.pdf.

31. Jacob Marschak (July 23, 1898–July 27, 1977), Kiev-born economist.

32. Robert Maynard Hutchins (January 17, 1899–May 14, 1977), dean of Yale Law School (1927–1929) and president (1929–1945), then chancellor (1945–1951), of the University of Chicago.

33. Letter from Marschak to Robert M. Hutchins, February 28, 1946, University of Chicago, Office of the President, Hutchins Administrative Records, 1892–1951, Box 73, pp. 3–4.

34. Letter from Friedman to Stigler, November 27, 1946, quoted in J. D. Hammond and C. H. Hammond, *Making Chicago Price Theory: Friedman-Stigler Correspondence 1945–1957* (Routledge, London, 2006).

35. Anna Jacobson Schwartz (November 11, 1915–June 21, 2012). Economist at the National Bureau of Economic Research and a writer for the *New York Times* who, with Friedman, wrote *A Monetary History of the United States, 1867–1960.*

36. The book was first published in Britain, where Hayek was living, in March 1944.

37. Friedman and Friedman, *Two Lucky People,* p. 158.

38. They found a fourth hand at bridge at the Mont Pèlerin meeting, the Norwegian singer and songwriter Trygve Hoff (July 7, 1938–December 2, 1987).

39. Friedman and Friedman, *Two Lucky People.*

40. Ibid.

41. Ludwig Heinrich Edler von Mises (September 29, 1881–October 10, 1973), Austrian School economist, historian, and sociologist. His *Socialism: An Economic and Sociological Analysis,* provided the logic that challenged the efficacy of government intervention in an economy.

42. A charitable trust, run by the eponymous Volker's nephew, which promoted free-market ideas and its thinkers. It seed-funded what became a burgeoning conservative and libertarian intellectual movement. The Fund funded Hayek's move to the University of Chicago and Director's Law and Society program there.

43. Interview with Friedman for the WGBH economics series *Commanding Heights,* 2002. http://www.pbs.org/wgbh/commandingheights/shared/minitextlo/int_miltonfriedman .html.

44. Quoted in Friedman and Friedman, *Two Lucky People,* p. 159.

45. After 1957, when his children were old enough to be left alone in America, Friedman, often accompanied by Rose, made the annual Mont Pèlerin meeting his summer vacation. He became president of the society in 1971.

46. Interview with Hayek, quoted in Alan Ebenstein, *Friedrich Hayek: A Biography* (Palgrave, New York, 2001.)

47. Pigou, Arthur (A. C.), *Economics in Practice* (Macmillan, London, 1935), p. 24.

48. Sidney Blumenthal, *The Rise of the Counter-Establishment: The Conservative Ascent to Political Power* (Union Square Press, New York, 1986), p. 91.

49. Joan Violet Robinson, born Joan Violet Maurice (October 31, 1903–August 5, 1983), British economist and leading member of Keynes's Cambridge Circus.

50. Friedman stood five feet two inches in his stockinged feet.

51. Richard Ferdinand Kahn, Baron Kahn (August 10, 1905–June 6, 1989), British economist. Befriended by Keynes when a student at King's College, as a member of Keynes's Cambridge Circus he became Keynes's closest collaborator on *The General Theory*. Guided by Keynes, he proved that the addition of public money into an economic system, through public works or other means, increased aggregate demand and resulted in predictable, measurable increases in economic activity. See *The Making of Keynes' General Theory* (Cambridge University Press, Cambridge, 1948).

52. (Edward) Austin (Gossage) Robinson (November 20, 1897–June 1, 1993), British economist and prominent member of Keynes's Cambridge Circus.

53. Kaldor helped Hayek write his assaults upon Keynes's ideas in *Economica* in 1931, and became a prominent Keynesian and advised Harold Wilson's Labour government 1964–1970.

54. Harry Gordon Johnson (May 26, 1923–May 8, 1977), Canadian economist.

55. Sir Dennis Holme Robertson (May 23, 1890–April 21, 1963), British economist. Like members of Keynes's Cambridge Circus, Robertson was intimately involved in critiquing Keynes's early drafts of *The General Theory*. He invented the term "liquidity trap."

56. Friedman and Friedman, *Two Lucky People*, p. 242.

57. The Bretton Woods Conference, formally the United Nations Monetary and Financial Conference, gathered 730 delegates from all forty-four Allied nations at the Mount Washington Hotel, Bretton Woods, New Hampshire, to regulate the international monetary and financial order after the conclusion of World War II. It was presided over and adjudicated by Keynes.

58. Friedman and Friedman, *Two Lucky People*, p. 248.

59. Ibid., p. 249.

60. Rupert Cornwell, "Paul Samuelson: Nobel Prize-winner widely regarded as the most important economist of the 20th century," *The Independent*, December 16, 2009.

61. Conor Clarke, "An Interview with Paul Samuelson," *The Atlantic*, June 17, 2009.

62. Michael M. Weinstein, "Paul A. Samuelson, Economist, Dies at 94," *New York Times*, December 13, 2009.

63. John Cassidy interview with Samuelson, *The New Yorker*, December 14, 2009.

64. Ibid.

65. Ibid.

66. Marie-Esprit-Léon Walras (December 16, 1834–January 5, 1910), French mathematical economist who formulated the marginal theory of value and pioneered the development of general equilibrium theory.

67. Letter from Samuelson to Friedman, August 25, 1950. Duke Samuelson archive.

68. Letter from Samuelson to Friedman, May 15, 1973. Duke Samuelson archive.

69. John Cassidy interview with Samuelson, *The New Yorker*, December 14, 2009.

CHAPTER 4: COUNTER KEYNES

1. Friedman and Friedman, *Two Lucky People*, p. 255.

2. After his scuffle with Keynes in 1931, Hayek spent years attempting to counter Keynes's *General Theory*. The eventual result, *The Pure Theory of Capital* (1941), was largely ignored, even by those opposed to Keynes's ideas.

3. Friedrich Hayek, *Hayek on Hayek: An Autobiographical Dialogue*, ed. Stephen Kresge and Leif Wenar (University of Chicago Press, Chicago, 2010), p. 145.

4. Friedman and Friedman, *Two Lucky People*, p. 222.

5. Ibid., pp. 229–30.

6. Ibid., p. 230.

7. Milton Friedman, *Capitalism and Freedom*, 40th anniversary edition (University of Chicago Press, Chicago, 2002).

8. Warsh, "The Rivals," *Economic Principals* blog, July 12, 2015. http://www.economicprincipals.com/issues/2015.07.12/1758.html.

9. https://www.jfklibrary.org/learn/about-jfk/historic-speeches/inaugural-address.

10. Friedman, *Capitalism and Freedom*, p 1.

11. Ibid.

12. Ibid., p. 2.

13. Ibid.

14. Ibid., p. 198.

15. Ibid.

16. Ibid., p. 199.

17. Ibid.

18. Blumenthal, *The Rise of the Counter-Establishment*, pp. 106–7.

19. Julius Henry "Groucho" Marx (October 2, 1890–August 19, 1977), American comedian, who made thirteen feature movies as part of the Marx Brothers.

20. Marx Brothers movie (1932) with screenplay by Bert Kalmar, Harry Ruby, S. J. Perelman, and Will B. Johnstone.

21. Friedman's libertarianism appears to owe little to other libertarian thinkers like von Mises, Ayn Rand, or Murray Rothbard, who are given little or no credit in his writings. Rather, his own libertarianism—which he preferred to call "liberalism"—appears to have stemmed from his own experience, in particular his observations when working for Roosevelt's New Deal.

22. "Liberty Is Winning the Battle of Ideas," *Register* (Santa Ana, Calif.), November 23, 1986. Reprinted in the Mont Pèlerin Society Newsletter, May 1987, pp. 8–9. Excerpted from a speech at a banquet celebrating the move of the Reason Foundation from Santa Barbara to Los Angeles, October 18, 1986.

23. Samuelson, *Economics: An Introductory Analysis,* 9th ed. (McGraw-Hill, New York, 1973), p. 848.

24. George Walker Bush (July 6, 1946–), forty-third president of the United States, 2001–2009. governor of Texas, 1995–2000.

25. Willard Mitt Romney (March 12, 1947–), United States senator from Utah since January

2019. Governor of Massachusetts from 2003 to 2007 and Republican nominee for president in the 2012 election.

26. Newton Leroy Gingrich, born McPherson (June 17, 1943–), Speaker of the U.S. House of Representatives, 1995–1999.

27. Rudolph William Louis Giuliani (May 28, 1944–), mayor of New York City, 1994–2001, personal attorney to President Donald Trump, 2018–2021.

28. Richard Bruce Cheney (January 30, 1941–), vice-president of the United States, 2001–2009. White House chief of staff from 1975 to 1977; U.S. House of Representatives member for Wyoming's at-large district, 1979–1989; secretary of defense, 1989–1993.

29. For once he found himself agreeing with J. K. Galbraith.

30. Friedman, "Why Not a Volunteer Army?" *New Individualist Review* (Liberty Fund, Indianapolis, Ind., 1981).

31. Friedman, "Prohibition and Drugs," *Newsweek*, May 1, 1972, p. 104.

32. Friedman first advocated this idea in "The Role of Government in Education," *Economics and the Public Interest*, ed. Robert A. Solo (Rutgers University Press, New Brunswick, N.J., 1955).

33. Friedman, "Decentralizing Schools," *Newsweek*, November 18, 1968, p. 100.

34. Ibid.

35. Barry Morris Goldwater (January 2, 1909–May 29, 1998). Five-term U.S. senator from Arizona (1953–1965, 1969–1987) and the Republican Party's nominee for president against President Lyndon Johnson in 1964.

36. Nelson Aldrich Rockefeller (July 8, 1908–January 26, 1979), American businessman and property developer, served as the forty-first vice-president of the United States from 1974 to 1977, and as the forty-ninth governor of New York (1959–1973).

37. William J. Baroody Jr. (November 5, 1937–June 8, 1996). White House Office of Public Liaison under President Gerald Ford and, later, president of the American Enterprise Institute (AEI).

38. Friedman and Friedman, *Two Lucky People*, p. 368.

39. *Saturday Evening Post*, August 31, 1963.

40. Goldwater's speech at the Republican National Convention, the Cow Palace, San Francisco, July 16, 1964.

41. http://www.cnn.com/2014/09/07/politics/daisy-ad-turns-50/index.html.

42. Friedman talk to University of Chicago faculty, "Schools of Chicago," reproduced in *The University of Chicago Record*, 1974, p. 6.

CHAPTER 5: DUELING COLUMNISTS

1. Paul A. Samuelson, *The Samuelson Sampler* (Thomas Horton and Company, Glen Ridge, N.J., 1973), April 1968, p. 65.

2. Ibid., January 1969, p. 168.

3. Interview with Samuelson by William A. Barnett, University of Kansas, December 23, 2003.

4. Friedman, *Newsweek*, November 9, 1970, p. 80. http://miltonfriedman.hoover.org/objects/56682/paul-samuelson?ctx=e20bfa6d-28ba-45c5-af74-e7802e94570f&idx=19.

5. Samuelson, *The Samuelson Sampler*, p. vii.

6. Ibid., November 1967, p. 39.

7. Ibid., January 1967, p. 34.

8. *Newsweek*, April 9, 1979.

9. Samuelson, *The Samuelson Sampler*, p. vii.

10. Samuelson, "Raising 1967 Tax Rates," *Newsweek*, December 1966.

11. Jean-Jacques Rousseau (June 28, 1712–July 2, 1778), eighteenth-century philosopher, writer, and composer from Geneva. His political philosophy influenced the Enlightenment, particularly in France, and the French Revolution. His *Discourse on Inequality* and *The Social Contract* are pillars of modern political and social thought.

12. Sigmund Freud, born Sigismund Schlomo Freud (May 6, 1856–September 23, 1939), Austrian neurologist and the founder of psychoanalysis.

13. Elwyn Brooks "E. B." White (July 11, 1899–October 1, 1985), American author of *Stuart Little* and *Charlotte's Web*, who wrote regularly for *The New Yorker*.

14. Joseph Rudyard Kipling (December 30, 1865–January 18, 1936), English journalist, novelist, and poet whose work includes *The Jungle Book*, *The Man Who Would Be King*, the poems *The Road to Mandalay*, *Gunga Din*, and *The White Man's Burden*.

15. Niccolò Machiavelli (May 3, 1469–June 21, 1527), Italian Renaissance historian, politician, diplomat, philosopher, and writer often credited with founding the study of political science.

16. Samuel Butler (December 4, 1835–June 18, 1902). British translator of classical Latin texts and author of the utopian satire *Erewhon*.

17. Charles John Huffam Dickens (February 7, 1812–June 9, 1870), English author and social critic whose works include *Oliver Twist, Nicholas Nickleby, A Christmas Carol, David Copperfield, Bleak House, Hard Times, Little Dorrit, A Tale of Two Cities*, and *Great Expectations*. His novels, such as *Great Expectations, Bleak House, A Christmas Carol*, and *David Copperfield*, brought to the public attention the profound inequalities of life in London in the mid nineteenth century.

18. Blumenthal, *The Rise of the Counter-Establishment*, p. 89.

19. John Davenport, "The Radical Economics of Milton Friedman," *Fortune*, June 1, 1967.

20. Conor Clarke, "An Interview with Paul Samuelson," *The Atlantic*, June 17, 2009.

21. Robert Merton Solow (August 23, 1924–), 1987 Nobel Prize–winning economist and MIT professor since 1949.

22. Solow quoted by Paul Krugman in "Who Was Milton Friedman?" *New York Review of Books*, February 15, 2007.

23. Quoted by Robert Sobel from a Samuelson interview in *Time* magazine, in Sobel's *The Worldly Economists* (Free Press, N.Y., 1980), p. 144.

24. Paul A. Samuelson, "My Life Philosophy," *The American Economist*, vol. 27, no. 2, Fall 1983, October 1, 1983. https://doi.org/10.1177/056943458302700202.

25. Michael M. Weinstein, "Paul A. Samuelson, Economist, Dies at 94," *New York Times*, December 13, 2009.

26. Ibid.

27. George Pratt Shultz (December 13, 1920–February 6, 2021), economist and business-

man. Nixon's secretary of labor, 1969–1970; director of the Office of Management and Budget, 1970–1972; and secretary of the treasury, 1972–1974. Reagan's secretary of state, 1982–1989.

28. Brad DeLong, obituary of Friedman. https://delong.typepad.com/sdj/2012/01/econ-1-uc -berkeley-spring-2012-why-we-are-reading-milton-friedman-and-rose-director-friedman -free-to-choose.html.

29. Sir Samuel Brittan (December 29, 1933–), English journalist. The *Financial Times's* first economics correspondent.

30. Samuel Brittan, obituary of Friedman, *Financial Times*, November 17, 2006.

31. Martin Anderson (August 5, 1936–January 3, 2015), economist, policy analyst, and author.

32. Martin Anderson, *Revolution: The Reagan Legacy* (Hoover Institution Press, Stanford, Calif., 1990), p. 172.

33. Robert Solow, "Why Is There No Milton Friedman Today?" *Econ Journal Watch*, vol. 10, no. 2, May 2013, pp. 214–16.

34. Brian Snowdon and Howard Vane interview with Friedman, in Snowdon and Vane, *Modern Macroeconomics: Its Origin, Development, and Current State* (Cheltenham, U.K, Edward Elgar, 2005.

35. Samuelson, *Economics*, 1st ed. (1948), p. 8.

36. John Maynard Keynes, *The Economic Consequences of the Peace* (Harcourt, Brace and Howe, New York, 1920), p. 235.

37. Keynes, *The Collected Writings of John Maynard Keynes*, vol. 4: *A Tract on Monetary Reform* (Macmillan for the Royal Economic Society, London, 1971), p. 16.

38. Ibid., p. 136.

39. Ibid., p. 65.

40. Arthur Neville Chamberlain (March 18, 1869–November 9, 1940), Conservative prime minister from May 1937 to May 1940. He is best known for his policy of appeasement and signing the Munich Agreement of 1938, conceding the German-speaking Sudetenland region of Czechoslovakia to Adolf Hitler's Nazi Germany, without recourse to the Czechs. When in 1939 Hitler invaded Poland, Chamberlain declared war on Germany and remained prime minister for eight months, being supplanted by Winston Churchill.

41. Keynes, *Collected Writings*, vol 19: *Activities 1922–9: The Return to Gold and Industrial Policy* (Macmillan for the Royal Economic Society, London, 1981), pp. 158–62.

42. Ibid., p. 229.

43. Ibid,. pp. 158–62.

44. Ibid., p. 220.

45. John Maynard Keynes, *The End of Laissez-Faire* (Hogarth Press, London, 1926), p. 47.

46. Paul A. Samuelson, *Readings in Economics*, 6th ed. (McGraw-Hill, New York, 1970), p. 85.

47. Friedrich Hayek, *Prices and Production and Other Works: F. A. Hayek on Money, the Business Cycle, and the Gold Standard*, ed. Joseph T. Salerno (Ludwig von Mises Institute, Auburn, Ala., 2008), p. 275.

48. Hayek, *The Road to Serfdom*, p. 125.

49. Letter from John Maynard Keynes to Friedrich Hayek, June 28, 1944. Reprinted in Keynes, *Collected Writings*, vol. 27: *Activities 1940–1946: Shaping the Post-War World: Employment*

and Commodities, ed. Elizabeth Johnson, Donald Moggridge (1980), pp. 385–87 (Macmillan for the Royal Economic Society, London, 1973).

50. Ibid.

51. Samuelson, *Economics,* 8th ed. (1970), p. 140.

52. Interview with Milton Friedman, *Playboy,* February 21, 1970.

53. Paul Krugman, "Who Was Milton Friedman?" *New York Review of Books,* February 15, 2007.

54. John B. Taylor interview with Milton Friedman, *Macroeconomic Dynamics,* February 2001, pp. 101–31.

CHAPTER 6: TO INTERVENE OR NOT TO INTERVENE

1. Samuelson, *Readings in Economics,* p. 86.

2. Samuelson, *Economics,* 1st ed. (1948), p. 284.

3. *Newsweek,* November 4, 1968.

4. Interview with Friedman, "Outspoken Economists Milton and Rose Friedman," *San Francisco Focus,* October 1984, pp. 70–78, 162–64.

5. Samuelson, *Economics,* 1st ed. (1948), p. vii.

6. Ibid., p 257.

7. Ibid., p. 617n.

8. Ibid. Samuelson notes that arguments that socialism was capable of managing an economy by "playing the game of competition" was challenged by "F. A. Hayek," who "has argued that this answer overlooks the problem of giving each man the initiative to better the existing order and that only with actual free enterprise do you efficiently utilize the dispersed information which each of us may possess." However, Samuelson, who took a critical interest in how the communist government in Russia addressed economic issues, adds this, as if to show that, notwithstanding Hayek, socialism could embrace a version of market forces: "See Chapter 40 for the movement in Soviet Russia to depend more on prices and profitability." Had Samuelson been more generous, he might have credited Hayek in part with the Soviet embrace of notions about the importance of prices.

9. Ibid., p. 207n. The note concerns research by Friedman, James S. Duesenberry, and Franco Modigliani about the lack of the newly rich to save compared to greater saving by the "old moneyed" who had enjoyed wealth for a long time.

10. Ibid., p. 272.

11. Paul Samuelson, contribution to a 1958 symposium sponsored by the Committee for Economic Development.

12. Friedman and Friedman, *Two Lucky People,* p. 341.

13. *Time,* December 31, 1966.

14. *Time,* February 4, 1966.

15. Sir William George Granville Venables Vernon Harcourt, KC (October 14, 1827–October 1, 1904). British lawyer, journalist, and Liberal Home Secretary, chancellor of the exchequer, and Leader of the Opposition.

16. Private letter from Samuelson to Friedman, May 17, 1966. Hoover Institution Friedman archive.

17. Letter from Friedman to Samuelson, May 11, 1987. Duke Samuelson archive.

18. Mark Skousen, "The Perseverance of Paul Samuelson's *Economics*," *Journal of Economic Perspectives*, vol. 11, no. 2, Spring 1997, pp. 137–52.

19. Interview with Friedman, quoted in Mark Skousen, "My Friendly Fights with Dr. Friedman," posted September 25, 2007. https://mskousen.com/2007/09/my-friendly-fights-with-dr-friedman/

20. Robert L. Hetzel, "The Contributions of Milton Friedman to Economics," *Economic Quarterly*, vol. 93, no. 1, Winter 2007, p. 2.

21. Milton Friedman, with the assistance of Rose Friedman, *Capitalism and Freedom* (University of Chicago Press, Chicago, 1962), preface to the 1982 edition.

22. Friedman and Friedman, *Two Lucky People*, p. 341.

23. Samuelson, *The Samuelson Sampler*, April 1973, p. 181.

24. Ibid., October 1966, p. 5.

25. Ibid., September 1968, p. 7.

26. Ibid., p. vii.

27. *Newsweek*, May 29, 1978. Quoted by Mark Skousen, "My Friendly Fights with Dr. Friedman," posted September 25, 2007. https://mskousen.com/2007/09/my-friendly-fights-with-dr-friedman/.

28. The quote is a lift from a chapter heading, "Inflation as a Method of Taxation," in Keynes's *Tract on Monetary Reform*.

29. *Newsweek*, April 9, 1979.

30. Friedman *Newsweek* column, "Because or Despite?" 28 October 1968, p. 104. https://miltonfriedman.hoover.org/friedman_images/Collections/2016c21/NW_10_28_1968.pdf.

31. Ibid.

32. These include: 1819, the first U.S. financial crisis; 1836, U.S. real estate speculation causes stock markets to crash in the U.K., Europe, then the U.S. The Panic of 1857, when the increase in money supply caused by the California Gold Rush dried up, a U.S. credit crisis crashed equity prices. 1866, "Black Friday" caused by railroad speculation. A bank panic led to a shortage of credit. 1907, U.S. bank panic spreads to France and Italy after stock market collapse. 1921, Commodity prices crash. 1929, the "Great Depression" starts after U.S. equities crash.

33. Friedman, "Whose Money Is It Anyway?" *Newsweek*, May 4, 1981, p. 64.

34. The Biblical story of the widow's cruse of oil that miraculously supplies Elijah during a famine (I Kings 17:8–16) was one of Keynes's favorite metaphors. See Keynes, *A Treatise on Money* (Macmillan, London, 1930), p. 139.

35. Friedman, "Whose Money Is It Anyway?" p. 64.

36. Ibid. http://miltonfriedman.hoover.org/friedman_images/Collections/2016c21/NW_05_04_1981.pdf.

37. Friedman, "What Belongs to Whom?" *Newsweek*, March 13, 1978, p. 71. http://miltonfriedman.hoover.org/friedman_images/Collections/2016c21/NW_03_13_1978.pdf.

38. Samuelson, *The Samuelson Sampler*, February 1971, p.191.

39. Samuelson, *Readings in Economics*, p. 90.

40. *Newsweek*, April 9, 1979.

41. Samuelson, *Readings in Economics,* p. 89.

42. *Newsweek,* August 29, 1977.

43. Samuelson, *Readings in Economics,* p. 86.

44. Ayn Rand, born Alisa Zinov'yevna Rosenbaum, (February 2, 1905–March 6, 1982), Russian-American novelist and screenwriter known for her best-selling novels *The Fountainhead* and *Atlas Shrugged.* Born and brought up in Russia, she moved to the United States in 1926.

45. Robert Emerson Lucas Jr. (September 15, 1937–). American University of Chicago economist and the central figure in the development of the new classical approach to macroeconomics. He received the Nobel Prize in Economics in 1995.

46. Gary Stanley Becker (December 2, 1930–May 3, 2014) American economist at the University of Chicago and the 1992 Nobel laureate in Economics.

47. Robert William Fogel (July 1, 1926–June 11, 2013), American economic historian and winner (with Douglass North) of the 1993 Nobel in economics.

48. Samuelson, *The Samuelson Sampler,* November 1968, p. 10.

49. Ibid. July 1972, p. 269.

50. Ibid., January 1970, p. 265.

51. Ibid., July 1972, p. 268.

52. Ibid.

53. Samuel Langhorne Clemens (November 30, 1835–April 21, 1910), American writer who wrote under the pen name Mark Twain. His best-known novels are *The Adventures of Tom Sawyer* (1876) and *The Adventures of Huckleberry Finn* (1885).

54. Samuelson, *The Samuelson Sampler,* July 1972, p. 269.

55. The Samuelson talk was collected in "Issues in Fiscal and Monetary Policy: The Eclectic Economist Views the Controversy; Original and Unpublished Papers," edited by James J. Diamond, DePaul University Department of Economics, November 1971, pp. 20–21.

56. Friedman, "Interest Rates and the Demand for Money," *Journal of Law and Economics,* vol. 9, 1966.

57. Letter from Friedman to Samuelson, November 15, 1971. Hoover Institution Friedman archive.

58. Letter from Samuelson to Friedman, December 1971. Hoover Institution Friedman archive.

59. Samuelson, *Readings in Economics,* p. 86.

60. Ibid., p. 142.

61. Friedman, "Whose Money Is It Anyway?" p. 64. http://miltonfriedman.hoover.org/friedman_images/Collections/2016c21/NW_05_04_1981.pdf.

62. In the 1927 case *Compañía General de Tabacos de Filipinas v. Collector of Internal Revenue,* Holmes wrote a dissenting opinion that included the phrase: "It is true, as indicated in the last cited case, that every exaction of money for an act is a discouragement to the extent of the payment required, but that which in its immediacy is a discouragement may be part of an encouragement when seen in its organic connection with the whole. Taxes are what we pay for civilized society, including the chance to insure."

63. Samuelson, *Readings in Economics,* p. 91.

64. Ibid., p. 90.

65. Ibid.

66. Ibid., p. 89.

67. Ibid., p. 88.

68. Paul A. Samuelson, *Economics from the Heart: A Samuelson Sampler* (Harcourt Brace Jova-novich, New York, 1983), p. 6.

69. Friedman, "Things That Ain't So," *Newsweek*, March 10, 1980, p. 79. http://miltonfriedman .hoover.org/friedman_images/Collections/2016c21/NW_03_10_1980.pdf.

70. Samuelson, *Economics from the Heart,* December 30, 1974, p. 5.

71. Ibid., April 19, 1979, p. 55.

72. Ibid., September 11, 1978, p. 53.

73. Samuelson, *The Samuelson Sampler,* February 1969, p. 16.

74. Leonard Trelawny Hobhouse (September 8, 1864–June 21, 1929). British advocate of social liberalism who was, along with Edward Westermarck, the first professor of sociology in a British university.

75. Samuelson, *Economics from the Heart,* December 30, 1974, p. 5. President Barack Obama was ridiculed by the campaign of his presidential opponent Mitt Romney in 2012 for mak-ing the same point as Samuelson. Obama said, "If you were successful, somebody along the line gave you some help. There was a great teacher somewhere in your life. Somebody helped to create this unbelievable American system that we have that allowed you to thrive. Somebody invested in roads and bridges. If you've got a business—you didn't build that. Somebody else made that happen."

76. Samuelson, *Economics from the Heart,* August 13, 1973, p. 34.

77. Samuelson, *The Samuelson Sampler,* September 1968, p. 7.

78. Robert Strange McNamara (June 9, 1916–July 6, 2009), former president of Ford Motor Company who became U.S. secretary of defense during the Vietnam War. President of the World Bank 1968–1981.

79. Samuelson, *Economics from the Heart,* July 23, 1979, p. 71.

80. Samuelson, *The Samuelson Sampler,* September 1968, p. 7.

81. Adam Smith (June 16, 1723–July 17, 1790), Scottish economist, philosopher, and author whose *An Inquiry into the Nature and Causes of the Wealth of Nations* (1776) is considered the first economics text.

82. Friedman's television series *Free to Choose,* 1980. https://thedailyhatch.org/2013/08/26/ milton-friedmans-free-to-choose-how-to-stay-free-transcript-and-video-60-minutes/.

83. Samuelson, "Modern Economic Realities and Individualism," in *Innocence and Power: Indi-vidualism in Twentieth-Century America,* ed. Gordon H. Mills (University of Texas Press, Austin, 1965), p. 55.

84. The first antitrust U.S. law, the Sherman Act, passed by Congress in 1890 as a "comprehen-sive charter of economic liberty aimed at preserving free and unfettered competition as the rule of trade." It offered the apparent paradox of government intervention to ensure that the market worked freely and fairly and did not, as all unfettered markets tend to do, result in monopoly providers.

85. Samuelson, "Modern Economic Realities and Individualism," in *Innocence and Power: Indi-vidualism in Twentieth-Century America,* p. 55.

86. Samuelson, *Readings in Economics*, p. 87.
87. Samuelson, *Economics from the Heart,* April 9, 1979, p. 55.
88. Samuelson, *The Samuelson Sampler,* April 1973, p. 181.

CHAPTER 7: MONEY, MONEY, MONEY

1. George Garvy (May 30, 1913–October 6, 1987), Latvian-born economist. With Martin R. Blyn, sought to discredit in 1969 Friedman's theory that changes in the supply of money are a key determinant of economic change.
2. Thomas S. Kuhn (July 18, 1922–June 17, 1996). American physicist, historian, and philosopher of science. His *The Structure of Scientific Revolutions* (1962) introduced the term "paradigm shift."
3. Robert Jacob Alexander, Baron Skidelsky (April 25, 1939–), historian of economic thought, biographer of Keynes, and Emeritus Professor of Political Economy at the University of Warwick.
4. Friedman's commentary accompanying the facsimile edition of Keynes's *General Theory*, 1936 (Verlag Wirtschaft und Finanzen GmbH, Dusseldorf, 1989). Reproduced in *Economic Quarterly* (Federal Reserve Bank of Richmond), vol. 83, no. 2, Spring 1997.
5. John O'Sulivan, filmed interview with Hayek, Films for the Humanities, 1985.
6. Keynes, *A Tract on Monetary Reform* (Macmillan, London, 1923), p. 80.
7. As described by Keynes in his equation, described in his *Tract on Monetary Reform* (1923), $n = p\ (k + rk')$, where n is currency notes in circulation, p is the cost of living index, k is the fraction of assets people keep as cash on hand, k' the fraction they keep in bank accounts, and r the fraction of deposits banks keep in reserve.
8. Keynes, *A Tract on Monetary Reform*, p. 80.
9. John Cassidy interview with Samuelson, *The New Yorker*, December 14, 2009.
10. With contributions from Phillip Cogan, John J. Klein, Eugene M. Lerner, and Richard T. Selden.
11. Keynes, John Maynard, *The General Theory of Employment, Interest, and Money* (Macmillan, 1936). See Chapter 21, "The Theory of Prices."
12. Friedman, Milton. "The Quantity Theory of Money—A Restatement." In *Studies in the Quantity Theory of Money*, edited by Milton Friedman (Chicago: University of Chicago Press, 1956), pp. 3–21.
13. In *The General Theory,* Keynes explained the interdependent relationship between consumer spending, industrial output, and investment, an assertion which became known as the income-expenditure model.
14. Interview with Samuelson by William A. Barnett, University of Kansas, December 23, 2003.
15. The data were compiled by Dorothy Brady and Margaret Reid, and Friedman also credited input from Rose Friedman.
16. This argument was used by conservative economists and lawmakers to question the value of the Obama administration's stimulus to revive the moribund U.S. economy after the 2008 financial freeze.
17. The *Encyclopædia Britannica* was owned by the Chicago store Sears and it depended for

many of its entries and editorial production work on the University of Chicago, which was offered ownership of the *Encyclopædia* as a gift in 1941. The university declined the offer.

18. The shorthand term M1 is made up of all cash in circulation, plus money equivalents like traveler's checks, as well as demand and checkable deposits held by the public in banks. M2 includes M1 plus short-term time bank deposits, small savings deposits, and retail money market funds. M3 includes M2 plus longer-term time deposits and money market funds with more than twenty-four-hour maturity. M4 includes M3 plus other deposits.

19. Letter from Samuelson to Friedman, December 8, 1964. Duke Samuelson archive.

20. Letter from Friedman to Samuelson, January 13, 1965. Duke Samuelson archive.

21. Piero Sraffa (August 5, 1898–September 3, 1983), Italian economist saved from Mussolini's fascism by Keynes appointing him the Marshall librarian at Cambridge. With Joan Robinson, founder of the Neo-Ricardian School.

22. Keynes, *Collected Writings*, vol. 13: *General Theory and After, Part 1* (Macmillan for the Royal Economic Society, London, 1973), p. 265.

23. Letter from Samuelson to Friedman, January 26, 1963. Duke Samuelson archive.

24. Letter from Friedman to Samuelson, February 2, 1965. Duke Samuelson archive.

25. Letter from Friedman to Samuelson, November 15, 1971. Duke Samuelson archive.

26. James Tobin (March 5 1918–March 11 2002), prominent American Keynesian economist who taught at Harvard and Yale and served on the Council of Economic Advisers.

27. Letter from Samuelson to Friedman, December 21, 1971. Duke Samuelson archive.

28. Allan H. Meltzer (February 6, 1928–May 8, 2017), American economist and Allan H. Meltzer Professor of Political Economy at Carnegie Mellon University's Tepper School of Business and Institute for Politics and Strategy in Pittsburgh, Pa.

29. Meltzer's obituary of Friedman for *Britannica*. http://blogs.britannica.com/2006/11/milton -friedman-1912-2006.

30. Letter from Friedman to Michael M. Weinstein, May 18, 1999. Duke Samuelson archive.

31. Friedman explained some of his and Schwartz's methodology, and assumptions about cash balances held by individuals, in a brief talk, "The Demand for Money," at the American Philosophical Society, Philadelphia, Pa., November 10, 1960.

32. Arthur Frank Burns (August 27, 1904–June 26, 1987), American economist at Rutgers, Columbia, and the National Bureau of Economic Research. Chairman of the U.S. Council of Economic Advisors 1953–1956 under Eisenhower, counselor to the president under Nixon, chairman of the Federal Reserve 1970–1978, and ambassador to West Germany 1981–1985.

33. A. F. Burns and P. A. Samuelson, *Full Employment, Guideposts, and Economic Stability* (American Enterprise Institute, Washington, 1967), pp. 92–93.

34. https://www.andrew.cmu.edu/course/88-301/phillips/friedman.pdf.

35. In a footnote to the published version of the speech, Friedman writes, "I am indebted for helpful criticisms of earlier drafts to Armen Alchian, Gary Becker, Martin Bronfenbrenner, Arthur F. Burns, Phillip Cagan, David D. Friedman, Lawrence Harris, Harry G. Johnson, Homer Jones, Jerry Hordan, David Meiselman, Allan H. Meltzer, Theodore W. Schultz, Anna J. Schwartz, Herbert Stein, George J. Stigler, and James Tobin."

36. The address was delivered in Washington, D.C., on December 29, 1967 and published in the March 1968 edition of *The American Economic Review*, vol. 58, no. 1.

37. In 1977, Congress amended the Federal Reserve Act, directing the Board of Governors of the Federal Reserve system and the Federal Open Market Committee to "maintain long run growth of the monetary and credit aggregates commensurate with the economy's long run potential to increase production, so as to promote effectively the goals of maximum employment, stable prices and moderate long-term interest rates."

38. Friedman speech to AEA published in the March 1968 edition of *The American Economic Review*, vol. 58, no. 1.

39. Knut Wicksell (December 20, 1851–May 3, 1926), Swedish economist whose work inspired the Austrian School.

40. Samuelson, *Economics*, 1st ed. (1948); (with William D. Nordhaus since 1985), 9th ed. (1973), pp. 393–94.

41. Friedman speech to AEA, *American Economic Review*, vol. 58, no. 1.

42. Alban William Housego "A. W." "Bill" Phillips (November 18, 1914–March 4, 1975), electrical engineer, economist, and sociologist, professor of economics at the London School of Economics.

43. https://www.andrew.cmu.edu/course/88-301/phillips/friedman.pdf.

44. P. Samuelson and R. Solow, "The Problem of Achieving and Maintaining a Stable Price Level: Analytical Aspects of Anti-Inflation Policy," *American Economic Review*, May 1960, pp. 177–94.

45. Samuelson and Solow introduced the "Phillips Curve" at the 1959 American Economics Association convention.

46. Vivek Dehejia, "How Milton Friedman and Edmund Phelps Changed Macroeconomics." https://worldview.stratfor.com/article/how-milton-friedman-and-edmund-phelps-changed-macroeconomics.

47. J. Daniel Hammond, "Friedman and Samuelson on the Business Cycle." *Cato Journal*, vol. 31, no. 3, Fall 2011.

48. A journalist took Friedman out to lunch and said, "One of your favorite sayings is 'There's no such thing as a free lunch.' Well, I'm here to disprove it today because I'm paying for yours." Friedman replied, "Oh, no, no, Mark, that wasn't a free lunch. I had to listen to you for two hours!" Mark Skousen, "The Rational, The Relentless," *Liberty Magazine*, September 2007.

49. Edmund Phelps, "Phillips Curves, Expectations of Inflation and Optimal Employment Over Time," *Economica*, vol. 34, no. 135, August 1967, pp. 254–81.

50. Letter from Samuelson to Friedman, May 15, 1973. Hoover Institution Friedman archive.

51. Samuelson was unimpressed by Friedman's methodology in drawing conclusions from the big data on money that he had compiled. He said, in 2003, "Particularly vulnerable is a scholar who tries to test competing theories by submitting them to simplistic linear regressions with no sophisticated calculations of Granger causality, cointegration, colinearities and ill-conditioning, or a dozen other safeguard econometric methodologies."

52. Friedman, *Capitalism and Freedom*, p. 135.

53. Friedman, "The Counter-Revolution in Monetary Theory," IEA Occasional Paper, Institute of Economic Affairs, London, 1970.

54. Perhaps the most famous was Friedman v. Walter Heller, Kennedy and Johnson's chairman of the Council of Economic Advisers, 1961–1964. See Milton Friedman and Walter W. Heller, *Monetary vs. Fiscal Policy: A Dialogue* (W. W. Norton, New York, 1969).

55. Richard Milhous Nixon (January 9, 1913–April 22, 1994), Eisenhower's vice president, 1953–1961, and thirty-seventh president of the United States, 1969–1974.

CHAPTER 8: NOT SO FAST

1. Even the term "stagflation" became the subject of bitter dispute between Friedmanites and Keynesians, with Friedman's collaborator Anna Schwartz slapping down the Keynesian *New York Times* columnist Paul Krugman for suggesting that Samuelson had coined the word. "[Krugman] erroneously suggests that the term 'stagflation,' which originated in the UK in 1965, was coined by Paul Samuelson after 1967," she wrote in a March 29, 2007 response to Krugman's "Who Was Milton Friedman?" in the *New York Review of Books,* February 15, 2007.

2. John Cassidy interview with Samuelson, *The New Yorker,* December 14, 2009.

3. Ibid.

4. *Newsweek,* May 29, 1978.

5. *Newsweek,* February 15, 1971.

6. *Newsweek,* October 15, 1973.

7. Samuelson and Barnett, *Inside the Economist's Mind* (Blackwell, Oxford, 2007), p. 147.

8. Samuelson advice to President Kennedy, 1961, "Text of Report to the President-Elect on Prospects for the Nation's Economy in 1961," *New York Times,* January 6, 1961.

9. Samuelson, *Economics,* 1st ed. (1948), p. 282.

10. Bureau of Labor Statistics CPI-All Urban Consumers. https://data.bls.gov/pdq/ SurveyOutputServlet.

11. The first recorded use of the term "hyperinflation" was in 1880, according to *Merriam-Webster.* The most famous examples took place in Austria and Germany in the immediate aftermath of World War I and in Hungary in the aftermath of World War II.

12. Samuelson, "Price Controls," *Newsweek,* December 1970.

13. Interview with Samuelson, *US News & World Report,* December 1960.

14. Samuelson, "Inflation Trauma (II)," *Newsweek,* May 21, 1973.

15. Samuelson, *The Samuelson Sampler* (*Newsweek,* November 1967), pp. 39–40.

16. Samuelson, *Economics,* 1st ed. (1948), p. 283.

17. Samuelson, *The Samuelson Sampler* (*Newsweek,* November 1967), p. 39.

18. Ibid., pp. 39–40.

19. Ibid.

20. Ibid., p. 41.

21. Ibid.

22. Ibid., p. 43.

23. Ibid.

24. Milton Friedman and Paul A. Samuelson, "How the Slump Looks to Three Experts," *Newsweek,* May 25, 1970, pp. 78–79.

25. Letter from Samuelson to Friedman, August 21, 1962. Duke Samuelson archive.

26. Samuelson, *Readings in Economics.*

27. Ibid., p. 144.

28. Ibid., p. 139.

29. Milton Friedman, *Inflation: Causes and Consequences* for the Council for Economic Educa-
    tion, Mumbai (Asia Publishing House, New York, 1963).

30. Ibid.

31. Samuelson, *Readings in Economics*, p. 142.

32. Ibid., p. 143.

33. Friedman, "The Relationship of Prices to Economic Stability and Growth," 85th Congress,
    2nd Session, joint Economic Committee Print, Washington D.C., U.S. Government Print-
    ing Office, 1958.

34. Samuelson, *Readings in Economics*, p. 384.

35. Ibid., p. 385.

36. Ibid.

37. Ibid., p. 386.

38. Ibid., p. 385.

39. Ibid., p. 386.

40. Ibid.

41. Ibid., p. 387.

42. Ibid.

43. Ibid.

44. Ibid.

45. Ibid., p. 388.

46. Although the AEA lecture is riddled with caveats, Friedman hardened up a central tenet of
    his monetarism, that the Great Depression was caused by money being "out of order" and
    that "every other major contraction in this country has been either produced by monetary
    disorder or greatly exacerbated by monetary disorder. Every major inflation has been pro-
    duced by monetary expansion."

47. Samuelson, *Readings in Economics*.

48. Samuelson counted James Tobin of Harvard and Yale, who was to win the Nobel Prize
    in Economics in 1981, and Franco Modigliani of the University of Illinois Urbana–
    Champaign, Carnegie Mellon University, Pittsburgh, and MIT, and the 1985 Nobel laure-
    ate in economics, as fellow post-Keynesians.

49. Samuelson, *Readings in Economics*, p. 148.

50. Ibid., p. 145.

51. Howard Sylvester Ellis (July 2, 1898–April 15, 1992), American economist, professor of
    economics at the University of California, Berkeley, 1938–1965.

52. Samuelson listed as graduates of Friedman's Chicago monetary-theory seminars economists
    such as Allan Meltzer at Carnegie-Mellon University of Pittsburgh, Karl Brunner (Febru-
    ary 16, 1916–May 9, 1989) of Ohio State University, Harry Johnson (May 26, 1923–May
    9, 1977) of the University of Chicago and the London School of Economics, the Federal
    Reserve Bank of St. Louis, several Chicago graduates who became bankers, and, briefly
    under the chairmanship of Senator William Proxmire (November 11, 1915–December 15,
    2005), Democrat from Wisconsin, the Joint Economic Committee of Congress.

53. Samuelson, *Readings in Economics*, p. 146.

54. Ibid., p. 145.

55. Ibid.

56. Ibid.

57. Ibid., pp. 145–46.

58. Ibid., 146n.

59. Ibid., p. 147n. 3.

60. Ibid., p. 147.

61. The process is commonly referred to as "printing money," though no actual printing of money is involved, and it has come to be known as "quantitative easing" or QE. Samuelson here contrasts the selling of government credit to a central bank that prints bank notes unsupported by new borrowing.

62. Samuelson, *Readings in Economics*, p. 148.

63. Ibid.

64. Ibid.

65. Ibid.

66. Samuelson's italics.

67. Keynes, *Collected Writings*, vol. 4: *Tract on Monetary Reform* (1923), p. 65. Keynes was frustrated by conservative economists who suggested that public spending to create jobs would provoke inflation "in the long run." His riposte was that "in the long run we are all dead."

68. Samuelson, *Readings in Economics*, p. 149.

69. Ibid., p. 150.

CHAPTER 9: TRICKY DICKY

1. Friedman and Friedman. *Two Lucky People*, p. 368.

2. Ibid.

3. Leo Brent Bozell Jr. (January 15, 1926–April 15, 1997), American conservative activist and Roman Catholic writer, who married Patricia Lee Buckley, sister of the conservative thinker and television celebrity William F. Buckley.

4. *New York Times* magazine, October 11, 1964. https://miltonfriedman.hoover.org/friedman_images/Collections/2016c21/NYT_10_11_1964.pdf.

5. Friedman and Friedman, *Two Lucky People*, p. 114.

6. Milton Friedman, "A Proposal for Resolving the U.S. Balance of Payments Problem: Confidential Memorandum to President-elect Richard Nixon," dated October 15, 1968, submitted to Nixon in December 1968. https://miltonfriedman.hoover.org/friedman_images/Collections/2016c21/Rowman_1988_a.pdf.

7. Friedman and Friedman, *Two Lucky People*, p. 376.

8. *Newsweek*, March 27, 1978.

9. Friedman and Friedman, *Two Lucky People*, p. 386.

10. Paul Winston McCracken (December 29, 1915–August 3, 2012), economist. Chairman of the Nixon's Council of Economic Advisers, 1969–1971.

11. The others Friedman credited with help were Armen Alchian, Gary Becker, Martin Bronfenbrenner, Phillip Cagan, David D. Friedman, Lawrence Harris, Harry G. Johnson, Homer Jones, Jerry Hordan, David Meiselman, Allan H. Meltzer, Theodore W. Schultz, Anna J. Schwartz, Herbert Stein, George J. Stigler, and James Tobin.

12. Herbert Stein (August 27, 1916–September 8, 1999), American economist, was chairman of the Council of Economic Advisers under Richard Nixon and Gerald Ford, 1972–1974.

13. Herbert Stein, *Presidential Economics: The Making of Economic Policy from Roosevelt to Reagan and Beyond* (Simon & Schuster, New York, 1985), p. 154.

14. Ibid., p. 145.

15. Many members of the CEA were also persuaded by Friedman's notions of a "natural rate of employment" that an economy could provide. It led them to approve Nixon's subsequent "full employment" budget in which the budget would be balanced as if the economy were at full employment.

16. Quoted in Denis Healey, *The Time of My Life* (Michael Joseph, London, 1989), p. 380.

17. Peter George Peterson (June 5, 1926–March 20, 2018), American investment banker, U.S. Secretary of Commerce from February 29, 1972 to February 1, 1973.

18. From taped conversation 546-2, July 26, 1971, White House Tapes, Nixon Presidential Materials Staff, National Archives at College Park, Md. http://millercenter.org/presidentialrecordings.

19. Stein, *Presidential Economics*, p. 138.

20. "A full employment budget" alluded to the amount of federal government stimulus spending needed to ensure full employment. By fixing spending as if full employment had been achieved, Nixon hoped to boost the economy and create jobs.

21. http://www.presidency.ucsb.edu/ws/?pid=3110. Nixon was expressing a commonly held simple Keynesian view that unemployment should be reduced by public spending and a budget deficit until full employment had been reached, when the budget should be made to balance to avoid overheating [inflation]. Nixon appeared to want it both ways: to continue spending despite full employment.

22. http://www.presidency.ucsb.edu/ws/?pid=3110.

23. Interview with Friedman, *Playboy*, February 21, 1970.

24. From taped conversation 547–9, July 27, 1971, White House Tapes, Nixon Presidential Materials Staff, National Archives at College Park, Md. http://millercenter.org/presidentialrecordings.

25. Friedman and Friedman, *Two Lucky People*, pp. 386–87.

26. John Bowden Connally Jr. (February 27, 1917–June 15, 1993), governor of Texas and U.S. Secretary of the Treasury. He was seriously wounded when riding in the car with Kennedy when the president was assassinated in Dallas in November 1963.

27. From taped conversation 268–5, August 2, 1971, White House Tapes, Nixon Presidential Materials Staff, National Archives at College Park, Md. http://millercenter.org/presidentialrecordings.

28. At the end of World War II, the U.S. owned more than half the world's official gold reserves—574 million ounces.

29. Nixon's White House chief of staff, H. R. Haldeman, told the president that "the British had asked for $3 billion to be converted into gold. If we gave it to them, other countries might follow suit. If we didn't, they might wonder if we had enough gold to support the dollar. In either case, it was a major crisis." Haldeman, *The Haldeman Diaries: Inside the Nixon*

White House (Putnam, N.Y., 1994). In the first twelve days of August, $3.6 billion of gold reserves were exchanged for paper dollars.

30. The pioneer in legally fixing prices of goods and labor was Harold Wilson, prime minister of the U.K., 1964–1970 and 1974–1976, an economist by training, who introduced a prices and incomes policy in 1965 that allowed the government to investigate wage agreements and overrule them if they were found to be undeserving.

31. From taped conversation 455–3, February 22, 1971, White House Tapes, Nixon Presidential Materials Staff, National Archives at College Park, Md. http://millercenter.org/presidentialrecordings.

32. From taped conversation 452–4, February 19, 1971, White House Tapes, Nixon Presidential Materials Staff, National Archives at College Park, Md. http://millercenter.org/presidentialrecordings.

33. From taped conversation 541–2, July 21, 1971, White House Tapes, Nixon Presidential Materials Staff, National Archives at College Park, Md. http://millercenter.org/presidentialrecordings.

34. From taped conversation 268–5, August 2, 1971, White House Tapes, Nixon Presidential Materials Staff, National Archives at College Park, Md. http://millercenter.org/presidentialrecordings.

35. Friedman email to Burton A. Abrams and James L. Butkiewicz of the Department of Economics, University of Delaware, Newark, Del.

36. Interview with Friedman, August 25, 1971, for Instructional Dynamics Incorporated's *Economics Cassette Series,* a biweekly, subscription-based series, 1968–1978. https://digitalcollections.hoover.org/objects/52346/the-presidents-new-economic-policy?ctx=6abc8261-3a8b-4aee-ad8e-2aec517ae55a&idx=13.

37. *Newsweek,* May 25, 1970.

38. Friedman and Friedman, *Two Lucky People,* pp. 383–84.

39. Friedman, "Why the Freeze is a Mistake," *Newsweek,* August 30, 1971.

40. Ibid.

41. Friedman and Friedman, *Two Lucky People,* p. 387.

42. Friedman, "Will the Kettle Explode?" *Newsweek,* October 18, 1971.

43. Samuelson wrote: "When I got on Nixon's enemy list it raised the prestige of myself within my own family and in my circle." MIT 150 Oral History. https://infinitehistory.mit.edu/video/paul-samuelson.

44. "How the Slump Looks to Three Experts" *Newsweek,* May 25, 1970, pp. 78–79.

45. Samuelson, "Coping with Stagflation," *Newsweek,* August 19, 1974.

46. https://miltonfriedman.hoover.org/friedman_images/Collections/2016c21/Gov_09_23_1971.pdf.

47. Ibid.

48. Hearings before the Joint Economic Committee, Congress of the United States, Ninety-second Congress, first session, Part 4, September 20, 21, 22, and 23, 1971, p. 735.

49. Ibid.

50. Ibid.

51. Ibid.

52. https://miltonfriedman.hoover.org/friedman_images/Collections/2016c21/Gov_09_23_1971 .pdf.

53. Samuelson, "Coping with Stagflation," *Newsweek*, August 19, 1974.

54. Ibid.

55. Ibid.

56. Stein, *Presidential Economics*, pp. 168–69.

57. Ibid., p. 207.

58. Friedman and Friedman, *Two Lucky People*, pp. 387–88.

59. *Newsweek*, September 8, 1980.

60. http://www.pbs.org/wgbh/commandingheights/shared/minitextlo/int_miltonfriedman .html#8.

CHAPTER 10: THE CHICAGO BOYS

1. Salvador Guillermo Allende Gossens (June 26, 1908–September 11, 1973), democratic socialist president of Chile, 1970–1973.

2. Kristian C. Gustafson, "CIA Machinations in Chile in 1970: Reexamining the Record." https://www.cia.gov/library/center-for-the-study-of-intelligence/csi-publications/csi -studies/studies/vol47no3/article03.html.

3. Nixon, quoted by Robert Dallek, in *Nixon and Kissinger: Partners in Power* (HarperCollins, New York, 2007), p. 234.

4. CIA spies played no direct part in the coup, but the agency generously funded Allende's opponents. See Dallek, *Nixon and Kissinger,* pp. 509–15.

5. Augusto José Ramón Pinochet Ugarte (November 25, 1915–December 10, 2006), Chilean general, politician, and dictator of Chile from 1973 to 1990; commander in chief of the Chilean Army until 1998; president of the government junta of Chile from 1973 to 1981.

6. Blumenthal interview with Friedman, quoted in Blumenthal, *The Rise of the Counter-Establishment,* p. 112.

7. Arnold Carl Harberger (July 27, 1924–), at the time chairman of the Chicago economics department.

8. Friedman and Friedman, *Two Lucky People*, p. 398.

9. Instead of introducing liberal measures to the economy gradually, Friedman insisted that all changes happen immediately. For Chile this meant the simultaneous sharp reduction in government intervention, an end to import tariffs, the deregulation of markets, taxes switched from direct to indirect, and the denationalization of state-owned industries. While Friedman denied that he had invented the term "shock therapy," in economics the first example of such radical action was recorded at this time in Chile.

10. Friedman and Friedman, *Two Lucky People*, p. 399.

11. See Appendix A of Friedman and Friedman, *Two Lucky People*, p. 591.

12. Friedman and Friedman, *Two Lucky People*, p. 400.

13. MIT 150 Oral History. https://infinitehistory.mit.edu/video/paul-samuelson.

14. Nobel Prize Paul A. Samuelson Facts. https://www.nobelprize.org/prizes/economic -sciences/1970/samuelson/facts/.

15. Quoted in Friedman and Friedman, *Two Lucky People*, pp. 444–45.

16. Letter from Samuelson to Friedman, November 5, 1970. Hoover Institution Friedman archive.

17. Letter from Friedman to Arthur R. Nayer, October 13, 1970. Hoover Institution Friedman archive.

18. Samuelson named Jacob Viner, Frank Knight, Paul Douglas, Joseph Schumpeter, Wassily Leontief, Gottfried Haberler, Alvin Hansen, Lloyd Metzler, Robert Solow, James Tobin, Lawrence Klein, Robert Mundell, Joseph Stiglitz, Bertil Ohlin, Gunnar Myrdal, Erik Lundberg, Ingvar Svennilson, Gustav Cassel, Erik Lindahl, and Knut Wicksell.

19. https://www.nobelprize.org/uploads/2018/06/samuelson-lecture.pdf.

20. Ibid.

21. Thorstein Bunde Veblen, born Torsten Bunde Veblen in Norway (July 30, 1857–August 3, 1929), economist and sociologist best known for his idea of "conspicuous consumption": people engage in conspicuous consumption, along with "conspicuous leisure," to demonstrate their wealth or to mark social status.

22. Samuelson, "A few remembrances of Friedrich von Hayek (1899–1992)," *Journal of Economic Behavior & Organization*, vol. 69, no. 1, January 2009, pp. 1–4.

23. Friedman and Friedman, *Two Lucky People*, p. 445.

24. Larry Martz, "A Nobel for Friedman," *Newsweek*, October 25, 1974.

25. Friedman and Friedman, *Two Lucky People*, p. 442.

26. Ibid.

27. *Newsweek*, October 25, 1976.

28. Friedman letter to Samuelson, October 20, 1976. Duke Samuelson archive.

29. Steven Lawrence Rattner (July 5, 1952–), financier and former journalist who served as lead adviser to the Presidential Task Force on the Auto Industry in 2009 for the Obama administration.

30. Quoted in Friedman and Friedman, *Two Lucky People*, p. 442.

31. Brian Snowdon and Howard Vane interview with Friedman, in *Modern Macroeconomics: Its Origin, Development, and Current State* (Edward Elgar, Cheltenham, U.K., 2005).

32. Friedman and Friedman, *Two Lucky People*, p. 442.

33. Ibid., p. 443.

34. Ibid., Appendix A, pp. 598–99.

35. Friedman was right. Inflation in Chile rose to an astounding 750 percent per annum. By May 1981–1982, it had fallen to 3.6 percent.

36. Friedman and Friedman, *Two Lucky People*, Appendix A, pp. 599–600.

37. Friedman's Nobel Banquet speech revised by Friedman and with graphs for the University of Chicago. https://www.nobelprize.org/uploads/2018/06/friedman-lecture-1.pdf.

38. Peter Jaworski interview with Friedman, *The Journal* (Queen's University, Canada), March 15, 2002, pp. 18–19.

39. Friedman's Nobel lecture, December 13, 1976. https://www.nobelprize.org/uploads/2018/06/friedman-lecture-1.pdf.

40. Friedman, "The Counter-Revolution in Monetary Theory," IEA Occasional Paper, no. 33, (Institute of Economic Affairs, London, 1970).

41. Friedman and Friedman, *Two Lucky People*, p. 458.

42. George J. Stigler, *Memoirs of an Unregulated Economist* (Basic Books, New York, 1985), pp. 33–34.

43. *Newsweek*, January 12, 1970.

44. Samuelson, *Economics*, 3rd ed. (1955), p. 316.

45. Samuelson, *Economics*, 5th ed. (1961), pp. 314–15.

46. Samuelson, *Economics*, 9th ed. (1973), p. 329.

47. Samuelson, *Economics*, 12th ed. (1985), p. 828.

48. Samuelson, *Economics*, 15th ed. (1995).

49. Samuelson, *Economics*, 5th ed. (1961), p. 318.

50. Samuelson, *Economics*, 18th ed. (2004), p. 41.

51. Samuelson, *Economics*, 8th ed. (1970), p. 140.

52. Samuelson, *Economics*, 11th ed. (1980), p. 761.

53. Ibid., pp. 761–63.

54. Samuelson, *Economics*, 15th ed. (1995), p. 372.

55. Samuelson, *Economics*, 18th ed. (2004), p .40.

56. Ibid., p. 41.

57. Quoted by Independent Institute, obituary of Friedman, November 18, 2006.

CHAPTER 11: FED UP

1. The pardoning of Nixon by Ford became the key issue rather than the Watergate events themselves.

2. https://en.wikipedia.org/wiki/File:Gallup_Poll-Approval_Rating-Jimmy_Carter.png.

3. *Newsweek*, May 29, 1978.

4. https://www.washingtonpost.com/archive/politics/1978/11/02/carter-moves-to-halt -decline-of-dollar/880b916b-24c7-4ce7-807f-1057b9ba40fd/.

5. "Recession: Made in Washington," *Newsweek*, December 24, 1979.

6. https://www.americanrhetoric.com/speeches/jimmycartercrisisofconfidence.htm.

7. https://news.gallup.com/poll/116677/Presidential-Approval-Ratings-Gallup-Historical -Statistics-Trends.aspx.

8. George William Miller (March 9, 1925–March 17, 2006), U.S. secretary of the treasury under President Carter.

9. Paul Adolph Volcker Jr. (September 5, 1927–December 8, 2019). Chairman of the Federal Reserve under Presidents Carter and Reagan from August 1979 to August 1987. He is widely credited with ending the high inflation of the 1970s and early 1980s. Chairman of President Obama's Economic Recovery Advisory Board, February 2009–January 2011.

10. William L. Silber, *Volcker: The Triumph of Persistence* (Bloomsbury Press, New York, 2012), pp. 145–46.

11. *New York Times*, July 29, 1979, p. F1.

12. Silber, *Volcker*, p. 148.

13. Personal Letters from 1979, Papers of Paul Volcker. Federal Reserve Bank of New York Archives, Box 95714.

14. Ibid.

15. Oskar Morgenstern (January 24, 1902–July 26, 1977), Princeton economist, who with mathematician John von Neumann founded the mathematical field of game theory and its application to economics.

16. Friedrich August Lutz (December 29, 1901–October 4, 1975), German-born Princeton economist who developed the expectations hypothesis.

17. Paul Volcker, "The Problems of Federal Reserve Policy since World War II," Princeton, 1949. https://catalog.princeton.edu/catalog/dsp019019s3255.

18. Minutes of Federal Open Market Committee Meeting, August 14, 1979, p. 1.

19. Denis Winston Healey, Lord Healey (August 30, 1917–October 3, 2015), British Labour Party Secretary of State for Defence, 1964–1970; chancellor of the exchequer, 1974–1979; and deputy leader of the Labour Party, 1980–1983.

20. Healey, *The Time of My Life*, p. 432.

21. Ibid.

22. Presidential address to the American Economic Association and the American Finance Association, Atlantic City, N.J., September 16, 1976. https://www.newyorkfed.org/medialibrary/media/research/quarterly_review/75th/75article7.pdf.

23. Ibid.

24. Paul Volcker, "The Role of Monetary Targets in an Age of Inflation," *Journal of Monetary Economics* 4, no. 2, April 1978.

25. Ibid., p. 331.

26. In particular the events in the spring and summer of 1977, when inflation leapt from 5 to 7 percent.

27. Paul Volcker and Toyoo Gyohten, *Changing Fortunes: The World's Money and the Threat to American Leadership* (Times Books, New York, 1992), pp. 164–65.

28. *New York Times*, September 19, 1979, p. 1.

29. Volcker and Gyohten, *Changing Fortunes*, p. 165.

30. Paul A. Samuelson and William A. Barnett (eds.), *Inside the Economist's Mind: The History of Modern Economic Thought, as Explained by Those Who Produced It* (Wiley-Blackwell, Hoboken, N.J., 2006), p. 180. http://www.library.fa.ru/files/Samuelson-Barnett.pdf.

31. The same was happening across the Atlantic, where Healey began publishing monetary estimates that were interpreted as targets. Healey wrote, "To satisfy the markets, I began to publish the monetary forecasts we had always made in private, and then described them as targets." Healey, *The Time of My Life*, p. 432.

32. Transcript of press conference with Volcker, the Federal Reserve Building, Washington, D.C., October 6, 1979, p. 3. https://fraser.stlouisfed.org/files/docs/historical/volcker/Volcker_19791006.pdf.

33. Volcker and Gyohten, *Changing Fortunes*, p. 167.

34. Ibid.

35. Samuelson and Barnett, *Inside the Economist's Mind,* p. 178. http://www.library.fa.ru/files/Samuelson-Barnett.pdf.

36. *Newsweek*, August 29, 1977.

37. Healey, *The Time of My Life*, p. 383.

38. Volcker and Gyohten, *Changing Fortunes,* p. 170.

39. Ibid., p. 166.

40. "Recession: Made in Washington," *Newsweek*, December 24, 1979.

41. Volcker and Gyohten, *Changing Fortunes*, p. 169.

42. Ibid., p. 170.

43. Ibid., p. 172.

44. *Newsweek*, May 12, 1969.

45. "Recession: Made in Washington," *Newsweek*, December 24, 1979.

46. "Living with Inflation," *Newsweek*, February 25, 1980.

47. http://www.pbs.org/wgbh/commandingheights/shared/minitextlo/int_miltonfriedman.html#8.

48. "Monetary Instability," *Newsweek*, June 15, 1981, p. 80.

49. Quoted in Samuelson, *The Samuelson Sampler*, p. 16.

50. "Living with Inflation," *Newsweek*, February 25, 1980.

51. Alan Stuart Blinder (October 14, 1945–), Professor of Economics and Public Affairs, Princeton; member of Clinton's Council of Economic Advisers, 1993–1994; vice-chairman, Board of Governors of the Federal Reserve System, 1994–1996.

52. Alan S. Blinder, *Hard Heads, Soft Hearts: Tough-Minded Economics for a Just Society* (Addison-Wesley, Reading, Mass., 1987), p. 78.

53. *The Wall Street Journal*, June 3, 1980, p. 6.

54. Ibid.

55. *Newsweek*, September 3, 1973.

56. "Monetary Overkill," *Newsweek*, July 14, 1980, p. 62.

57. Milton Friedman and Paul A. Samuelson, "Productivity: Two Experts Cross Swords," *Newsweek*, September 8, 1980.

58. Allen Wallis, quoted in Friedman and Friedman, *Two Lucky People*, p. 474.

59. Milton Friedman and Rose Friedman, *Free to Choose*, p. 299.

60. Ibid., p. 316.

61. Ibid., p. 330.

62. Ibid., p. 332

63. Ibid., p. 300.

CHAPTER 12: NO HOLLYWOOD ENDING

1. Friedrich Hayek, *Choice in Currency: A Way to Stop Inflation* (Institute of Economic Affairs, London, 1976), p. 16.

2. https://www.presidency.ucsb.edu/documents/address-behalf-senator-barry-goldwater-time-for-choosing.

3. Silber, William L. *Volcker: The Triumph of Persistence* (Bloomsbury Press, New York, 2012, p. 194.

4. M0 is a measure of "narrow money," i.e., the level of notes and coins in circulation added to the clearing banks' operational balances held by the Federal Reserve. For definitions of the other M measures of money, see Chapter Seven, note 18.

5. Samuelson interview with *The Atlantic*, June 17, 2009.

6. Samuelson, too, was against the federal government supporting failing companies. "The

burden of proof should go against governments keeping uneconomic business activities alive," he wrote, *Newsweek*, December 8, 1980.

7. "Election Perspective," *Newsweek*, November 10, 1980, p. 94.

8. The other members were Arthur F. Burns, Paul McCracken, Herbert Stein, Alan Greenspan, Arthur Laffer, James Lynn, William Simon, Thomas Sowell, and Charles E. Walker.

9. Anderson, *Revolution*, pp. 267–68.

10. Friedman and Friedman, *Two Lucky People*, p. 394.

11. Ibid.

12. "The Wayward Money Supply," *Newsweek*, December 27, 1982, p. 58.

13. *Meet the Press* (NBC), March 21, 1982.

14. Leo Calvin Rosten (April 11, 1908–February 19, 1997). American humorist, expert in Yiddish lexicography, and political scientist.

15. "More Double Talk at the Fed," *Newsweek*, May 2, 1983, p. 72.

16. Milton Friedman, "Lessons from the 1979–82 Monetary Policy Experiment," *American Economic Review* 74, May 1984, pp. 397–400.

17. Brian Snowdon and Howard Vane interview with Friedman, in Snowdon and Vane, *Modern Macroeconomics*.

18. Pioneers of the theory of supply-side economics include Robert Mundell (October 24, 1932–), professor of economics at Columbia University and Nobel Prize winner for economics, 1999; Arthur Laffer, whose Laffer Curve contends that there is a sweet spot at which a reduction in taxation can deliver higher revenues; and Jude Thaddeus Wanniski (June 17, 1936–August 29, 2005), economist and journalist.

19. Quoted in obituary of Samuelson, *New York Times*, December 13, 2009.

20. Attributed to the French economist Jean-Baptiste Say (January 5, 1767–November 15, 1832).

21. As Kevin Costner's character says in the movie *Field of Dreams* (1989), "If you build it, he will come."

22. *Newsweek*, December 15, 1980.

23. *Newsweek*, January 10, 1977.

24. Arthur Betz Laffer (August 14, 1940–). Member of Reagan's Economic Policy Advisory Board, 1981–1989, dubbed "the Father of Supply-Side Economics."

25. Laffer on the napkin story, https://www.heritage.org/taxes/report/the-laffer-curve-past -present-and-future.

26. Stein, *Presidential Economics*, p. 239.

27. Ibid., p. 245.

28. Samuelson, *Economics*, 7th ed. (1967), p. 343.

29. Samuelson and Nordhaus, *Economics*, 14th ed. (1992), p. 332.

30. Joseph Aaron Pechman (April 2, 1918–August 19, 1989), economist and taxation expert.

31. Emile Despres (September 21, 1909–April 23, 1973), adviser on German economic affairs at the U.S. Department of State, 1944–1945, and professor of economics at Williams College and Stanford University.

32. Samuelson, "Arthur Laffer: Here's my account." Duke Samuelson archive.

33. He was finally awarded a PhD by Chicago in 1972.

34. Quoted in Eric Alterman, *Sound and Fury: The Making of the Punditocracy* (Cornell, Ithaca, N.Y., 1999), p. 171.

35. Samuelson, "Arthur Laffer: Here's my account." Duke Samuelson archive.

36. The Economic Recovery Tax Act of 1981 cut the highest personal income tax rate from 70 to 50 percent and the lowest from 14 to 11 percent and lowered the highest capital gains tax rate from 28 to 20 percent, while the Tax Reform Act of 1986 cut the highest personal income tax rate from 50 to 38.5 percent, then to 28 percent in the following years, while increasing the highest capital gains tax rate from 20 to 28 percent.

37. "A Simple Tax Reform," *Newsweek*, August 18, 1980, p. 68.

38. *Newsweek*, September 24, 1973.

39. *Newsweek*, February 16, 1981.

40. "Deficits and Inflation," *Newsweek*, February 23, 1981, p. 70.

41. "Closet Keynesianism," *Newsweek*, July 27, 1981, p. 60.

42. Glenn Kesler, "Rand Paul's claim that Reagan's tax cuts produced 'more revenue' and 'tens of millions of jobs'," *Washington Post*, April 19, 2015. https://www.washingtonpost.com/news/fact-checker/wp/2015/04/10/rand-pauls-claim-that-reagans-tax-cuts-produced-more-revenue-and-tens-of-millions-of-jobs/?arc404=true.

43. "Deficits and Inflation," *Newsweek*, February 23, 1981, p. 70.

44. In fact, it was Republican presidents who have championed soaring deficits, among the main offenders being Reagan, George W. Bush, and Donald J. Trump.

45. This included attempts by Congress to oblige the executive to balance the books by law, including the Gramm-Rudman-Hollings Balanced Budget and Emergency Deficit Control Act of 1985, which sought to impose spending restrictions on executive authority. This was eventually deemed a violation of constitutional separation of powers by the Supreme Court.

46. William Jefferson Clinton, born William Jefferson Blythe III (August 19, 1946–). Forty-second president of the United States, January 20, 1993–January 20, 2001; governor of Arkansas, 1979–1981 and 1983–1992.

47. "Deficits and Inflation," *Newsweek*, February 23, 1981, p. 70.

48. From 1974 to 1979, a period of excessive money growth and roaring inflation, M1 grew by 7 percent. Between 1979 and 1984, M1 grew by 7.4 percent, yet it was a period of tight money and declining inflation.

49. Quoted in William Greider, *Secrets of the Temple: How the Federal Reserve Runs the Country* (Simon & Schuster, New York, 1989), p. 540.

50. See definitions of M measures 1 to 3 in Chapter Seven, note 18.

51. Interview with Friedman, July 19, 1984, quoted in Greider, *Secrets of the Temple*, p. 543.

52. William Poole (June 19, 1937–), chief executive of the Federal Reserve Bank of St. Louis.

53. Quoted in Greider, *Secrets of the Temple*, p 543.

54. Interview with Friedman, July 19, 1984, quoted in Greider, *Secrets of the Temple*, p. 684.

55. J. Charles Partee (October 21, 1927–February 15, 2007). Governor, Board of Governors, Federal Reserve, 1976–1986.

56. Quoted in Greider, *Secrets of the Temple*, p. 684.

57. James U. Blanchard III interview with Hayek, May 1, 1984. https://www.libertarianism.org/publications/essays/interview-f-hayek.

58. Ibid.

59. "Monetarism and hyper-inflation," letter from Hayek to *The Times* (London), March 5, 1980, p.17.

60. There are many causes for the collapse of the Soviet Union, including the Solidarity workers' revolt in Poland that confounded Kremlin ideologists, the bankruptcy of the Soviet economy because of its inherent inefficiency, pressure to spend on weaponry to counter U.S. challenges, the decision by Eastern European communist governments to allow free movement across borders, as well as moral pressure from influential individuals like "the Polish Pope" John Paul II, British prime minister Thatcher, and President Reagan.

61. Tom G. Palmer, "Why Socialism Collapsed in Eastern Europe," *Cato Policy Report,* September/October 1990.

62. Lech Wałęsa (September 29, 1943–), Polish politician and labor activist. He cofounded and headed Solidarity (Solidarność), won the Nobel Peace Prize in 1983, and served as president of Poland, 1990–1995.

63. Friedman, *Capitalism and Freedom*, p. 4.

64. Ibid., p. 9.

65. Friedman and Friedman, *Two Lucky People*, p. 396.

66. Friedman, *Capitalism and Freedom*, p. 3.

CHAPTER 13: END OF THE LINE

1. Samuelson, *Economics,* 5th ed. (1961), p. 819.

2. According to his son David Friedman, "He was probably in favor of the idea of free love early on, judging by something he once said, probably concluded it was a bad idea later, but would never have described it as socialism, since it obviously wasn't." Email to author, January 19, 2021.

3. Friedman and Friedman, *Free to Choose*, p. 25.

4. Friedman was an exception. As his son David Friedman explained, "From my father's point of view, describing how socialism works in practice was one way of showing things wrong with it." Email to author, January 19, 2021.

5. Samuelson, *Economics*, 1st ed. (1948), p. 595.

6. Quoted in obituary of Samuelson, *New York Times*, November 17, 2006.

7. Winston S. Churchill, House of Commons, November 11, 1947.

8. On his 1962 trip to Russia, Friedman had asked for data on the quantity of money in the Soviet economy, only to be told that "the central bank did not publish such figures: they were a state secret." Friedman and Friedman, *Two Lucky People*, p. 285.

9. Friedman thought Western intellectuals were soft on the despotism of communism while being robustly opposed to right-wing tyrants. Friedman's introduction to the University of Chicago Press's fiftieth anniversary edition of Hayek's *Road to Serfdom* contains this drive-by snipe: "Today, there is wide agreement that socialism is a failure, capitalism a success. Yet this apparent conversion of the intellectual community to what might be called a Hayekian view is deceptive. While the talk is about free markets and private property—and it is more respectable than it was a few decades ago to defend near-complete laissez-faire—the bulk of the intellectual community almost automatically favors any expansion of government

power so long as it is advertised as a way to protect individuals from big bad corporations, relieve poverty, protect the environment, or promote 'equality.'"

10. "An interview with Milton Friedman," *Reason*, December 1974.

11. Samuelson, *Economics*, 5th ed. (1961), pp. 825–31.

12. Herbert Spencer (April 27, 1820–December 8, 1903). English philosopher, biologist, anthropologist, sociologist, and classical liberal political theorist. Best known for coining the expression "survival of the fittest," after reading Charles Darwin's *On the Origin of Species*.

13. All points made by Friedman extensively.

14. Letter from Samuelson to Elliott, October 21, 1974. Duke Samuelson archive.

15. Letter from Edward Kosner to Samuelson, October 29, 1974. Duke Samuelson archive.

16. William Dodson Broyles Jr. (October 8, 1944–), journalist and screenwriter, editor of *Newsweek* from 1982 to 1984.

17. Letter from Friedman to William Broyles Jr., December 23, 1983. Hoover Institution Friedman archive.

18. Milton Friedman, *Bright Promises, Dismal Performance: An Economist's Protest*, ed. William R. Allen (Harcourt Brace Jovanovich, New York, 1983), preface, pp. ix–x.

19. Lester Carl Thurow (May 7, 1938–March 25, 2016), American political economist, dean of the MIT Sloan School of Management, 1987–1993.

20. Letter from Friedman to Richard Smith, January 26, 1984. Duke Samuelson archive.

21. Friedman wrote 300 columns for *Newsweek* between 1966 and 1984, 121 op-eds for the *Wall Street Journal*, and 22 op-eds for the *New York Times*.

CHAPTER 14: THE GROCER'S DAUGHTER

1. Healey, *The Time of My Life*, p. 377.

2. Ibid., p. 398.

3. Peter Jay (February 7, 1937–), British economist, broadcaster, and ambassador to the United States, 1977–1979.

4. "A General Hypothesis of Employment, Inflation and Politics," Occasional Paper, Institute of Economic Affairs, January 1976.

5. *The Times* (London), July 13, 1976.

6. http://www.britishpoliticalspeech.org/speech-archive.htm?speech=174.

7. Friedman and Friedman, *Two Lucky People*, p. 569.

8. Ian Gilmour, *Britain Can Work* (Martin Robertson, Oxford, 1983), p. 95.

9. Healey, *The Time of My Life*, p. 380.

10. *Meet the Press*, October 24, 1976.

11. *Sunday Telegraph*, October 31, 1976.

12. Gilmour, *Britain Can Work*, p. 95.

13. Keith Sinjohn Joseph, Baron Joseph (January 17, 1918–December 10, 1994), known as Sir Keith Joseph, 2nd Baronet, British barrister, and member of the Cabinet under four Conservative prime ministers.

14. Sir Alfred Sherman (November 10, 1919–August 26, 2006). Writer, journalist, political adviser to Margaret Thatcher. He sometimes failed to hide his unfashionable views. He told

Pravda, in 1974, "As for the lumpen proletariat, colored people and the Irish, let's face it, the only way to hold them in check is to have enough well armed and properly trained police."

15. Sir Alan Arthur Walters (June 17, 1926–January 3, 2009), British economist, chief economic adviser to Prime Minister Margaret Thatcher, 1981–1983 and briefly in 1989.

16. Full text of Joseph speech: https://www.margaretthatcher.org/document/110607.

17. https://www.theguardian.com/politics/1994/dec/12/obituaries.

18. Sir Keith Joseph, "Inflation is Caused by Governments." https://www.margaretthatcher .org/document/110607.

19. Joseph was highly intelligent but could not contain his reactionary views on subjects like the poor. In an October 19, 1974, speech at Edgbaston, Joseph deplored the fact that "a high and rising proportion of children are being born to mothers least fitted to bring children into the world. . . . Some are of low intelligence, most of low educational attainment. They are unlikely to be able to give children the stable emotional background, the consistent combination of love and firmness. . . . They are producing problem children. . . . The balance of our human stock is threatened." Joseph's failure to anticipate the likely offense a remark such as "human stock" would cause just thirty years after the defeat of Nazism, which murdered by the millions those they believed threatened the "human stock," immediately ruled him unsuitable for higher office. The speech was written by Alfred Sherman, of the Centre for Policy Studies. Joseph was aware of his own shortcomings. "Had I become party leader, it would have been a disaster for the party, country and for me. . . . I know my own capacities. Adequate for some jobs, but not for others," he said, as quoted in Morrison Halcrow, *Keith Joseph: A Single Mind* (Macmillan, London, 1989), p. 75.

20. Sir Edward Dillon Lott du Cann (May 28, 1924–August 31, 2017). British member of Parliament, 1956–1987; chairman of the Conservative Party, 1965–1967; chairman of the party's 1922 Committee, which represents the views of Tory backbench MPs, 1972–1984.

21. William Stephen Ian Whitelaw, 1st Viscount Whitelaw (June 28, 1918–July 1, 1999), Conservative politician who served in a wide number of Cabinet positions, including home secretary and deputy prime minister.

22. Gilmour, *Britain Can Work*, pp. 94–95.

23. Edward Heath, *The Course of My Life* (Hodder & Stoughton, London, 1998), p. 576.

24. Margaret Thatcher, *The Path to Power* (HarperCollins, London, 1995), pp. 566–67.

25. John Enoch Powell (June 16, 1912–February 8, 1998), classical scholar, soldier, Conservative member of Parliament (1950–1974), Ulster Unionist Party MP (UUP) MP (1974–1987), and Minister of Health (1960–1963), who oversaw the mass immigration of West Indians to man the National Health Service.

26. http://classics.mit.edu/Virgil/aeneid.6.vi.html.

27. https://www.telegraph.co.uk/comment/3643823/Enoch-Powells-Rivers-of-Blood-speech .html.

28. George Edward Peter Thorneycroft, Lord Thorneycroft (July 26, 1909–June 4, 1994), British Conservative chancellor of the exchequer, 1957–1958.

29. Evelyn Nigel Chetwode Birch, Lord Rhyl (November 18, 1906–March 8, 1981), British Conservative Secretary of State for Air, 1955–1957.

30. Enoch Powell, *Freedom and Reality* (B. T. Batsford, London, 1969.)

31. Keith Joseph, "Monetarism Is Not Enough," Stockton Lecture, April 5, 1976. https://www
.margaretthatcher.org/document/110796.

32. Richard Edward Geoffrey Howe, Lord Howe of Aberavon (December 20, 1926–October
9, 2015), Thatcher's longest-serving Cabinet minister. Chancellor of the exchequer, foreign
secretary, and leader of the House of Commons.

33. Heath, *The Course of My Life*, p. 585.

34. *Newsweek*, June 16, 1980.

35. On February 27, 1980, Thatcher held a small reception for Friedman and Friedman
attended by Geoffrey Howe, John Biffen, Nigel Lawson, Keith Joseph, Ian Gilmour, and
Patrick Jenkin.

36. Although the Conservative Party had fallen into the hands of a state-educated prime minister, it still ran with the ethos of a public (i.e., private) school, at which name calling and
bullying were par for the course. Thatcher divided her ministers into those who agreed with
her on monetarism—the "dries"—and those who remained Keynesian—the "wets."

37. Memorandum to U.K. Treasury and Civil Service Select Committee on "Enquiry into
Monetary Policy," June 11, 1980. Parliamentary Papers (Commons), Session 1979–1980,
720, part 1 (July 1980): 1–4, 55–61. https://miltonfriedman.hoover.org/friedman_images
/Collections/2016c21/1980juneHoCMemoOnMonetaryPolicy.pdf

38. Ibid.

39. Joseph, "Monetarism Is Not Enough," Stockton Lecture, April 5, 1976. https://www
.margaretthatcher.org/document/110796.

40. Halcrow, *Keith Joseph*, p. 160.

41. Quoted in Blumenthal, *The Rise of the Counter-Establishment*, p. 121.

42. Heath, *The Course of My Life*, p. 575.

43. Ibid., p. 576.

44. Ibid., p. 578.

45. Jürg Niehans (Bern, November 8, 1919–Palo Alto, Calif., April 23, 2007).

46. Peter Riddell, *The Thatcher Decade* (Blackwell, Cambridge, 1989), pp. 18–19.

47. Margaret Thatcher, *The Downing Street Years* (Collins, London, 1993), pp. 132–39. https://
www.margaretthatcher.org/document/110696.

48. *The Times* (London), March 30, 1981. Full list of economists: https://c59574e9047e61130f13
-3f71d0fe2b653c4f00f32175760e96e7.ssl.cf1.rackcdn.com/FECEBF1EA893413
EB9D3FA246218F30A.pdf.

49. Halcrow, *Keith Joseph*, p. 165.

50. Riddell, *The Thatcher Decade*, p. 19.

51. Nigel Lawson, Baron Lawson of Blaby (March 11, 1932), British Conservative, chancellor
of the exchequer, 1983–1989.

52. Riddell, *The Thatcher Decade*, p. 20.

53. Ibid., p. 21.

54. Ibid., pp. 21–22.

55. Brian Griffiths, Lord Griffiths of Fforestfach (December 27, 1941–), British Conservative
politician. Dean of the City University Business School.

56. Although she claimed inspiration from Friedman, he warrants only two mentions, en passant, in her 900-page memoir, *Margaret Thatcher: The Downing Street Years*, and a footnote.
57. The Campaign Guide 1987 (Conservative Research Department, London, 1986).
58. The Campaign Guide 1989 (Conservative Research Department, London, 1989).
59. Ibid., pp. 13–14.

CHAPTER 15: BEATING BIN LADEN WITH CHEAP MONEY

1. Friedman and Friedman, *Two Lucky People*, p. 391.
2. Ibid., p. 392.
3. Quoted in Jon Meacham, *Destiny and Power: The American Odyssey of George Herbert Walker Bush* (Random House, New York, 2015).
4. Friedman, "Oodoov Economics," *New York Times*, February 2, 1992. https://miltonfriedman.hoover.org/friedman_images/Collections/2016c21/NYT_02_02_1992.pdf.
5. Friedman and Friedman, *Two Lucky People*, p. 396.
6. William Jefferson Clinton, State of the Union address, January 23, 1996. https://clintonwhitehouse4.archives.gov/WH/New/other/sotu.html.
7. John Hawkins interview with Milton Friedman, Rightwingnews.com, September 15, 2003.
8. Interview with Friedman, *Wall Street Journal*, July 22, 2006.
9. Tom DeLay with Stephen Mansfield, *No Retreat, No Surrender: One American's Fight* (Sentinel, New York, 2007), p. 112.
10. Ibid.
11. David Asman interview with Friedman, Fox News, May 15, 2004. https://miltonfriedman.hoover.org/friedman_images/Collections/2016c21/2004mayfox.pdf.
12. Ibid.
13. Letter from Samuelson to Friedman, December 8, 1995. Hoover Institution Friedman archive.
14. Letter from Friedman to Samuelson, December 28, 1995. Hoover Institution Friedman archive.
15. Alan Greenspan (born March 6, 1926), American economist who served five terms as chair of the U.S. Federal Reserve 1987–2006. Once a close associate of Ayn Rand and a member of her inner circle.
16. Alan Greenspan, *The Age of Turbulence: Adventures in a New World* (Penguin, New York, 2007), p. 226.
17. Quoted in Henri Lepage, "Interview with Milton Friedman: The Triumph of Liberalism," *Politique internationale*, no. 100, Summer 2003, pp. 7–34.
18. Greenspan, *The Age of Turbulence*, p. 228.
19. Ibid.
20. Often attributed to Keynes, the phrase was delivered in 1935 by Congressman T. Alan Goldsborough, in a cross-examination of Federal Reserve governor Marriner Eccles in a meeting of the House Committee on Banking and Currency. Eccles: "Under present circumstances there is very little, if anything, that can be done." Goldsborough: "You mean you cannot push on a string." Eccles: "That is a good way to put it."
21. Owen Ullmann interview with Milton Friedman, "So, What's New? The 'New Economy'

Looks Like the Same Old Economy to the Nobel Laureate, Milton Friedman," *International Economy*, March/April 2001, pp. 14–17.

22. Samuelson, *Economics*, 1st ed. (1948), p. 277.

23. Quoted on CBS *60 Minutes*. https://www.cbsnews.com/news/bush-sought-way-to-invade-iraq/.

24. Interview with Friedman, *Wall Street Journal*, July 22, 2006.

25. John Hawkins interview with Friedman, Rightwingnews.com, September 15, 2003.

26. Louis Rukeyser et al. interview with Friedman, "Nobel Laureate Milton Friedman Discusses His Personal Views of How to Deal with the Economy," *Louis Rukeyser's Wall Street*, CNBC (television broadcast), September 20, 2002.

27. Nathan Gardels interview with Samuelson, *New Perspectives Quarterly*, January 16, 2006.

28. Ibid.

29. Ibid.

30. Alan Greenspan, "Rules vs. discretionary monetary policy" at the 15th Anniversary Conference of the Center for Economic Policy Research at Stanford University, Stanford, California, September 5, 1997. https://www.federalreserve.gov/boarddocs/Speeches/1997/19970905.htm.

31. Louis Rukeyser et al. interview with Friedman, September 20, 2002.

32. Friedman, "He has set a standard," *Wall Street Journal*, January 31, 2006.

33. Ibid.

34. "Milton Friedman: Why the Euro is a Big Mistake," *Scotland on Sunday*, August 18, 2002.

35. Conor Clarke, "An Interview with Paul Samuelson," *The Atlantic*, June 17, 2009.

36. Letter from Samuelson to Benjamin M. Friedman, March 10, 2008. Duke Samuelson archive.

CHAPTER 16: ALL GOING SWIMMINGLY

1. Ben Bernanke (December 13, 1953–), American economist, chair of the Federal Reserve, 2006–2014.

2. Ben Bernanke, at conference honoring Friedman, University of Chicago, November 8, 2002. https://www.federalreserve.gov/boarddocs/speeches/2002/20021108/default.htm.

3. It is telling that Bernanke refers directly to a central bank increasing "aggregate demand," the key phrase in Keynes's revolutionary diagnosis of what should be done to lift an economy out of recession.

4. Ben Bernanke, "Deflation: Making sure it doesn't happen here," remarks before the National Economists Club, Washington, D.C., November 21, 2002. https://www.federalreserve.gov/boardDocs/speeches/2002/20021121/default.htm.

5. Conor Clarke, "An interview with Paul Samuelson," *The Atlantic*, June 17, 2009.

6. Interview with Samuelson, *Wall Street Journal*, March 2009.

7. Interview with Samuelson by William A. Barnett, University of Kansas, December 23, 2003.

8. Letter from Friedman to Samuelson, October 25, 2001. Duke Samuelson archive.

9. Edward Teller (January 15, 1908–September 9, 2003), Hungarian-American theoretical physicist known, with Oppenheimer, as one of the two "fathers of the hydrogen bomb."

10. Julius Robert Oppenheimer (April 22, 1904–February 18, 1967), theoretical physicist and professor of physics at the University of California, Berkeley. Head of the Los Alamos Laboratory, along with Teller, considered one of the two "fathers of the atomic bomb" for his role in the Manhattan Project.

11. Letter from Samuelson to Rose Friedman, November 16, 2006. Duke Samuelson archive.

12. David Asman interview with Friedman, Fox news, May 15, 2004. https://miltonfriedman .hoover.org/friedman_images/Collections/2016c21/2004mayfox.pdf.

13. "Milton Friedman: Why the Euro is a Big Mistake," *Scotland on Sunday*, August 18, 2002.

14. Russell Roberts interview with Friedman. http://www.econlib.org/library/Columns/ y2006/Friedmantranscript.html.

15. Holcomb B. Noble, "Milton Friedman, Free Markets Theorist, Dies at 94," *New York Times*, November 16, 2006.

16. Samuel Brittan, "Iconoclastic economist who put freedom first," obituary of Friedman, *Financial Times*, November 17, 2006.

17. When Summers summarily resigned from the Harvard presidency after he condemned unthinking political correctness, Samuelson wrote a letter of condolence. "I grieve for you, for a hopeful crusade stymied, and (within the limits of human frailty), I also grieve for Harvard and thereby for the evolutions of universities globally. You were fighting the good fight. . . . Mob psychology can be much the same on college campuses as elsewhere. Sometimes even worse save the bloodshed." He advised Summers not to bear a grudge against Harvard for the small number there who had caused his ouster.

18. Lawrence Summers, "A Fond Farewell," *Time*, December 25, 2006.

19. Lawrence Summers, "The Great Liberator," *New York Times*, November 19, 2006.

20. Robert Joseph Barro (September 28, 1944–) economist. Paul M. Warburg Professor of Economics at Harvard University. One of the founders of new classical macroeconomics.

21. Martin Stuart "Marty" Feldstein (November 25, 1939–), economist. George F. Baker Professor of Economics at Harvard University, president emeritus of the National Bureau of Economic Research (NBER). President and chief executive officer of the NBER, 1978–2008 (except 1982–1984, when he was chairman of the Council of Economic Advisers and chief economic adviser to President Reagan).

22. Letter from Samuelson to Summers, November 20, 2006. Samuelson archive Duke University, Box 71. The italics are Samuelson's.

23. Greg Ip and Mark Whitehouse, "How Milton Friedman Changed Economics, Policy and Markets," *Wall Street Journal,* November 17, 2006.

24. Noble, "Milton Friedman, Free Markets Theorist, Dies at 94."

25. Letter from Samuelson to David Friedman and Janet Martel, August 20, 2009. Duke Samuelson archive.

26. Letter from David Friedman to Samuelson, September 8, 2009, Duke Samuelson archive.

CHAPTER 17: CAPITALISM TEETERS

1. Ben Bernanke, "Deflation: Making sure it doesn't happen here," remarks before the National Economists Club, Washington, D.C., November 21, 2002. https://www.federalreserve.gov/ boardDocs/speeches/2002/20021121/default.htm.

2. Court statement as part of lawsuit linked to 2008 bailout of AIG, quoted in *Forbes*, August 27, 2014. https://www.forbes.com/sites/timworstall/2014/08/27/ben-bernanke-the-2008 -financial-crisis-was-worse-than-the-great-depression/#25a4c8497684.

3. Ibid.

4. Ben Bernanke, at conference honoring Friedman, University of Chicago, November 8, 2002. https://www.federalreserve.gov/boarddocs/speeches/2002/20021108/default.htm.

5. Bernanke speech, "Four Questions about the Financial Crisis," Morehouse College, Atlanta, Ga., April 14, 2009.

6. Ibid.

7. BNP Paribas press release, August 7, 2007.

8. BBC Radio 4, "The Bailout," October 6, 2018.

9. Henry Merritt "Hank" Paulson Jr. (March 28, 1946–), Secretary of the Treasury, 2006–2009. Chairman and chief CEO of Goldman Sachs, 1998–2006.

10. Letter from Samuelson to Summers, July 29, 2008. Duke Samuelson archive, Box 71.

11. Letter from Summers to Samuelson, August 20, 2008. Duke Samuelson archive, Box 71.

12. Letter from Samuelson to Summers, August 20, 2008. Duke Samuelson archive, Box 71. The italics are Samuelson's.

13. Paulson press conference on federal government takeover of Fannie May and Freddie Mac, September 7, 2008.

14. Bernanke, "Four Questions about the Financial Crisis," speech at Morehouse College, Atlanta, Ga., April 14, 2009.

15. Ibid.

16. Nathan Gardels interview with Samuelson, *New Perspectives Quarterly*, January 16, 2006.

17. *Newsweek*, October 28, 1974.

18. An honorable exception was John B. Taylor of Stanford.

19. Gardels interview with Samuelson, *New Perspectives Quarterly*, January 16, 2006.

20. Ibid.

21. Ibid.

22. Letter from Samuelson to Bernanke, March 3, 2009. Duke Samuelson archive.

23. Friedman, *Wall Street Journal*, December 17, 1997.

24. Samuelson, "Farewell to Friedman-Hayek libertarian capitalism," Tribune Media Services, October 15, 2008.

25. J. Daniel Hammond, "Friedman and Samuelson on the Business Cycle," *Cato Journal*, vol. 31, no. 3, Fall 2011.

26. Samuelson, "Economic Policy is an Art," *New York Times*, October 30, 1970.

27. Conor Clarke, "An Interview with Paul Samuelson," *The Atlantic*, June 17, 2009.

28. Letter from Samuelson to Robin McElheny, associate director of the Harvard University Archives, November 9, 2006. Duke Samuelson archive.

29. Letter from Sidney Verba, director of the Harvard University Library, to Samuelson, November 14, 2006. Duke Samuelson archive.

30. Axel Leijonhufvud (1933–), Swedish economist. Professor emeritus at the University of California Los Angeles (UCLA) and professor at the University of Trento, Italy.

31. Don Patinkin (January 8, 1922–August 7, 1995), Israeli-American monetary economist

and the president of the Hebrew University of Jerusalem. His monograph *Money, Interest, and Prices* (1956) was for many years one of the most widely used advanced references on monetary economics.

32. Letter from Byrd to Samuelson, September 15, 1992. Duke Samuelson archive.

33. Letter from Byrd to Samuelson, April 18, 2005. Duke Samuelson archive.

34. Letter from Byrd to Samuelson, November 8, 2005. Duke Samuelson archive.

35. Letter from Samuelson to Robert L. Byrd, December 14 2005. Duke Samuelson archive.

36. Michael M. Weinstein, Samuelson obituary, *New York Times*, December 13, 2009.

37. Paul Krugman, "Paul Samuelson, RIP," *New York Times*, December 13, 2009.

38. *The Economist*, December 17, 2009.

39. Obituary, *Daily Telegraph*, December 14, 2009.

40. Chinese statistics, particularly economic data or the recording of embarrassing incidents such as the outbreak of diseases, are notoriously unreliable. Nor is the reporting of bad news welcomed. Li Wenliang and seven other doctors who express alarm at the spread of the disease were punished by Chinese authorities for "spreading false rumors."

41. By the end of July 2020, 35,107 Italians had died of COVID-19.

42. Steven Terner Mnuchin (December 21, 1962–), American investment banker. U.S. Treasury Secretary 2017–2021.

43. https://datausa.io/coronavirus.

44. In January, the total of reported unemployed in the U.S. was 74.8 million. https://nypost.com/2021/01/14/us-jobless-claims-965000-filed-amid-pressure-from-covid-19/.

45. Franklin Delano Roosevelt (January 30, 1882–April 12, 1945). Thirty-second president of the United States.

46. See Amity Shlaes, *The Forgotten Man: A New History of the Great Depression*, HarperCollins, 2007.

47. "The Impact of Covid-19 on U.S. Economy and Financial Markets," *Forbes*, https://www.forbes.com/sites/mikepatton/2020/10/12/the-impact-of-covid-19-on-us-economy-and-financial-markets/?sh=492d60322d20.

48. Tunku Varadarajan, "The Romance of Economics: The Weekend Interview with Milton (and Rose) Friedman," *Wall Street Journal*, July 22–23, 2006

49. David Director Friedman (February 12, 1945–); like Keynes, David Friedman did not achieve a degree in economics.

50. Robert Solow, "Why Is There No Milton Friedman Today?" *Econ Journal Watch*, vol. 10, no. 2, May 2013, pp. 214–16.

51. https://bradfordtaxinstitute.com/Free_Resources/Federal-Income-Tax-Rates.aspx

52. Donald John Trump (June 14, 1946–), real estate developer, television personality, and forty-fifth president of the United States.

53. First given before the Swedish-American Chamber of Commerce, New York City, May 10, 1972.

54. It is a mark of Trump's toxicity that his harsh criticism of free trade led to a marked swing in opinion towards free trade. At the end of Obama's presidency, Americans were in favor of free trade by a narrow margin of 51 percent to 41 percent. By August 2019, Americans

approved of free trade by 64 percent to 27 percent. https://www.cnbc.com/2019/08/18 /americans-support-free-trade----and-are-worried-about-the-trump-economy-poll.html.

55. *Newsweek*, June 10, 1968.

56. Robert Summers (June 22, 1922–April 17, 2012), economist and professor at the University of Pennsylvania from 1960.

57. Anita Arrow Summers (September 9, 1925–). Professor Emerita at the University of Pennsylvania, and authority on urban economic development, finance, and educational efficiency.

58. Kenneth Joseph Arrow (August 23, 1921–February 21, 2017), economist, mathematician, author, and political theorist. Joint winner with John Hicks of the Nobel Prize in Economic Sciences, 1972.

59. Quoted in obituary, *MIT News*, December 13, 2009.

60. Letter from Samuelson to Benjamin M. Friedman, May 7, 2008. Duke Samuelson archive.

61. Samuelson, "Hail to a Sage!" written for *Die Zeit*, June 1992. Duke Samuelson archive.

62. Ibid.

63. Horn, *Roads to Wisdom, Conversations with Ten Nobel Laureates in Economics*, p. 49.

Selected Bibliography

Alterman, Eric. *Sound and Fury: The Making of the Punditocracy* (Cornell, Ithaca, N.Y., 1999).

Anderson, Martin. *Revolution: The Reagan Legacy* (Hoover Institution Press, Stanford, Calif., 1990).

Arnold, Bruce. *Margaret Thatcher: A Study in Power* (Hamish Hamilton, London, 1984).

Backhouse, Roger E. *Founder of Modern Economics: Paul A. Samuelson*, vol. 1: *Becoming Samuelson, 1915–1948* (Oxford University Press, Oxford, 2017).

Blinder, Alan S. *Hard Heads, Soft Hearts: Tough-Minded Economics for a Just Society* (Addison-Wesley, Reading, Mass., 1987).

Blumenthal, Sidney, *The Rise of the Counter-Establishment: The Conservative Ascent to Political Power* (Union Square Press, New York, 1986).

Butler, David, and Dennis Kavanagh. *The British General Election of February 1974* (Macmillan, London, 1974).

———. *The British General Election of 1983* (Macmillan, London, 1974).

Bradlee, Ben. *A Good Life* (Touchstone, New York, 1995).

Brown, Gordon, *My Life, Our Times* (Bodley Head, London, 2017).

Buckley, William F. Jr. *God and Mammon at Yale* (Henry Regnery, Chicago, 1951.)

Cannon, Lou. *President Reagan: The Role of a Lifetime* (Public Affairs, New York, 1991).

Campbell, John. *Edward Heath: A Biography* (Jonathan Cape, London, 1993).

Congdon, Tim. *Money in a Free Society: Keynes, Friedman, and the New Crisis in Capitalism* (Encounter Books, New York, London, 2011).

Cosgrave, Patrick. *Thatcher: The First Term* (Bodley Head, London, 1985).

Cottrell, Allin, and Michael S. Lawlor. *New Perspectives on Keynes* (Duke University Press, Durham, N.C., 1995).

Cronon, E. David, and John W. Jenkins. *The University of Wisconsin: A History, 1925–1945*, vol. 3: *Politics, Depression, and War* (University of Wisconsin Press, Madison, 1994).

Dallek, Robert. *Nixon and Kissinger: Partners in Power* (HarperCollins, New York, 2007).

DeLay, Tom, with Stephen Mansfield. *No Retreat, No Surrender: One American's Fight* (Sentinel, New York, 2007).

Ebenstein, Alan. *Friedrich Hayek: A Biography* (Palgrave for St. Martin's Press, New York, 2001).

Ebenstein, Lanny. *The Indispensable Milton Friedman: Essays on Politics and Economics* (Regnery, Washington, D.C., 2012).

Edwards, Lee. *Goldwater: The Man Who Made a Revolution* (Regnery, Washington, D.C., 1995).

Fogel, Robert, and Stanley L. Engerman. *Time on the Cross: The Economics of American Negro Slavery* (W. W. Norton, New York, 1974).

Friedman, Milton, Ed. *Studies in the Quantity Theory of Money* (University of Chicago Press, Chicago, 1956).

———. *A Theory of the Consumption Function* (Princeton University, Princeton, N.J., 1957).

———. *Capitalism and Freedom* (University of Chicago Press, Chicago and London, 1962).

———. *Inflation: Causes and Consequences* (Asia Publishing House, New York, 1963).

———. *The Optimum Quantity of Money and other essays* (Aldine, Chicago, 1969).

———. *Bright Promises, Dismal Performance: An Economist's Protest*, edited by William R. Allen (Harcourt Brace Jovanovich, New York, 1983).

Friedman, Milton, and Rose D. *Friedman. Free to Choose: A Personal Statement* (Penguin, London, 1980).

———. *Two Lucky People: Memoir* (University of Chicago Press, Chicago, 1998).

Friedman, Milton, and Walter W. Heller. *Monetary vs. Fiscal Policy: A Dialogue* (W. W. Norton, New York, 1969).

Friedman, Milton, and Anna Jacobson Schwartz. *A Monetary History of the United States, 1867–1960* (Princeton University Press, Princeton, N.J., 1963).

Gilmour, Ian. *Britain Can Work* (Martin Robertson, Oxford, 1983).

———. *Inside Right: A Study of Conservatism* (Quartet, London,1978).

Goldwater, Barry, *Conscience of a Conservative* (Victor, Shepardsville, Ky, 1960).

Graham, Katharine. *Personal History* (Alfred A. Knopf, New York, 1997).

Greenspan, Alan. *The Age of Turbulence: Adventures in a New World* (Penguin, New York, 2007).

Greider, William. *Secrets of the Temple: How the Federal Reserve Runs the Country* (Simon & Schuster, New York, 1989).

Halcrow, Morrison. *Keith Joseph: A Single Mind* (Macmillan, London, 1989).

Hammond, J. D., and C. H. Hammond. *Making Chicago Price Theory: Friedman-Stigler Correspondence 1945–1957* (Routledge, London, 2006).

Harris, Kenneth. *Thatcher* (Weidenfeld and Nicolson, London, 1988).

Hayek, Friedrich. *The Road to Serfdom* (George Routledge, 1944).

———. *Choice in Currency: A Way to Stop Inflation* (Institute of Economic Affairs, London, 1976).

———. *The Collected Works of F. A. Hayek*, ed. Bruce Caldwell.

Vol. 2: *The Road to Serfdom, Text and Documents, The Definitive Edition, ed. Caldwell* (University of Chicago Press, Chicago, 2007).

Vol. 9: *Contra Keynes and Cambridge: Essays and Correspondence*, ed. Caldwell (University of Chicago Press, Chicago, 1995).

Hayek, Friedrich, ed. Joseph T Salerno. *Prices and Production and Other Works: F. A. Hayek on Money, the Business Cycle, and the Gold Standard* (Ludwig von Mises Institute, Auburn, Ala., 2008).

Hayek, Friedrich, ed. Stephen Kresge and Leif Wenar. *Hayek on Hayek* (University of Chicago Press, Chicago, 2010).

Healey, Denis. *The Time of My Life* (Michael Joseph, London, 1989).

————. *When Shrimps Learn to Whistle: Signposts for the Nineties* (Michael Joseph, London, 1990).

Heath, Edward. *The Course of My Life* (Hodder & Stoughton, London, 1998).

Horn, Karen Ilse. *Roads to Wisdom, Conversations with Ten Nobel Laureates in Economics.* (Edward Elgar, Cheltenham, U.K., 2009).

Hurd, Douglas. *An End to Promises* (Collins, London, 1979).

Hutchinson, George. *Edward Heath: A Personal and Political Biography* (Longman, London, 1970).

Kaldor, Nicholas. *The Economic Consequences of Mrs. Thatcher* (Duckworth, London, 1983).

Keller, Morton, and Phyllis Keller. *Making Harvard Modern: The Rise of America's Universities* (Oxford University Press, New York, 2001).

Kahn, Richard F. *The Making of Keynes' General Theory* (Cambridge University Press, Cambridge, 1948).

Keegan, William. *Mr. Lawson's Gamble* (Hodder & Stoughton, London, 1989).

Keynes, J. M. *The Economic Consequences of the Peace* (Harcourt, Brace and Howe, New York, 1920).

————. *A Tract on Monetary Reform* (Macmillan, London, 1923).

————. *The End of Laissez-Faire.* (Hogarth Press, London, 1926).

————. *A Treatise on Money* (Macmillan, London, 1930).

————. *The General Theory of Employment, Interest and Money* (Macmillan, London, 1936).

————. *The Collected Writings of John Maynard Keynes.*

> Vol. 5: *A Treatise on Money: The Pure Theory of Money* (1930) (Macmillan for the Royal Economic Society, London, 1971).

> Vol. 13: *General Theory and After, Part 1* (Macmillan for the Royal Economic Society, London, 1973).

> Vol. 17: *Activities 1920–2: Treaty Revision and Reconstruction* (Macmillan for the Royal Economic Society, London, 1981).

> Vol. 19: *Activities 1922–9: The Return to Gold and Industrial Policy* (Macmillan for the Royal Economic Society, London, 1981).

> Vol. 27: *Activities 1940–1946: Shaping the Post-War World: Employment and Commodities* (Macmillan for the Royal Economic Society, London, 1980).

Kiernan, Frances. *The Last Mrs. Astor: A New York Story* (W. W. Norton, New York, 2007).

Klein, Naomi. *The Shock Doctrine: The Rise of Disaster Capitalism* (Metropolitan Books, New York, 2007).

Kuhn, Thomas S. *The Structure of Scientific Revolutions* (University of Chicago Press, Chicago, 1962).

Lawson, Nigel. *The View from No. 11: Memoirs of a Tory Radical* (Bantam Press, London, 1992).

Ledbetter, James. *One Nation Under Gold* (Liveright, New York, 2017).

Leeson, Robert. *Keynes, Chicago and Friedman* (Pickering & Chatto, London, 2003).

Mackenzie, Norman, and Jeanne Mackenzie, eds. *The Diary of Beatrice Webb*, vol. 4: *The Wheel of Life*, 1924–1943 (Virago, London, 1985).

Meacham, Jon. *Destiny and Power: The American Odyssey of George Herbert Walker Bush* (Random House, New York, 2015).

Mirowski, Philip, and Dieter Plehwe. *The Road from Mont Pèlerin: The Making of the Neoliberal Thought Collective* (Harvard University Press, Cambridge, Mass. 2009).

Nelson, Robert H. *Economics as Religion: From Samuelson to Chicago and Beyond* (Pennsylvania State University Press, University Park, Pa., 2001).

Parker, Richard. *John Kenneth Galbraith: His Life, His Politics, His Economics* (Farrar, Straus and Giroux, New York, 2005).

Pigou, Arthur [A. C.]. *Economics in Practice* (Macmillan, London, 1935).

Pym, Francis. *The Politics of Consent* (Hamish Hamilton, London, 1984).

Powell, Enoch. *Freedom and Reality* (B. T. Batsford, London, 1969).

Reagan, Ronald, ed. Douglas Brinkley. *The Reagan Diaries* (HarperCollins, New York, 2007).

Riddell, Peter. *The Thatcher Decade* (Blackwell, Cambridge, 1989).

Samuelson, Paul A., *Foundations of Economic Analysis* (Harvard University Press, Cambridge, 1947).

———. *Economics: An Introductory Analysis* (McGraw-Hill, New York, 1948): 1st ed. 1948; 2nd ed. 1951; 3rd ed. 1955; 4th ed. 1958; 5th ed. 1961; 6th ed. 1964; 7th ed. 1967; 8th ed. 1970; 9th ed. 1973; 10th ed. 1976; 11th ed. 1980; with William D. Nordhaus: 12th ed. 1985; 13th ed. 1989; 14th ed. 1992; 15th ed. 1995; 16th ed. 1998; 17th ed. 2000; 18th ed. 2004; 19th ed. 2013.

———. *Principles and Rules in Modern Fiscal Policy: A Neo-Classical Formulation* (1951).

———. *Readings in Economics,* 6th ed. (McGraw-Hill, New York, 1970).

———. *The Samuelson Sampler* (Thomas Horton and Company, Glen Ridge, New Jersey, 1973).

———. *Economics from the Heart: A Samuelson Sampler* (Harcourt Brace Jovanovich, New York, 1983).

Samuelson, Paul A., and William A. Barnett, eds. *Inside the Economist's Mind: The History of Modern Economic Thought, as Explained by Those Who Produced It* (Wiley-Blackwell, Hoboken, New Jersey, 2005).

———. *Inside the Economist's Mind: Conversations with Eminent Economists* (Wiley-Blackwell, Hoboken, N.J., 2006).

Say, Jean-Baptiste. *A Treatise on Political Economy, Or, the Production, Distribution, and Consumption of Wealth* (first published in France, 1803; republished by Wentworth Press, New York, 2016).

Shlaes, Amity. *The Forgotten Man: A New History of the Great Depression* (HarperCollins, New York, 2007).

Shultz, George. *Turmoil and Triumph: My Years as Secretary of State* (Charles Scribner's Sons, New York, 1993).

Schultz, Henry. *The Theory and Measurement of Demand* (University of Chicago Press, Chicago, 1938).

Silber, William L. *Volcker: The Triumph of Persistence* (Bloomsbury Press, New York, 2012).

Skidelsky, Robert, ed. *Thatcherism* (Chatto & Windus, London, 1988).

Smith, David. *The Rise and Fall of Monetarism: The Theory and Politics of an Economic Experiment* (Penguin, London, 1987).

Stein, Herbert. *Presidential Economics: The Making of Economic Policy from Roosevelt to Reagan and Beyond* (Simon & Schuster, New York, 1985).

Stigler, George J. *Memoirs of an Unregulated Economist* (Basic Books, New York, 1985).

Szenberg, Michael, Michael Ramrattan, and Aron A. Gottesman, eds. *Samuelsonian Economics and the Twenty-First Century* (Oxford, 2006).

Tarshis, Lorie. *The Elements of Economics* (Houghton Mifflin, Boston, 1947).

Tebbit, Norman. *Upwardly Mobile: An Autobiography* (Weidenfeld and Nicolson, London, 1988).

Thatcher, Margaret. *The Downing Street Years* (HarperCollins, London, 1993).

———. *The Path to Power* (HarperCollins, London, 1995).

Volcker, Paul, and Toyoo Gyohten. *Changing Fortunes: The World's Money and the Threat to American Leadership* (Times Books, New York, 1992).

Von Mises, Ludwig. *Socialism: An Economic and Sociological Analysis* (Gustave Fischer Verlag, 1922). English translation by J. Kahane (Jonathan Cape, London, 1936).

Walters, Alan. *Sterling in Danger: The Economic Consequences of Pegged Exchange Rates* (Fontana/Collins, London, 1990).

Wanniski, Jude. *The Way the World Works: How Economies Fail—and Succeed* (Basic Books, New York, 1978).

Wapshott, Nicholas. *Ronald Reagan and Margaret Thatcher: A Political Marriage* (Sentinel, New York, 2007).

———. *Keynes Hayek: The Clash That Defined Modern Economics* (W. W. Norton, New York, 2011).

Wapshott, Nicholas, and George Brock. *Thatcher* (Macdonald, London, 1983).

Weintraub, E. Roy. *MIT and the Transformation of American Economics* (Duke University Press, Durham, N.C., 2014).

Winch, Donald. *Economics and Policy: A Historical Study* (Walker, New York, 1969).

Young, Hugo. *One of Us* (Macmillan, London, 1989).

Index

Note: Page references after 300 refer to endnotes.